RELIGION
IN A
SECULAR
CITY

RELIGION
IN A
SECULAR
CITY

Essays
in Honor
of Harvey Cox

EDITED BY ARVIND SHARMA

TRINITY PRESS INTERNATIONAL

Trinity Press International, P.O. Box 1321, Harrisburg, PA 17105
Trinity Press International is a division of the Morehouse Group.

Cover design: Trude Brummer

Library of Congress Cataloging-in-Publication Data
Religion in a secular city : essays in honor of Harvey Cox / edited by Arvind Sharma.
    p. cm.
  Includes bibliographical references.
  ISBN 1-56338-337-3 (hardcover)
  1. Christianity. I. Cox, Harvey Gallagher. II. Sharma, Arvind.
BR50.R386 2001
261 – dc21
                                            2001027904

Printed in the United States of America

01   02   03   04   05   06   10 9 8 7 6 5 4 3 2 1

48.00

CONTENTS

FOREWORD

One must be brief as many words follow these few. This volume is designed to felicitate Professor Harvey Cox on reaching, and happily exceeding, the biblically allotted span of three score and ten. As is well-known, such a text is usually a pretext for allowing scholars to express themselves freely on matters of choice without the shadow of the anonymous referee hanging over their shoulders. Peer review is good but peerless writing is even better! I hope the readers will enjoy these loose sallies of the mind.

In the course of assembling such a volume one incurs many debts, not all of which can be discharged or even acknowledged. My religious beliefs allow me the luxury of stretching my repayment over several lifetimes and ensure that I will, even if I happen to forget them! Notwithstanding such metaphysical solace, I would nevertheless like to express here my profound thanks to all the contributors. I would also like to acknowledge the help received from three persons in particular: Margaret Studier of the Harvard Divinity School, Barbara Karasinski of the Department of Afro-American Studies, Harvard University, and Mark Shields of the Faculty of Religious Studies, McGill University, in bringing this project to a successful conclusion.

PREFACE

Cornel West

Harvey Cox — my friend and brother — is one of the most significant religious thinkers of the late twentieth century. Unlike most American Christian theologians, his monumental work is international and ecumenical. Unlike most academic figures, his prophetic scholarship is accessible to a broad literate public. And in stark contrast to most of his fellow Baptists (including myself!), his pastoral engagement with the world embraces the secularisms, unbanisms, and technologisms of our postmodern world.

The story of Harvey Cox is the story of the flowering of a new kind of intellectual in mid-century America, deeply rooted in small-town Pennsylvania Protestantism, who was caught up by the emergence of the Black Freedom struggles, shaken by the realities of the Christian Left in Cold-War West Germany, challenged by the death-of-God ideologies and liberation theologies, and energized by the spiritualities of Buddhism and Pentecostalism. What makes Harvey Cox unique is that he wrestles with these diverse and disparate forces in light of his major theme: the idolatrous character of worldly goods and the liberating (though deeply worldly) content of the Christian gospel. In his fascinating intellectual travels through the thickets of texts — be they from Durkheim, Bonhoeffer, Bloch, Boff, Cone, Ruether, Ellul, or Tutu — Cox remains true to the anti-idolatrous sentiments of the Old Testament prophets and the courageous compassion of Jesus of Nazareth. The scope and delicacy of application of this theological consistency is rivaled only by Reinhold and H. Richard Niebuhr in twentieth-century American theology. And Cox's substantive concerns with race, gender, sexual orientation, and technology goes beyond them.

In this sense, Cox is an exemplary millennial thinker who immerses himself in the muddy, messy world of dynamic experiences without losing sight of the tears and laughter of ordinary people or closing his ears to the "cries of the wounded." Yet, he always sees these tragicomic realities through the lens of the cross at Calvary and hears these utterances of despair in light of the inexhaustible hope of ordinary and extraordinary resurrections.

HARVEY COX

A Short Biography

Harvey Cox was born in Malvern, Pennsylvania, on May 19, 1929. He attended public school there and then Berwyn High School. After high school he served briefly in the merchant marine on relief ships carrying horses and cattle to Europe. Returning, he received his A.B. with honors in history in 1951 from the University of Pennsylvania, where he also played saxophone in the marching band and was a member of the debate team. He received his first degree in theology from Yale Divinity School in 1955 and was ordained to the American Baptist ministry in 1956. He served as a Campus Minister at Temple University and at Oberlin College, then enrolled in the doctoral program at Harvard University. While studying at Harvard, he worked for the American Baptist Home Mission Society and taught part-time at Andover Newton Theological School. After studying with James Luther Adams and Paul Tillich, he competed his Ph.D. in the History and Philosophy of Religion at Harvard in 1962.

After receiving his doctorate Cox left immediately for Berlin, then divided by the Wall, and served for a year as an Ecumenical Fraternal Worker, traveling almost daily through Checkpoint Charley in an effort to maintain contact between the two sides of the divided city. Upon his return he worked actively with the Southern Christian Leadership Conference under the leadership of Dr. Martin Luther King, Jr. and was one of the founders of the Boston chapter of the SCLC. In the fall of 1963, he was arrested for participating in a civil rights demonstration and spent a few days in jail in Williamston and Washington, North Carolina.

In 1965 Cox published *The Secular City,* which became an international bestseller (nearly one million copies) and was translated into fourteen languages. In 1999 the Protestant Theological Faculty of Marburg University in Germany selected *The Secular City* as one of the two "most decisive" Protestant theological books of the twentieth century. The other was Karl Barth's *Epistle to the Romans.* In 1965 Cox joined the faculty of Harvard University, where he is now Thomas Professor of Divinity and chair of the Department of Religion and Society, offering courses both in the Divinity School and in the Religious Studies Program of the Faculty of Arts and Sciences. At present he is teaching, among other courses, one on "Contemporary Interpreters of Jesus," another on "Religious Values and Cultural

Conflict," and a jointly taught course on Science, Law, and Religion called "Thinking About Thinking" with Professors Alan Dershowitz and Steven J. Gould of the Harvard Law School and the Department of Paleontology, respectively.

Professor Cox has been a visiting lecturer or visiting professor at several universities around the world, including the University of Michigan; the Pontifical Catholic University of Lima, Peru; Kyoto University in Japan; the Naropa (Buddhist) Institute in Colorado; Brandeis University; the Gregorian University in Rome; and Moscow University in Russia. He has also taught during two semesters at the Seminario Bautista (Baptist Seminary) in Mexico City.

In addition to *The Secular City*, Professor Cox has published several books, including *On Not Leaving It to the Snake, The Feast of Fools, The Seduction of the Spirit* (which was a runner-up for the National Book Prize), *Many Mansions: A Christian's Encounter with Other Faiths, Religion in the Secular City* and, most recently, *Fire from Heaven*. He is currently at work on a book about Christian-Jewish relations. His articles have appeared in numerous publications, both scholarly and popular, including *The Yale Review, The Journal of Oriental Philosophy, Archives des Sciences Sociales de Religion* (published in Paris), *The Atlantic Monthly*, and the op-ed page of the *New York Times*. He also writes a regular column for *beliefnet.com*, the online interfaith religion magazine.

A lifelong tenor saxophonist, Cox plays with a Boston jazz-and-swing ensemble called "The Embraceables," and in November 1999 was featured as guest saxophone soloist with Mark Harvey's jazz orchestra "Aardvark" at the national meeting of the American Academy of Religion. He is also an enthusiastic member of the Boston Sailing Center.

Harvey Cox is married to Professor Nina Tumarkin, who teaches Russian history and heads the Russian Studies program at Wellesley College. He has four children and lives in Cambridge, Massachusetts.

AFTERWARD AND FORWARD

Harvey Cox

As I enter the eighth decade of life on earth, two intellectual temptations lure me. One is to gaze back over the many articles, books, reviews, courses, seminars, and lectures I have produced and try to discern some unifying pattern, some consistent — or at least vaguely constant — purpose at work. A *Festschrift* such as this feeds the temptation to grasp at closure. By exercising some mighty effort, could I help the puzzled reader to make out some overall configuration in what must appear to be a congeries of shifting interests and changing enthusiasms?

I could make a stab at it, and I might even convince a few skeptics. But I am not sure it would be worth the effort. It might be better to resort to Emerson's famous pronouncement that "consistency is the hobgoblin of little minds," a dictum which has comforted legions of mercurial people since he uttered it, including me.

The second apple that dangles before me as I enter my seventies is a different one, shinier and more succulent. It is to launch out onto some grand new enterprise, a vast undertaking — spacious in concept if not in pages written — that would draw on what I have learned in so many years of study, teaching, and travel and would permit me to tackle the most fundamental issues our species confronts today. Many years ago, when I first read Thomas Mann's *Doctor Faustus*, I saw myself in the young protagonist, who was attracted to the study of theology because it seemed to him to plumb the most primal and starkly critical human questions. I felt the same way in my youth, and I still do. Of course, Mann's hero later left theology, became a composer (modeled, it is said, on Arnold Schönberg), and eventually went mad. But I still believe that before he bade adieu, first to the "Queen of the Sciences," and then to his senses, the young hero had the right idea. Theology, which I understand to be the critical study of human spiritual traditions and faith, should indeed be concerned with the most underlying issues. I am glad there are scholars in other disciplines who also struggle with these axial themes. But theology, understood in the broadest sense, may be the only one that has a license, even a mandate to do so. Since, so far at least, I have not either turned to composing atonal symphonies or gone berserk, I still accept that mandate.

But one must be cautious. We inhabit an intellectual world that is now rightly suspicious of generalizations or of any hint of "essentialism." For two decades now scholars have been searching out and destroying spurious universalisms. This important mission has succeeded, however, mainly in clearing the ground. If anything, it has exposed the hiding places of those stubborn Big Questions, but it has rarely addressed them directly. Still, they have not gone away.

So, what are the Big Questions? More particularly, what are they from the perspective of a theologian like myself with a fascination for the rise and fall of civilizations and for the role religious traditions have played in those ascents and descents? Even as a college undergraduate I could not help musing on these mysteries. Reared in a not particularly pious family of Christmas and Easter Christians, I nonetheless found that church life in my small town opened a vast window both on the sweep of the past and on the persistent questions of human destiny. It might be hard to believe, but I first heard about Oswald Spengler's *The Decline of the West* when I was thirteen, from my Baptist Sunday School teacher, a serious young man in thick glasses. I was spellbound by Spengler's morose thesis, as our bespectacled mentor relayed it to us, that the whole of Western civilization was in inevitable decline and would be succeeded by a new civilization from the East.

I still carried Spengler's tragic scenario in the back of my mind when — after a brief stint in the merchant marine, I got to college (at the University of Pennsylvania). I immediately decided to major in history. The freshman course the department offered was called "Centers of Civilization," taught by a different instructor every two weeks. It vaulted from Athens under Pericles and Rome under Augustus to Baghdad under Haroun al-Raschid, and then back to Rome under Pope Innocent III. From there it moved on to Paris under Louis XVI, Berlin under Bismarck, and London under Victoria. It concluded, rather anti-climatically I thought, with Washington under Wilson.

We read secondary accounts, original sources in translation, and examples of the literature and poetry of these periods. We looked at slides of the Pantheon, St. Peter's, and Versailles, and the art of Phidias and Michelangelo. It was obvious to me that religion played a significant part in each of these hubs. Current critics would adjudge the syllabus hopelessly Eurocentric, and — with the exception of Baghdad — it was. But it captivated me and kindled a lifelong love of history.

Still, with my constant hankering for the questions historians raised but never seemed to answer, I also looked elsewhere. I took several courses in philosophy, dutifully beginning with the pre-Socratics and working my way, term after term, from Aristotle to Augustine to Aquinas to Kant and finally to John Dewey and Alfred North Whitehead. As a senior, I persuaded my adviser to allow me to take both the history and the philosophy senior honors seminars. Penn only initiated its Religious Thought offerings when I was a junior, and there was not yet an honors seminar, or I might have tried to squeeze that one in as well.

My college years were exhilarating, but they did not make me into a careful scholar, just a ravenously inquisitive one. I became fascinated with thinkers such as F. S. C. Northrop, whose *The Meeting of East and West,* with its intriguing frontispiece of Georgia O'Keeffe's "Two Blue Lines," offered a more hopeful scenario of East and West than Spengler had. Then there was Toynbee. I remember arguing with a Bryn Mawr student about his *A Study of History,* which had just made *Time* magazine. It was one night after we had both heard him lecture. Over too many cups of coffee, and on the basis of very little knowledge of his multi-volume opus, we energetically debated what we took to be his theorem. I thought his vision was sweeping and superb, but she, a serious Presbyterian, insisted his theology was woolly. (She was probably right.) I could not stay away from the Big Question people. I read Jacques Maritain on integral humanism and Crane Brinton on *Man's Fate.* I wrote a term paper on Nicholas Berdyaev, the Russian Orthodox philosopher who delved into things like time and eternity, freedom and slavery, and the destiny of man. Those were a heady four years.

After I graduated from Penn, I entered seminary at Yale just as the intellectual excitement of the "Neo-Orthodox" movement in Protestant theology was making its impact. Initiated by Karl Barth, it was flamboyantly represented in America by Reinhold Niebuhr and to some extent by his brother, Richard, whose *Christ and Culture* still shapes my thinking and whose famous course on Christian Ethics I took at Yale. These theologians emphasized biblical categories and Reformation themes, and they did it with flair and imagination. They certainly inspired me. But in doing their work so well, they concentrated on one particular tradition and tended to ignore the musings of that previous generation of thinkers I had grown to love in college and who had evidenced broader concerns. At first I thought that, in order to be up to date, I would have to bid farewell to these old mentors who appeared to the neoorthodox mind to be a hopelessly speculative and imprecise lot. Despite the neoorthodox pressure, however, I never gave up my secret vice, and I still read their books, scarred with underlining and marginal interpolations.

After my first assignment as a campus minister at Oberlin College, I entered Harvard in 1958 to pursue doctoral work in what was then called "The History and Philosophy of Religion." It was a new program, and it allowed me to stretch my wings once again. My doctoral adviser, James Luther Adams, a Unitarian who had been nurtured as a Baptist, encouraged me to follow my muse. Paul Tillich, whose famous "home seminar" I took twice, was busy writing his *Systematic Theology* but not too busy to try to rescue graduate students from Barth. While I was there, Gabriel Marcel, a quaint, gnome-like little man, came for a semester as a Visiting

Professor, and I was drawn to his phenomenological approach. I studied Merleau-Ponty with John Wild. I had an unforgettable seminar on theories of religion with the young Robert Bellah. I wrote my dissertation on "Religion and Technology from the Renaissance to the Present." It was an impossibly vast subject, one I would certainly warn a student today not to attempt, but the faculty encouraged me to tackle it.

When, after a few years of teaching at Andover Newton Theological School, I joined the Harvard faculty in 1965, the benefits and constraints of university life began to make their impact. I was surrounded by fascinating people who provided endless opportunities for absorbing conversations. During my first years on the faculty, for example, I sometimes ate my brown bag lunch with Wilfred Cantwell Smith, who had come to direct the Center for the Study of World Religions. His *The Meaning and End of Religion,* though densely written, boldly took on some of the issues neoorthodoxy had swept aside. He once actually had the audacity to offer a seminar on the possibilities of finding a "world faith." I suspect Smith welcomed me to our cheese on rye and coffee lunches even though I was a mere rookie in part because there were not many other people around who appreciated the awesome scope of his projects. He liked my book *The Secular City,* not because it was profound or even very original, I think, because it was neither, but because of its sweeping purview. It moved from the Stone Age to the twentieth century, across four continents, and from anthropology to religion to sociology with the kind of bold brush strokes only a work of youthful enthusiasm is permitted.

Harvard was a vortex of enlivening tensions for me. On the one hand, I could allow my inquisitiveness to run wild. But, on the other, I was expected to teach within the parameters of a particular field. And even though the title of mine seemed unbounded ("Religion and Society"), I felt I needed to narrow my focus, at least to some extent. I did, but for a variety of reasons I never succumbed completely to the lure of specialization. One of the reasons still embarrasses me: Though I loved biblical lore, I never perfected the skills to succeed as a biblical scholar, a historian, or a philosopher in the academic sense. For this reason I vastly admire my colleagues who have summoned the energy, intelligence, and perseverance to do so. I often shook my head in sheer admiration for a doctoral student in Old Testament who roomed in our home and who patiently worked his way through Greek, Hebrew, Ugaritic, Coptic, and hieroglyphics. He had, of course, already passed his exams in French and German, and since he planned to return to his native Malaysia, which is a predominantly Muslim country, decided he had better master Arabic as well. But he is only one example of the extraordinary people I have worked with for thirty-five years. I realize all too clearly that without their doing the hard digging and painstaking original research, I could not do the kind of teaching and writing I do. I have no gripe to make about people who specialize, even narrowly. I stand on their shoulders. And

I respect and at times even envy them. But what they do is not what I do, nor what I intend to do in whatever years remain for me.

It should now be evident why, at my age, I find the second apple — the Big Project — so seductive. In short, I crave to return to the large questions that fascinated me in Sunday School, in college, and in graduate school. I want to think again about the riddles that spurred the Toynbees and the Maritains and even the Max Webers to look at the Big Picture. I have been emboldened to do so by discovering recently a Harvard philosopher who was already gone before I arrived, William Ernest Hocking. He was the Alford Professor of Natural Religion, Moral Philosophy, and Civil Polity until his retirement in 1943. In 1915 Professor Hocking and his wife founded the Shady Hill School, which is still thriving in Cambridge today. His preoccupation was the relationship of religions and civilizations. As he matured in his career, he became increasingly interested in Buddhism and Hinduism, but had an especially strong fascination for Islam. As early as 1934 he wrote an essay on "Christianity and Intercultural Contacts." In 1938 he delivered the Hibbert Lectures at the Universities of Cambridge and Oxford. They were published in 1940 as *Living Religions and a World Faith*. In 1956 there appeared his *The Coming World Civilization*, which included a chapter entitled "Christianity and the Faith of the Coming World Civilization." But even before Hocking died, both philosophy and theology had left his agenda behind. Philosophy became preoccupied with semantic analysis, and theology — Christian theology at least — with tradition-specific issues. True, Reinhold Niebuhr did publish a book toward the end of his career entitled *The Structure of Nations and Empires*, but even his fondest admirers concede that it was one of his weakest efforts. He was more at home with the Hebrew prophets, Augustine, original sin, and Calvin.

But there are some hints that the tide may be turning, and they come from unexpected directions. When my colleague Samuel Huntington published his famous essay "The Clash of Civilizations" a few years ago, he was widely criticized for seeming to pit "the West against the rest." He argued that, in the new post–Cold War era, the old bi-polar division between America and the Soviet Union had fallen into the now somewhat overflowing dustbin of history. Now, he contended, civilizations would become the major players, and at the core of each civilization there is always a religious tradition. His vision implied the prospect of an ugly new era of holy wars.

Many of the criticisms of Huntington are quite valid, including the suggestion made by my colleague Diana Eck that Huntington's thesis does not take into sufficient consideration the fact that the world religions are now no longer as regionally defined as they once were. Muslims and Christians and Buddhists live everywhere on the globe, interspersed with a variety of peoples, creating a "marbling" effect that raises serious questions about whether they could inspire religious wars against another civilization. A second critique of Huntington, not as lofty as Eck's, is that all the various civilizations of the world are being drawn relentlessly into the maw of market culture and the religion of consumer consumption. Thus a unified, if tawdry, single world civilization is emerging, mucilaged together by McDonald's, The Gap, pop music, and Walt Disney, in which the classical religions are being reduced to folk artifacts and local color.

However this fascinating debate eventually sorts itself out, I am grateful to Huntington. He and his critics have reopened an intellectual Pandora's box which was, however, never fully sealed to begin with. The result is that the older, larger questions are decidedly back on the table. It is no longer merely quaint to think about such brow-furrowing issues as "religion and the coming world civilization." It has become a very shiny apple indeed.

To take up the agenda again, however, one must begin by recognizing that a few things have changed. For example, the world religious traditions themselves are mutating faster than ever. Shoe-horned by their new proximity and "marbling," the on-the-ground interaction among the adherents of the several spiritual traditions has accelerated. It takes place not just at conferences but also at kitchen tables and barbecues, around the water cooler, and at bars and pubs around the world. It has outdistanced the capacity of the theologians within those traditions to guide or control it. When they do, they often have to watch their step. Fifteen years ago the Vatican was still vexed about Latin American liberation theology, issuing silencings and warnings. Today Rome's worry is Catholic theologians in Sri Lanka and Africa who are trying to rethink Christian theology within the categories of those ancient civilizations. The Sacred Congregation for the Doctrine of the Faith, it would seem, is now more worried about the incursion of karma than about the threat of class struggle.

Little by little this cheek-by-jowl cohabitation among the global faiths has begun to influence Christian theology. When I was a seminarian at Yale, there were only a handful of courses on religions other than Christianity in the catalog, and none of them was required. Time was when Christian theologians could spin out a complete systematic theology, sometimes in many volumes, with no reference to other religions. Then, when the last chapter (usually on eschatology) was finished, they might devote a kind of appendix to "other religions." Even those who took the dialogue with these alternative faiths seriously wrote as though one could round out a complete Christian theology first, and then, fully provisioned, enter it into the larger conversation. The possibility that the very pillars of Christian theology — Christology, revelation, sin and redemption, and the rest — should be rethought in continuing conversation with analogous elements in other faiths had not yet seeped in.

But now the seeping has begun in earnest. It has occurred to some theologians, mainly younger ones, that it seems a bit idle to rehearse, for example, the Christian doctrine of creation without reference to a tradition like Buddhism, which flatly denies any creation. How can one discuss traditional

Christian teachings about death and resurrection without taking into account that here in America, an astonishing percentage of people polled tell interviewers (if not their priests and ministers) that they believe in some form of reincarnation? Or, to mention a topic that I have taught about for the last ten years, can Christian Christology proceed without reference to the appreciative portraits of Jesus Christ now being sketched by Muslims, Jews, Hindus, and Buddhists? I think not. The heightened religious pluralism of our time has done more than pose a new problem for Christian theology. It has thrown in doubt the basic method by which that theology has been pursued.

But what, an alert reader might wonder, does all this talk about religion have to do with a writer like myself who is still often identified, nearly four decades later, as the "theologian of secularization"? What does Athens have to do with Jerusalem? What does secularization have to do with religious proliferation and pluralism? The answer to both questions is the same. Athens and Jerusalem have created a whole history through their interaction with each other, and so have religion and secularization. In both cases, as soon as one achieves a kind of dominance, the other swoops back from exile to challenge it. When reason and intellect begin to ride high, they inevitably make unrealistic claims, and faith and intuition awaken to question their hegemony. Then, just as the sacral begins to feel its oats and reach out for civilizational supremacy, reason and cognition question its pretentiousness. In past eras, this seesaw battle often took centuries. Today events move more swiftly. Those, including myself, who adjudged certain expressions of secularization to be a healthy corrective to religion nonetheless welcomed religious critics who attacked these expressions when they tried to impose themselves as total worldviews. We cheered the courageous religious critics of Soviet oppression. But those who celebrated the recent resurgence of religion around the world are not so sure now. When, as in Iran and India, religious movements achieve political power, we find ourselves cheering for their more secular iconoclasts.

Will it ever be thus? Or does my analysis here reflect a "Western" separation-of-power bias, traceable back through Canossa, where an emperor forced the hand of a pope by kneeling in the snow, to the two-swords idea that seems implied in the New Testament itself? "There are two," the late John Courtney Murray, S.J., who was another of my youthful favorites, repeated time after time. This was, he said, the heart of Christian political theory. There is a justifiable autonomy to the secular realm, and the sacred thrives when it is the loyal critic of this realm, not when it casts envious eyes on the seats of power. I agree with the "there-are-two" theory. But other civilizations have had other histories of the dialectic of the sacred and the profane. Do we have anything to learn from them? Is ours so clearly the best? On what basis could such a claim be made?

Today the circumstances are further complicated. Movements that appear on the surface to be secular nonetheless demonstrate unmistakable religious characteristics. Both nationalism and communism became infamous for their shrines, saints, holy books, hymns, and *rites de passage.* At the same time, movements that appear to be religious frequently camouflage patently secular purposes. Still, despite these changed parameters and the confusing borders, the Big Questions, like a shiny cluster of apples, are heaving into view. Here are some of the premises on which they will have to be addressed:

First, we *will* have, willy-nilly and for blessing or for bane, a world civilization. That much is settled. When Hocking and Toynbee and their cohort talked about it, a world civilization was still a surmise or a hope. Today we are there, or nearly there. Some perceive its arrival with fear and trembling. Others greet it as a beneficent triumph, the golden dream of the centuries come true at last, and it is the good fortune of our generation to witness and enjoy it. Still others see it as a pell-mell process whose end product is still indistinct, but which is subject to mid-course correction. Whoever turns out to be right about this, hardly anyone now disputes the actuality: The global world civilization is upon us whether we like it or not.

Second, religions will play some role in the coming world civilization. Again, the question of what role is unclear. In some places, the sturdy rootedness of indigenous traditions stands as a bulwark against the incursions of the outside world, at least for a season. At the same time, some historians claim that the religions that are already global, especially Christianity, have laid some of the essential foundation for a worldwide society. Were he alive today, Arnold Toynbee would no doubt still be contending that no civilization, including presumably a world civilization, can exist for long without a core of symbols, myths, and narratives that preserve and transmit a set of values and meanings. In other words, no world religion, no world civilization. But others contend that, although this was certainly true in the past, the advent of modern science, mass literacy, and instant global communication, although they have not abolished religion, have rendered it superfluous. Some people may need or want religion, but civilizations can now get along quite well without it, thank you. This is an argument that could well continue not just for centuries, but for millennia. But it is tempting to puzzle over it, nonetheless.

Given all these elusive factors, it is obvious that exact answers to all the questions wrapped in the package "religion and the coming world civilization" are not available. But the opaqueness of mysteries has never discouraged theologians from plunging stubbornly ahead anyway. In this case, although answers are not at hand, rough guesses, alternative scenarios, and informed conjectures do not seem inappropriate. Indeed, the weight and gravity of the questions seem to demand some response. Here is an apple even the most docile Eve and the most dutiful Adam would have a hard time resisting. Besides, there is nothing essentially wrong with making informed guesses. It is done all the time in most fields of human endeavor. Where would economics be without it?

As I think about this emerging intellectual agenda, I am comforted by the realization that it is a good one to attack as I begin to collect Social Security and ride on the subway at reduced fare. It is a topic for senior citizens like myself for two good reasons. First, one has to have accumulated several decades of preparatory thinking before one is ready to wade in. Second, actuarial tables being what they are, one will not be on the scene to witness how it turns out, even in the short run. One is spared from being hymned as a "prophet before his time," which would undermine humility. But one is also delivered from the scorn and ridicule that are always the lot of mistaken prognosticators. There are certain comforts to aging.

It is also clear, I think, that even if the biggest picture resists comprehensive coverage, still, short-range projections are possible. Even these have to be qualified, of course, with the waiver that, *given present tendencies,* these are some things we might well expect of religion(s) and civilization(s) in the near-term future. If we are scourged by nuclear war, a worldwide economic collapse, or an ecological disaster, none of which is out of the question, then all bets are off. But if none of these does happen, here are a few such short-term projections:

1. The painful division *within* traditions between open and closed, experiential and doctrinal, hierarchical and congregational, dialogical and dogmatic, will continue and deepen. Fundamentalist Muslims and Jews and Christians will continue to reserve their most scurrilous polemic not for the adherents of other faiths, but for their fellow religionists who they believe are giving away the farm. These internal divisions, incidentally, make the kind of clash of civilizations Huntington anticipates even less likely.

2. Global communication will get faster and faster, while human attention spans get shorter and shorter. This will have critical significance for both civilization and for religion. The Romans knit together their civilization, which was nearly "global" for its time, with a system of highways the like of which the world had never seen. The British relied on sea lanes. America unified itself, geographically at least, with shining rails and the golden spike. Today we have the Internet. But the burden of the information overload is already taking its toll on our capacity to absorb, process, and evaluate the signals that assault us. Religion in the past has cultivated the long view and has often encouraged people, through meditation practices and institutions like the Sabbath, to slow down on occasion and let things sink in. I think we are already seeing the beginning of a backlash against speed up and overload. The evidence can be detected in the growing popularity of meditation techniques and retreat centers. But the danger is that religion could become no more than a service sector to the global civilization, no longer shaping its values but repairing the spiritual damage it inflicts.

3. The current direction of the global civilization will more than likely

lead to one of the nuclear or ecological calamities mentioned above unless some fundamental changes in that direction are introduced soon. And religions could play a role in that course alteration. First, perpetuating an economy whose logic is infinite expansion on a finite planet obviously invites disaster. Experts differ on when the first global catastrophe — of water, air, climate, or arable soil — might occur. But few disagree that, unless present consumption patterns change, it will occur sooner or later. China, which represents a market of over one billion people, has now been granted equal trading status with the United States. But the idea of one billion new customers consuming petroleum and other hydrocarbons, and then expelling their residues into the atmosphere, is enough to terrify any ecologist. Religions have traditionally taught that restraint and a recognition of limits are virtues to be cultivated, not antiquated habits to be outgrown. But will any religion, or all of them together, be enough to challenge the inner logic of planetary market capitalism? So far the evidence is not entirely encouraging.

Also, the capitalist market system has so far succeeded in making many promises of more wealth for all, but has produced instead more division and a wider gulf between haves and have nots. Religions, with very few exceptions, have traditionally counseled the rejection of excess riches, especially when they are won at the expense of others. For the most part, however, religions have addressed economic disparity with alms and charity. They have not, with some important exceptions, addressed the structural sources of inequality. It now appears that those exceptions, like Islamic notions of a righteous economy, the medieval Christian doctrine of the just price, the Social Gospel movement, Buddhist ideas of simplicity and scale, and liberation theology, need to be brought from the past and from the edges into the center of theological reflection on civilization.

4. It also appears certain that people shaped by a particular tradition will continue to engage in the selective retrieval of components not only of their own but of other traditions as well. More and more, larger numbers of people are unwilling to see the major traditions as discrete entities, each hermetically sealed off from the other. They view these traditions as wells from which to draw, or as tool-kits from which to choose the elements that give meaning to their lives. This often infuriates the guardians of these traditions who cherish them as indivisible wholes. But are they? In fact, have they ever been? Religious scholarship today questions the idea of "religions" as discrete entities, interacting at their edges if at all, sailing along through history like battleships in a fleet, with expanses of open sea churning between them. Instead, historians suggest that what we now call "religions," be they Christianity, Judaism, Islam, Buddhism, or any of the others, are in some measure constructions projected on a jumbled past in which the interaction was much more elemental and the separateness much less distinct. Was there, for example, something called "Judaism" in the first century C.E., and something else called "early Christianity," which separated

from it and was then in conflict with it? This is what I was taught in seminary. But now historians of the period such as Daniel Boyarin and Karen King question this tidy scenario. They demonstrate that the actual picture at the time was far more complex. The same could be said for the history of what we now call "Buddhism," which many Hindus see as simply another variant of their heterogenous tradition.

I am not one of those who believes, as some in Hocking's generation did, that a single world civilization will inevitably result, sooner or later, in a single world religion. If anything, we may be headed in a very different direction. As globalization seeks to spread its web to every last nook and cranny, it is evoking resistance from local, indigenous religions some had thought to be moribund. It might amaze Cortez to know that five hundred years after his conquest of Mexico ("for gold and for souls" as he put it), the spiritual traditions he thought he had defeated are staging a recovery. How else are we to explain the fusion of Catholic and Mayan images that inspires the Zapatista uprising in Chiapas? What is especially intriguing about this revival is that it is occurring not against but within Catholicism. This suggests another question for our growing agenda. Might the rebirth of highly local spiritualities — Native North American, Celtic, indigenous South American, Black African — take place *within,* and with at least the conditional approval of, the larger world traditions? There is some confirmation that it might.

5. Finally, the wild card. In every tradition women are exercising increased leadership. After millennia of living on the margin, they are now actively involved in ministerial and priestly functions, in teaching Torah, in the spiritual direction of Buddhist retreat centers, and in interpreting the Koran. What impact will this wholly new kind of liturgical and theological leadership have? The truth is that no one knows, but it is bound to have one, as the current evidence proves.

This inventory could undoubtedly be extended. What now unforeseen new factors will emerge? What rough and unshaped beasts are slouching toward Bethlehem, Benares, Kyoto, Mecca, and countless other places in between to be born? No one knows. Nonetheless, plainly there is no scarcity of questions to provide an ample agenda for the next phase of my thinking and writing. True, most of the people with whom I have discussed these ideas listen politely at first but then gently inform me that what I am talking about is so impossibly speculative and grandiloquent that I should go back to my drawing board and come up with a more modest idea. They have a point. And I do not want to remind them of the story of the innkeeper who once noticed Edward Gibbon writing by candlelight near the fire in his tavern and shook his head, chuckling, "Scribble, scribble, scribble, eh Mr. Gibbon?" I am not megalomaniac enough to suggest that comparison. Besides, whatever I write from here on will not be scribbling. I do have a Gateway 2000 equipped with Corel WordPerfect.

Despite the skepticism of some colleagues, I am not convinced that the time for looking at Big Pictures is over. And there are some friends who have encouraged me. I am happy to say that Professor Arvind Sharma, my old friend and the editor of this volume, was one of them. As with many of my previous projects, when I described my current scheme to him, he listened thoughtfully, offered some insightful observations, and then advised me to go ahead. Consequently, this paragraph provides me with opportunity to thank every single one of the contributors to this collection, all skillfully coaxed and cajoled by Arvind to take part. And I conclude by thanking Arvind himself for his many years of entering into active co-conspiracy with me, his frequent words of wise counsel, his encouragement and — not least — for having the patience and forbearance to see this volume through from its inception in his mind to the book the reader now holds.

Part One

1

PROFESSOR HARVEY COX

How I Came to Know Him

Arvind Sharma

I

Indian troops were poised to enter what is now Bangladesh when I arrived at the Harvard Divinity School on a comparatively peaceful mission.

The journey that had brought me to its door was a complicated one. I must rush through my life in India, the better to focus on my arrival at the University of Syracuse in the fall of 1968 to take aim at a doctorate in economics. This migration halfway around the globe was spurred by the starry-eyed belief that one might be able to solve India's problem of poverty this way — an act of academic optimism arising out of a curious amalgam of juvenile bravado (despite my age) and patriotic idealism. Three years into the program brought with them the twin realizations that (1) India's problems were probably insoluble and (2) economists in the West were more concerned with advancing their own affluence than alleviating poverty in the Third World. It was time to move on both literally and figuratively.

Disillusioned, I turned to religion, but in rational hope. By now I had concluded that the economic destiny of a nation was not determined solely by economic forces. Paul A. Baran, the German economist, made this point with the help of homespun German wisdom: that there is meat in the kitchen is never decided in the kitchen. Even though a vegetarian then, I had relished the saying, although not without a trace of Gandhian guilt. But I digress.

It was with mixed feelings that I surveyed the imposing architecture of the Harvard Divinity School, as I stood in front of it one fall morning in 1971. What was a good Hindu like me doing in a place like this?

II

"Who is the most eminent Christian theologian of our times?"

When I asked my fellow Christian students this question I did so in the expectation of a straightforward answer. I was unprepared for their response.

3

I thought they would just mention a name, as I might mention the name of
S. Radhakrishnan if someone asked me for the name of the most prominent
contemporary Hindu thinker. They did anything but. Instead, a thundering
silence ensued, broken by a few barely audible gasps, some smiles, some
smirks, some laughter; some just seemed perturbed and some even looked
stricken.

The audacity of my inquiry now of course amazes me; at the time it
seemed perfectly natural. Forthrightness has a simplicity to it apparently
unknown to deliberation.

I had almost begun to wonder if I had committed a *faux pas* in this
new environment I now found myself in, if I had "said something," if I
had ignorantly broken some unwritten rule, like never mentioning women,
religion, or politics at a British army mess, when someone, perhaps taking
pity on me, said: "Well, there is Professor Harvey Cox, for instance, and..."
A few German-sounding names followed that I had trouble registering (I
hadn't taken my German exam yet).

"Where does he live?" I asked, making a mental note.

Some of the students at the table gave me an amused look — the kind of
look I was to get from my colleague at Sydney University in Australia when
I was to ask him later: "Has there been any progress in Western philosophy
in the course of this century?"

"Where does he live?" He repeated the question. Was it repeated
rhetorically, I had begun to wonder, when he ended the suspense by saying:

"Here."

"Here?" I asked again.

"Professor Cox teaches here at the Divinity School. He is the author of
the book, *The Secular City.*"

III

My experience of the Harvard Divinity School still consisted mainly of
disconnected sentence fragments, when another piece was added to this
fragmented universe in the form of Zen.

"Zen. What is Zen?" I had asked my newly acquired Jewish friend. I
hadn't heard of Zen yet, even though orientally inclined.

She cast a look of excited horror at me, at my abysmal ignorance. She
might even have wondered how this guy even got admitted into an M.T.S.
program. Then in a tone dripping with intellectual pity she said, "Come
with me," taking me by the hand.

Where is she going to take me, I wondered. My Tantrika fantasies were
just beginning to take shape, when I found myself with her in what I would
later discover was known as the Braun Room.

We joined a sizable group of people, who sat facing two obviously prominent people. "He is Alan Watts," she said, pointing him out with a graceful

movement of the neck, "and the person reading is Professor Harvey Cox." Yes, Professor Harvey Cox was then in the midst of reading a passage. We were a trifle late.

"So he is Professor Harvey Cox," I said to myself, as I immersed myself in the words. It was an account which, I learnt later, is a celebrated one in Zen annals — the meeting of the Zen patriarch Bodhidharma, freshly arrived from India, with the Chinese Emperor. It had to be some version of the following incident and could well have been this very passage:

> ...the Emperor described all that he had done to promote the practice of Buddhism, and asked what merit he had gained thereby — taking the popular view that Buddhism is a gradual accumulation of merit through good deeds, leading to better and better circumstances in future lives, and finally to *nirvana*. But Bodhidharma replied, "No merit whatever!" This so undermined the Emperor's idea of Buddhism that he asked, "What, then, is the sacred doctrine's first principle?" Bodhidharma replied, "It's just empty; there's nothing sacred." "Who, then, are you," said the Emperor, "to stand before us?" "I don't know."[1]

Everyone laughed, and none more than Watts.

Not bad, I said to myself as we broke up after the talk. A Jew and a Hindu in the audience with an American expounding "Zen," with a Christian theologian in the chair, not bad at all. What is this drumroll about Christian intolerance we hear in India all the time? I see an open discussion of Buddhism in a Christian setting. Quite a few weeks into the term and I do not recall anybody asking me to convert to Christianity!

What I was experiencing, without knowing it as such, was the distinction between proselytizing Christianity and liberal Christianity, and liking it. So what if Christianity started out with an exclusionary soteriology, at least they wondered what to do with Socrates. In any case, what really matters is not where you begin but where you end up. Perhaps this is the message of that common saying in India: Do not probe into the origins of a sacred river or a sacred person. Does this also apply to a religious tradition? I did not know where such Christianity was going but liked the direction it was headed in — or at least pointing to.

Life may still have its puzzling aspects at a Divinity School for a Hindu, but it had also become gratifying.

IV

I came to know Professor Harvey Cox more when I ended up taking the mandatory courses in Christianity with him, before we could earn the academic epaulette of M.T.S. (Masters in Theological Studies).

One session stands out in memory. I don't know how it all started but soon Professor Cox was summarizing Reinhold Niebuhr's book entitled *The*

Nature and Destiny of Man for the class. It was a *tour de force*. I grant that I was an impressionable middle-aged Hindu, but still it was masterly. The summary was followed by an equally masterly explanation of how it came to be "spun" to undergird the ideology of the Cold War. (We were still into it then.) I do not remember the details now, only the impression, which was lasting, as one can see.

It is perhaps difficult for anyone to escape the shadow of his or her past, either as biography or as history. So when the time came, I decided to make my oral presentation in one of the classes given by Professor Harvey Cox on the association of Christianity with imperialism. It might seem like free associating to an American, but for an Indian the association is hardly free — it is forced on him by history. While recently cleaning the Augean stables of my accumulated papers, I came upon the following comment on it by Professor Cox in a document contained in my dossier. This is what it said:

> In his oral presentation he effectively documented the relationship between the prevailing Christian ideology in Britain in the nineteenth century and its influence on British imperial expansion in India, showing the extent to which the Christian ideology promoted that expansion and the extent to which it checked it. It was a lucid presentation and showed an ability on his part to relate theological ideas to historical events.

I must wonder to what extent this element of identifying "the extent to which it checked it" was the result of the impact that my new environment was having on my thinking. For much as we may like to imagine that our minds inhabit a point of Archimedean objectivity, situatedness is hard to escape. Be that as it may, intellectual forces were in this way set in motion which would gradually mature into the belief that to characterize any tradition as this or that may ultimately involve a misrepresentation, as most traditions conceal a number of perspectives, and even contradictory perspectives, within their horizons.

From the view that religions may be this or that ("Hinduism is tolerant, Christianity is not.") one graduates to the view that most religions contain elements of both this and that ("Strands of tolerance and intolerance are present within both Hinduism and Christianity and their proportions can vary over time."). If one keeps moving along this trajectory, then ultimately any labelling of any tradition as this or that — "Hinduism . . . Christianity . . . Islam . . . is patriarchal." — begins to sound mildly offensive. Each tradition is many things — a polychrome. Sure there is patriarchal Hinduism, patriarchal Christianity, or patriarchal Islam. But can one label Hinduism, or Christianity, or Islam "patriarchal" without prejudice to those elements in these traditions which might not be so?

V

One must now fast-forward to 1992. It must have been the 7th of December 1992. It can be no other, for it was the day after the demolition of the Babri Mosque in Ayodhya.[2]

The demolition was not yet a settled fact in my mind as I walked into the office with the local newspaper tucked under the armpit. I had heard some rumors to the effect the previous day, but they were too fantastic to be considered credible, even with the reputedly lower cultural Hindu threshold in the matter. There was though this quizzical call from an excited friend late in the evening, letting me know that the Mosque had been razed to the ground.

As I wondered and went through the news report it became apparent that what until a moment ago I had dismissed as incredible, was indeed true. Once more the unbelievable had happened.

I began to feel nervous. I am not sure why. This was simply something too cataclysmic to elicit a normal reaction. Its magnitude was paralyzing, but only mentally; emotionally, it was devastating.

"This is too much," I muttered to myself when my eyes fell on another news item: The Indian prime minister had announced that the mosque will be rebuilt on the very spot!

I believe I have never before or after experienced such an emotion of unmitigated outrage. Very briefly, I went ballistic. I think it had to do with my short stint as a civil servant in India. I could scarcely believe my eyes. Is the prime minister of India, the nation's CEO, out of his mind? Does he not realize the effect such a statement will have in a situation such as this—add fuel to fire? For a brief moment I viscerally felt as if the country were about to come apart, and I along with it.

If the effect of the news had been devastating, the effect of reading the Indian prime minister's statement was catastrophic.

Just then the phone rang. Brushing aside any qualms about answering it in my condition, I lifted the receiver.

It was Professor Harvey Cox on the line.

Events were happening in such quick succession that I was spooked and breathless. I don't recall what our initial conversation was all about, although I am certain that my contribution to it must have been minimal.

Whatever it was, it was soon overtaken by recent developments.

"By the way, I am sorry to hear about the reports of religious conflict from your country. I hope it settles down soon."

I do not remember the content of our conversation with any claim to exactitude, but I can recall vividly its tone. It was designed to put me at ease. I am certain that I was out of breath for most of it.

I was extraordinarily tense before and during the call. It is not exactly every day that these three things happen: a mosque is razed to the ground; your prime minister commits what you think is a Himalayan blunder (Gandhi's expression), and you get a direct call from Professor Harvey Cox, while you are trying to come to terms with these. The saving grace was that the third had acted like an antidote to the first two. It was reassuring in some indescribable way.

It was an extraordinary forenoon. That is how I remember it even today.

Things, of course, had been building up in India for a while. And whenever I would see Professor Harvey Cox we would talk about them. By the time he visited Montreal in the fall of 1990, to speak at our Faculty, the explosive potential of the developments back in India had become obvious. My own protracted reflection on these had brought me to the unlikely conclusion that few others seemed to reach or at least articulate — that it all went back to partition: the partition of British India into the two nation-states of India and Pakistan. Partition is the Wailing Wall of my generation, and yet partition in secular India has the status of the "love that dare not speak its name" in Victorian England. However, to talk of current developments without talking of partition was, for me, like talking about the American Civil War without talking of slavery, or about Nazi Germany without mentioning the Holocaust. Fortunately I was not entirely alone in this — at least a handful of Indians in Montreal thought similarly. We drew up the following statement.

An Appeal for Referendum on Partition

News from around the world today indicates that tectonic changes are under way across the globe. Two items have figured prominently, among others: the call for a plebiscite in Kashmir and the right to self determination of peoples of Eastern Europe.

Inhabitants of the subcontinent of India are poignantly reminded at this moment of the grave injustice done to them in 1947, when the then British India was partitioned without taking the wishes of its inhabitants into account. We, the undersigned, therefore, urge that a plebiscite be held over the entire territory which comprised British India on the question of its partition into India and Pakistan. We regret that the fate of a quarter of the population of the globe was decided arbitrarily by the representative of an imperial power and by those who were not even duly elected by adult franchise. We attribute the current malaise on the subcontinent to the fact that a political decision of such momentous significance as the vivisection of a country's body politic was imposed upon it without taking its corporate wishes into account through a referendum.[3]

I showed it to Professor Harvey Cox as we sat in the lounge of the Chateau Versailles. I remember the location because he mentioned how he had honeymooned in the same hotel with Nina.

He read it over. I wondered aloud if he would be willing to endorse it. After all, if it could have the support of a Christian, not only of a Christian but of a Christian theologian, not only of a Christian theologian but of an internationally renowned Christian theologian. . . .

I was awakened from the fantasy by a monosyllable: "Yes." Then he said, with equal simplicity: "I think it has been a great tragedy."

I was quite stunned. I am not sure what stunned me more, his willingness to signify his support for the appeal or his pronouncement that partition was a great tragedy. Not everyone sees it that way. Many who feel that way do not say it that way. But here was someone who said it as he saw it.

Of course others may see it differently. But my frustration was not with them, but with those who, even when they saw it as a tragedy, were somehow prevented from stating it as such. Why, we could get only a handful of Indians to sign on. And here was someone who was not even from India but could yet sense its tragic dimension in an unencumbered way.

VI

To talk of partition is to talk of Mahatma Gandhi. We talked about him often, often enough for Professor Harvey Cox to invite me to address his class on one of my visits to Cambridge from Montreal. Subject: Mahatma Gandhi as a Liberation Theologian.

I don't remember now exactly what I said, but I do remember a moment during the talk which was theologically liberating. I was dwelling on the theme of Mahatma Gandhi's leadership of the struggle for Indian independence in the course of my talk, when all of a sudden out of nowhere, I heard myself say, "India became free on August 15, 1947. We were slaves in our country and the Lord freed us with a mighty hand!"

This line was completely unplanned; totally unrehearsed. I didn't know what I had said until I heard it. And then I panicked, hearing myself say it. I had really gotten carried away by the moment. I cast an anxious glance in the direction of Professor Harvey Cox. (Will he ever invite me to speak again — a Hindu carrying coal to Newcastle as it were, presumptuously, if spontaneously, waxing biblical at the Harvard Divinity School itself?)

He smiled and nodded. I continued: "Gandhi was for us Moses and Christ rolled into one. . . . "

VII

These days I seek out opportunities to participate actively in discussions of religion and human rights. But this was hardly the case in the summer of 1993. I had just returned from a trip overseas and casually begun to catch up with my calls. I was startled by a message from Professor Harvey Cox, which laid out the details of a Project on Religion and Human Rights. At the end I was asked to let him know whether this interested me.

Initially I did not know what to think. Human rights? Isn't that just another reformulation of the White Man's Burden? Another manifestation of imperialism — and this time moral at that? And the West talking of human rights — this is surely risible, after having deprived the rest of the world of them for three centuries! But then the flow of thoughts would make a U-turn. Are you sure? Don't knock it until you try it. Do you doubt that people of genuine goodwill exist all over the world? (This is something I have had no reason to doubt so far in my life.) Do you think that Indians are the only people called upon by Gandhi not to look on inertly when injustices are being committed? How do you account for your own majestical pessimism in relation to the moral sensibilities of "other" people? One cannot just live in the world, one must live in a just world.

The fact that the inquiry had come from Professor Harvey Cox tilted the balance of the scales in its favor. I signed on...and on...and on.

Looking back, I am now struck by the fact that Professor Harvey Cox never ever said that I *should* be concerned about human rights. The question simply was: was I or not? It was not even so much an ethical as an existential matter. Albert Schweitzer says somewhere that example is not the main thing, it is the only thing. Surely another formulation of Gandhi's response, when asked for his message: "My life is my message."

VIII

What has it been like to know Professor Harvey Cox? I could try to say a lot of complimentary things or I could say just this: Back in India, it is said that merely to know some people is to improve the quality of one's life. This volume attests that I am not the only person to feel this way upon coming to know Harvey.

Notes

1. Alan Watts, *The Way of Zen* (New York: Pantheon Books, 1957), 86.
2. Edward A. Gargan, "Hindu Militants Destroy Mosque, Setting Off a New Crisis in India," *New York Times* (December 7, 1992): A1, A10.
3. *Pragati* (Montreal: August–September 1990): 15. This text also subsequently appeared as the substantial part of a letter to the editor in the *New York Times*, December 16, 1992, under the heading "Time to Undo Damage of Indian Partition."

2

A REMINISCENCE

Robert McAfee Brown

Harvey and I were members of a seven-person "Mission of Desperation" at the very end of 1972, when President Nixon had given the go-ahead to drop as many bombs on Haiphong Harbor as would be needed to pummel the Vietnamese into submission. Participation in this mission was one of the few times Harvey and I had ever met; for a number of years we had been involved in war protest, but only occasionally at the same time and in the same place. I had privately decided that there was no such person as "Harvey Cox," and that what I had observed on a few occasions was a kind of portable anti-war icon, programmed to give speeches and engage in actions that would inspire the rest of us not to lose heart or head.

But now, thanks to the Nixon bombings, we actually shared each other's company both corporeally and ideologically, flying together to such places as London, Stuttgart, Utrecht, and Rome, hoping to persuade Christian and Jewish leaders to speak out strongly against the bombing, since our own government clearly would pay us no heed.

Harvey had a special assignment, albeit a self-imposed assignment. This was to carry, in his overcoat pocket, a present for the pope, the shell of an expended anti-personnel weapon, that ugly instrument of modern warfare that does intensive harm to people, while leaving buildings untouched. We hoped the pope would accept this symbol of what our world had become and would challenge the human family to reverse course and once again turn swords into ploughshares, or, in our case, an anti-personnel weapon into a candle holder.

Harvey was clearly the point man on our trip. Whenever our group was introduced and the name "Harvey Cox" was spoken, there was an intake of breath, as Europeans for the first time put together the name and the face. Cardinal Alfrink of Utrecht, not one to leave anything to chance, responded in cordial tones, "Yes, I have heard of you." As had they all.

We were unable to secure a papal audience. A few local folk intimated that the papal household was fearful that Harvey was planning to talk the rest of us into a sit-in on papal property, which would have been unseemly. This conjecture, whether accurate or not, was far ahead of what any of us

11

might have dreamed up as a possible attention-getter with the Holy Father. Even so, Harvey got one of the papal attendants to accept the bomb-casing-become-a-candleholder, and to relay to the pope our hope that he would light the candle and keep it lit at least until the ending of the bombing of Haiphong Harbor.

All that, however, pales to insignificance in comparison to what else was going on with the bomb, for it played a creative role throughout the trip. It had apparently not occurred to Harvey that to transport a bomb casing onto an airplane was at best "unlawful" and at worst "unethical." That it went safely through the JFK and Heathrow metal detectors without happenstance would have been a signal event without further embellishment, save that Harvey repeated the performance at each of the twelve remaining gates on our itinerary.

Now bombs, whether detonated or not, are not supposed to make it past safety devices of the sort present at all airports. And what would it have done to our trip if, at any of the fourteen gates, the "peacemakers from overseas" had been discovered to be transporting bombs, whether explodable or not?

After we had gotten through a half dozen such gates without mishap of any sort, I decided that the neutralized bomb had some kind of *mana*, or sacred power, emanating from it, so that under the protection of such *mana*, the chances were pretty good that no mere human contrivance, such as a fence or a gate, could deter it from the completion of its task.

Fair enough, I mused, but something was still missing from the equation. For the bomb obviously had to have what can be designated as a "bomb carrier," a participant endowed with another form of power, namely *chutzpah*, about which it is often said that if you have to ask what it means you'll never understand the answer. *Chutzpah* may not be describable, but it can be observed, and in the present instance, Harvey's decision to carry a highly volatile instrument of war (even if only symbolically) through fourteen ever-so-sensitive turnstiles was an example of *chutzpah* to the highest degree, demonstrated in our very presence.

Conclusion: when *mana* and *chutzpah* come into contact, under skillful leadership, there is no calculating what such a combination could finally do for the cause of peace.

Which Harvey has been doing ever since.

3

THE TIMES, GOD, AND HARVEY COX

John C. Cort

In 1984 Harvey Cox published a follow-up to *The Secular City* entitled *Religion in the Secular City*. At the publication party we sang a song to the tune of the old hymn: "Love Lifted Me":

> I was sunk in doublespeak
> Back in the modern age,
> Secularity seemed bleak,
> Religion an empty stage.
> Now at last I've found a book
> That says I can have it all,
> Harvey says that God is back
> And standing tall.

The *New York Times* ran the review of this book on the first page of its Sunday Book Review. Subsequently a reviewer in a much smaller publication closed his review with these words, "God bless Harvey Cox. When he tells the world that God is back and standing tall, he does it with so much style and *élan* that even the *New York Times* has to take notice."[1]

The Times did not, however, at that time acknowledge that God was back and standing tall. Sitting upright, perhaps. Standing tall, at least in *The Times*' political opinion, would have to wait another thirteen years, until December 7, 1997, when it devoted a whole issue of its *Sunday Magazine*, with splashy red cover, to the subject of "God Decentralized." Actually, that title and the subtitle served notice that Americans may be among the most religious people in the world, but that they are "inventing unorthodox ways" to express their religious faith or feelings, or whatever might pass for religion in this crazy mixed-up world. And these qualifications indicated that *The Times* at least was not convinced that God was more than about 5′10″ tall. Tall perhaps if you yourself were 5′6″. Otherwise, no.

Still, a whole issue devoted to any kind of religion? And not a bad issue at that. In fact, quite comprehensive and fair to all parties, including a section for atheists, and the Endpaper, without which no magazine is complete these days, devoted to humorous remarks about "the afterlife" by assorted cynics. But on balance not a bad issue.

For that I think Harvey Cox deserves some of the credit. For he is one of the theologians who has kept alive the notion that one could be intelligent, have a sense of humor, be a conscientious scholar, write in a clear, graceful style, and still believe in God. This has not always been self-evident.

True, there was a time when he favored Bonhoeffer's notion of "a religionless Christianity,"[2] which was a little difficult to understand. But in that 1984 book he wrote that "the Resurrection of Christ... is coming to supply a focal motif in the theology of postmodern Christianity."[3] He gave no evidence that this trend was displeasing to him and thereby left the impression that it might even be pleasing. And this issue of the *Times Magazine* confirms his prophecy, for the two best, most persuasive writers in the issue proclaim their faith in the Resurrection, what St. Augustine called "God's supreme and wholly marvelous work."[4] This would not have happened ten years ago, not in the *New York Times*. More about these two writers later. For now let us examine this extraordinary issue, "God Decentralized," in some detail.

The lead article is by Jack Miles, author of *God: A Biography,* which won a Pulitzer Prize. His conclusion seems to be that the religious revival is not so much the result of a growth of faith in God as it is the result of a loss of faith in life without God. That is, more and more thinking people "have looked at what their society has become and recoiled" (p. 58). The fact that many people can drive their new Mercedes to the shopping mall and drive it home loaded with goodies, while children elsewhere go hungry and homeless, does not fill these people with delight but rather with disgust. And even intellectuals in comfortable ivory towers are finding that comfortable ivory can become acutely uncomfortable in time. So they turn to God, but often to a God of their own making, or to another God than the one in whose image they were raised.

For this purpose the United States has become a convenient locale. The next piece is devoted to statistics, and what stands out is our religious diversity, "God Decentralized." The number of Hindus in this country is approaching one million, up from 70,000 in 1977. There are 3.5 million Muslims, about as many as there are Presbyterians. Nearly a million are African-Americans.

Although 87 percent of Americans consider themselves Christians and most of these attend church, at least on occasion, the identity of the church has been changing dramatically. Mainline Protestant membership is down significantly, Roman Catholics are down slightly but still comprise 22 percent of the population, and the more evangelical Protestant sects are up sharply. The Church of God in Christ, for example, is up 863 percent in the last thirty years. These sharp increases have been powered in large part by the 400 megachurches (up from ten in 1970) that you can see on TV, with congregations in the thousands, massive choirs, beautiful soloists, and always a spell-binding preacher who can raise the short hairs on the back of your neck.

My own superficial observation is that in these churches the line between entertainment and religion becomes somewhat fuzzy. The theology, what there is of it, tends to be traditional, the social message conservative, the intellectual content minimal, the emotional appeal maximal, and the financial appeal likewise and continuous. It takes money to put on this kind of a show.

What the mainline Protestants and Catholics can learn from these churches is that traditional theology has a strong appeal, as does good music and good preaching. Intellectual content need not, and must not, be sacrificed. The human animal is a rational animal before and above all, and at no time should the impression be left that reason may be subordinated to feeling, to the emotions, however warm and sexy they may be. At the same time, the mainline churches can only ignore the element of emotion at their own peril. This underlines the importance of music and good preaching, which have traditionally been the media by which feeling has been communicated to the faithful in a religious service.

Some of the statistics in "God Decentralized" are puzzling. For example, we learn that 96 percent of Americans say that they believe in God, compared with 95 percent fifty years ago. The same percentage (41) still attend church once a week and 63 percent regularly say grace before meals, compared with 43 percent in 1947. At the same time, 60 percent of the respondents in a recent poll said that religion is a waning force in American life. In short, while religious faith seems to be either constant or increasing, keeping the U.S.A. up among the most religious countries in the world, most of us seem to agree that the secular city is becoming even more secular with the passage of time. Somehow our faith, or faiths, are not reflected in our lives. Or at least not in the lives and/or actions of those who control, dictate, dominate, shape, or otherwise mess up the general construction of our society. Those at the top, the rich and powerful, are either losing faith or their faith is placed in some pretty distorted, self-indulgent kind of religion. Their secularism is not the kind of positive phenomenon that Harvey Cox wrote about in *The Secular City.*

Peter Steinfels contributes a thoughtful piece, "When is a Catholic Not a Catholic?" centered on the Catholic students at Purdue University in Indiana and the studies of James Davidson, a sociologist of religion at that institution. Davidson draws a pretty grim picture: "Young Catholics are less religious in childhood than their parents and grandparents; they report fewer experiences of God's presence in their lives, and they are less committed to the Church. . . . Unless steps are taken (they will continue) to disagree with traditional faith and morals and to embrace religious ideas that are incompatible with Church teachings." This tendency, Davidson concludes, threatens "the long-term viability of the Church" (p. 63).

Steinfels's own observations, however, reveal a much more cheerful picture. The chapel of St. Thomas Aquinas Center on the campus, not a megachurch but still seating 1200, is filled three times on Sundays and Steinfels writes, "Judging from these numbers, and from the energy with which the young people pray, sing, and proclaim the Scriptures, it's easy to conclude that the Roman Catholic Church in the United States has little to worry about when it comes to passing on its faith to another generation" (p. 63).

Grim or cheerful, take your pick. And of course there are some, both in and out of the Church, who would pick grim because they find it more cheerful to believe that what is known as "cafeteria Catholicism" may be more popular in the future than the single, fixed menu of us oldsters.

Steinfels also reports that there are some of the Purdue students who prefer the fixed menu. These are not so likely to be found at the free-swinging Thomas Aquinas Center, but at St. Boniface Church, which is off campus. Adam Gretencord, one of the students, insists that "I am a *Roman* Catholic" and this means "the whole business, no picking and choosing" (p. 64).

Steinfels spoke to other young folks, both on and off the Purdue campus, and was impressed with their commitment to the traditional faith. But Davidson insists that the data show that the trend away from the traditional may have slowed but it has not stopped.

The American Jewish population is close to the same size it was in 1980, about 5.5 million, but as a percentage of the total population it has slipped from 3 percent to just over 2 percent. The main reason for the slippage seems to be intermarriage. One estimate is that in 1997 some 50 percent of the marriages were outside the Jewish faith, or Jewish culture, if that is a better term. Before 1960 it was about 10 percent.

Rodger Kamenetz tells us what is happening within the community of religious Jews. He is the author of *Stalking Elijah: Adventures with Today's Jewish Mystical Masters,* which recently received a National Jewish Book Award, and *The Jew and the Lotus,* which will soon appear as a documentary film. These titles, and their popularity, indicate a significant trend within that community. It is illustrated nicely by a story from Kamenetz's own experience:

I knew something was up when I gave a lecture for the United Jewish Appeal in New York. U.J.A. is a bulwark institution of secular American Judaism, yet here I was fielding questions about Jewish spirituality — meditation, the renewal movement of Rabbi Zalman Schachter and *kabbalah* (Jewish mysticism). Finally, a bewildered older gentleman asked, "What does this have to do with supporting the state of Israel?" I smiled and thought, absolutely nothing.

The old exoteric (outward looking) agenda of institutional Judaism focused heavily on supporting Israel, along with such enduring issues as anti-Semitism, the Holocaust, and the rescue of Soviet and Ethiopian Jewry. But for a new generation, for whom the immigrant experience is a fading memory, the outward struggles have turned inward (p. 84).

"Perhaps, indeed," Kamenetz admits, "there is only anecdotal evidence that I, and others like me, exist." But there is some convincing evidence. He points to the success of Rabbi Jonathan Omer-Man, the crippled, English-born founder of Metivta (Aramaic for "academy") in Los Angeles, which in seven years has taught more than 3,000 Jews the rudiments of Jewish prayer and meditation. His success and the reasons he gave Kamenetz for his success tie in with the reasons given by Jack Miles for the current religious revival. This is how Rabbi Omer-Man expressed it:

> Most people past age 20 have broken hearts. There's no way you can't. Whether [because] of people very important to us dying, going mad, abandoning us or just, "I don't like the life I'm living, I'm disappointed, my life seems meaningless," nobody denies having a broken heart.

Kamenetz believes that the cure for Jewish broken hearts lies in a return to the spiritual and prayerful treasures of that ancient faith. He makes a good case for this belief.

There are other articles about pilgrimages, about a family headed by a Catholic mother and a Buddhist Japanese-American father, about and by a black female Unitarian minister, about faith healing, about a New Age woman who has (so far) successfully combined religion and real estate, about a thriving black Baptist church in Louisville that has grown from 97 members in 1983 to 2,439 today. Much of this thriving is due to the charismatic minister, but another reason was well put by his assistant: "The key is, once they come in, you've got to get them involved. You don't do that, you lose them" (p. 100). And so Canaan Missionary Baptist Church offers involvement for every talent: a youth ministry, a sports ministry, a men's ministry, a food pantry, Bible study, a youth choir, a Community Development Corporation.

Finally, let us return to "the two best writers," who not only confirm Harvey Cox's dictum that "the Resurrection of Christ . . . is coming to supply a focal motif in the theology of postmodern Christianity," but also help us to see how intelligence or reason can be combined with feeling and imagination to make a case for religious faith.

Thomas Aquinas used to say that "art is the use of right reason in the making of things."[5] Yes and no. More than reason seems to be involved. Pascal used to say with typical exaggeration that "imagination governs all; she created beauty, justice and happiness. . . . "[6] Both are partly right. And so was Goethe, who has Faust saying that "feeling is all in all."[7]

Barbara Grizzuti Harrison is the Catholic author of *Italian Days* and *An Accidental Autobiography.* Her short piece is entitled "Alone in a Lofty Place." The first paragraph sets the stage:

> It is late at night.... My usually lovable apartment is untidy. (There are, for reasons I have no wish to discuss, pork chop bones, mail order catalogues and heaps of German Art Deco jewelry on my dining room table.) My mind is untidy too. Even my computer, companion and co-worker, feels alien: illness has kept me from it for a long time, and it seems like a recalcitrant stranger. Woe, in other words, is me.

Consider the brilliance of the phrase: "for reasons I have no wish to discuss." Impossible not to feel a surge of sympathetic feeling for this woman. She is honest and humble enough to reveal her abandoned pork chop bones, but proud enough not to reveal why she abandoned them. The picture is one of classy and humorous, but solid, misery and loneliness.

In this misery and loneliness she can still "enter into joy and light" by thinking upon Jesus Christ and the company of His saints. Others insist that "Jesus was merely a Son of God, not God himself; but how very much less desirable and attractive He is if He is only Daddy's brave best boy, prophet, social worker, revolutionary. It is because God suffered in His flesh and soul that we, broken and askew, are able to cast ourselves upon Him" (p. 73).

It is this same appeal of the suffering Christ that sounds most clearly in that other best writer, Benjamin Cheever. Cheever is the son of John Cheever, another brilliant writer whose *New Yorker* stories, as I vaguely remember them, gave no evidence that he would raise a religious son. The son sounds more like a traditional Episcopalian, but that is only a guess. He comes on as embarrassed and almost ashamed of his religiosity and his faith that Jesus was the Son of God who rose from the dead.

He gets to you, and here again feeling is a powerful element, by telling the story of a cynical, unbelieving college friend who in a moment of total misery asked the question that Jesus, quoting from Psalm 22, asked on the cross, "My God, my God, why hast thou forsaken me?" Cheever ends his piece:

> So what does this story mean? That we're all closet Christians? I don't think so. What it means, I think, is that we often don't know what we believe. What we do know, what we can know, is what we *mean* to believe.
>
> And I mean to believe in the man they called the King of the Jews. I mean to believe in his courage. I mean to believe in his love.
>
> And that he suffered terribly (p. 44).

The only fault I could find with Cheever's piece is what I think is an unnecessary concession: "To repeat the Apostles' Creed is to abdicate the rational mind. I know that" (p. 42).

I don't know that. I don't believe that. Maybe it's just my background as a curious newspaperman and lifelong journalist. Reading the Gospels, I recognize trustworthy reporting. Of course there are contradictions and inconsistencies, but nothing that the failure of honest memories or the natural disagreement of honest witnesses cannot explain. The overall effect is one of truth.

But the best thing ever written about the credibility of the Resurrection was written by the fourth-century saint John Chrysostom, who, unfortunately, seems also to have been anti-Semitic. After highlighting the fact that the first disciples of Jesus were mostly uneducated, unsophisticated men from the Galilean sticks and that they were totally terrified and demoralized by the crucifixion, John Chrysostom concludes:

> How then account for the fact that these men, who in Christ's lifetime did not stand up to the attacks by their fellow Jews, set forth to do battle with the whole world once Christ was dead — if, as you claim, Christ did not rise and speak to them and rouse their courage? Did they perhaps say to themselves: "What is this? He could not save himself but he will protect us? He did not help himself when he was alive, but now that he is dead he will extend a helping hand to us? In his lifetime he brought no nation under his banner, but by uttering his name we will win over the whole world?" *Would it not be wholly irrational even to think such thoughts, much less to act upon them? It is evident then that if they had not seen him risen and had proof of his power, they would not have risked so much* (emphasis added).

It *is* evident. Common sense, the product of reason reflecting on experience, tells us that it is evident. If it is "wholly irrational" not to believe, then it is wholly rational to believe. To repeat the Creed you don't have to abdicate the rational mind. Neither do you have to take refuge in subtleties to the effect that it is not contrary to reason, it is rather above or beyond reason. Christian faith is wholly reasonable.

I could be wrong, but I get the impression that Harvey Cox has come more and more to a similar conclusion.

Notes

1. John C. Cort, *Religious Socialism* (Winter 1984): 9.
2. Daniel Callahan, ed., *The Secular City Debate* (New York: Macmillan, 1966), Harvey Cox in "An Exchange of Views," 118.
3. Harvey Cox, *Religion in the Secular City* (New York: Simon & Schuster, 1984), 214.
4. St. Augustine, cited in *Christian Prayer: The Liturgy of the Hours* (Jamaica Plain, Mass.: Daughters of St. Paul, 1976), 1039.
5. Thomas Aquinas, *Summa Theologica* (Chicago: Encyclopaedia Britannica, Great Book Edition, 1990), Part 1 of Second Part, Article 4, Question 57, 38.
6. Blaise Pascal, *Pensées* (New York: Pantheon, 1950), 43.
7. Johann Wolfgang von Goethe, *Faust* (New York: Modern Library, 1930), 132.

4

BUILDING ALLIANCES

Cox and Levenson

JORGE PIXLEY

Harvey Cox, besides being a distinguished Harvard theologian, is also a Baptist minister. In May of 1997 we had the privilege of having him as the speaker for our Frank Pais Lectureship[1] at the Baptist Theological Seminary of Nicaragua. After recognizing that the "consumer culture" fostered by the global market is the main threat to humans living today and drawing attention to the explosive growth of Pentecostalism around the globe, he issued a call for an alliance among religions to challenge the consumer culture and especially urged that we as Baptists maintain an openness to the evangelical values of the Pentecostal movement. Both the prophetic recognition of the principal threat to human life and the generous openness to the "other" of Protestantism were typical of the minister and professor we honor with this book.[2]

In this article I would like to examine the public position of Professor Cox's Harvard colleague Jon Levenson with respect to liberation theology, specifically my Exodus commentary. Dr. Levenson is Albert A. List Professor of Jewish Studies at the Harvard Divinity School. The polemic he has carried on with liberation theology goes back to a faculty paper read in the spring of 1988 in Cambridge, which went through several versions of lectures at diverse universities and ended up as the last chapter of a 1993 book, *The Hebrew Bible, the Old Testament, and Historical Criticism*.[3] In the present article I would like to respond to that chapter from a position that prizes alliance-building of the sort Harvey Cox proposed in Managua. Polemics may have a legitimate place in alliance-building when deviations which threaten one group in the alliance are being exposed. Levenson's book is polemical; is it also constructive in our current climate, where all religions and peoples are threatened by a market gone wild?

Levenson's Reading of My Exodus Commentary[4]

Let me begin this reading of Levenson's reading of my reading of the biblical Book of Exodus by stating that the Pixley in Levenson's reading is not recognizable by me. The commentary is not engaged at any depth and the Pixley in his reading is a straw man.

Neither does Levenson engage Marxism at any depth. I do not deny that my commentary is Marxist as well as Christian. But the Marxism which Levenson attacks, which was the ideological support of the bureaucratic government of the USSR, is not the Marxism I use in my analyses of the historical situation that evoked the exodus nor that professed by myself or other liberation theologians.

Levenson emphasizes the surprise I express that the tribes of Israel make allowance for personal slavery in the laws of Exodus (p. 134). He takes my surprise as an indication of failure to understand the true nature of the Exodus, which he reads me to be taking as a movement "from slavery to freedom, either freedom in the older, liberal sense of emancipation from external constraint for the purpose of self-determination, or freedom in the newer, Marxist sense of liberation from oppression and alienation for the purpose of equality, solidarity, and community" (p. 146). While it is true that I speak in my commentary of Egypt and pre-Israelite Canaan as class societies, I never identified slavery as the basis of these societies. Using the category of the Asiatic Mode of Production which Marx outlines in the *Grundrisse* of 1857–58, I make it clear that the oppressive class was identical with the monarchical State (p. 4). The villages preserved a measure of autonomy in their internal affairs, but were linked to the State by the obligation to pay tribute in kind. The two classes involved in the production and reproduction of life were the State (the king and his functionaries) and the peasants (the sum of villages in the king's territories).

That the exodus from Egypt can be understood as a revolutionary movement depends not on the equal human rights of all citizens and foreign residents, men and women, but on the suppression of human kingship, for the king personified in a religious, transcendent manner, and hence legitimated, the oppression which autonomous villages experienced in the tribute they were forced to render in kind and in forced labor. The legal codes in the Pentateuch (if we make the exception of Deut 17:14–20, generally taken to be a late law) make no provision for human kingship and thus establish the basis for a classless society of a primitive sort, a primitive communism. This is revolutionary and not simply a primitive social organization, because it arises as a rejection of societies in Egypt and Canaan which had monarchical States.

My surprise at Israelite slavery, then, reflects a sadness that this people had not understood the inhumanity of this reduction of persons to merchandise, a sadness which I also feel that the place of women is not equal to that of males. But this is a historical fact that must be accepted as one of the characteristics of this revolutionary society. Revolutions are historical movements with the specificities of any historical movement. That slavery was tolerated in this revolutionary rejection of kingship does not cancel its revolutionary

character. What does reflect a counterrevolutionary movement in Israel is
the creation of kingship with Saul and the introduction of forced labor with
Solomon. Although the book Levenson reads was a commentary and not a
systematic argument, the reading of passages like pp. 113–16 should have
made clear the basis for my considering the exodus a revolutionary movement. Levenson, unlike Marx and (in a modest reflection of Marx) myself,
unhistorically would require of an ancient social movement that it conform
to modern liberal or Marxist definitions to qualify as revolutionary. Had he
wished to understand, surely my commentary had enough clues to disabuse
him of such an unhistorical definition, and had he read my *God's Kingdom*
of 1983[5] or Marx's *Grundrisse* of 125 years before, the historicity of any
revolution would have been clear enough.

It is absolutely astounding to find Levenson making very much the same
point I make in my commentary about Israel's subjection to YHWH — as
if this undercut my argument. Israel rejected service to Pharaoh in order
to become the servant of YHWH. This Levenson develops at length in the
chapter we are discussing, and I concur. This would relativize a reading of
the exodus as the emancipation of personal slaves for a slaveless society, but
this was not the basis of my identification of the exodus as revolutionary. In
the sociological reading of the exodus that underlies my commentary (and
which is explicitly argued in *God's Kingdom*), YHWH takes the place of
the king in State societies of the time, those of Canaan and Egypt. So that
in fact the servitude to YHWH allows the tribes to free themselves from the
various forms of tribute which human kings require. Allow me to quote a
passage from the commentary:

> The principal theoretical text of this ancient revolution is profoundly reli-
> gious. A secular revolution was not a real option for the peasants of Canaan
> who could no longer tolerate the taxation imposed on them by the kings.
> They thought that gods sent rain, they thought that gods delivered them from
> plagues. The alternatives they faced were not like those facing the Russian
> revolutionaries at the beginning of this century — between a religion that le-
> gitimated an oppressive social order, and a revolutionary doctrine that made
> workers the agents of their own history. The Canaanite peasants depended on
> gods for their survival. The option was between the gods of the kings, Baal
> and his minions, and the God of the poor, Yahweh.... Only, they would have
> to tender to Yahweh their exclusive loyalty (121).

The revolution of the Moses people from Egypt and the tribes of Israel
from Canaan was obviously not patterned on modern liberal or Marxist
theories of emancipation from slavery or a classless society. Any attempt to
understand it so would be naively ahistorical. These peasants were rejecting
gods that supported kings and surrendering themselves to YHWH the God
who rejected kings. This was revolutionary, and it is theorized in the parable
of Jotham in Judges 9, not in social-scientific language but in the language
of fable.

Levenson interprets the relation of Israel to YHWH by three terms, enthronement, covenant, and dedication. I find no problem in agreeing, and believe that had he read my commentary with a will to understand, he would have found these elements there. Certainly, he would have found the first and the second, and the third in an implicit fashion. The kingship of YHWH has a very important sociological place in my commentary and its revolutionary interpretation of the exodus, for which I acknowledged my debt to Martin Buber. Covenant was not fully developed, although I acknowledged my debt to George Mendenhall. I can only conclude that Levenson's preconceptions about revolution did not allow him to read my commentary with a clear mind.

Listening and Reading

If religions are going to make a contribution to the defense of human life from the threats that confront our survival in the next generation, we must learn to listen to each other and discover the commonalities behind our diverse pieties. Let me quote from a remarkable case of inattention in Levenson's book:

> It is this antipathy to forced labor that stands behind much and perhaps most of the criticism of monarchy in the Hebrew Bible. The kind of liberation typified by the exodus from Egypt represents a transition from a regime of centralized government and state domination to one in which authority is located in village elders administering traditional law within a clan structure. In these narratives, one important end-result of the exodus is political and social decentralization and local control (137).

Absolutely! This is very much what I had in mind when I interpreted the exodus as a revolution, and it is indeed what I meant in my *God's Kingdom* by the replacement of a tributary mode of production in Egypt by the clan organization of extended families in tribal Israel. Forced labor, according to the text of the book of Exodus, was the specific form of the tribute which provoked the people of Moses to revolt against Egyptian kingship.

Let us continue with Levenson:

> If this is a point that would have embarrassed a Northern abolitionist like Weld, it should devastate an exegete of Marxist sympathies like Pixley. For if there is one thing that the Communist revolutionaries to whom Pixley likens Moses could not tolerate, it was the persistence of traditional modes of association outside state control (137).

There is some truth to Levenson's accusation against "Communist revolutionaries," and I did in fact compare Moses to Lenin and Castro, both of whom embraced a democratic centralism which requires total acquiescence once the party had reached a position. Those of us who move intellectually and politically within the Marxist heritage have to rethink our understanding of democracy to allow space for the existence of opposition associations of various sorts, not just within any society governed by a socialist party, but also within the party itself.

Within the writings of Marx, especially the middle-Marx of the *Grundrisse* and his late reflections on the Paris Commune and his correspondence with Vera Zasulich about the Russian peasant communes, we can appreciate the rich possibilities Marxism as theory and practice has to offer.[6] The debate about Marx and his views of various modes of production, and especially capitalism and socialism, is important.[7] Marx continues to be the inspiration of the Marxist tradition of social-scientific and political thought, and Lenin's revolutionary policies and those of the twentieth-century communist revolutions is only one possible development, and one that is not at all dominant in Marx's writings.

It remains a fact that Marxists have to repent from the centralism of twentieth-century "really existing socialism" and make their repentance credible. In the current political climate the existence of socialist parties that are coalitions, notably the Workers' Party (PT, Partido dos Trabalhadores) and the armed struggles of the indigenous Zapatistas in Mexico, illustrate the possibilities. The PT is a coalition of labor unions mostly based in São Paulo's heavy industries with Christian base communities, native Brazilians, feminist groups, African-Brazilians, ecological groups, and others. Obviously, this kind of politics requires continual readjusting as the interests of the various constituent groupings must be listened to. Many Latin American Marxists see the PT as the model of leftist politics of the future.

The Zapatistas in Chiapas are carrying out an armed insurrection which does not aim to take over the Mexican government and exercise State power. The aim in the struggle is to pressure for democratic rights for all Mexicans, with the understanding that in a country of as many people as Mexico, the first democratic right is the right to preserve the peoplehood of each nation within the country. One could argue about whether the Zapatistas are Marxist or not. At the very least, the historical manner in which they think about politics derives from Marx, the first social scientist to think about societies in a thoroughly historical manner. The Zapatista struggle for the rights of peoples is also a struggle for the Jewish people.

Reading liberation theology or listening to the PT in Brazil or the Zapatistas in Mexico requires some attention to the historical specifics of each case. But of course this is a discipline we must cultivate if we are to find our allies in the difficult struggle we face to live humanly and to create the conditions in which other people different from ourselves can also live humanly.

Reading the Bible

Levenson and I have some important differences about how it is that the Bible is an authoritative text for faith and how it should be read. But there is some common ground in our effort to find nourishment for our faith in these texts, and there is also common ground in the understanding that there is diversity within the texts with which the reader must come to terms. He writes,

> It is, in short, too convenient to portray Mesopotamian society as brutal and degrading and biblical law as a time-conditioned effort to mitigate the brutality and degradation. Rather, honest investigation of the Bible requires us to recognize that the parts we like and the parts we do not are *both* biblical and that *both* these components have roots and parallels in the larger ancient Near Eastern world (p. 139, Levenson's italics).

This "honesty principle" is an important one, because it keeps us from manipulating the text to serve our own or our group's interests at the expense of other communities, ancient or modern.

There is, however, a difference in the way we approach these contradictions in the Bible or between the Bible and other cultures. The difference has to do with the place of timeless principles in dealing with sacred texts. For Levenson, the issue in the case of the exodus is slavery or emancipation, and on the issue the biblical text does not speak with one voice. "The embarrassing fact [is] that the Bible was long invoked in support of both slavery and its abolition" (Levenson, 139). This is a genuine concern of biblical interpretation when the issue we are facing is slavery. That, however, is no longer a germane issue in the U.S. or in Latin America. Nor was it historically the issue in the exodus from Egypt, if by slavery we mean the kidnapping of people to sell them as private property, as in the case with the African slavery we knew in both North and South America. We have seen that both of us agree that the issue for Moses and his followers was State or generalized slavery, which really had to do with the nature of the clan's relation to the king. So the issue of slavery in the Exodus is a false issue, even though it was important in the context of a society which practiced systematic kidnapping of Africans which is, thank God, a thing of the past.

Nevertheless, there remain some major issues of conflict with the biblical text. Within the book of Exodus one thinks of the different interpretations of the plagues and of the revelation at Sinai. Within one strand of the plague narratives, which classic biblical scholarship identifies as Yahwist, God and Moses use the plagues as pressure in the negotiations for the release of the people of Israel. Here it is the children of Israel, not the Hebrews of whom we hear in Exodus chapter 1. In the other major strand of the plague narratives, the plagues are demonstrations of YHWH's power, and in order to have a chance to make the full grand performance, it is necessary to harden Pharaoh's heart so that he will not yield prematurely and so cut off the demonstration. In my commentary, I read these different interpretations of the plagues that we find within the text as the readings of different social groups within different contexts. On the one hand, the Yahwist version reads as the political class of advisors to the kings of Israel who are interested in the power of kings. The other strand is interested in religious authority and, in the hypothesis I used, was composed by the post-exilic priestly class, whose power had a religious legitimation.

The two strands of tradition can also be identified in the text about the Sinai revelation, one being found in the Covenant Code in Exodus 20–23 and the other in the prescriptions for the construction of the Tabernacle in Exodus 25–31. Was YHWH revealing the norms for social life to the children of Israel, or was YHWH giving the plans for the place where the glory would appear to the people? As in the case of the plagues, in my commentary I situate these strands in different hypothetical social groupings which need not concern us here.

The specifics of the social locations of the two strands of the plagues narrative are debatable and are not the issue here. However, the idea that within the Holy Bible we have the legitimation of different social groupings in ancient Israel is an issue. In reading the Bible as a support for a faith that feels the need to organize for actions aimed at transforming social structures, it is critical to see the ideological expressions of diverse social groups and sometimes groups opposed to each other. The authority of the text undergoes a shift as what we read is no longer a timeless message, such as one that might condemn slavery in principle, but rather a lesson about the ideological struggles of God's people in the past. This lesson can help religious groups today, Catholic, Protestant, or Jewish, to "read" the struggles in which they are engaged, and to understand the perspectives of their oppressors. So, in an expression often attributed to Saint Augustine, we were given the Book of Scripture by the Creator in order to learn to read the other book of the Creator, the book of Life. In the images of Carlos Mesters, the Bible is like the guidebook at a museum, which makes little sense by itself but which can be immensely helpful in enabling us to place in context the paintings we are viewing on the walls of the museum.

Is Liberation Theology Intrinsically Anti-Jewish?

We Christians are not in a comfortable position when we try to defend ourselves against charges of anti-Judaism. And this is where Levenson culminates his argument against my liberation reading of the exodus story. Anti-Judaism is indeed very deeply encrusted in Christian theology from its very beginnings, and none of us is free from it, as least as a residual and unintended function of the theological language we have inherited and which we use. Liberation theology is an effort to read the Bible from the midst of a faith-struggle of believing communities to transform the societies of which they are part. It seems perfectly natural that the Jewish people should appropriate liberation theology for their own family purposes, considering their long history of oppression by Christians and others. And this is in fact what Marc H. Ellis has attempted.[8]

When Levenson states that "this type of liberationism, whether intentionally or not, taps into wells of Jew-hatred that are as deep as they are ancient" (pp. 157–58), liberation theologians would be ill advised simply to deny the accusation and probably ought to seek refuge in the unintentional character of this well-tapping, which Levenson allows may be the case.

Let me plead the need for common ground between the Jewish people and other oppressed peoples of the world. It is not an example of "Jew-hatred" to read the exodus as a revolutionary struggle of peasants who felt oppressed by kingship of the variety Marx called Asiatic, which more properly can be called Tributary. Because of their national struggle during the monarchy and because of the centuries of struggle for survival in diaspora, the Jewish family have read this as their story. Of course! Why not? But does this mean that Christian workers in São Paulo or Tojolobal peasants in Chiapas should not read it also as their story? We must grant that ancient Israel and the Jewish diaspora read it as their story first. But, must that reading be exclusive of other oppressed peoples struggling to come together around new historical projects? Surely, it is hyper-sensitivity to interpret our reading of the exodus story as just another example of Christian Jew-hatred.

There is an exclusivity in Levenson's reading of liberation theology that is offensive. He says at one point, "Suffering alone does not qualify a people for an exodus. Even in Egypt, no other slaves are redeemed, only Israel" (152). The second sentence begs the question about who were the subjects of the exodus and also forgets that it was not exactly slavery that was involved but a social system of tributary kingship suffered by all the peasants in Egypt, both those who followed Moses (Israelites? Hebrews? a mixed multitude?) and those who were afraid to do so. The least we can say about the first sentence quoted is that it lacks the generosity we should hope to find from fellow religious believers. Amos was much more generous: "Are you not like Cushites to me, children of Israel? says YHWH. Did I not bring Israel out of the land of Egypt [no slavery mentioned], the Philistines from Caphtor, and the Aramaeans from Kir (Amos 9:7)?"

Conclusion

In this volume we are recognizing the contribution of Harvey Cox to academic theology and to the Christian and religious world. An outstanding characteristic of Cox's work has been his ability to listen to various other religious voices, as illustrated in his works on Eastern religion and on Pentecostalism, among others.[9] While not claiming his approval for my response to his Jewish colleague, I do wish to appeal to the spirit of his generous reading of other pieties as we reach the end of another century in the Christian accounting of chronology. We must build bridges, and then we must use them!

Notes

1. Frank Pais, an active Baptist in Santiago, Cuba, was a leader in the 26th of July movement against President Batista. He was shot by the police on the streets of Santiago on the 30th of July of 1956.

2. The lectures and much of the wonderful discussion they evoked were published in our journal *XILOTL,* number 20, of October 1997.

3. Jon Levenson, *The Hebrew Bible, the Old Testament, and Historical Criticism* (Louisville: Westminster John Knox Press, 1993).

4. George V. Pixley, *On Exodus: A Liberation Perspective* (Maryknoll, N.Y.: Orbis Books, 1987).

5. *God's Kingdom* (Maryknoll, N.Y.: Orbis Books, 1983).

6. On the latter, see Teodor Shanin, ed., *Late Marx and the Russian Road: Marx and "the Peripheries of Capitalism"* (New York: Monthly Review Press, 1983).

7. I refer especially to the pioneering work of liberation theologian Enrique Dussel, *Elementos fundamentales para la crítica de economía política (Grundrisse) 1857–1858,* 3 vols. (Mexico City: Siglo XXI, 1971).

8. Marc H. Ellis, *Hacia una teología judía de la liberación* (San José, Costa Rica: DEI, 1988), a translation of an English original published by Orbis.

9. *Turning East: Why Americans Look to the Orient for Spirituality — and What the Search Can Mean to the West* (New York: Simon and Schuster, 1977), and *Fire from Heaven: The Rise of Pentecostal Spirituality and the Reshaping of Religion in the Twenty-First Century* (Reading, Mass.: Addison-Wesley, 1994).

5

TRAINING PROPHETS

Reconciliation and Ministry in Civil Society

RODNEY L. PETERSEN

Harvey Cox epitomizes a historical era at Harvard University and its Divinity School. His ministry and work have helped to shape the direction of ministry for the twenty-first century. This paper is structured around these two contentions. In making this argument we will touch on a number of Cox's important works that illustrate and substantiate the nature of his significance for the conception and practice of ministry.

Cox came to a school that would soon become embroiled in the social crises that opened the latter third of the twentieth century. He came to a school in a period marked by factors that included, first, a crisis in religious and social authority. Second, it was a time marked by a growing awareness of the complexities of human community. Third, the scholarship of the period became more deeply attuned to ideological perspective and more conscious of the limits of human objectivity. Each of these three issues is part of a longer story in American cultural history, but each was galvanized in a fresh way by the maturation of particular post-war (World War II) developments, the American Civil Rights Movement and the War in Vietnam. Cox's work reflects this turbulence and these changes in the University and the way in which seminary education became shaped at Harvard's Divinity School. What makes it all the more noteworthy, however, is not just the attention to contemporary issues which his work illustrates, but the way in which he draws us to the task of the pastoral theologian as concerned with reconciliation in a variety of manifestations. Furthermore, the locus of this work became not only the Christian Church in its diversity, but also social service agencies and voluntary associations. The latter institutions, often daughters of the churches, would increasingly play a significant role in pursuing and advocating social policy in a nation more firmly divided through the period between Church and state.

Harvey Cox was born in Phoenixville, Pennsylvania (1929). He joined the faculty at the Divinity School in 1966. He received his A.B. from the University of Pennsylvania in 1951, and having served as Protestant chaplain

at Temple University in downtown Philadelphia, 1953–54, received his B.D.
at Yale in 1955. He then became director of religious activities at Oberlin,
1955–58. It was in this context that he wrote his first publication, *Our World
is God's World* (1959), early setting forth his vision of the church in the
world, his life's theme.[1] Cox carried these interests into his doctoral studies
at Harvard under James Luther Adams, serving as a lecturer at Andover and
as program associate with the American Baptist Home Mission Society.

After preparation as a graduate student, he began to teach in an era
that would soon be marked by a kind of academic "Ground-Zero" for the
world of the university as it would be largely defined after 1969. He was
initially seen, in part, as working in the tradition of his mentor James Luther
Adams's theology of culture, teaching first in the Department of the Church,
then in Theology, and then in Theology and Ethics. Cox's doctoral thesis
under Adams was on "Religion and Technology" (1963). Out of this came
his world bestseller in numerous languages, *The Secular City* (1965). The
transition from this doctoral work to writing *The Secular City* was natural.
It was clear that the rise of the modern metropolis was possible only through
the technological innovations that made urban life in the twentieth century
technically possible. Although the work on technology was never published,
he observes that he may have invented the word "technopolis" as a way of
referring to the modern city. As Cox explains:

> What I was striving to say in *The Secular City* was that God is present also
> in technopolis. This is not an environment that the church needs to flee or
> fear or condemn out of hand. What we need to do is look for and discern
> the Spirit which is our God and know that certain parts of the technopolis
> are destructive of human life and are demonic. I was not at all hesitant in
> using the term "demonic" because one of my teachers was Paul Tillich who
> reintroduced the whole idea of the demonic into academic theology.[2]

Cox's argument in the book, that the secular is not outside the realm of
God's action or God's presence, influenced as it was by Dietrich Bonhoeffer,
would serve to shape his further scholarship and ministry. On the strength
of this book and his developing scholarship Cox was called back to the Divinity School from his position as assistant professor at Andover Newton
(1963–65).[3] The renown he began to enjoy made Cox something of a Department in himself, with his own distinctive approaches, large courses open
to undergraduate students of the Yard, and also the graduate students from
other faculties. The passion alluded to above would enable Cox to become
a religious spokesperson for the Divinity School and issues confronting the
churches as they would be opened up in the tumultuous years ahead.

In an interview conducted in the spring of 1997 with Harvey Cox the
question was asked of him, "What is your passion?" His reply was revealing. His passion, a phrase used in *The Secular City* and elsewhere, "is to try
to determine what God is doing in human history and to respond appropri-

ately to this activity of God, and to help the community of faith discern the presence and passion of God and to take the appropriate measures to get in step with the action of God. Therefore all the theology that I have ever done I think of as pastoral theology."[4] In so doing he was soon to become in the eyes of the world the single most heeded professor in religion at Harvard.

With these opening remarks in mind, we will turn our attention to a few of the more salient features of Cox's work and then, briefly, to the topic of reconciliation and to the place of the voluntary association in Cox's work and in American life.

Scholarship through Change and through Storm

Cox's teaching and written scholarship have arisen out of a period of social and intellectual turmoil in the life of the University. Broadsides published by *The Harvard Crimson* from what have often been called the "turbulent" years of student unrest in the contemporary history of Harvard College, the years running from 1968 to 1972 more or less, include headlines that read as follows:

> "Students Occupy University Hall, Eject Deans, Staff from Offices" (*The Harvard Crimson,* April 9, 1969).

> " 'Cliffe' Finally Proposes Marriage to Ten Thousand Men of Harvard" (*The Harvard Crimson,* February 23, 1969).

> "Police Raid Sit-In at Dawn; 250 Arrested, Dozens Injured" (*The Harvard Crimson,* April 10, 1969).

Amid the tumult marked out by these *Crimson* broadsides the Divinity School often came to be identified with Harvey Cox, a school both erudite and radical in its theological sanction of social change. The first broadside asks us to recall new attitudes toward authority that became evident in the 1960s. Revolution in sexual practices, changes in family relationships, and turmoil in the church and in society were well underway by this point. Each made itself felt differently in the University — for example, the cessation of parietal rules (*in loco parentis*) in the College dormitories and elimination of the coat and tie rule in its various House dining facilities. Student participation on a multitude of administrative and faculty committees became a part of university life into the 1970s. Many of the changes alluded to above had been subsumed in social thinking since the 1930s by the effects of the Depression, Second World War, and post-war preoccupation with Communism. However, by the late 1960s we were moving as a society into a period of social transition brought about, in part, by the movement for Civil Rights and controversy surrounding the War in Vietnam. The times were opportune for rethinking accepted social mores and patterns of authority. Cox's work sought to do this both in what he would call the "Apollonian" and "Dionysian" dimensions of this work.

The second of our broadsides reminds us of the deeper recognition to which we have been asked to come respecting meaningful participation in the community of men and women with regard to women, part of a larger multiculturalism which has grown in significance since the 1960s. Harvey Cox became a kind of pioneer for Liberation Theology as it would soon be called and for other forms of inclusivity.

Finally, our third broadside symbolizes a kind of academic revolution, not unrelated to the crisis in authority alluded to above, a postmodern scholarship frequently referred to as "deconstruction" in the literary world, certainly a deconstruction of a privileged and established worldview. In the theological world this became associated with the work of Hans-Georg Gadamer and then with that of Paul Ricoeur, among others. Pictured not only in the takeover of University Hall, a symbol of the liberal yet authoritarian aspect of the older world of scholarship, this loss of the older sense of objective authority might be depicted even more clearly in the fear felt by many at the time that Widener Library itself might be destroyed in the midst of the unrest. On the day that University Hall was taken over, many academics and staff linked arms forming a human wall around the Library to protect it from the anger and frustration of the crowd. Local police and Massachusetts State Troopers marched down Boylston (now Kennedy) Street and Massachusetts Avenue to control the riot. In the all-university assembly which followed in the Harvard stadium, many feared that the University itself would be shut down.

Crises in social authority, our understanding of community, and a widening global perspective with a changing conception of objectivity would become a kind of corrective to modernity and help to mark out the scope of Cox's work after *The Secular City*. The first two of these points would be taken up with Gustavo Gutiérrez in *A Theology of Liberation*. Gutiérrez draws out the point that secularization in the economically developed capitalist countries tends toward a cultural form, challenging the hegemony of traditional religion with the pluralism of other worldviews. Whereas in the poorer countries, secularization assumes a different expression, challenging the misuse of religion by ruling elites who tend to use religion in order to sacralize their privileges.

Religious and Social Authority

Taking Gutiérrez's first point for the moment, we can see how Cox continued to follow out this idea in the domain of religious and social authority. Although Cox would consistently argue that praxis should be the "first moment" of an appropriate response to God, the context for this moment was set for Cox within an existential crisis in religious and social authority often epitomized for him by the philosopher and novelist Albert Camus. In 1967 Albert Camus received the Nobel Prize for Literature. Earlier, in 1965, in

The Secular City, Cox had written of Camus and of how he was helping to point the way humanity was trying to live with direction and integrity without recourse to something beyond this world. How do we live with values without God?

Concerned about the erosion of values. Cox taught a course for a couple of years on "religious values and cultural conflict." As Cox would comment, moral values do not just float along. They are embedded in narrative, in religious narrative.

"So, how do you get along without those is a very, very serious challenge, I think. I simply do not believe you can reinstitute a religious narrative in a culture in which it has lost its grip on people. How do you do that? God might be able to do it, but I think we cannot say we must get back to the religious values. They have to have their own self-certifying power."[5]

This concern not only marks out Cox's "praxis-oriented" "first moment," but it would also shape his theology after *The Secular City.* Cox writes of the formative experience he had living in Berlin, working as an ecumenical fraternal worker, living on the edge of the two worlds then defined by the Cold War. One of the experiences that became very clear to him was that you could not make a claim for the validity or truth of the Gospel based upon the supreme moral performance of Christians. Camus was a very good illustration for Cox of one who could live compassionately with genuine commitment to human decency and justice without any transcendental reference point.

Cox's new approach to theology would come with his book, *The Feast of Fools* (1969), originally presented as the William Belden Noble Lecture of the spring of 1968. By a special arrangement with the Preacher to the University, the lectures were given in Andover Hall at the Divinity School, replete with slides, movies, balloons, and dance, amid music at times deafening in its joyous beat and syncopation, the celebrant himself already familiar around Harvard Square. Cox, playing tenor saxophone with a jazz ensemble later to be named "The Embraceables," spoke of *The Secular City* as having been his "Apollonian" work now to be celebrated differently by the evident "Dionysian" endeavors.

The era marked by Cox's early work at the Divinity School witnessed the crumbling of theologies and church practice in the wake of social upheavals throughout the country. The first such seminary reaction was that of biblical conservatives meeting in a Thanksgiving workshop on evangelical and social concerns in Chicago in November 1973. Talks from this conference and responses were published by Ronald Sider in *The Chicago Declaration* (1974).[6] This was followed by the Hartford Declaration, shaped by conferees in January 1975 who gathered at the Hartford Seminary Foundation. The Hartford Declaration identified thirteen themes concerning the involvement of the Church in the world, published as *An Appeal for Theological Affirmation.*[7] The subtext to this document pointed at some excesses in contemporary theologies of liberation for churches growing weary of the political activism appearing in theological schools and even in the churches at that time. The Hartford Declaration found a critic in Harvey Cox who called its themes "flaccid" and its promoters "fellow backsliders." Cox went on to criticize the theological failings of the Declaration against an agenda being set by God in the context of the world.

A Task Force of the Boston Industrial Mission drafted the "Boston Affirmations" in 1976 which Cox signed. This Mission had as its goal aiding the economy to move away from its dependence on military procurement and toward peacetime production. With an explicitly Trinitarian undergirding, the Task Force looked in the "Affirmations" to "hopeful participation" on the part of churches in the contemporary issues confronting society. Under the leadership of Scott Paradise and Norman Faramelli, the Task Force included Roman Catholics, Episcopalians, Lutherans, Presbyterians, Baptists, and members of the United Church of Christ with Harvey Cox and Sister Mary Hennessey (then Executive Director of the Boston Theological Institute, BTI) playing vital roles.[8]

The thesis of *The Secular City*, developed in relation to contemporary crises of meaning, had moved Cox to search for the wider activity of God in the world. In relation to the tension reflected in the two documents, the so-called *Hartford Declaration* and the "Boston Affirmations," Cox would say in retrospect,

> I can quite honestly say that it is God who sets the agenda — and God from the biblical perspective. God is not just active exclusively within the Church. There are ecclesiocentric theologies and there are cosmocentric theologies. I think that the Bible is a wonderful example of a God who works in history and works in the world. The Church is the community of faithful who respond to celebrate, demonstrate, and proclaim the initial activity of God. It is not a choice between the world and the Church.... Where does the Word really speak to us? In my experience as a Christian throughout the years, it surely has come in church many times, but not always. There have been times when the Word of God has come to me in places which we might classify as secular or worldly or profane. I do not think that it is in any way anti- or nonbiblical. I think it is exactly what the biblical figures are always being accosted by and address, by unusual and unforeseen circumstances coming out of God's world.[9]

As observed on the dust cover of *The Secular City*, the book was "A celebration of its liberties, and an invitation to its disciplines." While sympathetic with the cultural critique of evangelicals like Francis Schaeffer, politically Cox had become more radical, placing himself "near the right fringe of the New Left," and certainly distant from evangelical political conservatives like Carl Henry.[10] Cox adds that "there is an unnecessary gap in today's world between the world-changers and the life-celebrators." Apollonian and Dionysian theological motifs would be garnered in support of what Cox called a "proleptic liberation as a festive radical." In the absence of a clear word from God, human engagement was to be with movements of human liberation modeled on the experience of Moses before the mystery of the Burning Bush. Cox's engagement was not, as for Camus, from an agnostic existentialism, but from a deep confidence in an undergirding meaning.

The Complexities of Human Community

Cox would write in the Preface to the twenty-fifth-anniversary edition of *The Secular City* that "Liberation theology is the legitimate, though unanticipated, heir of *The Secular City*."[11] His concern for the vitality of faith communities was a topic to which he would continue to return.[12] The deeper awareness of the complexities of human community was a topic of sustained reflection in Cox's work. One of the most significant books to influence him during the writing of his doctoral dissertation was Emile Durkheim's *The Elementary Forms of Religious Life*. Having worked with Robert Bellah, then an assistant professor at Harvard, in the interpretation of Durkheim, Cox reflects, "It has never left me, the idea that all social and cultural structures are somehow ultimately grounded in implicit religious affirmation, even the most allegedly secular. That is a theme in *The Secular City*. That it is called 'the secular city' really has a grounding in religious or quasi-religious or pseudo-religious understanding."[13]

Such liberation would be sought in a variety of areas raised up for social consideration by technology and changing social patterns, addressed by Cox from the perspective of his earlier doctoral work. One of the first issues to be dealt with was the way by which the modern world was to approach areas of biological necessity, most explosively in the 1960s the area of the "New Morality." This issue was alive with controversy as Cox joined the Divinity School faculty, for in 1965 the Department of the Church tackled the question in a symposium on "The Church and the New Morality." Two years later Cox participated in another symposium with *Playboy* editor Hugh Hefner.[14] Across the Common, at Episcopal Theological School, Joseph Fletcher III held forth on the topic and, together with Cox, collaborated in the *Situation Ethics Debate*.[15]

Debate over the nature and place of human sexuality was not, however, the area where Cox would leave his greatest mark. Cox's real work would become associated with Liberation Theology as the field began to develop in relation to greater attention paid to ethnicities and social classes previously marginalized in establishment cultures.[16] Cox promoted the concept of Jesus as Liberator, and the idea of God's preferential option for the poor and the oppressed. Having become discouraged and distraught by the assassinations of Martin Luther King and Robert Kennedy, in whose presidential campaign in the spring of 1968 he had worked, Cox traveled that summer to a missionary training center in Latin America where he became fluent in Spanish and in "liberation theology." Excited by the idea of Jesus Christ the Liberator, the action of God in the world and the "preferential option for the poor" as put in the influential statement of the Catholic bishops of Latin America (1968), Cox began to think through this perspective in some of the first courses offered in North America on Liberation Theology. As he writes reflectively, although hardly aware of it at the time, his closing paragraph in *The Secular City* proposed an agenda that would be taken up by and defined in Liberation Theology, i.e., that the first "moment" in theology for us, as it was for Moses, is "an act of engagement for justice in the world, not a pause for theological reflection," and that "accompanying" the poor in their pilgrimage is ethically responsible and theologically promising.[17]

When reflection on human sexuality returned in a new guise, now as the women's liberation movement, Cox was inadvertently at first in the center of debate. With students and faculty seeking to make the Divinity School a more fully inclusive institution, a group of women, led by E.D.S. (Episcopal Divinity School) feminist Emily Culpepper, in a course on "Christianity and Rapid Social Change," based on the World Council of Churches study document, felt that the course was not critical enough. The group made it clear that they were not going to take over the administration building, making reference to the Student Strike of 1969, but rather to take over the class. After consultation with Dean Krister Stendahl, Cox turned over the course to Culpepper and her associates, in the end impressed with the serious nature and outcome of their work.

Cox kept up with the rapid pace of social criticism that continued unabated into the early 1970s. The weekend when Mary Daly staged her famous walkout from Harvard's Memorial Church in the fall of 1971, Cox had been at the Air Force Academy sitting in with a group of nuns, priests, ministers, and young people sponsored by Clergy and Laity Concerned trying to call attention to the bombing of North Vietnam by giving out copies of the Prayer of St. Francis as people were coming to the Chapel. The same issue of the *Boston Globe* reported a Harvard professor arrested at the Air Force Academy trying to get *into* the Chapel while another story reported on Mary Daly *walking out* of the Memorial Church.

Cox would bring his ethical thinking to bear upon American society in the Vietnam era together in a volume entitled, *Military Chaplains: From Religious Military to a Military Religion.*[18] Whether with respect to the poor and marginalized or the powerful and established, Cox's social critique was based in a deeply religious perspective on the world. As he would comment later, "I think for me the operative theological principle was and continues to be anti-idolatry." Cox underscores the importance of one's understanding of the Gospel or of the community of faith to be corrected, criticized, and called into question by others. Underscoring the importance of such a critical stance, Cox adds,

I think the ecumenical movement is not a club where we can do things better together. It is a theologically necessary essential corrective to the tendency toward idolatry. Now, I started thinking that on the basis of different Christian traditions. I have now expanded this in two ways. One of them is to say that people who understand the Gospel from a perspective of a different cultural tradition or background or a different gender perspective correct my biases. I correct theirs too. I think that it is theologically essential that that conversation, though it is very rough and angular at times, can continue. I would go on and say the same now about the multitude of other religions. I think the other religions have something to teach us without our relapsing into a kind of relativism. I think there is something we have to learn.[19]

Cox's theology would come like that of the civic Reformers of the sixteenth century both to the poor and marginalized, oppressed by stultifying structures, and to the privileged and wealthy, blinded and captured by wealth and position. An illustration of the former was to come in the 1980s. Cox was clearly influenced by and appreciative of the fresh theological vitality in the Roman Catholic Church under the impact of its papal leadership from John XXIII through John Paul II, and from Latin American liberation theologians and such German counterparts as Hans Küng and the Flemish Catholic reformer Edward Schillebeeckx. Nevertheless, Cox rose to the defense of papally disciplined Father Leonardo Boff, writing *The Silencing of Leonardo Boff: The Vatican and Future Christianity*.[20] An illustration of Cox's prophetic criticism of those captured by wealth and position would follow later in an article analyzing the market as God, excoriating those captured by a business theology whose credo is limitless expansion.[21] As the civic theologians of the early Reformation might have cried in the streets of Strasburg, Zürich, or Geneva, Cox wrote from Cambridge that God's call is simple and clear: "Believe and Follow."[22]

The Limits of Knowledge and Global Religious Revival

While the final paragraph of *The Secular City* opened us to the developments of Liberation Theology, the final chapter of Cox's *The Secular City* marks out for us his approach to the phenomena of the worldwide revival of religion today. The chapter, something of a polemic against the so-called "death of God" theologians, scopes out the reality of God in secular as well as religious realms of life. If our conception of social order is susceptible to idolatry, so, too, Cox was arguing, is the spiritual and ecclesial realm. The implication is that people of faith need not flee the secular world nor that religion, simply by being religion, is necessarily good.[23] Cox developed the latter point with respect to the new religiousness of the 1970s in *Turning East: The Promise and Peril of the New Orientalism*.[24] The former argument became one of deepening reflection for Cox both with respect to religions other than Christianity as well as with respect to Christianity as

Cox, together with other scholars in the field, became more deeply attuned to ideological perspective, more conscious of the human limits to objectivity.

Opportunity for reflection on the many dimensions of human religiousness came for Cox and others at the Divinity School in part through the new Center for the Study of World Religions organized under Dean Krister Stendahl. Cox, as world traveler, had long pondered over the engagement of academic Christianity with the plurality of religions in the world. He now wrote on the Christian encounter with religious pluralism in *Many Mansions: A Christian's Encounter with Other Faiths.*[25] In this work he encouraged Christians to speak in dialogue from a strong sense of their own Christian identity, not engaging in discussion from the perspective that one's own identity need be suppressed for a meaningful and spirited dialogue to occur. In this he fully agreed with faculty colleagues Wilfrid Cantwell Smith and John Carman.

Cox's encounter with the revolutionary changes occurring within the Christian movement came, most notably, in his study of Pentecostalism, entered into in part with the assistance of Eldin Villafañe of Gordon-Conwell Theological Seminary, illustrating in this way not only concerns developing within the Boston Theological Institute community but also patterns of cooperation as earlier viewed with Andover Newton Theological School and Episcopal Theological Seminary [now Divinity School]. Here was a form of Christianity that transcended earlier theologies, jumped across the barriers of "establishmentarian" Catholicism, Orthodoxy, and Protestantism, and appeared indicative of alternative cultural rootings. Commenting on the work of missiologist Andrew Walls, Cox would later add that we should not see such different perspectives as alternatives or revivals but as cultural settings within which the Gospel takes shape and therefore we can see how much our understanding of the Christian Gospel is in fact parochial, ethnocentric, and patriarchal. Cox wrote open-mindedly about the global phenomenon in his *Fire from Heaven: The Rise of Pentecostal Spirituality and the Reshaping of Religion in the Twenty-First Century.*[26] He had come to discern in this movement something challenging to the ethos and structures, not only to the mainline denominational churches, but notably to the Roman Catholic charismatics in Latin America. He wrote the book, as he had his others, not merely as an exercise for academic theologians, but also for a broad readership. Cox was intrigued by the way in which Pentecostalism addressed some of the basic and elemental needs of people first learned from sociologist Emile Durkheim in terms of ritual, practice, and one's relationship to the world.

Reconciliation as the Work of Pastoral Theology

"All the theology that I have ever done I think of as pastoral theology." If we keep this statement by Cox in our minds and understand his work in the context of the events of the latter third of the twentieth century, we might conclude that the mark of Cox's efforts has been to make possible the work of reconciliation in society. The three factors that shaped the period also shape his work: the crisis in religious and social authority, a growing awareness of the complexities of human community, and attention to ideological perspective and the limits of human objectivity.

This interest in a ministry of reconciliation thus contextualized helps to explain his concern for the shape of theological education with attention given to the complexity of worldviews that one might expect to encounter in any contemporary society. Fresh attention was given to the curriculum of the Divinity School under Dean George Rupp, successor to Dean Krister Stendahl. Rupp sought to reshape the curriculum into three concentric circles. He asked Cox to chair the committee and move the proposal along through faculty support. The idea was to get faculty talking to each other and across departmental lines, putting Scriptural Studies at the center, and then Christianity and Culture in the next band, and finally World Religions. Eventually the idea was passed. Cox's involvement was based not only on his commitment to dialogue across natural boundaries, but also upon his viewpoint concerning the identity of the Divinity School itself. Convinced that Christians should conscientiously maintain their identity within interfaith dialogue, Cox would come to assert:

> I think you get a better education in a school with a theological and value position that is up front and one of the things I have tried to contribute to Harvard Divinity School, with some failure, some success, is that we are an ecumenical school, not a nondenominational school. We are a school where people come from different traditions, representing different traditions, being explicit about that and making that part of the mix, and not pretending that we have some generic Christianity or generic religion.[27]

This concern for informed dialogue among the varieties of Christian expression and reaching toward interreligious dialogue extended to conversation within the university and among its various faculties. It is an example of his attempt to hold together a conversation within a university as traditionally conceived and, more specifically, a dialogue between the Church and the world. With a dialogic as well as prophetic cast of mind, Cox would add,

> We have as a Christian theological obligation the responsibility of addressing parts of the university which are not explicitly religious — economics, business, law. It is a vast task and not everyone can to it. The main danger you fall into if you try is being thought of as "holier than thou," or moralizing or preaching.... However, the opposite danger is that you accept the pathological subdivision of the university into tinier and tinier departments all doing their own thing and poring over narrower and narrower issues and problems with their own language about those problems — the language about the language — so that the shaping centers of the culture and of the university just do not have the criticism, support, or critique of a theological voice.[28]

Cox has carried this prophetic desire to cross boundaries to his support of the Divinity School's Center for the Study of Values in Public Life initiated under Dean Rupp's successor, Dean Ronald Thiemann. All of this, Cox argues, calls for sensitive dialogue, not an impositional attitude, in a university that is quite different from the one he came to in 1965.

This concern for reconciliation as a form of ministry in the secular city extends beyond directly epistemic concerns expressed in the shape of a divinity school curriculum. It extends to a recognition of the ways in which religion can be distorted and used for purposes that in fact deny its ideals. While all of Cox's work breathes an irenic spirit, this sensitivity to instrumentalizing religion is clearly seen in his Preface to the revised edition of *The Secular City* (1990). Cox notes the persistent quality of human religiosity. It is a point directly made in the article, "World Religions and Conflict Resolution," which he wrote with Arvind Sharma and others.[29] There he and his co-authors scored the instrumental use of religion in ethnocultural and national rivalries. While appreciating along with others the resurgence of religious sentiment as a resource for conflict resolution, Cox worried over the way in which religion seems to add complications to conflict situations.

Indeed, Cox has been a part of the faculty committee of the B.T.I. International Mission and Ecumenism program which has sought to understand how religion is implicated in regional violence and how churches, mosques, synagogues, or other places of worship can be sources of reconciliation. He and his fellow authors noted the importance of reference to a larger moral universe to transcend the interests of contending parties in dispute, that politics is not an autonomous sphere of human endeavor, and that statecraft exists within the envelope of encompassing moral values and underlying religious worldviews. Religion, as it becomes involved in regional disputes, calls forth what social theorist and mediator Louis Kriesberg defines as a dissensual as opposed to consensual conflict, the former involving disagreements about beliefs or values and the latter disagreement over the apportionment of ends.[30]

The boundaries between relevant social categories become more intractable (dissensus) insofar as the issues in contention concern different beliefs or values. Such differentiation occurs frequently easily between races and ethnicities, sexes, and persons of different class. Such dissensus easily plays into the hands of persons who would exacerbate difference for purposes of political gain. Cox's work with Douglas Johnston and Cynthia Sampson draws real and symbolic attention to issues of regionalism violence, increasingly characteristic of a day when new forms of nationalism or regional identities are playing upon elements conducive to dissensual conflict, history, language, and religion, reinforced by a system of passports that locks people into given regions.

In his "mid-course correction," embodied in the preface to the new edition of *The Secular City,* Cox notes the role of "religious revival and secularization" as "morally ambiguous processes."[31] Distinctive values or beliefs are a necessary condition for dissensus conflict, but they are not sufficient. In addition, the differences must be such that the values or beliefs are perceived as incompatible. Incompatibility has two sources. One is that the persons with different views be in a social relationship that places the views in opposition. The other is that persons with one set of views assert objectionable claims upon persons not sharing the views. To illustrate the first point, if social groups do not have the opportunity to interact with one another, social conflict may not develop. There can be no conflict with groups that have nothing to do with one another. When groups of people enter into a social relationship that requires joint action or actions that affect both groups and they hold different views pertinent to that relationship, the basis for a dissensual conflict exists.

For Cox and many who are like-minded, religion, and Christianity in particular, should serve as an avenue for reconciliation. However, such is not always the case. While grounding a Christian understanding of reconciliation in the three theological realities of Christology, ecclesiology, and even cosmology, Robert Schreiter writes that the legitimacy of Christianity is and often has been compromised by its silence and complicity with victimizers in the interest of *Realpolitik*. Thus all the more intriguing are Schreiter's remarks about the reality (perhaps prophetic necessity) for communities of Christians to distance themselves (for a while) from the larger church in their search for and discovery of reconciliation — particularly if that larger church is implicated in the very violence it seeks to overcome.[32] Here might be found the germinal ideas of what can be called a psychological history of organizations — or what an earlier generation referred to as the spiritual history of the Church. We might also locate here Cox's own struggle with Bonhoeffer and a "religionless" Christianity. This is not the absence of faith but rather a prophetic distancing from faiths and churches and creeds that appear to have taken on the appearance, despite themselves, of idolatries.

Again, we might ask the question: Can the Church (as concrete congregations of Christians) participate in the ministry of reconciliation among groups in deep dissensual conflict? With an appropriate sense of its own sin and limitations, Cox's answer appears to be in the affirmative through the way in which he has continued to work with churches as Harvard's pastoral theologian *par excellence*. With this it might be said that there is a need to more carefully define remembrance, forgiveness, reconciliation, restorative justice, and other terms that illustrate attitudes that move beyond retribution to deeper patterns of community reconstruction and conversation.

Civil Society as the Locus of Ministry

Cox's conception of ministry is to do the work of reconciliation in a social context defined by the contemporary crisis in religious and social authority,

a growing awareness of the complexities of human community, and attention given to ideological perspective and the limits of human objectivity. The
context for that ministry is not only the Church but also voluntary associations in service to civil society. This is seen not only in the nature of his
writing as considered above and in his support for Center for the Study of
Values in Public Life at the Divinity School, but also in the nature of his
studies with his mentor James Luther Adams. Adams's work and theology
of culture have helped to illustrate the manner by which voluntary associations have come to be in American cultural life and the debt that they owe
to the churches and other religious communities.[33]

Cox's argument in *The Secular City,* as outlined earlier, that the secular is
not outside the realm of God's action or God's presence, offers further warrant for ministry in the context of voluntary associations. Such associations
are often formed in relation to immediate needs in society and so are sensitive to that praxis which should be the "first moment" of an appropriate
response to God. Such organizations provide a way to deal with the place of
values in a context characterized by an apparent erosion of values or where
values are subject to debate and arise out of different religious and cultural
traditions.

Voluntary associations arise out of a principle of religious volunteerism.
They are most often grounded in immediate social needs, or praxis. Furthermore, they operate in a unique social "space," one long occupied almost
exclusively by the churches in Western societies, that is, between the state
and the family. Cox was influenced by James Luther Adams in this, as earlier
in his career he had learned from the French social theorist Emile Durkheim
that the shape of ministry is not only grounded in a faith community but
also reaches beyond into new forms of social organization appropriate to
the organization of society.[34]

In an article entitled "Forces of Civility," John Tirman, executive director
of the Winston Foundation for World Peace, writes of the meteoric growth of
non-governmental organizations, or NGOs, in the last third of the twentieth
century. He refers to this growth as a "quiet revolution rumbling beneath the
surface of global politics."[35] They have arisen to propound universal ideals,
environmental concern and that of global sustainability, human rights, and
an array of humanitarian causes. In fact, one might say that on a global
scale the contemporary period is in some ways reminiscent of the period
following the Second Great Awakening in North America, when voluntary
organizations burst forth to live out the idealism of that awakening with
concern and advocacy directed to social ameliorization. They act to anticipate and work with social conflict. They focus on the needs of refugees and
immigrants and all of the activity taken note of above. They are venerable
institutions like the American Friends Service Committee, the Mennonite
Conciliation Service, Peace Now, the Communità di Sant'Egidio, Moral Re-
armament, Fellowship of Reconciliation and more recent associations or

institutions like Common Cause and the Carter Center of Emory University. The effectiveness of these organizations comes from a variety of factors. Tirman cites, for example, their self-conception as global citizens interested in peace, justice, and equality without reference to national interests.

The genius of voluntary associations, furthermore, comes from their effectiveness in providing ways to break down social cleavages in society. Social conflict often emerges as groups begin to see themselves as groups of people in isolation from other groups and united around a common grievance. Such a base of conflict has the potential to grow into overt social violence if the grievance is not attended to or if apparent and contentious goals begin to become articulated. Voluntary associations can be the means for the articulation of such goals, but they can also provide additional social space and opportunity for people in different groups to develop common interests. In this way they provide for cross-cutting conflict strategy.[36]

In Conclusion: By Way of a Tribute

This paper has been structured around the argument that Harvey Cox's work epitomizes the religious and cultural milieu in which he found himself and that his response has been to create a vision for ministry in the twenty-first century. The character of that ministry is one given to reconciliation and set in the context of both churches and voluntary associations. His work has been shaped by cultural challenges that can be summarized as a crisis in religious and social authority, a growing awareness of the complexities of human community, and by attention to the importance of ideological perspective and the limits of human objectivity.

Cox's own genius has been to develop a pastoral theology and model for ministry for churches faced with the rapidly urbanizing and secularizing culture of the North Atlantic community in the last third of the twentieth century. It is a theology that works to break down social cleavages in society and amongst people. It draws out of the Bible a vision of partnership between humanity and God "in organizing the world."[37] This vision and work is seen early, in *The Secular City,* and is carried out through his career. It is a historical perspective that challenges the way in which church history has been perceived at least since Flacius Illyricus, Caesar Baronius, and the wars of religion in the early modern period, i.e., a historical perspective that has tended to draw a dichotomy between sacred and secular history between the holy and the profane. Although nurtured in Baptist polity, Cox's theology is grounded in a radical monotheism that finds its human response in stewardship: It is God who sets the agenda for both the "city" and for the Church.

Notes

1. He would later give an account of himself, *Just As I Am* (Nashville: Abingdon, 1983).

2. Cox goes on to explain that he wanted to call the book "God and the Secular City." However, the publisher thought to call it just "The Secular City." Cox felt that if they had gone with his initial idea there might have been less misunderstanding about the book on the part of a large number of people who never read it or felt that Cox was a celebrant of everything secular.

3. The book was reviewed by Charles West, Paul Lehmann, David Little, L. Kilmer Myers, and Michael Novak in successive issues of *Christianity and Crisis*, 25, nos. 12–13 (1965): 147–53, 165–66. Commenting on the book, Talcott Parsons wrote, "The new American 'secular city,' as Harvey Cox (1965) has called it, despite its complex strains, conflicts, and imperfections (which from any religio-ethical point of view are many and serious), has been legitimated as a genuine holy community in the ascetic [Weberian] Protestant sense." See Cox's reply in *Christianity and Crisis* 25, no. 21 (1965): 274–75.

4. The interview was conducted by the author of this article for the as yet unpublished manuscript by George H. Williams on the history of religion at Harvard University, May 7, 1997. The Church takes up its prophetic stance in relation to, and often at odds with, the secular city. In responding to the pastoral needs of the Church in the world, and of the Church's prophetic involvement with the world, Cox considers himself to be a "church theologian," much influenced by Karl Barth and his· *Kirchliche Dogmatik*. See his piece in *Barth, Barmen and the Confessing Church Today*, ed. James Holloway (Lewiston, N.Y.: Mellen, 1995).

5. Interview with Harvey Cox, May 7, 1997.

6. Ronald Sider, ed., *The Chicago Declaration* (Carol Stream, Ill.: Creation House, 1974).

7. Alfred Krass recounts the story of these and other declarations in *Evangelizing Neo-Pagan North America: The Word that Frees* (Scottdale, Pa.: Herald, 1982). *The Worldview Symposium and Hartford Appeal*, text, critique, and further responses, was made available in pamphlet form. The participants and respondents, in their broad confessional groupings, included: Catholics: Gregory Baum, David Tracy, George Tavard, Gabriel Moran; Protestants: Richard Neuhaus, John Bennett, John C. Cobb, Wolfhart Pannenberg (of Munich, but at the time in the United States), Robert Jewett, Richard Mouw, and George Forell; and Orthodox: Thomas Hopko and Alexander Schmemann.

8. The "Boston Affirmations" appeared simultaneously in the March 1976 issues of *Worldview* (45–53) and the *Andover Newton Quarterly;* the latter edition edited by Max Stackhouse, also a student of James Luther Adams. The *Quarterly* "Affirmations" were accompanied by additional responses illustrative of reflection from within the Boston Theological Institute (BTI) community of which the Divinity School was an integral part.

9. Interview with Harvey Cox, May 7, 1997.

10. *Secular City*, vii. While reflecting on positive aspects in the theological "Foundationalism" of then apologist Francis Schaeffer, Cox noted the "consistent cultural critique" offered by Schaeffer. Schaeffer's strength was seen by Cox to lie in his confrontation with the stories, myths, lies, fables, and values of the culture.

Cox's criticism of Schaeffer was in Schaeffer's unnecessarily, from Cox's perspective, "absolutely blind insistence on the verbal inspiration of the Bible."

11. 25th Anniversary Edition, xv.

12. See his foreword to *Seek the Peace of the City,* ed. Eldin Villafañe (Grand Rapids: Eerdmans, 1995).

13. Interview with Harvey Cox, May 7, 1997.

14. See James Luther Adams, *Autobiography,* ch. 29.

15. Philadelphia: Westminster Press, 1968. See Cox's *On Not Leaving It to The Snake* (New York: Macmillan, 1967).

16. *Secular City,* xiv.

17. Ibid.

18. New York: American Report Press, 1971.

19. Interview with Harvey Cox, May 7, 1997.

20. Oak Park, Ill.: Meyer-Stone Books, 1988.

21. Harvey Cox, "The Market as God. Living in the New Dispensation," *The Atlantic Monthly* (March 1999): 18–23.

22. Such was the theme of much of the preaching of Heinrich Bullinger. See my *Preaching in the Last Days* (New York: Oxford University Press, 1993), chapters 5–6.

23. *Secular City,* xii–xiii.

24. New York: Simon and Schuster, 1977, 1984.

25. Boston: Beacon Press, 1988.

26. Reading, Mass.: Addison-Wesley, 1995.

27. Interview with Harvey Cox, May 7, 1997.

28. Ibid.

29. *Religion, The Missing Dimension of Statecraft,* ed. Douglas Johnston and Cynthia Sampson (New York: Oxford University Press, 1994): 266–82.

30. *Social Conflicts* (Englewood Cliffs, N.J.: Prentice-Hall, 1982), 28–42.

31. *Secular City,* xi–xii.

32. Robert Schreiter, *Reconciliation. Mission and Ministry in a Changing Social Order* (Maryknoll, N.Y.: Orbis Books, 1993).

33. J. Ronald Engel, ed., *Voluntary Associations: Socio-Cultural Analyses and Theological Interpretation* (Chicago: Association Press, 1986). See in particular, "Voluntary Associations in Search of Identity" (160–70); "The Voluntary Principle in the forming of American Religion" (171–200); and "Voluntary Associations" (250–53).

34. See also on this, Hans Küng, *Christianity.*

35. "Forces of Civility: The NGO Revolution and the Search for Peace," *Boston Review* (December–January 1998–99): 49–53.

36. Louis Kriesberg, *Constructive Conflicts: From Escalation to Resolution* (Lanham, Md., and Oxford: Rowman & Littlefield, 1998), 42–53.

37. The term is that of Charles West used in his review of Cox's *Secular City* in *Christianity and Crisis* 25, no. 12 (1965): 148.

6

HARVEY G. COX

Socio-Theological Critical Conscience and
Prophet/Friend of Third World Christianity

VICTOR F. WAN-TATAH

A Personal Reflection

When Rudolf Otto describes the numinous feeling in *The Idea of the Holy*, he refers to an elusive quality that draws one to the numinous object of great attraction. In many ways, Otto's idea explains why I sought out Harvey Cox the moment I arrived at Harvard from my home in Cameroon in the fall of 1977.

There is truly something mysterious but equally enticing about both the power of knowledge and the imparting of knowledge. This explains why the opportunity to work with an intellectual hero like Harvey, who embodied my ideal of theological scholarship and social activism, was a dream come true for me. Concomitantly, however, the anticipation of gaining knowledge and wisdom guided by such a venerable scholar and teacher as Harvey Cox provoked many emotions in me. Although I felt a profound sense of awe and elation at the prospect of meeting and working with Harvey, this was accompanied by an abiding awareness of dread and a fear of failure. These feelings arose because I also was aware of the challenge that this dream created and all that was required of me to realize this dream. Now, upon reflection I truly can say that the whole experience was an epiphany.

Bonds of Affinity

My social activist background in Cameroon as a press and radio minister in the Communication Department of the Presbyterian Church in Cameroon (P.C.C.) predisposed me to the practical and political aspects of ministry and scholarship which I highly valued and came to appreciate at the Harvard Divinity School. My varied academic interests fell within the Department of Applied Theology, headed by Harvey Cox, the Department of Systematic Theology, and the Department of Social Ethics. My decision to major in the area of Religion and Society at both the M.T.S. and Th.D. levels was therefore natural and predictable.

The practical dimensions of theological education which I pursued can be understood both in the Kantian sense of the practical consequences of human action as a "free" moral agent, and also in the Weberian sense of reciprocity between institutional processes and various levels of consciousness. It is from these perspectives that I developed my interest in the study of religion and society with an eye to the mediational role of sociology and cultural Anthropology. my requirements for the Th.D. degree. At this time, I never entertained any thought of teaching in an American university. Since, however, the authorities of my sponsoring Church in Cameroon, through the Basel Missionary Evangelical Society, refused to send me financial aid following the completion of my M.T.S. degree, I was compelled to reassess my professional goals after admission to the doctoral program. I was excited to continue working with Harvey, who, before I received official notification that I was accepted into the doctoral program, had indirectly indicated that he was looking forward to working with me. I understood that even though Harvey's research agenda made him unavailable at times, he would be available when I needed him most.

Dedicated to working with Harvey, I concluded that preparation for this association should begin with an attempt to captivate the spirit of *The Secular City* and to try to understand its relevance for my intellectual pursuits. This book broke new ground in its socio-theological and cultural analysis by its affirmation and celebration of modernity in a world-come-of-age. For my own academic endeavor, I was interested in whether the principles and ideas contained within this book could appropriately provide a framework from which I could analyze the African Christian experience in urban areas.

African cities are in many ways different from Western secular cities. Even the most urbanized and secular of African cities are only deceptively areligious or harbingers of freedom and human development. In West, East, or Southern Africa, whenever Africans move to the cities out of economic necessity or for want of a better life, they bring their religion and traditions with them.

The anonymity and freedom that are celebrated in the Western metropolis do not necessarily carry the same significance in Africa. Tribal quarters or "settlements" in African cities like Douala in Cameroon, or Lagos or Ibadan in Nigeria, exemplify what John Mbiti and other African scholars have identified as the foundational philosophy of African existence: "I am, because we are." The African in the city might be physically far removed from his/her family and tribe, but spiritually, they still continue to nourish family and tribal links whenever possible by sending messages and valuable material gifts through intermediaries to family members in the village. Their identity is still essentially determined by their extended family and tribal belonging via an interesting network of contacts. The frequency of such contacts is greatly enhanced by the weekly or monthly social meetings of tribal members, many of whom are successful businessmen and -women, government workers, or professionals who come into the city for employment of some sort. This traditional though somewhat modified surrogate tribe in the city, has proven to be an indispensable factor in the adaptation of many Africans to city life. Ordinarily, young immigrants to the city would prefer to remain anonymous, but when people, especially youths, encounter financial crisis or severe illness, they have nowhere to turn for help but to their surrogate tribal elders in the city.

The most meaningful insight for me in *The Secular City* is the fourth chapter, which deals with the secular city in a crosscultural perspective. As Harvey observes, secularization is a worldwide phenomenon. Harvey is fully aware of some of the unique features of secular life in the so-called Third World. His reflections on the multicultural expressions of the liberating Gospel in his teaching and scholarship mark his unique theological acumen and status among other Western theologians. I say this knowing that for the past three decades or so, Western theology has more or less worn cultural blinders by not only minimizing the priceless value of nonwestern theological endeavors, but also by failing to include Third World theological discourse and training as an integral part of theological education and not as a peripheral discipline.

Unlike a majority of prominent Western theologians, Harvey has, with firm conviction, kept pace with the monumental explosion and growth of Third World theology. This is exemplified in his book *Turning East,* with its focus on Asia, in which he has shown that Christianity is in practice a truly world religion. Additionally, in *The Silencing of Leonardo Boff,* he captured the soul of Latin American liberation theology, making him one of the most critical and most effective theological witnesses of the twentieth century. This book, although it reflects Harvey's crosscultural perspective, also presents a critical discourse in which he discusses liberation theology as a means to effectively confront liberation issues within the Catholic Church itself and society in general.

Contribution to Euro-American Liberation Theology

Harvey's understanding of liberation theology in the Third World as a theological discourse which can provide the political and economic framework for a Christian grassroots movement, proves that he is more than an armchair theologian. The skills required for this praxis-focused approach are undoubtedly field oriented, since the theologian's objective is to participate in the different communities of faith and in the community's faithful witness to Christ. In order to carry out this type of research, Harvey saw the need to make special arrangements with the University to devote every other year to field research.

In his lectures and presentations at conferences which I attended, this trend toward the practical dimensions of religious experience was palpable as I listened to him. Armchair theology may have its place in the sterile walls of the academy, but a theologian with a critical understanding of the faith of real people must stay close to the scriptures while discerning how the scriptures relate to different historical contexts. Theology cannot pretend to be apolitical in a world where politics and politicians make sweeping decisions that affect people's lives or when corporate executives amass extreme wealth in salaries and corporate fringe benefits at the expense of poorly paid workers. These modern sins have not been sufficiently denounced or "challenged" in the contemporary theological powerhouses of the West. Rather, some religious conservatives choose to engage in theological discussions on single ethical issues like abortion and capital punishment. In doing so, they unwittingly tend to obscure the praxis-oriented message of the Gospel, unlike Harvey whose work demonstrates his awareness and application of this message.

Long before it became fashionable to talk about "solidarity with the poor" in the liberation theological circles of Latin America, Harvey Cox was already living in solidarity with the poor in his neighborhood of Roxbury. Harvey's move to Roxbury perhaps could best be understood if we reflect on his earlier childhood experiences while growing up in Malvern, Pennsylvania, where he had been exposed to one of two black churches in that area. As a young boy, Harvey's mother, Maud, took him to the African Methodist Episcopal Church. This exposure to black culture as a youth may have impacted his decision to move out of the white middle-class neighborhood in which he was living in Boston and move to Roxbury where there is a substantial number of black churches. His reminiscing concerning his missed opportunity to have become acquainted with the other black church in Malvern indicates his interest in the black culture and in particular, the black church.

"It stood across the bridge, not much more than a shack clinging to a corner of land near the abandoned section of the old Lincoln Highway. It housed a Baptist congregation made up mostly of the poor, mainly darker-skinned, dark people who lived nearby. It represented then, I suppose, the end of the class-ethnic spectrum opposite the Quaker meeting. Maybe that's why it is the only other church in Malvern I have never been inside. *But I still feel sad and cheated about that.* I went to school and played and fought with kids who went to that church, but not until I was in my teens did I see anything odd about their having completely separate ways to God. I sometimes wonder now if that strangeness ever struck them."

Eco-Theological Insights

The prophetic qualities evident in Harvey's scholarship on secularization in the Third World also can be discovered in his eco-theological insights. His reflections on the global ecological dilemma were light years ahead of his time, and they bring a fresh perspective to the ongoing debate concerning the religious sources expressed in the discourse regarding the preservation of the environment.

Harvey's diagnosis of the problem was as true and as relevant in the early seventies as it is today. In a ringing criticism of ecological writers, he strikes at the root of our contemporary problem:

> Ecological writers who criticize Christianity and Judaism for their overwhelm-
> ing emphasis on the relations between God, man and neighbor, with little
> emphasis on the rest of "nature," are partially right. These faiths emerged in
> history at a time when nature was no longer seen as such a terrible threat and
> the religious question focused on man and God. It was a time when human be-
> ings were going through that crucial evolutionary stage of understanding their
> uniqueness as creatures who, though clearly a part of "nature," also in some
> ways transcended it. . . . But what the ecological critics of Christianity overlook
> is that our present crisis is not *primarily* one of our relations to "nature." It
> has to do with man, with whether we can begin to control the runaway growth
> of technology, redirect the use of energy to compassionate purposes, reorder
> our institutions to a more humane scale and design habitations that will not
> strangle or suffocate their inhabitants. It has to do with how we can devise
> an economic system which does not exist by creating false needs, using up
> non-renewable resources to assuage them, and poisoning the planet with the
> effluvium of the process. So this challenge to our survival obviously requires a
> faith that helps man deal not so much with "nature" but with choice, power,
> institutional corruption and corporate greed. Though our questions today are
> very much like the primitive man's, it would merely hasten the disaster to em-
> ulate his answers. Our job is not to return to the forest but to turn around a
> juggernaut (Cox, 1973:61–62).

Harvey is undoubtedly aware that the yearning for a simplistic primitive ecological theology to solve our ecological problems greatly obscures
the misuse of political and economic power. The blatant abuse of power,
the unbridled deforestation of virgin forests and the disappearance of rare
plants and animals in the Third World by Western corporations in their
quest for profit, speaks volumes to the abuse of Western corporate and governmental power. Third World Theology definitely needs socio-theological
tools to expose the sins of the industrialized world that have been committed against the powerless in these countries. It cannot, however, ignore the
God of history who is involved in the liberative struggles of God's people.

The Holistic Harvey

The attempt I have made to highlight Harvey's great contribution to theological and religious scholarship definitely does not exhaust all of his works.
A perusal of his works reveals other writings which stimulate theological in-

sight and commitment to holistic change in church and society. For example, Harvey's *The Feast of Fools* (1969) is an exploration of festivity and fantasy in theological imagination which deals with anti-establishment religion and theology. Moreover, his theological adventure into the joys and dynamism of the people's religion can be discovered in *The Seduction of the Spirit* (1973), which makes his theology somewhat humorous and adventurous to read and contemplate. And to those who have known him for some time, it is a true reflection of the thoughtful and happy apostle that he embodies in other dimensions of his life.

In his most recent book, *Fire from Heaven* (1996), Harvey provides a timely and definitive socio-theological analysis of the rise of the Pentecostal movement in our time. Among the most rapidly growing churches in Africa are African Independent Churches, most of which are Pentecostal in their enthusiasm and liturgical expression. Many of these churches, as Harvey recognizes, provide prominent leadership roles for women, while some of the women prophets and priests also are healers.

Although Harvey is a very dedicated and erudite scholar, he is able to devote some time to preaching. Harvey occasionally preaches at the Old Cambridge Baptist Church in Harvard Square. He values his church roots and preaches in other churches when his busy schedule permits. Once when he reflected on his Baptist tradition and what he thought he had missed, he wished he had been able to preach like the homiletically adept Baptist preachers did. Not that he did not know how to preach or had not mastered the craft of the sermon, but he concluded that there was not enough fervor and conviction in the oratory of clergy whose formal preparation for the ministry lacked the conviviality and charisma of homegrown preachers.

Harvey's interest in the church extended outside of his Cambridge parish and other local churches. Like his theological hero Dietrich Bonhoeffer, who saw himself as a minister-theologian and activist, Harvey, through his ecumenical work, has relentlessly summoned the mainline churches in the West to be more cognizant of their myopic perception of ministry which excludes the silent minority.

The Utility and Relevance of World Religions

Most Western theologians engage eager students in various types of God-talk within the traditional settings of the University or Seminary. Here the majority of students are exposed to comparatively more religious education than the typical student in a liberal arts college or state university. It is fair to say without exaggeration that most theological schools do include in some ways the study of world religions. But students who are really grounded in the complex ecumenical issues of inter-faith dialogue are those who already plan to major in ecumenical and mission fields. The general student population may occasionally encounter representatives of other religions in special lectures or seminars.

Rather than treating world religions as a peripheral component of the curriculum, it ought to occupy a prominent and permanent place in the traditional theological curriculum of every theological school or seminary. Already in many state and private universities the different religions of the world are being taken very seriously. We live in a pluralistic society and world where knowledge of other religions especially among future leaders of communities of faith must be deepened and contained in the basic course offerings for students preparing for ministry or for a career in teaching.

At the college level, a variety of courses in world religions are offered at the undergraduate level. These courses for the most part are offered as electives for students meeting their humanities requirements or for a limited number who might be majors in philosophy or religious studies, depending on the size of the college or university. At Youngstown State University where I am an Associate Professor in Religious Studies, Introduction to World Religions is taught as a humanities requirement and the Department of Philosophy and Religious Studies justifies its services to non-majors and minors as a means of facilitating critical thinking and multiculturalism. On a more limited basis, specialized courses in ethics are offered to serve specialized and professional programs and majors like engineering, environmental studies, peace studies, and nursing.

These goals make perfect sense in a department, which as recently as fifteen years ago, did not emphasize diverse religions as an inherent component in its course offerings. In the past, a largely Roman Catholic faculty catered to the needs of students who had been exposed to a Catholic high school education, and who, for academic and spiritual or faith-related reasons, saw the religion and philosophy department as one way of satisfying course needs. Our department, however, has changed significantly in its diverse mix of both faculty and course offerings. The religious studies side of the department of philosophy and religious studies at Youngstown State University is made up of five full-time faculty with doctorates from Graduate Theological Union, Brown, University of Wisconsin, and two from Harvard. We offer a wide range of courses from Introduction to World Religions to specialized courses and seminars in Buddhism, Christianity, Islam, and Ethics of Judaism. As a state institution, we can no longer "nurture" the faith of believers or of former believers who want to recover the faith they once treasured. We must remain "objective" and non-committal in our presentation of the religions we teach.

Ideal as that may be, and as confident as we as teachers and scholars feel that we are achieving our objectives, there are certain issues that compelled me to question some of my assumptions about our mission. I have frequently run into students of all age groups in my classes who have shared their doubts about faith in God, notwithstanding their Christian upbringing. These were questions that they have been wrestling with for some time, but which could not be satisfactorily answered by their priests or ministers. I remember, for example, an elderly couple who at one time belonged to a Protestant congregation where the minister lived and adhered to traditional values. They had no problem with the minister's preaching because his old-time religion sermons were inspiring and gave them a sense of security and constancy. But when the demographics of the neighborhood changed and a new minister arrived, emphasis shifted from spirituality and individual Christian growth to "contemporary" sermons, laced with doses of social and political activism or of the Social Gospel. The couple believed that their waning faith might be reinvigorated if they returned to school and took some courses in the Department of Philosophy and Religious Studies.

I have also met some very bright young students who take our courses hoping to find some kind of moral and spiritual compass in a rapidly changing society where familiar pictures of traditional intact families and the workplace are constantly challenged by modern technology and information overload from the mass media. Upon reflection, I identified some of my students' problem with the pluralization of urban consciousness. This phenomenon affects the processes of primary socialization to the extent that for some people, going back to school gives them an opportunity to reassess and reconstruct the spiritual foundations of their "home world."

How can we as teachers of religion lend some guidance to students who are searching for answers and meaning in an increasingly complex world beyond the confines of our specific departmental missions while at the same time maintain objectivity and fairness to all religions? Could I continue to ignore the specific faith-related questions of my students who would be exposed to only a brief introduction to world religions? Invariably, when I teach Introduction to World Religions, I stress the need for fairness, objectivity, and empathy in learning about other religions. I have, however, been equally critical of world religions' devotees when it comes to their application of certain religious doctrines to real life. This is especially significant when there are obvious theological contradictions which require a critical assessment.

For want of a clear direction or orientation, some students ask me, "What do you yourself believe?" "Do you mean my priest or minister was wrong?" I generally avoid the question by claiming that my personal religious belief has nothing to do with what I consider to be phenomenological observations about religious practice in real life.

After reading Harvey's *Many Mansions* (1988), however, I realized that there might be another way of addressing this question without claiming objectivity. This book focuses on the issues of honesty and sincerity in inter-religious dialogue. The irony born of Harvey's personal experience is that people prefer to play it safe when talking about their religion with someone of a different faith, just as my colleagues have to avoid being too personal in their teaching of world religions. Many Christians in dialogue, myself included, tend to avoid their basic core beliefs in Christ. We fail to realize that we might be more credible and effective if we share our deepest beliefs and convictions while listening attentively to our interlocutors, whether they be students or religious specialists, to share what makes their own faith special and meaningful.

Harvey's *Many Mansions* adequately addresses the relevance of the need to engage in an interfaith dialogue. His own interfaith encounters, for example, are global and represent contemporary experiences of members of different religions struggling to relate their beliefs to essential or common ideals in Christ.

Harvey's christological model adequately provides the concepts and ideas from which I can create my own conceptualization of the African Christ. There are two varieties of the Black Christ, all aimed at empowering black people in America to deal with the problem of institutional racism in the Christian imagery, doctrine, and theology. When Marcus Garvey became increasingly aware of the hopelessness of the people's efforts to gain full citizenship and dignity in America, he initiated the Back to Africa Movement. A centerpiece of his strategy included the renunciation of white Christianity in general and the white Christ in particular. The same theme has been elaborated by Albert Cleage in *The Black Messiah,* which is an eclectic commentary on biblical passages which enhance Afrocentric interpretations of the Gospel.

It is James Cone who has systematically brought out the cardinal theological implications of the symbolism of the Black Christ in *God of the Oppressed* (1975). The defining criterion for asserting that Jesus is black is based on the sad reality of institutional racism in American society and the dominance of racist religious and theological discourse in contemporary white American culture.

Conclusion

Recently, a good friend of mine posed a character check question about another mutual friend of ours. "Is she 'for real'?" she asked. "Yes," I said. "She is true and genuine, you can count on her." I began my reflection on the life and work of Harvey by expressing my sincere admiration for his work and recalling the positive influence he personally had on me. In spite of his worldwide reputation and busy schedule, I believed that he would be there for me if I had an issue or problem that needed to be addressed. I asked myself a few times if he was "for real." Time and experience has proven to me that he is more than real. He is not only a great teacher, scholar, and mentor, but he is also a person of outstanding character and humility.

My interactions with Harvey as a student and teaching fellow in his always popular courses, Jesus and the Gospels and Latin American Liberation

Theology, provided rare opportunities for me to draw inspiration and gain knowledge from rich and diverse sources. He sowed and watered the seeds of my career then, and, in his ever gracious manner, he continues to express interest in my academic and personal future.

Before I moved to Ohio, Harvey took me out for a sumptuous lunch in Harvard Square during which we discussed many issues of common interest, and he gave me names of important contacts in Youngstown. One of the individuals he encouraged me to meet was Bishop James Malone, then past president of the Catholic Bishops' Conference. During this conversation, I was greatly impressed to find that Harvey had been involved in the local ecumenical effort to stave off the devastating effects of the steel mill closing in the Mahoning and Shenango Valleys. His visit to Youngstown State University in March 1998 as a guest speaker sponsored by the Department of Philosophy and Religion was a very special experience for me both personally and academically. I indicate personally because I ferried him from the airport and I transported him to Hiram College, where he also was directing a seminar to a group of clergy. That was truly a precious and memorable occasion for me. The academic experience also contains some elements of the personal. When I first met Harvey, I was the student and he was the professor. He was a role model for me then, and I had hoped that some day I could become as effective a teacher and scholar as he is. I guess you can say that I wanted Harvey to be proud of me and my achievements. His visit to Youngstown State University gave me the opportunity to share some of my accomplishments with him.

In conclusion, Harvey's scholarship and life have set a model for my own work in many important ways. For me, the most significant part of his scholarship that I have been able to integrate into my own work is his model of christological enculturation and interpretation. I have employed this framework to approach critical theological issues in African and African American religious scholarship. The method is both refreshing and useful in constructing liberative or oppositional theological discourse while upholding complementary traditional beliefs and practices of the people's religion.

It is indeed a joyous event to celebrate the life and work of one of the greatest and innovative theological teachers and scholars of the twentieth century. This is even more meaningful when that individual happens to be a true friend, teacher, and mentor for life. Congratulations, good health, and many more years to your exemplary service to God's people.

Part Two

7

THE SECULAR AND THE RELIGIOUS UNDER THE SHADOW OF THE CROSS

*Implications in Christoph Blumhardt's
Kingdom Spirituality for a Christian Response
to World Religions*

Frank D. Macchia

Harvey Cox's classic, *The Secular City*,[1] challenged my understanding of the relationship of the church to its social context at a very formative stage in my development as a student at a Pentecostal college. When I later pursued doctoral research into the work of Christoph Blumhardt, the pietist pastor who "turned to the world" and became involved as a socialist in secular politics, I was pleasantly surprised, but then not so surprised, to find that Blumhardt had made an impact on the thinking of Harvey Cox. When David Little described Cox's *The Secular City*, as simply another rendition of Walter Rauschenbusch's social gospel, Cox responded that he wrote more directly under the European interpretations of *sich realisierende Eschatologie*, particularly in the light of the influence that Christoph Blumhardt and Leonard Ragaz (one of Blumhardt's disciples) exercised on Bonhoeffer's world piety.[2] Of course, Bonhoeffer was not the only one so influenced by Blumhardt. Paul Tillich stated that Christoph Blumhardt opened up for him and others of his generation "in an unheard-of way" "a new understanding of the relationship of the church to society."[3] As is better known, Karl Barth learned from Christoph Blumhardt a way of understanding the impact of the Kingdom of God on society without forsaking the sovereignty and freedom of the divine action.[4]

Even after *The Secular City*, Harvey Cox continued to share insights similar to Barth's and Blumhardt's into the ambiguity of both religious and secular movements in relation to the possibility of bearing witness to the Kingdom of God and its liberating presence in the world. Of course, as Cox

has noted in his subsequent writings, there are radical ecumenical implications in this refusal to absolutize any human "faith" (religious or secular),
particularly for enhancing our capacity to hear the voices of the oppressed
and for opening Christianity up to religious voices other than its own.[5]
There are other contemporary theologians besides Cox, such as Jürgen Moltmann, who were fundamentally shaped by the ecumenical implications of
the "Kingdom spirituality" and "world piety" of Christoph Blumhardt.[6]
Even the ecumenical vision of German writer Hermann Hesse may have
been influenced by Christoph Blumhardt and the world vision of southern
German Pietism, since Hesse spent some time as a troubled youth under
Blumhardt's care and was connected to various streams of radical Pietism
through his father.[7] As I think even the relatively brief exposition that follows will show, the work of Christoph Blumhardt in the light of its setting
in Württemberg or southern German Pietism, especially in the light of the
influence exercised on him by his father, Johann Christoph Blumhardt, provides one important theological context for understanding Cox's work on
the secular city and interreligious dialogue. I offer this exploration of the
world piety of Christoph Blumhardt and its significance for interreligious
ecumenism in honor of Harvey Cox's provocative work and the influence
that it has had on my development as a Pentecostal theologian.

Kingdom Spirituality in the Pietist World
of Christoph Blumhardt

K. Blaser made the provocative observation that the "Kingdom of God on
earth" has been the central theological problem of the twentieth century,[8]
and such was the case already in the context of Christoph Blumhardt's
world in nineteenth-century Württemberg Pietism. Much earlier than that,
and further north in Germany, Jakob Spener, usually referred to as the
progenitor of German Pietism, rooted his hope for a "better time for the
Church" in the expectation that the Kingdom of God will soon break
in upon us in great strength. In fact, one can refer to "an explosion of
similar eschatological, especially chiliastic, thoughts everywhere in early
Pietism."[9] Early Württemberg Pietism was especially characterized by various more-or-less separatistic cell groups that promoted a fervent expectation
of the soon-coming Kingdom of God. They tended to view the oppression caused by royal absolutism, political corruption, and moral laxity on
all levels of society that characterized seventeenth- and eighteenth-century
Württemberg as a sign that the end was near. Unlike the earlier Pietism further north, Württemberg Pietism was not led by theologians and students
but was more *Volkstumlich,* led originally by lay people of humble and even
poor surroundings. Their inspiration came largely from sermons, biographies, and devotionals rather than from theological treatises. Württemberg

Pietists called into question the monopoly on truth assumed by academic theologians and leaders of the institutional church, opening the way for fresh impulses that led to the socially and ecumenically relevant Kingdom spirituality of Christoph Blumhardt.

There were, of course, theological minds that influenced Christoph Blumhardt. Christoph learned from Albrecht Bengel and F. C. Oetinger to understand the breaking in of the Kingdom of God in broad historical and cosmic dimensions. He also learned from Zinzendorf and his Herrnhuter (and others) that personal devotion to Jesus as Liberator and Redeemer would serve the prophetic ministry of the people of God for the Kingdom of God more fruitfully than eschatological or metaphysical speculation. But it was his father's battle for the healing of a tormented woman that focused his attention on the healing and liberation of the suffering and oppressed as the most significant locus for the breaking in of the Kingdom of God in power. The elder Blumhardt, Johann Christoph, prayed unceasingly for the deliverance of Gottlieben Dittus from "demonic oppression" and connected her recovery in 1843 to the breaking in of the Kingdom of God and a yet-future outpouring of the Holy Spirit. In this understanding of the Kingdom of God as a liberating force, the elder Blumhardt was fulfilling the direction started by his uncle who emphasized the plight of the sick and the evils of racism in his understanding of the mission of the Church in the world. Johann Christoph's passion for the Kingdom of God was thus expressed primarily in "groaning" with the suffering creation for the redemption to come (Rom 8:26) as well as in working with those who suffer toward wholeness and the discovery of new life in the Spirit.

Johann Christoph's prophetic passion for the breaking in of the Kingdom of God was qualified, however, by a realistic evaluation of the bondage to sin and oppression that still gripped the world and the Church so tightly. He became a "theologian of hope" striving to be a channel for the breaking in of the Kingdom of God but also awaiting a time of grace in which the Holy Spirit would be poured out upon the world, causing the Kingdom of God to make a global impact toward liberation, healing, and righteousness before Christ returns.[10] His spirituality "between the times" was one of patient waiting (*Warten*) and impatient hurrying (*Eilen*) toward the divinely initiated realization of the Kingdom of God in the world. Karl Barth characterized Johann Christoph's spirituality as "action in waiting."[11]

Christoph Blumhardt's Turn toward the World

The controversial ministry of Christoph Blumhardt began in 1880 when his father blessed him from his deathbed with the leadership of Bad Boll near Stuttgart, a spiritual retreat center founded by the elder Blumhardt for the holistic care of the sick. From early on, Christoph was reared in the spirituality and message of the coming Kingdom of God that were formed in the pastoral experiences of his father. He attended the University of Tübingen to prepare for the ministry, but struggled there to find consistency between what he had learned under his father and the theology on which he was to be examined. He once remarked about his professors that if they had only really known the One about whom they were pontificating, "their faces would turn as white as chalk from terror!"[12] After he entered the ministry and took over the leadership of Bad Boll, he wrote, "I stand firm in the particular calling as successor of my father's thoughts, which for me were inspired of God."[13] Such a stand would be a tall order. Blumhardt inherited his father's eschatological expectation of a soon-coming worldwide outpouring of the Holy Spirit for healing from sickness and liberation from the oppression of sin and unrighteousness. He was left with the task of explaining the delay in the fulfillment of his father's hope and a way of interpreting this fulfillment that, in the true spirit of his father, would not be bound to the past but open to new insights inspired by the Spirit of God.

The new breakthrough for understanding the fulfillment of his father's hope would come for Blumhardt nearly two decades after he took the helm of the ministry at Boll in his "turn to the world" and entry into socialist politics. Throughout part of the 1880s, the first decade of Blumhardt's leadership at Boll, his mother, Doris, served as an advisor to him. Upon her death in 1886, he lamented that all of his advisors were gone. He needed to find a new direction in his service to the Kingdom of God. In the late 1880s, he began to see that the global outpouring of the Holy Spirit would not occur within the confines of Bad Boll, nor Europe for that matter, nor within Pietism or even Christianity. A more secular and social understanding of spiritual themes began to emerge. The elder Blumhardt's groaning for the suffering creation was then specified as a groaning for oppressed farmers.[14] The "sin against the body" was no longer chiefly demonic oppression or sickness but the terrible conditions of the factories.[15] The evil that distorts creation was not simply described as an alienation from the Creator but specifically in the industrial poisoning and killing of the forests.[16] The elder Blumhardt's hesitancy to deal explicitly with the economy is replaced by a sweeping criticism of riches and of capitalist systems as part of the spirit of Antichrist. Blumhardt's battle was not just for the healing of individual people but was to be worldwide "down the streets everywhere the poor, abused, and miserable are."[17]

Blumhardt made his decisive turn to the world in his decision to join the Social Democratic Party (*Sozialdemokratische Partei*), which was at that time more communist in orientation than was to be the case in later decades. His decision to join the Socialists shocked the pietist world. But his desire to side with the workers in their struggle for justice was the major motivation for this shocking move into secular politics. Furthermore, he also saw in the Socialists a way of understanding the outpouring of the Spirit in witness to Jesus Christ among all of the downtrodden of the earth outside the confines of isolated pietist cell groups or the walls of churches removed from the suffering of humanity. His involvement with the Socialists was not motivated by party loyalty but by faithfulness to suffering humanity and to the values advocated by the Socialists which he came to regard as secular analogues of the pietist values that he had learned from his father. He said of the Social Democrats: "At base, the Socialists are not a party nor a class loyalty, but a loyalty to humanity. Hence, I can be nonpartisan within the Socialist Party."[18] He was particularly attracted to the potentially international, intercultural nature of the Socialist movement. He remarked, "Finally, finally, my heart finds satisfaction in an international arena. Now I can go to all people regardless of their nation or religion; but the churches are closed to me because of this."[19] For Blumhardt, "God is not a god of the Germans or Russians, or Chinese; God is a world God, a God of the entire creation."[20] National identities are idolatrous.

Blumhardt stood head and shoulders above others of his day who were wrestling with the German "social question." Unlike J. H. Wichern and A. Stoecker, Blumhardt did not associate the Kingdom of God with German chauvinism or antisemitism. Unlike F. Naumann, neither did he assume a dualism between the Kingdom of God and earthly affairs, so that the demands or presence of the Kingdom of God are no longer felt in one's cultural life or social action. Christoph Blumhardt saw the need to bear witness to the Kingdom of God in the midst of human life but without any identification of the former with the latter. The Kingdom of God is neither identified with nor separated from cultural life or social action for Blumhardt. The Kingdom of God is free and sovereign, and yet, intimately at work in human striving for liberation and redemption. Human action, religious and secular, is seen for all of its ambiguity and fallenness. But, by God's grace primarily, and secondarily by human determination, such action can be made to bear witness to, or provide analogues of, the Kingdom of God breaking in among us.[21] Karl Barth best described the uniquely prophetic way that Christoph Blumhardt connected the divine and the human involvement in the realization of the Kingdom of God on earth:

> The unique element, and I say it quite deliberately, the prophetic, in Blumhardt's message and mission consists in the way in which the hurrying and the waiting, the worldly and the divine, the present and the coming, again and again met, were united, supplemented one another, sought and found one another.[22]

The judgment of the Kingdom of God on the Church was thorough. Blumhardt's attack on the Church, including its institution, sacraments, and missionary efforts, became sharp and relentless. He went out into to the world among the "heathens" and unbelievers to find faithful followers of the Kingdom of God. But Blumhardt was to learn that there were dark powers at work not only in the witness of the Church but also in Socialist politics. During his Socialist years, he was optimistic about the progress of the Kingdom of God in the world through the work of the Social Democrats, leading one theologian to argue later that Blumhardt had abandoned his father's "theology of hope" for a heretical association of the Kingdom of God with social progress.[23] This judgment is extreme and inaccurate. Blumhardt never associated the Kingdom of God with any notion of social progress, religious or secular. There is an optimism during the political years that the Spirit was using the Socialist movement to provide the most profound witness to the Kingdom breaking into society for liberation and righteousness in Blumhardt's day. But he was to become less optimistic at the eve of his life about the role of the Socialists as vessels of the Kingdom of God in the world. After six years of service for the Social Democrats on the Stuttgart *Landtag,* Blumhardt became somewhat disillusioned with party politics and less optimistic about his capacity to witness the future transformation of the world through the Socialist movement.[24] After he removed himself from the turbulent storm of party politics, he remarked that what was familiar at that point was not "a rough wind but a growth in stillness."[25] Yet, he still believed that the fundamental reality of Christ's presence may be felt in both the agony and the ecstasy of life, whether it be secular or religious. And he never abandoned the values that motivated his prophetic criticisms of the Church and attracted him to side with the poor and to reach out to people of other religions. We will briefly explore in greater detail both the christological and the pneumatological foundations of Blumhardt's ecumenism, as well as his consequent attitudes toward the Church and other faiths.

From the Incarnation to the Cross: The Christological Foundation of Blumhardt's Ecumenism

Blumhardt's ecumenical openness to people of other religions did not preclude for him a strong christological concentration to the Gospel of the Kingdom of God. The emphasis of the elder Blumhardt on the outpouring of the Holy Spirit as the end-time period of grace was replaced in the younger Blumhardt's thought by a stress on the entry of God decisively into human history in the human life, death, and resurrection of Jesus. He maintained that without God's redemptive deeds in history "we would only be able to speak of God philosophically." Blumhardt wrote further of the fulfillment of God's mighty deeds in history: "But in Jesus God is revealed in the flesh. Now we can experience God in deepest misery."[26] In Jesus, God is revealed in fullness: "God should be recognized in Christ, through whom the entire radiance of the righteousness and truth of God is revealed to us."[27] He recognized the Kingdom of God was essentially the liberating and redemptive presence of God that broke into history decisively in the person of Jesus.

Blumhardt insisted that God's activity in the liberating story of Jesus was the criterion for judging the work of the Kingdom of God in the world, a point that Christians did not always appreciate. Blumhardt stated to the Pietists, "We still have religion, we still have Christian morals. But that Jesus has come in the flesh, that our God is here, that has often disappeared from us."[28] In fact, Blumhardt's involvement outside the Church with the Socialists was largely motivated by his conviction that Jesus sided with the poor, something which Blumhardt felt, with justification, the Church had not done sufficiently. For example, Jesus' feeding of the 5,000 was not so important because of its miraculous nature but because of its dramatic revelation of the fact that the Kingdom of God comes through Jesus "as a help to the hungry, as well as to the sick and the miserable."[29] He argued that Jesus came from among the poor and will illuminate the world through the poor today.[30] Jesus was one among the "lowly" and was himself a "socialist," who "chose twelve apostles from among the proletariat."[31] Blumhardt came at one point to so stress the significance of the human-life example of Jesus that he described Jesus as only being a man: "Jesus is here! He was just a man and you should be one too."[32] The emphasis here, however, is on the genuine humanity of Jesus as the locus of God's work toward initiating a new humanity and a new creation. The fact that he begins the remark with "Jesus is here" implies that Jesus had to be in some sense more than "just a man." Though Blumhardt said in one place that Jesus was not his God,[33] his dominant belief throughout his life was in the exclusive deity of Jesus.[34]

In his ecumenism, Blumhardt does not limit the significance of Jesus to the work of God in and through the Church, but neither does he abandon the Church's confession that includes the scandal of particularity involved in granting eschatological finality exclusively to the life, death, and resurrection of Jesus. The "Christ" is not cut loose from its exclusive and inseparable connection with the historical Jesus for the sake of ecumenical dialogue with those who would not locate God's decisive and final redemptive act in the crucified and risen man of Nazareth. There is an exclusivity to Blumhardt's Christology. But this exclusivity is not of a sectarian spirit which arrogantly associates the Kingdom of God on earth with Christianity or the Church. As Jan Milic Lochman pointed out, the *exclusivity* of Christ as the only Savior and Lord is unique in that it is also disturbingly *inclusive*.[35] For Blumhardt, Christ is alone Savior and Lord because only in him does God decisively reach out to all of humanity, both the religious and the godless, in both judgment and hope.

The cross was for Blumhardt the most significant revelation of God's redemptive act in Jesus of Nazareth and the focus of following Jesus in solidarity with humanity, especially the suffering and the oppressed. Particularly in the years directly preceding his involvement in politics, Blumhardt developed a spirituality of the cross, focusing on the crucifixion of Jesus as the supreme revelation of the way of the Kingdom of God in the world. The cross became the place where idolatrous exclusivity dies and the scandal of

God's all-embracing judgment and grace is accepted. "Die that Jesus may live" was his exhortation to all who wanted to be citizens of the Kingdom of God, regardless of their religious affiliation. All that mattered for people of other religions was not that they convert to the Christian religion but that they "die so that God, the Most High and Creator, can live in Jesus."[36] The most important decision for anyone of any religion to make is following Jesus to the cross, for only through the cross can one find life.

One may understandably consider as extreme Blumhardt's effort to point nonchristian people to the crucified Christ in the midst of their own religious faith without implying that they ever need to consider themselves "Christian." Largely missing from the ecumenical implications of Blumhardt's focus on the cross is the call to public evangelism, a call that will seek to offer to others the Gospel of the Lord Jesus Christ that exists at the heart of what it means to be Christian, with all of the scandal that this may provoke within many nonchristian faiths. But Blumhardt does remind us that the Gospel is not the Gospel of Christianity or the Church primarily, but the Gospel of the crucified Christ who gave of his own life in solidarity with the world in order that the world might come to know life. Blumhardt saw clearly that the evangelism of the people of God must look to the cross as the place where Christianity is relativized and stripped of its idolatrous self-exaltation. He remarked, "We must take the cross seriously, but not with Constantine as a flag of the sinful world. 'Love your enemies,' 'Do good to those who hate you.' "[37]

Furthermore, there is a place for saying that God will use people of faith and hope outside of Christianity as vessels of the coming Kingdom even without their first being Christianized or ecclesiasticized. As Jürgen Moltmann noted,

> If it is Christianity's particular vocation to prepare the messianic era among the nations and to make ready the way for the coming redemption, then no culture must be pushed out and no religion extinguished. On the contrary, all of them can be charismatically absorbed and changed in the power of the Spirit. They will not be ecclesiasticized in the process, nor will they be Christianized either; but they will be given a messianic direction towards the kingdom.[38]

Though this process of praying and working for the Spirit to prepare for the messianic era by transforming all people (including Christians) should not exclude evangelism, Blumhardt has shown us that this process will also exceed, and provide external insight and blessing for, the evangelistic work of the Church in history.

Blumhardt stressed that Christians of various confessions will not know the life at the source of their Gospel without the way of the cross.[39] The Pietists are concerned about the coming of the antichrist, but, according to Blumhardt, "the antichrist is he who wants to be comforted by Christ before he puts to death what must die." Both Catholic and Protestant Christians "grind their teeth" because something distinct to their traditions must die in their faithfulness to the cross.[40] This is why Blumhardt called the life of the Gospel a "dying life." He remarked: "What is the Gospel? Dying life, my dear people! And God will provide the power for this."[41] The cross is to shape one's entire life after the example of Jesus. The responsibility and privilege of living the way of the cross are great. Following the crucified Christ allows us to participate in the liberation and redemption of the world. "God helped the world at the cost of Jesus Christ, and at the cost of our lives as well if we are bound to Christ."[42] He even stated boldly that salvation was "by our blood through Christ's blood."[43]

The Progress of the Kingdom of God through the Holy Spirit

For Blumhardt, God and Christ can be present redemptively in the world only through the Holy Spirit. Despite Blumhardt's accent on the important human participation in the redemption wrought by the Kingdom of God in the world, he does not hesitate to locate the power of this work in the Spirit and grace of God alone. "Then God becomes hallowed as the only Father and Jesus as the only Lord and Savior through the deeds of the Holy Spirit. No knowledge or piety can give rise to this divine deed."[44] One is reminded of the "waiting and hurrying" spirituality of Blumhardt's father. If the "waiting" referred to liberation and redemption through the grace and Spirit of God alone, the "hurrying" pointed to the important role that humanity and creation are allowed to play in bearing witness to, and functioning as channels of, the divine action in the world. Especially during the political years, Blumhardt developed a vision of the "progress" of the Kingdom of God in the world through the work of the Holy Spirit and the positive response of creation.[45] This development of the pneumatological dimension of the Kingdom of God, allowed Blumhardt to complement his prior emphasis on the way of the cross, which was never abandoned entirely. He stated, "We are finding a desire for progress, for further development, everywhere among people. This is the Spirit."[46]

The implication of the cross emerges in Blumhardt's conviction that nature and history are fallen and are drawn into the progress of the Kingdom in order to participate in, and bear witness to, the work of God. As Blumhardt stated, "The Kingdom develops from within itself. We walk alongside it and are happy to recognize this great movement of the reign of God."[47] The Kingdom progresses "alongside" of history because of the sovereignty and freedom of the divine action. Yet, the Kingdom's movement "alongside" also impacts history as it moves ahead. Blumhardt explained this impact more precisely in a letter to the pastor and Socialist, Leonard Ragaz, in which Blumhardt wrote of a movement of the Spirit of Christ proceeding through the times and presenting us with a kernel of truth that will push us ahead into that which is new.[48] In this way the historical and cultural development of peoples gets "pulled up into" the progress of the Kingdom, which creates new avenues of growth not present before.[49] This understanding of the work of the Kingdom through the Spirit in history seems very similar to Paul Tillich's "kairos" event, particularly in its more dynamic and progressive form implied in *The Socialist Decision.*[50]

Blumhardt eventually reinterpreted his father's hope for a future, worldwide outpouring of the Holy Spirit to mean that God is already involved through the presence of the Spirit in the world to transform all of creation.[51] As his father before him, Blumhardt argued that the Kingdom of God does not just transform people within but impacts outward life, including society and creation. He wrote: "Grace is not something subjective, a comfort within, but something objective, or external to us in the appearance of new life. There are genuinely new situations created by the Spirit into which we enter."[52] God is revealed through the Spirit in the world as the One who is near to create new possibilities for life. Blumhardt stated: "As Creator, God is at the same time the Preserver and Redeemer of the world. God's sovereignty does not imply a divine distance from life and not at all an opposition to the world. Nature is God's palace."[53] He stated further, "What then is God? Look at heaven, look at the earth. There is pure life, resurrection, restitution; and if the world becomes a desert, it must be renewed — this is God."[54] His father's emphasis on the miraculous is now replaced by a notion of God's remarkable power exercised for redemption within the realm of the natural. "The self-disclosure of God lies precisely in the natural."[55]

Blumhardt placed a particular focus on the role of persons as channels of the divine life throughout creation. "The Holy Spirit will be recognized there, where people become human."[56] Becoming human is the goal of everyone in the Kingdom of God, regardless of one's religion. Blumhardt told the missionaries, "Do not seek Christians. Seek human beings!"[57] Though Blumhardt did not want to exclude the need at times to teach or to preach the Gospel, he came to view the major witness of the people of God to be through transformed persons who bear witness to the love of Christ. "The witness through one's person is the greatest truth of the Bible and remains from God the greatest reality that people have experienced."[58] The point of inquiry into both the historical Jesus and the present work of Christ through the Spirit is primarily the life of a person shaped by the Spirit of Christ. Blumhardt exhorted his son-in-law who worked as a missionary to China that "Jesus must become understood in your person before you can tell the Chinese of the historical and present existence of Jesus. The unity of Jesus and our person can alone effect the beginning."[59]

Blumhardt provided some guidance for discerning that which is a genuine work of the Spirit and an expression of Jesus from that which is not by refusing to separate the work of the Spirit today from the life, teachings, death, and resurrection of Jesus in history. Throughout Blumhardt's writings, one finds numerous references to the life, teachings, and death of Jesus. For example, concerning the hope for the progress of the Spirit in history, Blumhardt stated concerning Jesus, "he was against everything that belongs to the world of sin and hoped for a new development through the Spirit."[60] Blumhardt was emphatic about the significance of the life of Jesus as a liberating event for current praxis: "Our person must enter the history of Jesus, our entire being must find something there in the person of Jesus and, with this, become more like him, have what he had, and conquer as he did. Otherwise, our Christianity is worth nothing."[61]

The work of the Spirit in the historical life, death, and resurrection of Jesus was foundational for Blumhardt and of ongoing criteriological significance for discerning the present work of the Spirit. The direction of Jesus toward the poor, the sick, and the oppressed, inspired Blumhardt to see the Spirit of Christ at work in social liberation and progress in the secular realm. Such a devotion to the secular and liberating thrust of Jesus' ministry provided Blumhardt with insights into the Spirit's work in culture and society that were unique for his day. For example, in writing to his son-in-law about the progress of the Spirit of Christ in Chinese history and culture, he recognized that growing secularity is pushing religion out of public life. But even so, he noted that the Spirit of the Kingdom is still at work in the increasingly secularized world. Unknown by the people of such cultures, the Kingdom of God "rumbles" beneath the surface of human culture and history, "taking hold of" the different areas of human activity and opening up new opportunities of life. He stated further, "Will not the binds be loosed and the chains be broken asunder?" As proof that such hope is finding fulfillment, Blumhardt remarks, "Who could have thought thirty years ago that the women of China are now having the doors open to them that once only belonged to men?" Such may not seem religious on the surface, but "first the Spirit must be free to be understood in a worldly way before knowledge of God can come."[62]

Helmut Gollwitzer is correct in stating that for Blumhardt "Christology becomes pneumatology," meaning that the Spirit of the Kingdom of God is a dynamic force for liberation and redemption that breaks into history decisively with the incarnation of God in Jesus and culminates with the Parousia.[63] Indeed, because of the importance of pneumatology for Christology, Jesus "is not like a man who lived once and then passed away; we can only compare him to a Spirit who always creates something new and wills that which is good for each time period."[64] At the end of history, nonchristian peoples, who may not realize that they are serving the Spirit of Christ in history, will be able to look back and recognize that they have indeed glorified Christ.[65] One can say that, for Blumhardt, pneumatology fulfills Christology by defining Christ's eschatological work in history, from its foundation in the life of the historical Jesus to the end of history and the fulfillment of the Kingdom. But Jesus provides the foundation and ongoing criterion for understanding pneumatology for Blumhardt as well. This mutual contribution of Christology and pneumatology implied in Blumhardt's work is more Eastern than Western and, as we will note, implies significant ecumenical implications for interreligious dialogue.

The Kingdom Relativizes the Church and Its Mission

Blumhardt was convinced that the churches had fallen woefully short of the example of Christ in their missionary efforts. "Right from the start," he wrote to his son-in-law in China, "the mistake seems to me to have been that missionaries presented themselves to the Chinese like professors to students." Blumhardt suggested that an approach more respectful of the Chinese would be to discover "the way of the Savior" who approaches them as "one human being among others" while pointing toward the Kingdom of God through a self-giving life.[66] Consistent with the example of Christ, the doctrine of the Apostles is to be "personified" in our Christ-like lives to be authentic.[67]

Forbidden among those who follow Christ will be any future reference to the Chinese as "the yellow devil." They are to be referred to instead as people valued as much by God as any other people.[68] In this way, we also avoid the "missionary and ecclesiastical coercion" that the churches in Europe and North America have exercised in foreign missions.[69] No effort is to be made to conform the Chinese to European culture. The Gospel is to be lived out in a way that respects Chinese culture and interests, encouraging them "to unite with the truth and to deal justly with the Asian world."[70] The Chinese will be able to sense in the context of their own history and progress "what Jesus is, the Person of God's power and love, without any religious trimmings."[71] Instead of associating missions with "europeanizing and christianizing," the people of God will seek to witness "the essence of God and Christ emerge in every people naturally and truly in their own language and morals, so that we Europeans might learn from this and be revived through it."[72] Such humility will occur as we are "taken up with the Savior instead of Christianity, with the Holy Spirit instead of our spirit, be taken up with God." "Then," he claimed, "we will experience the Kingdom of heaven."[73]

Blumhardt was convinced that "the pride of Christians cannot endure forever."[74] The Kingdom of God was breaking in with such elemental force that a decisive change was occurring with respect to God's plan for the Church. In fact, Blumhardt was convinced that the present Church and its missionary efforts were already superseded by the impact of the Kingdom of God in the world. He exhorted his son-in-law in China not to fear being called a "heathen among the heathen" as long as he supports the work of Christ and the Spirit of God. This is so because, "the concept of the Church is now done away with; the harvest has begun." There is therefore not to be any dogmatic or liturgical separation of Christians from the world.[75]

The sacraments of the Church have lost their original connection with the Kingdom of God. They have become "tools of power for the Church." The sacraments have thus exhausted their historical purpose. Blumhardt quoted Luke 22:18 to suggest that the eucharist is now unnecessary and is replaced by the future Messianic banquet.[76]

Blumhardt came to regard baptism as unnecessary since it had also lost its connection with the Kingdom of God and had become a source of division and alienation from the world. But the baptism in the Holy Spirit is still to be cherished, since this experience brings us into solidarity with the world.[77] Blumhardt was willing to allow baptisms to occur among those who wished to publicly express their devotion to Jesus Christ.[78] He even praised those Chinese who did have the courage to identify openly with Christ through baptism, since they provide a sign of what it can mean to become Christian in a cultural setting different from that of Europe.[79] What he seems to have been against was the institutional function of baptism in a triumphalist Church that all too often distinguished itself from the world not to be for the Kingdom and, therefore, for the world, but in order to be for itself. For the People of God, "the sacrament is secondary; but what really matters is whether or not we are just human beings."[80]

There is no question about the fact that Blumhardt detached the work of Christ through the Spirit from the Church and attached it instead to the Kingdom of God. There is no *Christus Prolongatus* in the Church for Blumhardt. The incarnation of God in Christ by the Spirit proceeds in history as the Kingdom of God and is served by anyone devoted to the Kingdom, whether or not such a one goes under the title of "Christian." But Blumhardt also gives hints of not abandoning the notion of the Church and its unique elect purpose entirely. If there is to be a "church" in the world, it is to look and act much differently than it has in the past. "Pity on us," Blumhardt wrote, "if we were to preach the forms of the Christian religion in baptism, confirmation, and the eucharist and regard this as sufficient for becoming Christian! We should be a church in the Spirit not forms, and not in the human spirit, but God's Spirit."[81] Such a Church will be "a channel of the living God, where the revelation of God can find a place in which to occur."[82] The danger here, of course, is in a platonic notion of the Church that regards its external forms and institutional expressions as irrelevant. But, to his credit, Blumhardt understood the fallenness and ambiguity of the Church as an institutional body and placed his emphasis on the true "soul" of the Church, namely, its faith, hope, and love in the Spirit of Christ and in service to the Spirit of the Kingdom of God in the world.

The Kingdom Relativizes Religions

If there is to be no absolutizing of the Church in the light of the Kingdom of God, there was to be for Blumhardt no absolutizing of faith, whether it be Christian or of some other religion.[83] He was just as averse to identifying the world's religions with the Kingdom of God as he was the Church. Though, as we have noted, other religions can bear witness to the life of the Gospel of Christ, they also belong to the life of fallen humanity according to Christoph.[84] The question for Blumhardt had to do with the power of new life in relation to these religions. All religions including Christianity are useless if no such power proceeds from them. "The situation is no longer religion against religion, but righteousness against sin, life against death."[85] Religion is meant to bear witness to new life, for Blumhardt lamented, "Oh the unholy separation of religion and life!"[86] Christ has come "to solve the question of life, and not religion." Hence, a missionary should bring life in the name of Jesus, and not religious disputations.[87] The central issue is not dogma but life, "life that cannot be defined."[88] Indeed, "the devil has a way of laughing at merely religious ideas or viewpoints." And all religion must lead to new life on earth, whether it be "Buddhist, Catholic, or Pietist."[89] All too often, one only asks "what brings profit" instead of "what belongs to life?"[90] Blumhardt makes his fundamental conviction in the light of the Kingdom of God dawning in the world as follows:

> We neither want to see the heathen remain eternally as heathen nor Christians as eternally in Christendom. We seek something new, a life in God through the Spirit of Christ which will be created by the Spirit of God.[91]

Even the secular world falls under the judgment that proceeds from Christ toward religion, for, with Jesus, both science and religion cease.[92] Through Christ, humanity is being freed from both secular and religious rules.[93] Blumhardt defines the prophetic in distinction from both the religious and the moral: "The prophets break free of all rules and risk forsaking all human entanglements in order to freely trust in the living God instead of proceeding further in stagnant religious morals."[94] This distinction of the prophetic from the religious and the moral is rooted for Blumhardt in the freedom of God and the divine commandments. He stated, "human morals must not remain as God's eternal commandments. We must not proceed from human morals."[95]

The decisive revelation of the demands of the Kingdom and of the divine commandments is in the cross of Christ. Thus, "the only thing that counts from religion is following Jesus to the cross. Only through the cross is there life."[96] Christ is the truth from which all religions draw their life and authenticity as witnesses of the Kingdom of God. One abandons the Kingdom of God if Christ is simply viewed as being the same as Buddha, or as simply one religious leader among others.[97] Confucius and Buddha are not revelations of God next to that which comes through Christ. Blumhardt stated conclusively that Jesus "is not a historical figure similar to the leading figure of a world religion. He is the practical, graspable, personal presence and in this way the ensemble of a new humanity in the making."[98]

Conclusion

The work of Christoph Blumhardt is certainly not the final word on the challenge among Christians of relating the Gospel of the Kingdom of God to world religions. His radical separation of Christ, the Spirit, and the Kingdom of God from the Church and his rejection of the Church's worship and sacraments are one-sided and extreme. He came close to rejecting the relevance of the Church entirely, though he did hint here and there that the Church may bear witness to the coming Kingdom in its worship, sacraments, and external witness. But, regardless of such hints, there is little effort to provide the kind of constructive biblical theology of the Church in a secular and pluralistic context that one finds begun in Harvey Cox's *The Secular City*.[99] It is interesting to view Cox's *Secular City* as a response to Blumhardt's challenge to redefine the Church and its mission in the midst of an increasingly secular context.

Furthermore, Blumhardt is justified in placing praxis above dogma. But lacking is an appreciation of dogma and theology for guiding praxis as well as ecumenical dialogue. After all, any effort to develop an ecumenical openness to world religions from the vantage point of a confession of Jesus as Lord will raise certain theological and dogmatic questions that cannot be avoided. Helpful are his remarks concerning a Christian witness through love and good deeds that exists in ecumenical openness to the legitimacy of other religions as witnesses to the Kingdom of God. But his near replacement of evangelism with a witness through life comes close to denying the Church its important kerygmatic function in the world.

But it is important to note again that Blumhardt's criticisms were also directed outside of the Church to other religions. Blumhardt was just as clear about refusing to absolutize faiths of other religions as he was with regard to the faith of Christianity. The focus on the cross in Blumhardt's work recognized the fallenness of religion. This theology of the cross was to find a certain affinity with the modern criticism of religion, a criticism which, as Barth was to develop later, was the great contribution of atheists like Ludwig Feuerbach. Later, in the spirit of Blumhardt, Moltmann spoke of the cross as an "unreligious" act, since it cancels out all patterns of religious projections. "The modern criticism of religion can attack the whole world of Christianity, but not this unreligious cross."[100]

Through difficult years of party politics, Blumhardt also came to be leery of confidence in secular movements to adequately bear witness to the coming Kingdom. He understood the ambiguity of both religious and secular movements and institutions in bearing witness to the Kingdom of God in human redemption and liberation. He was more willing to find signposts of the coming messianic Kingdom in contexts beyond the Church, both religious and secular, than he was within the Church. But, as Werner Jackh noted, Blumhardt's sharp stance *against* the Church was really *for* the Church.[101]

From Blumhardt we also learn that Christians can utilize a christological criterion in embracing the work of the Kingdom of God in the world today without neglecting the fundamental role of the Spirit both in the shaping of the christological criterion and in the present direction that it may take. Blumhardt teaches us that we can be centered on Christ and the Spirit without falling into ecclesiocentrism. But we must not forget that this was a man who loved the Church. His strong criticisms toward the Church were part of a sibling rivalry which was motivated by a deep love for the Church that was injured through disappointment with its failures as a historical and fallen religious body. In the midst of Blumhardt's strong "No" toward the church, there are echoes of an affirming "Yes." The grace implied in this "Yes," as well as the judgment implied in the "No," will continue to guide the Church in its ecumenical relations with other communities of faith and with people of goodwill everywhere.

Notes

1. Harvey Cox, *The Secular City: Secularization and Urbanization in Theological Perspective* (New York: Collier Books, 1990 reprint).

2. Daniel Callahan, ed., *The Secular City Debate* (New York: Macmillan, 1966), 69–74; 87.

3. Observe what Tillich says of Blumhardt in Carl Braaten, ed., *A History of Christian Thought: From Its Judaic and Hellenistic origins to Existentialism* (New York: Harper & Row, 1967), 532. For the connection between Blumhardt and Bonhoeffer, notice Vernard Eller's Introduction to *Thy Kingdom Come: A Blumhardt Reader* (Grand Rapids: Eerdmans, 1980), esp. xiv, and Gerhard Sauter, *Die Theologie des Reiches Gottes beim alteren und jungeren Blumhardt* (Zurich: Zwingli Verlag, 1962), 117, 223.

4. See especially Karl Barth, "Past and Future: Friedrich Naumann and Christoph Blumhardt," in J. A. Robinson, ed., *Dialectical Theology,* trans. K. R. Crim (Richmond: John Knox, 1968).

5. "The Secular City Twenty-Five Years Later," in *The Secular City* (1990 reprint), xi–xxiii.

6. Jürgen Moltmann, *The Church in the Power of the Spirit* (New York: Harper & Row, 1977), 282ff.

7. See Walter Hollenweger's remarks about the influence of the communist Pietistic village, Korntal, on Hesse: *Umgang mit Mythen, Interculterelle Theologie,* vol. 2 (Munich: Chr. Kaiser Verlag, 1982), 195; concerning the time Hesse spent with Blumhardt, see Werner Jackh, *Blumhardt: Vater und Sohn und Ihre Welt* (Stuttgart: J. F. Steinkopf Verlag, 1977), 144–48.

8. "Mission und Erweckungsbewegung," in M. Brecht et al., eds., *Pietismus und Neuzeit* (Göttingen: Vandenhoeck & Ruprecht, 1981), 7:144.

9. Philip Jakob Spener, *Pia desideria,* trans. T. G. Tappert (Philadelphia: Fortress Press, 1964), 76; see also quotes from Spener in M. Greschat, ed., "Die 'Hoffnung besserer Zeiten' fuer die Kirche," in *Zur Neueren Pietismus Forschung* (Darmstadt: Wissenschaftliche Buchgesellschaft, 1977), 288.

10. Frank D. Macchia, *Spirituality and Social Liberation: The Message of the Blumhardts in the Light of Württemberg Pietism* (Metuchen, N.J.: Scarecrow Press, 1993), ch. 2.

11. Karl Barth, *Action in Waiting* (Rifton, N.Y.: Plough, 1969, 1979).

12. Quoted in Werner Jackh, *Blumhardt*, 112.

13. Christoph Blumhardt, *Ansprachen, Predigten, Reden, Briefe: 1865–1917* (Neukirchen-Vluyn: Neukirchener Verlag, 1978), 1:76.

14. *Ansprachen*, 2:16.

15. Ibid., 39.

16. Ibid., 113.

17. Ibid., 84.

18. Ibid., 187.

19. Ibid.

20. Ibid., 25.

21. Macchia, *Spirituality*, 128–33.

22. Barth, "Past and Future," 45.

23. Paul Schuetz, *Sakuläre Religion* (Tübingen: J. C. B. Mohr, 1932).

24. Macchia, *Spirituality*, ch. 3.

25. *Ansprachen*, vol. 3, 70–71.

26. *Ansprachen*, vol. 2, 101.

27. Ibid., 163.

28. *Ansprachen*, vol. 1, 123.

29. *Christus in der Welt* (Zurich: Zwingli Verlag, 1958, reprint), 131.

30. Ibid., 41.

31. *Ansprachen*, vol. 2, 184.

32. *Ansprachen*, vol. 1, 118.

33. *Ansprachen*, vol. 2, 237.

34. See for example, Ibid., 8.

35. Jan Milich Lochman, "My Pilgimage as an Evangelical Theologian," currently unpublished.

36. *Ansprachen*, vol. 2, 33.

37. *Ansprachen*, vol. 1, 74.

38. Moltmann, *The Church*, 163.

39. *Ansprachen*, vol. 2, 254.

40. Ibid., 30.

41. Ibid., 130.

42. Ibid., 141.

43. Ibid., 9–10.

44. *Christus in der Welt*, 40.

45. Macchia, *Spirituality*, 133–36.

46. *Ansprachen*, vol. 2, 298.

47. *Ansprachen*, vol. 3, 70.

48. Ibid., 61.

49. *Christus in der Welt*, 233.

50. Paul Tillich, *The Socialist Decision*, trans. F. Sherman (New York: Harper & Row, 1977).

51. *Ansprachen*, vol. 1, 85–86; 105.

52. *Ansprachen*, vol. 2, 55.
53. Ibid., 295.
54. Ibid., 168.
55. Ibid., 67.
56. Ibid., 139.
57. Ibid., 33–34.
58. *Christus in der Welt*, 215.
59. Ibid., 38.
60. *Christus in der Welt*, 86.
61. *Ansprachen*, vol. 1, 63.
62. *Christus in der Welt*, 233.
63. Helmut Gollwitzer, "Christoph Blumhardt neu sichtbar," *Evangelische Theologie* 41 (1981), 259ff.
64. *Ansprachen*, vol. 2, 287.
65. *Christus in der Welt*, 242–43.
66. Ibid., 27.
67. *Ansprachen*, vol. 1, 113.
68. *Christus in der Welt*, 140.
69. Ibid., 38.
70. Ibid., 157.
71. Ibid., 164.
72. *Ansprachen*, 224.
73. *Ansprachen*, vol. 1, 160.
74. Ibid., 155.
75. *Christus in der Welt*, 68.
76. *Ansprachen*, vol. 2, 152.
77. *Christus in der Welt*, 111, 170.
78. Ibid., 199.
79. Ibid., 158–59.
80. *Ansprachen*, vol. 2, 177.
81. *Ansprachen*, vol. 1, 112.
82. *Ansprachen*, vol. 2, 69.
83. I am grateful to Jürgen Moltmann for his discussions about the problems associated with absolutizing the Church or faith, *The Church*, 153–55.
84. *Ansprachen*, vol. 2, 175.
85. *Christus in der Welt*, 22.
86. Ibid., 153.
87. Ibid., 29.
88. Ibid., 91.
89. Ibid., 114.
90. Ibid., 39.
91. *Christus in der Welt*, 157.
92. Ibid., 165.
93. *Christus in der Welt*, 212.
94. *Ansprachen*, vol. 2, 32.
95. Ibid., 58.
96. Ibid., 54.

97. Ibid., 153.

98. Quoted by J. Harder in his Introduction to *Ansprachen,* vol. 1, 13.

99. *The Secular City,* Part Two.

100. Jürgen Moltmann, *The Crucified God: The Cross of Christ as the Foundation and Criticism of Christian Theology* (New York: Harper & Row, 1974), 37.

101. Werner Jackh, *Blumhardt,* 14.

8

THE WHITENESS OF GOD

The Unintended Theological Legacy of James Baldwin

WILLIAM HAMILTON

Nor, in some things, does the common, hereditary experience of all mankind fail to bear witness to the supernaturalism of this hue. It cannot well be doubted, that the one visible quality in the aspect of the dead which most appalls the gazer, is the marble pallor lingering there; as if indeed that pallor were as much the badge of consternation in the other world, as of mortal trepidation here. And from that pallor of the dead, we borrow the expressive hue of the shroud in which we wrap them. . . . But not yet have we solved the incantation of this whiteness, and learned why it appeals with such power to the soul; and more strange and far more portentous — why, as we have seen, it is at once the most meaning symbol of spiritual things, nay, the very veil of the Christian's Deity; and yet should be as it is, the intensifying agent in things the most appalling to mankind.

—Herman Melville, *Moby Dick,* chap. 42

James Baldwin was probably not a novelist of the first rank, but as a writer of essays, polemical and autobiographical, he was as fine as anything the last half of our century has produced. It is mainly his nonfiction that I will examine to try to define his strange and important theological legacy.[1]

James Baldwin was born in the same year I was, and the gulf between us can be established by comparing two wildly dissimilar events that happened to each of us when we were fourteen years old, worlds apart. When I was fourteen, I put on my scout's uniform and travelled to New Salem, Illinois, from which I walked alone the twenty-one miles to Springfield, repeating the journey that Abraham Lincoln had made nearly a hundred years earlier to study law. After completing the walk, a friend and I saw "Lost Horizon," and I fell in love with Jane Wyatt and decided I wanted to be like Robert Conway when I grew up.

If I fled to Shangri La the summer I was fourteen, Baldwin fled to God in a conversion experience that had a permanent effect and did, I suspect, permanent damage. Under the influence of a gifted black woman minister, after an all-night session of music and prayer, Baldwin fell down at the foot of the church altar and gave himself to a God he (later?) discovered to be white. That summer night, Baldwin established an identity he never relinquished: Christianity = God = white. All Christianity, even black Protestantism, is white. This is the key that unlocks the theological legacy of this remarkable man and writer. The gulf illustrated by these two 1938 tales, one wildly trivial, one desperately important, is one I will try to bridge by that kind of understanding and love that Baldwin so often demanded of himself and of his readers.

Baldwin's conversion experience bears one striking similarity to that of Augustine of Hippo. Augustine was not simply converted to Christianity (or neoplatonism or neoplatonized Christianity or whatever) under that tree in Milan, he was converted to celibacy, in effect, to the priesthood. Baldwin, at the foot of a cross, not a tree, was not only converted to a white God, but to the "ministry." For three years after that summer evening, Baldwin was a very successful boy preacher. He admits that in many ways he never left the pulpit (*The Price of the Ticket*, p. xviii). His relationship to his readers was invariably homiletic, confrontational, prophetic. To read a Baldwin essay is to be indicted for sin.

I

Before we come to the white God, we must first examine the general understanding of Christianity (religion, Protestantism — black and white) that his fateful, temporary, summer conversion brought him. Here is the center of Baldwin's description of this event: "the universe is simply a sounding drum; there is no way whatever, so it seemed then and has sometimes seemed since, to get through a life, to love your wife and children, or your friends, or your mother and father, or to be loved. The universe . . . has evolved no terms for your existence, has made no room for you, and if love will not swing wide the gates, no other power will or can. And if one despairs — as who has not? — of human love, God's love alone is left. But God — and I felt this even then, so long ago, on that tremendous floor, unwillingly — is white. And if His love was so great, and if He loved all His children, why were we, the blacks, cast down so far?" (*The Fire Next Time*, p. 344. For the full description of the experience, see pp. 337–52).

This is an experience of God, without question. But is the God that found young Baldwin evil or good? He made him afraid, "afraid of the evil within me and afraid of the evil without."[2] I think his God was evil, but that he did not fully know it at the time. His brief obedience to that evil God gave him his fear, and also gave him (leading him into his calling as a preacher) the first form of his vocation as a writer. That evil God and that fear provided two firm convictions that never left James Baldwin and that became the linchpins of his unintended theological legacy. (1) Christianity, whether black or white or black-and-white, is to be radically rejected. Thus, for Baldwin, black Christian theology is simply an oxymoron. (2) The Christian God is indelibly white, even in Harlem in 1938, and that is why Christianity is an evil to be rejected.

These principles do not liberate Baldwin, they haunt him for the rest of his life. Yet he cannot resist doing a kind of theology in spite of them. For example, his solution to the problem of the black and the Jew is not anecdotal (New York City as "hymietown") or sociological, it is theological. The black *must* be anti-Semitic, he insists, because the Jew is white. I don't think he ever exactly states it, but he surely may — even must — conclude that blacks are also obliged to be anti-Christian because Christians are white — indeed, even black Christians are apparently white when they worship the white God. God's color can no more be changed than his gender (Baldwin's word to the feminist theologies of our day).

So, this true conversion to the inevitably evil white God both helped and wounded the gifted adolescent. It gave him an experience of community he had never known:

> The church was very exciting. It took a long time for me to disengage myself from this excitement and on the blindest, most visceral level, I never really have, and never will. There is no music like that music, no drama like the drama of the saints rejoicing, the sinners moaning, the tambourines racing, and all those voices coming together and crying holy unto the Lord. There is still, for me, no pathos quite like the pathos of those multicolored, worn, somehow triumphant and transfigured faces, speaking from the depths of a visible, tangible, continuing despair of the goodness of the Lord. I have never seen anything to equal the fire and excitement that sometimes, without warning, fill a church, causing the church, as Leadbelly and so many others have testified, to "rock." (*The Fire Next Time,* p. 345)

Yet this same Church was also loveless and cruel: "the orgasm of the mob is drenched in the blood of the lamb" (*The Price of the Ticket,* p. xviii). Baldwin's hatred of the Church is clearly connected to his hatred of his father.

> I was frightened of all those brothers and sisters of the church because they were all powerful.... And I had one ally, my brother, who was a very undependable ally because sometimes, I got beaten for things he did and sometimes he got beaten for things I did. But we were united in our hatred for the deacons and the deaconesses and the shouting sisters and of our father. And one of the reasons for this is that we were always hungry and he was always inviting those people over to the house on Sunday for an enormous banquet and we sat next to the icebox in the kitchen watching all those hams, and chickens, and biscuits go down those righteous bellies, which had no bottom. ("Notes for a Hypothetical Novel," p. 239)

Now Baldwin kept the emotional content of that conversion experience and jettisoned (almost, but not quite completely) the superstructure of Church, God, Christianity. Somehow, out of this encounter with the evil white God, a permanent link was forged in his mind between Christianity and slavery: "I am called Baldwin because I was either sold by my African tribe or kidnapped out of it into the hands of a white Christian named Baldwin, who forced me to kneel at the foot of the cross" (*The Fire Next Time*, p. 369). Which is exactly what he did at the moment of his conversion.

Christianity has delivered, Baldwin argues again and again, two lethal blows to the black. First, in the form of the white missionary movement in Africa, it destroyed his natural pagan faith. He quotes, with approval, the words of the Anglican priest, Marcus James: "Christianity, as practiced by Europeans in Africa, is a cruel travesty" ("Princes and Powers," p. 55). Baldwin's anger over this missionary rape is intense.

> In the case of the Negro the past was taken from him whether he would or no; yet to forswear it was meaningless and availed him nothing, since his shameful history was carried, quite literally, on his brow. Shameful; for he was heathen as well as black and would never have discovered the healing blood of Christ had we not braved the jungles to bring him these glad tidings. Shameful; for, since our role as missionary had not been wholly disinterested, it was necessary to recall the shame from which we had delivered him in order more easily to escape our own. As he accepted the alabaster Christ and the bloody cross — in the bearing of which he would find his redemption, as, indeed, to our outraged astonishment, he sometimes did — he must, henceforth, accept that image we then gave him of himself: having no other and standing, moreover, in danger of death should he fail to accept the dazzling light thus brought into such darkness. It is this quite simple dilemma that must be borne in mind if we wish to comprehend his psychology. ("Many Thousands Gone," p. 69)

Second, Christianity not only ruined the black in Africa, it ruined him once again when he was brought over here:

> Thus, the African, exile, pagan, hurried off the auction block and into the fields, fell on his knees before that God in whom he must now believe; who had made him, but not in his image. This tableau, this impossibility, is the heritage of the Negro in America: "Wash me," cried the slave to his Maker, "and I shall be whiter, whiter than snow!" For black is the color of evil; only the robes of the saved are white. It is this cry, implacable on the air and in the skull, that he must live with. ("Everybody's Protest Novel," p. 33)

In America, blacks at once perceived the hypocrisy of the Christian church:

> My ancestors and I were well trained. We understood very early that this was not a Christian nation. It didn't matter what you said or how often you went to church. My father and my mother and my grandfather and my grandmother knew that Christians didn't act this way. It was as simple as that. And if that was so there was no point in dealing with white people in terms of their own moral professions, for they were not going to honor them. ("A Talk to Teachers," p. 330)

But Baldwin does not spare black Christians.

> ... part of the dilemma of the Christian Church is the fact that it opted, in fact,
> for power and betrayed its own first principles which were a responsibility to
> every living soul, the assumption of which the Christian Church's basis, as I
> understand it, is that *all* men are the sons of God and that *all* men are free in
> the eyes of God and are victims of the commandment given to the Christian
> Church, "Love one another as I have loved you." And if that is so, the Church
> is in great danger not merely because the black people say it is but because
> people are always in great danger when they know what they should do,
> and refuse to act on that knowledge. ("White Racism or World Community,"
> p. 438)

That summer conversion finally led Baldwin to the fixed conviction that
all Christians, black and white, are hypocrites governed by "blindness, loneliness, and terror" (*The Fire Next Time*, p. 345). But if the white God and
the black and white Church began to die on that summer night in 1938,
the emotional legacy of the moment never left Baldwin. So, after hypocrisy,
Baldwin's second indictment of Christianity was that it failed to comprehend
the sensual delights of this life. He finds this especially in the South.

> Everything seems so sensual, so languid, and so private. Desire can be acted
> out here; over this fence, behind that tree, in the darkness, there; and no one
> will see, no one will ever know. Only the night is watching and the night
> was made for desire. Protestantism is the wrong religion for people in such
> climates.... ("Nobody Knows My Name," p. 189)

There is bitter truth, Baldwin argues, in the joke about what a pity it
was that the Plymouth Rock didn't land on the Pilgrims instead of the other
way around ("Nothing Personal," p. 382). "Christianity not only extracted
the energy out of the black in Africa and here under slavery, it buried a
vital energy at the time of its beginning" (*The Fire Next Time*, p. 351).
"That energy must return. We can hear it in jazz, in the blues, where irony,
despair, and rejoicing in the force of life, all come together" (ibid., p. 349,
350). Baldwin comes very close, as we shall shortly note, to the claim that
because of his special connection to jazz, blues, and the ironic love of life, the
black may be able to turn around, even to "redeem," Christians, Churches
of all colors, even the white God himself.

II

What did the young James Baldwin mean when he discovered, on that summer night, that God — even the God in that black church — was white?[3]
When a traditional idea of God distresses you — turns out to be white, as in
this case — you can do one of two things. You can jettison God altogether
but stay with the attributes, like righteousness or love. This is the way of
William Blake in his "Songs of Experience." Or, if you are concerned about

being acceptable to the pious, you can try out some new definitions of the old theological terms. Baldwin falls between these two stools, but tilts definitely toward the first.

Baldwin's America is "mercilessly pinned beneath the thumb of the Puritan God" ("The New Lost Generation," p. 311). God has made his people both hypocritical and joyless.

Baldwin says he approves of Bobby Seale's glib comment that white people have a terrible idea of God: "they have never accepted the dark gods, and their fear of the dark gods, who live in them as surely as the white God does, causes them to distrust life" ("No Name in the Street," p. 520). What raises the theological critique of Baldwin well beyond the journalistic silliness of Seale is that when he is criticizing God, he is criticizing the God of white and black alike. What Baldwin wants for himself and his people is love, and he is not quite clear whether God can deliver that love to anyone: "Love takes off the masks that we fear we cannot live without and know we cannot live within. I use the word 'love' here not merely in the personal sense but as a state of being, or a state of grace — not in the infantile American sense of being made happy but in the tough and universal sense of quest and daring and growth" (*The Fire Next Time*, p. 375). That desired love has an almost redemptive character, apparently replacing the white God who has failed to bring love to the world:

> The really terrible thing, old buddy, is that *you* must accept *them* [i.e., the white that have placed blacks in the ghetto so they could be forgotten and die]. And I mean that very seriously. You must accept them and accept them with love. For these innocent people have no other hope. They are, in effect, still trapped in a history which they do not understand; and until they understand it, they cannot be released from it. (Ibid., pp. 335–36)

For all of his bitter anger against the loveless white God of the Christians, Baldwin cannot quite let him go. One can feel this anguish in one of his most eloquent passages.

> It is not too much to say that whoever wishes to become a truly moral human being (and let us not ask whether or not this is possible; I think we must *believe* that it is possible) must first divorce himself from all the prohibitions, crimes, and hypocrisies of the Christian church. If the concept of God has any validity or any use it can only be to make us larger, freer, and more loving. If God cannot do this, then it is time we got rid of Him. (Ibid., p. 352)

But not quite yet? Baldwin, as we shall see, is unexpectedly optimistic about human destiny, and here he seems almost optimistic about the possible transformation of the white God into One who can make us truly loving. Our love is a kind of test for such a God. If we can love, then perhaps He can as well. But for now, that white God, discovered at the foot of the cross in 1938, is, and must continue to be, dead. But something may emerge from the ashes. Baldwin can almost sound mystical.

I suggest that the role of the Negro in American life has something to do with our concept of what God is, and from my point of view, this concept is not big enough. It has got to be made much bigger than it is because God is, after all, not anybody's toy. To be with God is really to be involved with some enormous, overwhelming desire, and joy, and power which you cannot control, which controls you. I conceive of my own life as a journey toward something I do not understand, which in the going toward, makes me better. I conceive of God, in fact, as a means of liberation and not a means to control others. Love does not begin and end the way we seem to think it does. Love is a battle, love is a war; love is a growing up. ("In Search of a Majority," p. 234)

Baldwin's mature theology is a dynamic ditheism. Two Gods are in combat: one, the white God who has deeply damaged all Christians, black and white; the other God, probably not Christian, is not much more than a possibility or a hope. This other God, if we let him, may make us able to love one another and he will do this by first working his way with blacks, who then will turn to love the whites who, until they are loved by blacks, are unable to love anyone, even themselves. Out of this ditheism, Baldwin fashions, for all of his anti-Christian anger, a serious note of redemption. We will conclude with a look at Baldwin on sin, redemption, and the redeemer.

III

Just as we have confidently defined James Baldwin's theological legacy as a terrible portrait of the evil white God of the Christians that converted him and damaged him at the same time, just as we think we have caught him falling down the Christian mountain to a placid secular-humanist valley below, something happens. Baldwin reaches out his hand, grabs on to a root, breaks his fall, and brandishes before us, of all things, a strange and even partly Christian structure of redemption. Alongside the ditheism, Baldwin has a doctrine of sin, of redemption, of the redeemer, and even, strange to say, an eschatology both this-worldly and other-worldly.

I'll never forget the day. It was over forty years ago and I was teaching my first Introduction to Theology class. There I was, sometime around Halloween, earnestly selling my version of the Niebuhrian doctrine of man (as we called it then) to a class that had six or eight able black students. One day, after class, a young man stayed behind to instruct his instructor about sin. It went something like this: "All this stuff about pride and self-righteousness sounds very white to a black today, Professor. Don't forget, our historic experience of sin is of sin that has been exercised upon us by proud and self-righteous men. Can't you see how we have come to see ourselves as more sinned against than sinning?"

This is Baldwin exactly; a doctrine of being sinned against. Here is Tish in *The Fire Next Time:* "Sometimes, I admit, I'm scared — because nobody can take the shit they throw on us forever. Sin is not 'me,' it is 'the man,' 'fighting the man' " (p. 339). Notice how Baldwin construes the nature of a proper black-white dialogue: "On the one hand they [whites] can scarcely dare to open a dialogue which must, if it is honest, become a personal confession — a cry for help and healing which is, really, I think, the basis of all dialogues and, on the other hand, the black man can scarcely dare to open a dialogue which must, if it is honest, become a personal confession which fatally contains an accusation" ("White Man's Guilt," p. 412).

If whites are honest they cry for help, if blacks are honest they accuse. (This has a long way to go before it can be called a true dialogue, I suspect.) In a tribute to Norman Mailer, Baldwin is reminded that Mailer once remarked to him that he wanted to know how power really works. Baldwin finds such a desire very white, wryly commenting that *he* knows how power works, it works on (i.e., against) him, and if he didn't know how power works he'd be dead. Sinned against, not sinning. The First Letter of John just doesn't apply: "If we say we have no sin, we deceive ourselves and the truth is not in us" (1:8). Small wonder that whenever Baldwin reaches out for evidence for his doctrine of being sinned against, it is not to the Yahwist, nor to Calvin or Milton, but to Bessie Smith and her unforgettable cries of violation and courage.

But even though the black does not sin, he is still doomed. He is, like Bigger Thomas, damned ("Many Thousands Gone," pp. 77–78) and alienated — from Europe and Chartres and culture, from whites, and even (such is the damage whites have done) from other blacks ("Stranger in the Village," pp. 83, 88–89). It is hard to resist the impression that Baldwin's doctrine of sin entails the presupposition of the innocence, at least the *relative* innocence, of the black. The doomed, innocent redeemer.

If there is something like sin in Baldwin's post- or almost-Christian theology, there is also redemption. Just as sin is both absent and present, so with redemption. It seems pretty clear that Baldwin doesn't think he needs or wants redemption, particularly if that means a redemption delivered by whites. He locates himself and his people as "beyond the disciplines of salvation," apparently repudiating the whole Christian salvation scheme. He doesn't want white "acceptance" or "tolerance"; he wants only to be recognized as a human being ("Stranger in the Village," p. 84).

But what Baldwin is really rejecting is not the idea of redemption itself, but the idea that redemption has to come from God. "It is important to bear in mind that we are responsible for our soul's salvation, not the bishop, not the priest, not my mother, ultimately it is each man's responsibility alone in his own chamber before his own gods to deal with his health and his sickness [notice the rare note of personal contrition], to deal with his life and death. When people cannot do this with themselves, they very quickly cannot do it with others" ("White Racism or World Community?" p. 441). This is a human redemption achieved by human agents, and it is striking

to observe that Baldwin can boldly describe this view of redemption as an
expansion and transformation of "God's nature which has to be forever
an act of creation on the part of every human being" (Ibid.). The human
redeemers make over God in their own image.

There is more. If redemption is what human beings do for each other,
it is also what blacks must do for whites, even for those whites who think
they are called upon to save the blacks. Baldwin has a deeply christological
vision of the black in America: "For these innocent people have no other
hope" (*The Fire Next Time*, pp. 335–36). There is a content to the black's
redemptive power. Sometimes Baldwin will speak of jazz or Bessie Smith or
irony. But the main thing the black redeemer delivers to the bewildered white
is the fact that life is tragic (*The Fire Nest Time*, p. 373). At times Baldwin
seems to suggest that the black redeemer can do for everybody everything
that churches and mosques have so ineptly attempted: "Perhaps the root
of our trouble, the human trouble, is that we will sacrifice all the beauty of
our lives, will imprison ourselves in totems, taboos, crosses, blood sacrifices,
steeples, mosques, races, armies, flags, nations, in order to deny the fact of
death, which is the only fact we have" (*The Fire Next Time*, p. 373). It is
the function of the black to rejoice in the fact of death in the presence of
the white American who, Baldwin insists, does not believe in death. For to
rejoice in death is to celebrate and delight in the conundrum of life.

Yet at the powerful close to *The Fire Next Time*, Baldwin seems to set
aside his black Christology and his redemptive claims for himself, and to
come to a different, and more satisfactory, vision is which each of us needs
the other: "In short, we, the black and white, deeply need each other here
if we are really to become a nation — if we are really, that is, to achieve
our identity, our maturity, as men and women" (p. 375). No more special
claims for the black's redemptive vocation. We need each other, and it may
be too late. Baldwin's hope has never seemed so wan, nor his apocalyptic
conclusion (to *The Fire Next Time*, 1962) so possible as today.

> If we — and now I mean the relatively conscious whites and the relatively
> conscious blacks, who must, like lovers, insist on, or create, the consciousness
> of the others — do not falter in our duty now, we may be able, handful that
> we are, to end the racial nightmare, and achieve our country, and change the
> history of the world. If we do not now dare everything, the fulfillment of that
> prophecy, recreated from the Bible in song by a slave, is upon us: "God gave
> Noah the rainbow sign, No more water, the fire next time!" (p. 379)

Against this background of redemption, Baldwin struggles to hold on to
Jesus. He was presented to him, even in the Black Church, as white. But he
really wasn't white, he was a "disreputable, sun-baked Hebrew" (*The Fire
Next Time*, p. 351), "born in Nazareth under a very hot sun … [spending]
his life beneath that sun" ("White Racism or World Community?" p. 346).
Jesus has to be rescued from whiteness, because Baldwin will not let him

go. The resurrection goes, and the crucifixion and the nonresistance to evil. But Matthew 25:40 remains in Baldwin's blood and pen, and the sun-baked Jewish teacher has a bit of redemptive work to do after all: "as you did it to one of the least of my brethren, you did it to me." This is what Jesus said and did, this is what we are still obliged to do.

The mixture of Christian and post-Christian in Baldwin's theology, the mixture of anger and love, of arrogance and humility, can be finally seen in this almost eschatological climax:

> The word "revelation" has very little meaning in the recognized languages: yet, it is the only word for the moment I am attempting to approach. This moment changes one forever. One is confronted with the agony and the nakedness and the beauty of a power which has no beginning and no end, which contains you, and which you contain, and which will be using you when your bones are dust.... To love in connection with a life beyond this life means, in effect — in truth — that, frightened as one may be, and no matter how limited, or how lonely, and no matter how the deal, at last, goes down, no man can ever frighten you. This is why blacks can be heard to say, "I ain't got to do nothing but stay black, and die!..." The custodian of an inheritance, which is what blacks have had to be, in western culture, must hand the inheritance down the line. So, you, the custodian, recognize, finally, that your life does not belong to you: nothing belongs to you. ("The Devil Finds Work," p. 631)

There are three powerful black theological voices in the second half of our century. Each differs radically from the other two, and each is of decisive importance. They are Malcolm X, Martin Luther King, Jr., and James Baldwin. Malcolm X is representative of a profound religious orthodoxy, a man killed by (and because of) heresy. The American Nation of Islam had put the pieces of his early life together, but its separatism, if not racism, slowly got to him until, under the influence of a pilgrimage to Mecca, he ended his life convinced of the interracial, intercultural vision in the Sunni Muslim tradition. Malcolm reminds us that an orthodox faith, sure of its own correctness, can sometimes heal broken lives, and need not be intransigent or evil. Here is a portion of a lecture given by Malcolm X in Rochester, New York, several day before his murder. It is the clearest statement I know of his ultimate Muslim faith.

> One of Islam's main principles is the pilgrimage to Mecca. I was fortunate to make it in April 1964, and I went back again in September of the same year. It was on the pilgrimage to Mecca that I was able to see the real spiritual power of Islam and to see its ability to produce and create real brotherhood. While I was in Mecca during one of the days of the ritual, I was sitting on a mountain called Mount Arafat in a huge tent. I was fortunate to be the guest of the government at the time, and of the Crown Prince who is now the King. In this tent were people from different parts of the world, most of them dignitaries. In addition, when you looked outside the tent at the passing pilgrims, they too were of every color. In this tent, I looked out at those who in the West would

be considered white. Probably they had been born in America and would call themselves white. Now when I was in the Black Muslim movement we had been thoroughly convinced that it would have been impossible for a white person to move to Mecca, to become a Muslim and to practice Islam. Most of us who were in the Black Muslim movement absolutely believed that. We believed exactly what Elijah Mohammed had taught us. So being over there and seeing those people — white, black, brown, red, and yellow — I sat there trying to ask myself: "What is the difference between these white people here beneath this tent, and those that I had just left behind in the states?" Because there was a difference. And after a couple of days of careful observation it dawned upon me that the basic difference between those over there [i.e., in the United States] who were white and those here who are white was not in color but in attitude. The person there [i.e., Mecca] — when he says he's white, with him it's just an adjective. He uses it to describe a color, his color, which is for him incidental. The difference is that in the western hemisphere where I was raised, when a person says he's white he means something else. He means more that just color. In the western hemisphere, when a person says he's white, he has a different sound to his voice. He means he's boss; it is a badge of superiority, as in the phrase "I'm free, white, and twenty-one." It [i.e., the word "white"] has the same connotation in every walk of life when white people use it. So I came to see that the religion of Islam absolutely removes from the person who is white the tendency to think that because he was white he was better than someone who was black or brown or red or yellow. His [i.e., the white person under the influence of Islam] whiteness was just something incidental, while, as I have already pointed out, in the West "white" had become a badge of authority, of acceptance. Whereas in that [i.e., Islamic] society, a person was permitted to go forward on the basis of his deeds, his actions, his conscious behavior. Whereas in this [i.e., the West, the United States] society, a person is permitted to go forward is he's white, and he is held up if he is not white. In that society [i.e., the society he experienced in Mecca, during the pilgrimage] color had nothing to do with one's acceptance or rejection whatsoever. This is what I learned; these were the thoughts going through my mind as I was over there making this pilgrimage.

It should not be forgotten that Martin Luther King's theological contribution to Christianity and America was at least as important as his often and rightly praised moral and prophetic gifts. He was more than the great Birmingham letter and the "dream" speech. If Malcolm X is the power of orthodoxy, Dr. King shows the importance of liberal or revisionist theology. What he did was to take the other-worldly eschatology of slavery Protestantism and the spiritual and then, without altering any of the traditional language, he radically broadened its range, bringing it from the next world to this. The product is a secularized, politicized, radicalized version of the traditional theology of the Black Protestant church. Two examples:

> When I git to heaven,
> Gonna take off my shoes,
> And walk all over God's heaven.

In the spiritual, the singer has no shoes, and he or she is restricted as to where he or she can walk. Heaven will be different. Dr. King's comment is a simple one: "What you have expected, in your songs and prayers, from heaven, you must now learn to expect and demand from this world. I will show you can accomplish this."

Or, in the words of a spiritual Dr. King often quoted:

> Free at last, free at last.
> Lord God Almighty,
> Free at last.

Originally, of course, this is about dying and going to heaven, where there will be a freedom unknown to earth. But, Dr. King insisted, do not wait for heaven's freedom; it can be achieved here and now. Dr. King shows how traditional religious language can be rescued from its other-worldly quietism and put to work in the present struggles of this world.

James Baldwin's theological voice (I suspect he would not have enjoyed that phrase!) is neither orthodox nor revisionist. Malcolm X lived comfortably in the Muslim world he finally found at the end of his life. Dr. King was a comfortable and willing child of his inherited Protestant theological culture, however bravely he tried to expand it. Baldwin stands on the boundary between the Christian and the — what? — anti-, post-, non-Christian worlds. Sometimes all of God, Christianity, and the churches of all colors seem to be the unmitigated enemy. Yet a kind of God remains (or arises) after the old white God is killed. It has to do with love and whatever it takes to make us all more human.

He has a doctrine of sin from which he virtually excludes both himself and his people, and an even stranger doctrine of redemption in which sometimes the black takes over from Jesus the function of redeeming the white, and sometimes the black and white together — alone, without God or sons of God — redeem each other.

James Baldwin seems to be one of the most recent of those modern religious thinkers who cannot do with Christianity as it is, and who yet cannot quite do without it. His theological work is a hand stretched out to us, and I am inclined to grasp it.

Notes

1. Baldwin's collected nonfiction can be found in *The Price of the Ticket: Collected Nonfiction, 1948–1985* (New York: St. Martin's/Marek, 1985). Citations in the text will contain the page reference to this collection and the title of the original volume or article: e.g., p. 333, *The Fire Next Time*.

2. "Evil within me" is an important and unusual phrase. This is the only place I have found in Baldwin's nonfiction where sin is described as within as well as without. In general, Baldwin's "doctrine" of sin is a doctrine of being sinned against —

by whites. Slavery is never far from Baldwin's theological reflections. Now that the effects of slavery are making a fresh appearance in our country, "playing the race card," the attack on affirmative action, Baldwin's slave-haunted theology may be more than ever needed.

3. The deep anger associated with the idea of the white God can be illustrated from Baldwin's first novel, *Another Country*. Rufus is about to achieve climax in Leona, and the narrator remarks: "And, shortly, nothing could have stopped him, not the white God himself nor a lynch mob arriving on wings."

9

STORIES AS ARROWS

The Religious Response to Modernity

ROBERT N. BELLAH

Since *The Secular City*, Harvey Cox, as a Christian theologian, has pioneered in finding the religious relevance of the secular and the secular implications of the religious. He has also helped open the door to nonchristian religions as participants in the inquiry about the nature of contemporary society. I would like this paper to be a contribution to the dialogue he has so significantly widened.[1]

The thought of a leading contemporary defender of modernity, the philosopher/sociologist Jürgen Habermas, provides my point of departure. For Habermas the primary virtue of modernity is autonomy: men and women come of age, capable of rational thought and of the rational public discussion through which they are to determine their common fate. I believe this is a noble ideal but an incomplete one.[2]

In his single most important theoretical distinction Habermas divides society into lifeworld and systems. The characteristic feature of the lifeworld is that it is organized in terms of language. The use of language, in formal and informal ways, is the core of how the lifeworld functions. The lifeworld includes things like family, local community, and religious groups, but in a complex society it also includes the realm of public discourse. It is by no means exclusively private: it is that part of our lives where language, expressing what is important to us, is at the center. For some of us, what we mean by community is virtually identical with the lifeworld, but for reasons that will become clear later on, Habermas resists such an identification and does not use the term community.

The systems, according to Habermas, are organized primarily not through language but through nonlinguistic media. The great archetypal systems that have so much to do with our lives today are the market economy, where the steering mechanism is money, the bottom line is the profit-and-loss calculation, and the administrative state, where the steering mechanism is power.

In Habermas's view the process of modernization involves two comple-

mentary processes: the rationalization of the lifeworld and the differentiation of the systems from the lifeworld. The distortions of modernity, and
it should be remembered that Habermas is a critic as well as a defender
of modernity, arise from blockages in the process of rationalization of the
lifeworld, something I will explain shortly, and a reversal of the proper relation between lifeworld and systems. The differentiation of the systems from
the lifeworld should allow them to operate more effectively so as to serve
the lifeworld better. However if the systems, the economy and the administrative state, become autonomous to the degree that they are no longer
anchored in the norms and values of the lifeworld but seek to subordinate
the lifeworld to their own quest to maximize money and power, something
Habermas vividly characterizes as the colonization of the lifeworld by the
systems, then we have a distorted modernity indeed, one in need of radical
reform.

Let me return to the question of the rationalization of the lifeworld, the
quintessential project of the Enlightenment. As I have indicated, for Habermas, a true child of the Enlightenment, autonomy is the central modern
value. The rationalization of the lifeworld is that process through which
individual autonomy is continuously increased and the barriers to it diminished. It is in this context that we can understand Habermas's antipathy to
community and his doubt about the value of religion.

Community for Habermas involves taken-for-granted assumptions that
are essentially unarguable and that limit the freedom of the individual. Thus,
for Habermas, the individual and community exist in a zero-sum situation:
the stronger the one, the weaker the other. I will reserve my criticism of this
idea of community until later. Habermas's view of religion is representative
of much contemporary thought. Habermas is not unsympathetic to religion;
indeed, he gives it considerable importance in his notion of social evolution.
Religion, in his view, has made a significant contribution to the progressive
sequence of enhanced social learning capacities, which is what he means by
social evolution. It is just that with the advent of modernity, religion's role
has come to an end. Its conception of the sacred and of religious truth is
too "frozen," too closed to critical examination, too limiting of individual
autonomy, to be viable in the modern world. Conceptions of the sacred and
of religious tradition, according to Habermas, need to be "thawed" or "liq-
uefied" if we are to have a genuinely modern culture based on undistorted
communication, which he defines as the open argumentative redemption of
validity claims concerning issues of truth, rightness, and authenticity where
the best argument carries the day. From Habermas's perspective, the pernicious survival of frozen religious forms blocks free communication and
interferes with the autonomy of individuals.[3]

Without being able to put it so elegantly, many of our contemporaries,
particularly in the university but quite broadly in the well-educated middle
class, would agree with Habermas's position. Many of them would hold,

however, that if religion confines itself to private life and the expressive concerns of individuals, eschewing any claim to influence public life and public decisions, then it may have a justifiable and harmless role to play in contemporary society, for those who continue to be interested in it.

This understanding of religion, more common than we might think within as well as without the churches, is not only the result of cultural forces associated with the Enlightenment. It is rooted in critical social changes associated with the emergence of modern society. All the terms that we confidently use in discussion of related issues today, such as religion, civil society, and the state, are products of a specifically European history that it might be useful for us to consider, even if briefly, before we go on.

Many people know that sociology is a quite recent term, coined by Auguste Comte in 1837. We are perhaps not so aware of the fact that society and religion are also, in their current meanings, quite modern terms. Society is not only a new term, but it is also only intelligible as a contrast term to two other relatively new terms: state and economy. It is worth remembering that the ancient Greek word *polis,* from which comes a rich variety of modern words, for example, in English, politics, policy, police, and others, meant simultaneously city, state, society, and community, so that we have no modern word that really translates it. Economy is also Greek in origin, but in ancient Greek it meant household management; economy in our sense was for them just one more aspect of the *polis.*

It was the rise of the modern Western nation-state, beginning in the seventeenth century but maturing in the eighteenth and nineteenth centuries, that gave rise to the notion of society as something different from the state. In early notions of "civil society," society and economy were not clearly differentiated, but with the rise of industrialization the realms of society and economy came to be seen as different from each other and both of them as different from the state. It is this process to which Habermas points when he speaks of the differentiation of the systems from the lifeworld. Religion is also a term that takes on its modern meaning at about the same time the terms state, society, and economy are differentiating out from each other.

If we go back to ancient Greece, religion is simply the cultic life of the *polis,* and not conceivable outside it. It is true that Christianity developed the idea of the Church, interestingly enough borrowing the word *ecclesia,* the assembly of the citizens, from Greek political life to denominate itself. But the Church, though having an independent identity, a concept only barely foreshadowed by earlier Greek religious associations, was nonetheless very much embedded in the whole of society. Religion as a separate sphere was in considerable part itself the product of the rise of the nation-state system which, in turn, was in part a reaction to the religious wars between Protestants and Catholics in the early seventeenth century.

From the time of the Peace of Westphalia in 1648, religion was seen as a matter for each state to decide for itself and no longer a valid cause of international warfare.[4] From this idea there developed in the eighteenth century the idea that religion could be separated from the state altogether, being a matter of individual conscience. Thus emerged the idea of religion as something separate from other spheres and rooted in the experience and conscience of individuals which most of us take for granted in our modern usage of the term.

Serious conceptual difficulties occur when we take these terms, arising from a specific history, but now common not only to social science but to modern discourse around the world, and apply them as universal categories. When we look at tribal societies that do not have a differentiated state or economy, then we can plainly see that religion cannot be a separate sphere of largely private experience. Rather religion permeates and expresses the whole way of life of the tribal people. When we seek to study their rituals, we soon find we are learning about their kinship relations, the exchange of goods, the hierarchies of power and influence, such as they are, and many other things. Indeed singling out something we call "religion" from other things that tribal people do may be convenient for our analysis, but it is reading into their way of life a category which is not separated in that way by the people we are studying.

When we look at what are frequently called the world religions (what I have called "historic religions"),[5] we find significant differences from tribal religions, in that there are written religious texts, groups of priests or religious teachers, religious associations, and schools, all things unlikely to be found in tribal societies, except in incipient form. Yet religion is still deeply embedded in the whole way of life of the people. It is certainly not a matter primarily of private experience and conscience, and it is not a sphere of life separate from others, for none of the spheres of life that we take as separate in modern society is all that separate from the others. Since Judaism and Christianity are themselves "historic" religions, they exist somewhat uncomfortably in modern society. Protestant Christianity, with its strongly individualistic tendencies, has gone farthest in accepting the place to which modern culture assigns religion, but even there we will find more than a little unease. Religions that believe that God created heaven and earth and is the Lord of all do not easily accept being assigned to a delimited sphere.

On the other hand, the very nature of modern life, whatever our beliefs, tends to assign our religion to a highly private sphere. Most modern states guarantee our religious freedom but tend to assume that that freedom will only be used within that private sphere. This assumption does not derive from some arbitrary prejudice against religion: it has a real historical source, namely, early modern wars of religion. We should not forget that in Europe the first half of the seventeenth century was the most terrible period until the twentieth century because of the wars of religion. The modern nation-state came into existence in part as an effort to calm religious passions and end religious wars. In the twentieth century, nation-states have been responsible for the most horrible wars in human history, so we must consider them ambiguous projects at best, but we cannot entirely forget their initial connection to the search for peace. Particularly in religiously plural-istic societies, the salience of a national rather than of a religious narrative, and the national solidarity that such a narrative has created, has to some de-gree overcome the possible hostility that could and did divide nations along the lines of different religious communities. Where such national narratives have failed, as in Northern Ireland, Lebanon, or most recently the lands that were once Yugoslavia, the possibility of religious warfare, so obvious in the seventeenth century, becomes actual again. I point out these uncomfortable facts to help us understand why descendants of the Enlightenment are so nervous about any role at all for religion in public life, and why they would like religion to remain safely ensconced in the private sphere.

We have come a long way from Habermas, but I want to return to his argument for a moment. How can one answer Habermas when he says essen-tially that religion is outmoded in modern culture or can at best be a purely private consolation? I think it is possible to answer by showing that Haber-mas himself has no adequate reply to the distorted modernization that he criticizes, what he sometimes refers to as the depletion of nonrenewable cul-tural resources. Habermas's response to the distortions of modernity involves controlling the economic and political systems that impinge on what he calls the lifeworld, that part of our life that is steered by language. So far so good, but when one asks how the lifeworld is supposed to provide a moral anchor-age to the systems and prevent the systems from, as he puts it, colonizing the lifeworld, then his answer, namely a further rationalization of the lifeworld itself, seems unconvincing. The lifeworld, as Habermas at times seems to know, involves a balance between the taken-for-granted, the traditional, and that which is open to question. But instead of seeing that relation as a vital and dynamic one, Habermas tends to see it as a zero-sum relationship in which advance lies in the continuous increase of areas of life controlled by voluntary and autonomous action responding to the criterion of reason, and the continuous decline of everything else. I believe Habermas gets himself into an impossible and ultimately self-defeating position because of an inad-equate philosophical anthropology and ultimately an inadequate conception of rationality. I would argue that the Enlightenment has been strong on cri-tique but singularly weak in producing new forms of solidarity. More than thinkers like Habermas have been willing to admit, religion has provided the social coherence which has allowed the constructive side of the Enlight-enment project to proceed. Further, religion may be crucial in transforming the distortions of modernity that Habermas has so acutely analyzed.

In moving toward a constructive answer to the problems that Haber-mas has raised, one which without rejecting the Enlightenment nonetheless reaffirms the indispensability of community, tradition, and religion, let me return to the situation of tribal societies which I mentioned above, for their situation vividly illustrates our problems and provides resources for their solution.

To put it bluntly, tribal societies can be characterized as lifeworlds without systems. For a long time that fact was taken to be a negative judgment on tribal societies. It was seen as a sign of their backwardness: no money, no market economy, no powerful bureaucratic state. Tribal societies were seen as marginal, remnants of a past that progress and modernity have left far behind. At this point in human history we have begun to have second thoughts about that characterization. When we recognize that the lifeworld is threatened everywhere, we can take tribal societies and their travail in the modern world as a metaphor for the whole human condition. One of the points the authors of *Habits of the Heart*[6] tried to make is that even among the people who profit most in our society, the lifeworld, which is composed of those relationships that give meaning and integrity, is severely eroded. The price exacted by becoming a functionary in the economic and bureaucratic systems of our current society is the undermining of one's ability to live in a coherent lifeworld. Many of those with whom we talked have come to see that that price is too high.

Just because the systems are minimal in tribal societies we need not romanticize them. Christians can recognize that the systems are the projection and externalization of disordered desires that are characteristic of all of us, whether we live in tribal societies or any other. What Augustine called *concupiscentia,* the inordinate desire to possess, and what he called *libido dominandi,* the will to control other people, things that contribute to the childish omnipotence of wishes that makes us want to be like God — these are the motives that attract us to the power, the wealth, the control that are promised us by modern economies, modern states, and modern technology.

Members of tribal societies also have these disordered desires; their societies are not perfect: there is bullying and domination; there is intertribal warfare; there is personal tragedy. One doesn't have to indulge in romantic fantasies, nonetheless, to see that those disordered appetites have not yet been externalized into structures that take on a life of their own, become like monsters, and are no longer the servants of our wishes but dominate, control, and subjugate us. That hasn't happened yet in tribal societies. For those of us who live in a world where money, power, and technology more and more set the terms for everything about our lives, it is worth thinking about societies where that is not the case. I want to illustrate how such societies work, recognizing that no tribal society in the world, and certainly not in North America, is free of the impingement of the systems. My first example comes from the distinguished Laguna Pueblo Indian author Leslie Marmon Silko. She writes:

> Even now, the people at Laguna Pueblo spend the greater portion of social occasions recounting recent incidents or events which have occurred in the

Laguna area. Nearly always, the discussion will precipitate the retelling of older stories about similar incidents or other stories connected with a specific place. The stories often contain disturbing or provocative material, but are nonetheless told in the presence of children and women. The effect of these inter-family or inter-clan exchanges is the reassurance of each person that she or he will never be separated or apart from the clan, no matter what might happen. Neither the worst blunders or disasters nor the greatest financial prosperity and joy will ever be permitted to isolate anyone from the rest of the group. In the ancient times, cohesiveness was all that stood between extinction and survival, and, while the individual certainly was recognized, it was always as an individual simultaneously bonded to family and clan by a complex bundle of custom and ritual. You are never the first to suffer a grave loss or profound humiliation. You are never the first, and you understand that you probably will not be the last to commit or be victimized by a repugnant act. Your family and clan are able to go on at length about others now passed on, others older or more experienced than you who suffered similar losses.[7]

What I want to bring out from this passage is how language, how the telling of stories, gives meaning, identity, and social coherence, and operates to organize a lifeworld that isn't dependent on external control systems. When this kind of linguistic expression is working well it strengthens the coherence of society by exchanging stories, by telling what happened in the past. It makes sense of what is happening now by telling stories that are still rooted in the specific places that surround the people where they live. Aboriginal peoples are rooted in their particular localities in a way that those of us who more recently came to the land have difficulty understanding.

For even clearer examples of how stories rooted in places act to defend the tribal lifeworld I want to turn to the Western Apache, a group I studied in my undergraduate honors thesis, *Apache Kinship Systems,*[8] and have never forgotten. Keith Basso, an anthropologist who has long worked with the Western Apache, quotes several of them to show how places and their stories work in their lifeworld. According to a seventy-seven-year-old woman, "the land is always stalking people. The land makes people live right. The land looks after us. The land looks after people." A fifty-two-year-old man tells what can happen when one leaves the land, when one no longer has the land and its people to look after one: "One time I went to L.A., training for mechanic. It was no good, sure no good. I start drinking, hang around bars all the time. I start getting into trouble with my wife, fight sometimes with her. It was *bad*. I forget about this country here around Cibicue. I forget all the names and stories. I don't hear them in my mind anymore. I forget how to live right, forget how to be strong."[9]

Basso worked with a Western Apache named Nick Thompson to get his understanding clear about how these stories work, translating back and forth between Apache and English. Thompson was satisfied with the following version which summed up his understanding, thinking of stories as arrows which are told to hit you when you have been acting in ways that hurt other people:

> So someone stalks you and tells a story about what happened long ago. It doesn't matter if other people are around — you're going to know he's aiming that story at you. All of a sudden it *hits* you! It's like an arrow, they say. Sometimes it just bounces off — it's too soft and you don't think about anything. But when it's strong it goes in deep and starts working on your mind right away. No one says anything to you, only that story is all, but now you know that people have been watching you and talking about you. They don't like how you've been acting. So you have to think about your life.
>
> Then you feel weak, real weak, like you are sick. You don't want to eat or talk to anyone. That story is working on you now. You keep thinking about it. That story is changing you now, making you want to live right. That story is making you want to replace yourself. You think only of what you did and what was wrong and you don't like it. So you want to live better. After a while, you don't like to think of what you did wrong. So you try to forget that story. You try to pull that arrow out. You think it won't hurt anymore because now you want to live right.... Even so, that place will keep on stalking you.[10]

A lot of what goes on in our society through the formal procedures of lawsuits and trials and jail sentences is going on in the lifeworld of these Western Apaches through stories. Through language, through these stories that are arrows, they pull people back from doing wrong things. In this way the lifeworld is maintained without being colonized by the systems, although to the degree the Apache are part of the larger society they can by no means escape the systems.

It might be helpful to look at biblical religion from the perspective that we have begun to develop by considering tribal peoples. Even in the earliest parts of the Hebrew scriptures we are dealing with people who have come up against powerful systems, not as differentiated as modern ones, but strong enough to threaten the lifeworld. If we ask when the systems began — because they weren't always around, they do begin at a certain point in history — they probably began somewhere in the third, but certainly in the second millennium B.C.E. Their first appearance in the Bible came in the great bureaucratic, military empire of Egypt, which could mobilize vast forces of chariots and spears and had subjugated a tribal people, Israel. Moses was the leader of what we might call a renewal movement in this subjugated tribal people on the verge of losing its identity under the coercion of the Egyptian regime. Somehow Moses was able to lead his people out of that empire into the wilderness and to be the channel of the word of God which allowed them to renew their tribal solidarity under Yahweh, but not under any king or emperor. Moses was not a king: he was the leader of a tribal people trying to regain a sense of who they were in part through remembering the stories of the patriarchs, Abraham, Isaac and Jacob, stories that linked them to the land to which they were returning.

If we look at the New Testament, we see that Jewish Galilee was not a land of tribal people. Through a thousand years of pressure the systems had gained ever increasing power. Jewish Galileans were a peasant people pushed almost to the verge of destruction by the Roman occupying power with its taxes, by the Greek landowners living in the cities and extracting their income from their tenants, and even by the emissaries of the temple aristocracy in Jerusalem who also had to be paid. Poverty, misery, and destruction were widespread. As in the case of Moses, contemporary biblical scholarship speaks of the Jesus movement initially as a renewal movement among those very impoverished peasants in Galilee in the face of the power of economic, bureaucratic, and military systems.

If we know one thing about Jesus we know that he was executed by Roman imperial troops as a political criminal. The Romans were afraid of him because they saw him as an agitator of a subject people. But Jesus had not advocated violence; his message was a reassertion of the ethic of peasant reciprocity, pushed to the limit of self-giving love in an almost unbelievable response to the kind of pressures that the people he was speaking to were under. What did Jesus have in the face of the military and economic power of the established authorities, Jewish, Greek, and Roman? He had language. The disclosing word was all on earth he had: parables and stories. Many of the stories he told were arrows, pointed stories that had a message that called people to change their lives. "Repent," he said, or, as the Western Apache put it, "Replace yourselves."

Through most of human history the great traditional societies have lived in a balance between the lifeworld and the systems. Religion, because it is fundamentally linguistic and narrative, has operated as a bulwark of the lifeworld, but it has often been coopted by the systems so that it has on occasion been an agent of the colonization of the lifeworld by the systems, especially when an alien religion has been imposed by imperial power on a subject people. Again and again, new religious movements or revivals have arisen to nurture, defend, and strengthen the lifeworld and to reassert lifeworld identities. But the systems have never relented their pressure.

During the last two or three hundred years, the pace of change has increased dramatically. The balance has begun to shift decisively in ways unknown in all previous history. One crucial factor was the emergence of the market economy in its most radical form, where not only materials and money were part of the market, but land and labor also became its components, with devastating consequences for the lifeworld. We can see the shift vividly in what was happening in England at the end of the eighteenth century and the early nineteenth century. We can see it in the poetry of Wordsworth and Blake and the novels of Dickens: the dispossessed peasants driven into the cities, pushed to the wall economically, but, more importantly, deprived of their culture, of their lifeworld, of everything that made sense to them. Here too there were renewal movements, one of the greatest of which was Wesleyan Methodism, which was an effort to reform the life-world in the cities among the displaced peasants. It was a difficult task and not always successful.

The market economy, wherever it goes, and by now there is nowhere it has not penetrated, undermines the lifeworld, whether in Europe or Africa or Asia or the New World. We heard in the voices of the Western Apache in Cibicue the way in which it undercuts the ability of the lifeworld to survive. The market economy is so destabilizing that it sets off deep political and ideological movements in response. Karl Polanyi's *The Great Trans-formation*[11] shows how in many respects the modern nation-state in its bureaucratic form arose as an effort to defend its population from the devastation created by the market economy. It has been an ambiguous response, however, for while defending its population in some ways, it has developed a whole series of mechanisms that in their own way also intrude on and destabilize the lifeworld. Modern politics seem to oscillate between believers in the free market and believers in the bureaucratic state. If those are the only options, then our outlook is bleak indeed, for both destroy the lifeworld if they have their way unimpeded.

I have painted a rather dark picture of modernity, and yet I do not consider myself an antimodernist. With Habermas I celebrate the positive achievements of modernity and the Enlightenment through the rationalization of the lifeworld: the criticism of oppression and injustice, the assertion of individual rights, the unleashing of energy that comes from free speech and free discussion without any censorship or dogmatism. I also celebrate the achievements of the modern economy and the modern state. They have created the possibility, unfortunately not yet the reality, of a degree of fulfillment and cultural enrichment of everyone that in all previous societies were reserved only for a few.

And yet the modern scenario has never gone the way its most ardent proponents have hoped. The twentieth century has seen the most terrible wars, and they still continue, and the most brutal despotisms (fortunately the worst of them have fallen) that the world has ever known. But now, with the collapse of Fascism and Communism and the end of the Cold War, why are we not entering a golden age? Why is the world increasingly divided between rich and poor nations and between rich and poor within each nation? Why, instead of sharing our abundance, are we abandoning whole sectors of the population to misery and despair, in the United States to a vast and rapidly growing apparatus of police and prisons?

For quite some time it has become evident that modernity is not leading unambiguously to human liberation but has some rather different consequences. Nobody sums it up better than George Orwell, in a paragraph that is quite stunning in the way it uses language, we could say language as arrows:

> For two hundred years we had sawed and sawed and sawed at the branch we were sitting on. And in the end, much more suddenly than anyone had foreseen, our efforts were rewarded, and down we came. But unfortunately there had been a little mistake. The thing at the bottom was not a bed of roses after all, it was a cesspool filled with barbed wire.

If I may interpret Orwell's metaphor: the branch of religion, tradition, and community on which we had been sitting and that we thought we could saw off because we would land in a bed of roses turned out to be a lot more important than many people thought.

Putting it this way poses a very big question. Our task is greater than the defense of the remnants of the lifeworld, although if there weren't many remnants it is doubtful that we would even be here. No one can live by the dollar sign and the power quotient alone. We still are who we are because religion, tradition, and community have somehow managed to survive in the face of all the disruptions of the last two hundred years. But our task is not simply, through nostalgia, to preserve the remnants. It is somehow or other to revivify the lifeworld and help it regain control over the systems. If we fail, we will simply commit suicide as the human race. That is why that most unutopian of statesmen, Vaclav Havel, speaks of our need at the present for a politics of the impossible.[12] And for those who dismiss him as unrealistic, I would remind them of the many years of persecution, including four years in prison, which he experienced under Communism. If he is a man of faith, it is because his faith has been tested in a way that few of ours have.

So, in outlining a politics of the impossible I will argue that we have two huge tasks: (1) to revivify the lifeworld, and (2) to reintegrate the lifeworld and the systems.

In seeking to revivify the lifeworld we must come to terms with the Enlightenment project of rationalization of the lifeworld, the project that, in Habermas's terms, involves the melting or liquefying of the sacred, tradition, and community. At the same time that we need to affirm rational criticism, we must also see that rational criticism has never created a viable spiritual or ethical vision. We need to affirm the healthy function of doubt at the same time that we see that doubt only makes sense in relation to effective belief. Rational criticism and doubt are indispensable weapons in the struggle against all oppressive dogmatisms, but they cannot create a world, they can only destroy one. The source of vision, of reason in its classical, not its modern sense, is story, is myth. The myth gives rise to thought.[13] And the stories that transform us, replace us, are not only spoken but enacted, as tribal peoples know so well. But not only tribal peoples: "On the night he was handed over to suffering and death, our Lord Jesus Christ took bread...." The words of institution become the embodied acts of priest and congregation.

The words that are also enacted and that put us in touch with the sacred do something else that rational criticism and doubt can never do: they create a community, they bind us to one another and tell us who we are. Enlightenment criticism reminds us that stories and ritual actions and the communities they create can become closed, hardened, oppressive to those within as well as those without, and that is a lesson that we can never forget. But Enlightenment criticism is wrong to see such hardness and closure, such frozenness, as the essence of religion, tradition, and community. For a tribal people still in touch, however tenuously, with its life-giving past, every retelling of a sacred story is related to present need, is reshaped to meet present challenges and open the way to present solutions. For the biblical religions there is a living God who has spoken continually to current need throughout history and who still speaks anew if we could but hear. Only a dead tradition is closed. A living tradition is always an ongoing argument seeking to "gain knowledge of the New by reanimating the Old," as Confucius put it.[14] A genuine community is not based on uniform and unquestionable consensus. It shares a past which gives it a sense of identity and a future which gives it hope, but it is open to argument, even conflict, about what its shared history and its future engagements mean and should be. A genuine community does not crush but empowers individuals.

In a deeply anxious and divided world we know that distorted communities based on fear and paranoia are all too common. But an enlightened effort to destroy communities and reduce them to their constituent individuals is more likely to produce such distorted communities than to eliminate them. What I am trying to argue is that the modern project, so far as it attempts to follow Descartes in his incredible wish to be born at the age of twenty with no childhood and no history and to base his life on clear and distinct ideas alone,[15] has been radically mistaken. Nor has it been only an intellectual mistake, for it has given rise to a "Cartesian savagery" when we moderns have attempted to wipe clean the slate of all cultures less "come of age" than our own. We must open our eyes to see that we are in the midst of a wonderfully unfolding story of life on this planet and we will only then find our way within it, not by trying to jump outside our skins into a realm of pure reason.

If revivifying the lifeworld under modern conditions is difficult, reintegrating the lifeworld and the systems would seem to be impossible. It would take far more space than this article even to sketch some beginnings. The basic point is that the market economy and the state exist to serve human beings, not to enslave them. That is a mantra we can never repeat often enough. Habermas argues that we must "re-anchor" the systems in the lifeworld, that is, in a normative order that gives them human purposes. I think that is a useful metaphor but not a sufficient one. A modern lifeworld needs to constitute itself as a democratic community, a community that can spin a living membrane around the economy and the state so that they are not just anchored in but permeated by the values and meanings of the lifeworld.

This would mean not abandoning power, but a new kind of power: replacing regardless power[16] with careful power, patient power. How to do that is, of course, an enormous challenge. Here all I can do is point to the idea of subsidiarity, familiar in the Catholic social teachings, which has a rich set of implications for this project.

Everything I have said is based on a different intuition of our present moment religiously from that of Samuel P. Huntington, with his notion of the reemergence of conflict between the great religious civilizations of the world.[17] I believe the modern religious situation is one in which we can be open to all the great traditions, including the tribal traditions, without falling into eclecticism or relativism. The better we understand other traditions, the better we understand our own. The better we understand other traditions, the better we see that we are engaged in a common struggle to create a more human world.

To close by pointing once again to the central place of language in my argument, let me adapt some biblical language: They that live by the sword shall perish by the sword. They that live by the Word shall have eternal life.

Notes

1. I would like to acknowledge a grant from the Lilly Endowment that helped make research for this paper possible.

2. Here and in what follows my discussion is based mainly on volume 2 of *The Theory of Communicative Action* (Boston: Beacon Press, 1987; first German edition, 1981).

3. This discussion of Habermas's view of religion is based on volume 2 of *The Theory of Communicative Action*, especially Ch. 5, Sec. 3, "The Rational Structure of the Linguistification of the Sacred," 77–111. In his concluding chapter to *Habermas, Modernity, and Public Theology*, Don S. Browning and Francis Schüssler Fiorenza, eds. (New York: Crossroad, 1992), "Transcendence from Within, Transcendence in this World," 226–50, Habermas modifies these views to some extent, recognizing the practical contribution of some Christians and some theologians to the public struggle for social justice. But with respect to the place of religion in modern culture he leaves us with only this rather agnostic statement: "As long as religious language bears with itself inspiring, indeed, unrelinquishable semantic contents which elude (for the moment?) the expressive power of a philosophical language and still await translation into a discourse that gives reasons for its position, philosophy, even in its postmetaphysical form, will neither be able to replace nor to repress religion" (237).

4. The importance of the transition symbolized (but certainly not caused) by the Treaty of Westphalia was pointed out to me in an unpublished paper of Bryan Hehir in 1992.

5. For this term see "Religious Evolution" in Robert N. Bellah, *Beyond Belief* (Berkeley: University of California Press, 1991 [1970]), 20–50.

6. Robert N. Bellah, Richard Madsen, William M. Sullivan, Steven M. Tipton, and Ann Swidler, *Habits of the Heart* (Berkeley: University of California Press,

1985). See especially the Introduction, "The House Divided," to the new paperback edition (Berkeley: University of California Press, 1996).

7. Leslie Marmon Silko, "Landscape, History, and the Pueblo Imagination," *Antaeus,* no. 57 (Autumn 1986): 93.

8. Robert N. Bellah, *Apache Kinship Systems* (Cambridge: Harvard University Press, 1952).

9. Keith H. Basso, "Stalking with Stories," Ch. 2 of *Wisdom Sits in Places* (Albuquerque: University of New Mexico Press, 1996), 39.

10. Basso, *Wisdom Sits in Places,* 58–59.

11. Karl Polanyi, *The Great Transformation* (Boston: Beacon, 1957[1944]).

12. Vaclav Havel, *The Art of the Impossible: Politics as Morality in Practice, Speeches and Writings, 1990–1996* (New York: Knopf, 1997).

13. Paraphrased from Paul Ricoeur's well-known remark, "The symbol gives rise to thought," in *The Symbolism of Evil* (Boston: Beacon, 1969 [1967]), 347.

14. Herbert Fingarette, *Confucius: The Secular as Sacred* (New York: Harper Torchbook, 1972), 68.

15. Eugen Rosenstock-Huessy, *Out of Revolution* (Windsor, Vt.: Argo, 1969), 754, 756. The passage of Descartes on which Rosenstock-Huessy is elaborating is *Discourse on Method,* trans. John Veitch (LaSalle, Ill.: Open Court, [1637] 1946), Part 2, 13.

16. Albert Borgmann in his *Crossing the Postmodern Divide* (Chicago: University of Chicago Press, 1992) defines regardless power as "the determination to prevail aggressively regardless of physical resistance, to prevail methodically regardless of complexity, and to prevail socially regardless of traditions" (123).

17. Samuel P. Huntington, *The Clash of Civilizations and the Remaking of the World Order* (New York: Simon and Schuster, 1996).

10

MAÑANA IS TODAY

A Socio-Theological Reflection on the Latino Journey

REV. ELDIN VILLAFAÑE

Introduction

" 'What happens tomorrow?' asked the wide-eyed little boy after a perform-ance of *The Oxcart*."[1] That question is often raised by many as the curtain comes down on René Marqués's heart-wrenching depiction of the Immigrant experience — this time of the Puerto Rican journey.

The Oxcart is a story of cultural bonds based on dignity and mutual respect. It's a story of hope and family, of courage and struggle; but also of distress, disillusionment, and of tragedy. Doña Gabriela, Luis, and Juanita must leave the *finca* (the rural farm) by oxcart to live in "La Perla," a slum district in San Juan. They hoped to better their condition in San Juan. Yet no one in the family is able to find work or adapt to the San Juan slum. They migrate from "La Perla" to New York City. The journey this time takes them to the Morrisania *barrios* of the Bronx.

In the living room of their cold and dark Bronx flat is a carved model of an oxcart, sitting on top of a radio. The oxcart is the symbol of their search for freedom and happiness. An oxcart, after all, brought them away from the *finca* to the city. It represented a journey of freedom and happiness — or so they thought.

In the last tragic scene of *The Oxcart,* Juanita must have remembered the words of her brother Luis, as he contemplated bringing his family to New York City. Words that reflect the hopes and dreams of many immigrants: "They say there's plenty o' work. They pay good. An' the poor man's as good as the rich...a country where a man can do somethin' to stop bein' poor.... Where all the machine in the world come from, and all the money in the world, and the good things that make all the people in the world happy."[2]

For Luis, the oldest child and man of the house, it was not a happy jour-ney. An accident at the factory he worked in took his young life. Just before the curtains come down on this play, Juanita, with tears, yet courageously

105

and defiantly, utters words that many who have taken similar journeys have valiantly expressed: "Now we know the world don't change by itself. We're the ones who change the world. And we're gonna help change it."[3]

What happens tomorrow? For many immigrants and Latinos that have been in the United States for many generations *Mañana* (Tomorrow) is Today!

  - For many *Mañana* is Today speaks of a vision of tomorrow too long deferred.

  - For others *Mañana* is Today speaks of a sustaining vision of hope in an apparently hopeless future.

  - And for all *Mañana* is Today speaks of the moral claim that the immigrant, the poor, and the stranger places on the Church "to help change the world" for all the Juanitas in our *barrios*.

Under three correlated themes I will address my reflections on the Latino journey: First, I will look at *la Realidad* (Reality) of Latinos in the United States; second, I will present Latino religiosity by what I call *Salsa* Christianity; and finally my remarks will focus on a Latino call for justice.

La *Realidad* of Latinos

Mañana is Today speaks of a vision of tomorrow too long deferred.

In Storm Lake, Iowa, there is a large influx of immigrants from Mexico, that according to the *U.S. News & World Report* (September 23, 1996) is creating "The New Jungle." This magazine alludes to the turn-of-the-century book *The Jungle* (1900), by Upton Sinclair, and its exposé of the meatpacking industry, that parallels the exploitative and miserable conditions of present Latino workers. On the other hand, in the latest *Hispanic Business* magazine, we have a listing of the top one hundred Latino-owned companies and also their annual listing of the one hundred most influential Latinos; both magazines highlight the emergence into national consciousness of a peculiar "pueblo" — the Hispanics or Latinos. This emergence into national consciousness has significantly challenged the political, economical, educational, and religious structures and leadership of North American society.

The exponential growth of Latinos in the United States is one of the critical factors, with its social implications, that make for this significance. According to the Census Bureau, between 1980 and 1990, Latinos increased 53 percent, reaching 22.4 million. Presently, many estimate that there are over 30 million Latinos, and that by the year 2013, according to the projections by demographers, Latinos will number 43 million. Latinos, according to Moisés Sandoval, "will not only have surpassed African-Americans as the largest 'minority,' but they will also be the majority of the [sixty-plus million] Catholics in the Nation."[4]

This phenomenal growth is further noted by research at the Texas Data Center, which estimated the 1996 Latino population in the Lone Star State at 28 percent, but projects the Latino growth to 43 percent by the year 2030. Florida's Latino population, for example, is expected to grow from 13.1 percent in 1993 to 21.5 percent in the year 2020, according to the Census Bureau projections.[5]

Latinos are a highly urbanized people, concentrated in the largest cities of America. A million or more live in each of the metropolitan areas of New York, Chicago, and Los Angeles. Demographers also note hundreds of thousands in each of at least a dozen other cities. Equally important is that every major city in the nation has a sizable community.

Yet, the demographic phenomenon does not tell the whole story. To paraphrase Charles Dickens in *A Tale of Two Cities,* "It is the best of times for Latinos, and it is the worst of times."

One can celebrate the many achievements of Latinos — and there are many — in many fields. One can celebrate:

> The outstanding figures in the Latino theater, such as: Miriam Colon, Ivan Acosta, and Luis Valdez.

One can celebrate:

> Latinos in Film: Anthony Quinn, Jose Ferrer, Rita Moreno, Andy Garcia, Edward James Olmos, Rosie Perez, Cameron Diaz, Jennifer Lopez, and yes, Raquel Welch (Raquel Tejada).

One can celebrate:

> The great contributors to music: From the Tejano music of la Mafia, Gloria Estefan, Tito Puente (Latin Jazz), Carlos Santana (Latin Rock), Celia Cruz, Ruben Blades, and Marc Anthony (Salsa) to Edward Mata, conducting the Dallas Symphony.

One can celebrate:

> Outstanding Latino literary figures: Oscar Hijuelos, Pulitzer Prize for fiction (1990), *The Mambo Kings Play Songs of Love,* Victor Villasenor, *Rain of Gold,* Ana Castillo, *Loverboys,* Esmeralda Santiago, *When I Was Puerto Rican,* and the Brooklyn born Puerto-Rican poet, Martín Espada, *Trumpets from the Islands of their Eviction.*

One can celebrate:

> Latinos success in business and politics: In business: Henry Cisneros (now President/CEO of Univision, one of the largest T.V. stations in the Americas); and the just deceased chairman of the board/CEO of Coca-Cola Roberto Goizueta. In politics: Federico Peña, Nydia Velazquez, and U.S. Ambassador to the United Nations Bill Richardson (Mexican-American).

One can celebrate:

> Latinos in baseball: Well, just name any major league baseball team — we are living in the era of the Latinization of baseball. From the N.Y. Yankees' Puerto-Rican Bernie Williams to Cuban refugee pitcher and World Series MVP, Miami Marlin Livan Hernandez.

Indeed one can celebrate — in many large and small ways — the contributions Latinos are making to American society.

Nonetheless, a sampling of the most vital socioeconomic statistics reveals that the condition of most Latinos is grim! In the strong words of the late Orlando Costas, "the overwhelming majority of Hispanics have been condemned, along with the majority of [African-Americans], to be the permanent underclass of North American society."[6]

Recent reports by the Census Bureau showed that, in 1995, median household income rose for every other American ethnic and racial group, but for the nation's 27 million Latinos, it dropped 5.1 percent. The downturn, which affects the American-born as well as the newly arrived across a broad spectrum of socioeconomic indicators, has baffled social scientists. And it has prompted some to warn that many Latinos, members of the nation's fastest growing ethnic or racial group, may become entrenched as America's working poor.

Census data show that for the first time the poverty rate among Latinos in the United States has surpassed that of blacks. Latinos now constitute nearly 24 percent of America's poor, up 8 percentage points since 1985. Of all Latinos, 30 percent were considered poor in 1995, meaning they earned less than $15, 569 for a family of four. That is almost three times the percentage of non-Hispanic white people in poverty. Of the poorest of the poor, those with incomes of $7,500 or less for a family of four, 24 percent were Latinos.

These are not just statistical blips. Overall, household income for Latinos has dropped 14 percent since 1989, from about $26,000 to under $22,900, while rising slightly for blacks. Experts acknowledge that the influx of millions of Latin American immigrants over the last twenty years — two million between 1990 and 1994 alone, the Census reports — has pulled income numbers down because immigrants tend to be poor.

Researchers also remind us that the Latino population is an amalgam of people, and their descendants, from nearly twenty-four countries. They range from typically prosperous Cubans of Miami to Puerto Ricans, largely concentrated in New York and the nation's poorest ethnic group.

Generalizations, then, are often of limited use. Nonetheless, the growing group of scholars who study America's Latinos point to several factors that affect most Latinos:

– Structural changes in the economy that have drastically reduced well-paid blue-collar jobs.

- The failures of institutions like schools to retain Latino students and provide them with a marketable education, resulting in a widening gap in graduation rates from both high school and college. Latinos have by far the highest high school drop-out rate of any group in the nation.

- Discrimination among employers who see Latino immigrants, particularly those who speak poor English, as disposable workers.[7]

In the words of Arturo Vargas, head of the National Association of Latino Elected Officials (NALEO), "It is the American nightmare, not the American Dream."[8]

The oxcart is stuck in the mud. Or should we say the asphalt!

Latino and *Salsa* Christianity

Mañana is Today speaks of a sustaining hope in an apparently hopeless future.

In the midst of this grim picture there are signs of hope! Latinos, notwithstanding the so-called fatalism of their heritage, are a people of hope, of joy, of fiesta, and of intense religiosity! Many Latino institutions, and other institutions and people, have been a source of help, strength, and empowerment for the Latino community. Of particular interest to me has been the role of religious institutions. As I have noted elsewhere, the Latino is a *homo religiosus* (a religious being). There is no area of life, no matter how trivial, that is not touched by the religious sentiment. The depth of Latino religiosity cannot be fathomed by mere statistical quantification of church attendance, or for that matter, by statistical surveys or religious profiles. The Latino culture and person cannot be understood apart from this religious dimension.[9]

For me, at the dawn of the new millennium, *Salsa* is emerging as the metaphor "par excellence" for Latino reality and Christianity. It can be heard in most corners of the *barrios* — and for that matter, in many venues of our great cities in America. It's *salsa* — not the condiment, but that unique blend of Latino rhythms — that has been both a source and demonstration of solidarity and identity among the many new Caribbean and Latin American immigrants and established Latinos. *Salsa* as a particular musical style is an urban creation. With its genesis and popularization in New York City at the end of the sixties and beginning of the seventies, it represents not so much a new rhythm discovered, but the integration of different musical forms and experiences. In similar fashion to jazz, it has the power to express the deep personal and social longings of a people.

José Luis Méndez reminds us that:

> In amalgamating (blending) in one musical expression common to all [meaning: Puertorriqueños, Dominicanos, Cubanos, Venezolanos, Centro- y Suramericanos], *salsa* has created a space for understanding and action that must

not be overlooked. In effect, *salsa* is not only music. It is emotion, experience and communication. It is discovery and affirmation of cultural and human identity in which politics, social reality and daily life are mixed with the same intensity as the musical rhythms.[10]

The Latino church, like its *salsa* music, "has created a space for under-standing and action that must not be overlooked."[11] The *salsa* metaphor is instructive here. *Salsa's* musical rhythms are a mixed or *mestizaje* of "bolero, guaracha, plena, rumba, cumbia, guajira, chachachá, bomba, seis y aguinaldo."[12] And some would add, jazz and rock. Its mostly Afro-Cuban, Nuyorican, and urban beat discloses and underscores the three root-streams or three distinct strands of Latino cultural identity. For Latinos the *salsa* rhythm is one that emerges from the historical and biological convergence of African, European (Spaniards), and Amerindian heritage. This first or early *mestizaje* is further developed by what we call the second *mestizaje* — the encounter of Latinos with white/anglo and mostly urban North American reality.

The Latino church, like its *salsa* music, represents the blending or *mes-tizaje* of colors, customs, and commitments from many nationalities. It too has amalgamated into one distinct religious expression — *salsa* Christianity!

In a context of marginalization and poverty the *salsa* Christianity that has emerged in the Latino church, in its most active and social significant expressions, plays for Latinos and models for society at large at least the following three vital social-spiritual rhythms: (1) the rhythms of Survival; (2) the rhythms of Signpost; and (3) the rhythms of Salvation. These three S's (Survival, Signpost, and Salvation) give us a picture of the Latino church and the rhythms of its urban ministry.[13]

The Rhythms of Survival:
A Place of Cultural Survival and Affirmation

The Latino church in the *barrios* has been the locus of cultural validation. Family values, language, music, art, customs, and symbols of the Latino *pueblo* have been sustained, nourished, and affirmed in the Latino church. When the dominant culture pressed for a forced assimilation, many found their Latino culture and values safeguarded in the enclaves of our Latino churches.

No one can visit a Latino Protestant church today (particularly indige-nous Pentecostal congregations) without being impressed by the *salsa* nature of their *fiesta* (celebration) expressed in the blending of their music and na-tive instruments — guitar, maracas, and bongos — and thus savor the depth of the Latino soul, of *salsa* Christianity! The experience of *salsa* Christianity in the "cultos" by Latinos is one that "reaches beyond the levels of creed and ceremony into the core of human religiousness, into what might be called 'primal spirituality.' "[14]

Virgilio Elizondo makes "Fiesta" a central theological category. Though he speaks about Mexican-Americans, what he says can be applied equally to all Latinos:

> The happiness and joy — is immediately obvious to outsiders. The tragedies of their history have not obliterated laughter and joy — fiesta is the mystical celebration of a complex identity, the mystical affirmation that life is a gift and is worth living....In the fiesta the [Latino-a] rises above the quest for the logical meaning of life and celebrates the very contradictions that are the essence of the mystery of human life.[15]

It is in the many Latino churches in our *barrios* that many find their culture — their lives — affirmed. Amid the experience of oppression, domination, and the struggles for mere survival, the fiesta — with games and rituals, music and dance, food and "familia" — speaks eloquently of joy, hope, and life.

The Rhythms of Signpost:
A Signpost of Protest, Resistance, and Priestly Presence

To the dominant Church the Latino congregation is often a "foreign enclave," a possible "threat to the unity of the universal Church," or a "mission station." This paternalistic view is shattered by the persistent presence of the Latino church, which does not go away, but stands, in the words of Orlando Costas, "as a disturbing sign on the fringes of an unjust society — a prophetic indictment against the racism, political oppression, economic exploitation and sociocultural marginalization which have been such a constituent part of the American way of life."[16]

Stated differently: The mere presence of the Latino church in the *barrios* is:

- A prophetic witness: to the principalities and powers, interpreted as either institutions and/or people who dehumanize God's children;

- A prophetic witness: to the other churches and denominations who have left or refuse to enter our *barrios;*

- A prophetic witness: to the *barrios* members themselves, who are challenged to forgiveness, hope, and community; and

- A prophetic witness: to the Latino believers themselves, who are challenged and called not to accept their *status quo.*

The Latino church's presence as *a priestly community* in a deep and mysterious way sacralizes the *barrios,* providing space or context for the gathering of God's people for intercession, prayer, and strength. The Puerto Rican author Piri Thomas, referring to his Tia's (aunt's) Pentecostal church,

speaks to this reality: "It was a miracle how they could shut out —
the...horrors of decaying rotten tenement houses and garbage-littered
streets, with drugs running through the veins of our ghetto kids. It was
a miracle that they could endure the indignities poured upon our *Barrios*.
I knew that every one of them didn't get weaker. They got stronger. Their
prayer didn't get shorter. They got longer."[17]

The Rhythms of Salvation:
A Liberated and Liberating Community

The Latino churches which literally dot the many inner-city *barrios* of America are communities of hope and liberation. These churches can be found
in a storefront or a converted synagogue, or perhaps a traditional church
building "abandoned" by its "sister" anglo church. There one finds a simple
but powerful proclamation of the gospel of Jesus Christ. There one finds
a gathering of God's church, providing a community of freedom, dignity,
self-worth, comfort, strength, hope, joy — abundant life!

Once again Orlando Costas is on target when he states: "Indeed the prophetic genius of the minority church is that it has learned to 'sing the Lord's
song in a strange land' (Psalms 137:4). It has been able to give its respective
communities a vision of a more fraternal, just, and peaceful world, enabling
them to hope even when there seems to be no hope. Its ethic has been clearly
one of liberation."[18]

As a liberated community, the Latino church lives out the Gospel both
in its life and in its liberating mission. Though poor by the standards of the
world, it witnesses to a richness of faith, hope, and love (1 Cor 13:13).

A Latino Call for Justice

Mañana is Today speaks of the moral claim that the immigrant, the
poor, and the stranger places on the Church 'to help change the world'
for all the Juanitas in our *barrios*.

To the rhythms of *salsa* Christianity one must add the rhythms of the many
people groups and churches that make up our cities. The oxcart still sits,
not on the radio, but perhaps on top of the televisions of many Latinos. It
calls out for justice this time, particularly to the Church at large. It calls out
to all who have taken to heart Amos's ringing call: "But let justice roll on
like a river, righteousness like a never-failing stream" (Amos 5:24).

There are many Latino justice issues, some of which I have noted explicitly, while alluding to others. Among the many issues that are relevant to the
barrios, to Latinos, are: Immigration policy issues, employment and under-
employment (jobs), housing, health care, drugs and substance abuse, AIDS,
discrimination and racism, youth gangs, affirmative action, high drop-out

rates, bilingual education, problems of inequity in education, and economic and political empowerment.

There is one issue that I believe has emerged as one of the most critical to all Latinos — be they recently arrived immigrants or, for that matter, fourth and fifth generation Latinos — an issue about which I believe the Church can do much. It is also an issue that impacts all the other issues noted. The issue is the education of Latino children. It's not a new issue, but given the global economy and high-tech society in which we live, the "American dream" — if that is the direction of the "oxcart" — will not be justly realized by Latinos if we do not address the problems of inequity in education.

Recent issues in *Time* (October 27, 1997) and *Newsweek* (October 27, 1997) magazines featured educational articles titled, "How Johnny Should Read," and "Why Andy Couldn't Read," respectively. The justice issue for Latinos and for the Church is "Why Juanito doesn't go to School!"

A few years ago — notwithstanding recent achievement, but still relevant in its projections — Jane Moore and Harry Pachon noted the following dismal portrait of Latino educational status:

> For every 100 Latino children who entered Kindergarten only 55 graduate from high school, 25 enter college, and 7 completed college. Only 4 will enter graduate school and 2 will finish.[19]

Recently a call to action was given by the President's Advisory Commission on Educational Excellence for Hispanic Americans. The purpose for the call to action is to "compel local, state and federal policy makers to take serious and immediate action to improve the educational attainment of Hispanic Americans."[20]

The Commission found that the lack of educational attainment by Latinos can be attributed to several factors: inadequate school funding at all levels; the segregation of students into inadequate schools; and the treatment of bilingualism as a liability instead of a rich cultural and economic resource. It noted that the lack of representation at policy-making levels by Latinos makes it difficult to address the educational disparities.

The Commission also underlined the following trends threatening equity in education: it was noted that unless programs targeted to Latinos were federally mandated and expected to uphold national performance standards, the state and local enforcement was only superficially effective. Another trend was the changing attitudes on race and ethnicity, including changing perceptions of affirmative action and immigrant policies which have the potential to reverse thirty years of proactive legislation.[21]

What can the Church do? How can Christians of all persuasions show solidarity with Latinos in their quest for educational justice? Public educational issues are political issues. As such we have much to learn from the leadership of the Roman Catholic Church in this matter. The U.S. Conference of Catholic Bishops' statement "On Political Responsibility," for example, defines the Church's role in the political order to include the following:

- Educating the faithful regarding the teaching of Christ and their responsibilities
- Analyzing issues for their social and moral dimensions
- Measuring public policy against gospel values
- Participating with other concerned parties [Christians or non-Christians] on the public issues involving human rights, social justice and the life of the Church in society[22]

Focusing on education, let me suggest four basic steps the church can take, and I'll do so in normative terms:

1. Christians, and all people of goodwill, should be in *solidarity* with Latinos regarding educational justice issues.

2. Anglo and Latino churches should *partner* to address educational issues, participate in local school boards, and attend PTA and other school functions.

3. Individual churches should form *task forces* to study the issues and strategize action plans that are in keeping with Gospel values and biblical justice.

4. A *prophetic call to justice* on behalf of Latinos should infuse the Church's teaching, preaching, and concrete witness.

The Holy Spirit is moving among many in our cities to articulate a clear and coherent vision of values and spirituality in the public sphere. The challenge to the Church is to participate in the Spirit's historical project. The strategy of the Spirit is to empower its people to incarnate its love in *just actions* in the world. We must discern the signs and join the Spirit in its action in the world in anticipation of his reign. We must discern the role of the Church in its engagement with Latinos in its quest for justice and biblical liberation. Orlando Costas has stated it well:

> The near future is always a foretaste of the distant future. We do not have to wait for the consummation of the Kingdom in order to discern its justice in the social and political sphere and the presence of its liberating power in social structures. The Holy Spirit is showing us already signs of social and political justice and structural liberation in many places and situations. We know that an event is a sign of the justice of God when it enables the poor and oppressed to experience a measure of economic, sociocultural, and political liberation.[23]

Mañana is Today!

Notes

1. René Marqués, *The Oxcart* (New York: Charles Scribner's Sons, 1969), v.
2. Ibid., 81–82.
3. Ibid., 154.
4. Moisés Sandoval, "Hispanics in the United States: Between Conquest and Liberation," in Ana Maria Pineda and Robert Schreiter, eds., *Dialogue Rejoined: Theology and Ministry in the United States Hispanic Reality* (Collegeville, Minn.: Liturgical Press, 1995), 4.
5. Eunice Moscoso, "Hispanic Leaders Seek Security at Planned October March; Raise Immigration Issues with Justice Officials," *Cox News Service/Latino-Link Enterprises, Inc.* (June 5, 1996): 2.
6. Orlando Costas, *Christ Outside the Gate: Mission Beyond Christendom* (Maryknoll, N.Y.: Orbis Books, 1982), 113.
7. Carey Goldberg, "Hispanic Households Struggle as Poorest of U.S. Poor," *Times News Service/LatinoLink Enterprises, Inc.* (January 30, 1997): 1–3.
8. Ibid., 3.
9. See especially chapter 2, "Hispanic American Religious Dimension" in Eldin Villafañe, *The Liberating Spirit: Toward an Hispanic American Pentecostal Social Ethic* (Grand Rapids: Eerdmans, 1993), 41–132.
10. José Luis Méndez, "Puerto Rico y La Cultura de la Salsa," *Entre el Limbo y el Consenso: El Dilema de Puerto Rico para el Proxímo Siglo* (San Juan, P.R.: First Book Publishing of P.R., 1997), 83 (my translation).
11. Ibid., 83.
12. Ibid., 88.
13. For an elaboration of this material see Eldin Villafañe, "The Power of the Powerless: A Paradigm of Partnership from the Underside," in *Seek the Peace of the City: Reflections on Urban Ministry* (Grand Rapids: Eerdmans, 1995), 29–39.
14. Harvey Cox, *Fire from Heaven: The Rise of Pentecostal Spirituality and the Reshaping of Religion in the Twenty-First Century* (Reading, Mass.: Addison-Wesley, 1995), 81.
15. Virgilio Elizondo, *Galilean Journey: The Mexican-American Promise* (Maryknoll, N.Y.: Orbis Books, 1983), 43.
16. Orlando Costas, "Social Justice in the Other Protestant Tradition: A Hispanic Perspective," in Frederick Greenspahn, ed., *Contemporary Ethical Issues in the Jewish and Christian Traditions* (Hoboken, N.J.: Ktav, 1986), 223.
17. Piri Thomas, *Savior, Savior, Hold My Hand* (Garden City, N.Y.: Doubleday, 1972), 19–20.
18. Costas, "Social Justice," 224.
19. Jane Moore and Harry Pachon, *Hispanics in the United States* (New York: Prentice-Hall, 1988), 68.
20. Angelina Mercado, "Hispanic American Education Caught on the Nation's Fault Line," *The NPRC Report* (October–November 1996): 5.
21. Ibid.
22. Jeffrey L. Brown and Eugene F. Rivers, "The Urgent Responsibility of Black Churches," in *Boston Globe* (November 10, 1996): Op-Ed page.
23. Costas, *Christ Outside the Gate*, 30.

11

THE HOLY SPIRIT AND THE THEOLOGY OF LIFE

Seven Theses

JÜRGEN MOLTMANN

1

"Come, Creator Spirit" (*Hrabanus Maurus*). Prayers to the Holy Spirit are mostly Maranatha-prayers as the liturgical epiclesis as well as the epicatic existence of human beings as beings in expectant hope show. When we pray for the "coming" of the Holy Spirit, we pray that the all-embracing presence of God may come out of the distanced divine counterpart. We then experience God the Spirit as both counterpart and presence, as any child experienced the mother as both encompassing presence, in which it lived, and as counterpart, to which it cried. It follows that we understand God the Spirit as divine person and divine element at the same time. The special, unique, and own personality of the Spirit is a streaming, self-communicating, and outpouring presence (Ps 139), not the closed self-existence, the *individua substantia* of Boethius, traditionally used for the concept of the trinitarian persons. When God the Spirit is — as the biblical metaphor says — "poured out on all flesh," the Spirit is spreading her uncreated divine energies on all creatures, glorifying and divinizing them by participation. The embracing and penetrating presence of the divine Spirit is an energy-field of vibrating, vitalizing, and erotic forces, if we follow Gregor Thaumaturgos and call the divine, the cosmic, and the human love "eros." The relationship between God the Spirit to the divine energies of being and to the vigor of life is a relationship of emanation, not creation.

2

The question of the origin of the energies of the Spirit is by no means a speculative one. According to the Old Testament, the Spirit that makes alive arises from the "shining countenance" of God (Ps 51; 104; 139). The "countenance of God" is a symbol for the affection, the alert attentiveness,

116

and special concern of God. In human analogies, too, the "face" is the place of the special revelation of inner movements: joy and pain are shown in laughing and crying. The "hidden face of God" (*hester panim*) is regarded as symbolic of the judgment of God, as "turned away" as divine condemnation and eternal death. But the "shining (illuminating) face of God" is seen as the source of divine life, love, and blessing. The Aaronite blessing — "let your face shine upon us" — is in fact a prayer for the vitality of the Holy Spirit. Seen physically, our eyes only receive light; physiognomically, however, our eyes "shine" and "beam" at the sight of love and as expression of deep joy.

According to the apostle Paul, the glory of God shines forth from the "face of Jesus Christ" throwing "a bright shine in our hearts" (2 Cor 4:6). The believers will therefore also reflect "the glory of the Lord" with "un-veiled faces" (2 Cor 3:18). This has deep anthropological consequences. Our "hidden faces" make us "hidden" to ourselves, incapable of knowing our-selves truly: We are *homo absconditus*. Our groaning for self-encounter and self-experience arises from our concealment, the mystery we are to ourselves and others, and will find fulfillment in the apocalypse of our selves in the "seeing God from face to face" (1 Cor 13:12). "Then I shall know even as also I am known": *homo revelatus*. The experience of the Spirit of God is combined with the inner self-experience of that "bright shine in our hearts": God within us. As Augustine once confessed, *"Interior intimo meo."* And here our true self-encounter begins in the apocalypse of our selves in God and God in our selves.

3

According to the New Testament, the Spirit of God comes into the world through the Christ story, because the Christ story emerges out of the divine Spirit. We celebrate in the ecclesiastical year Christmas — Good Friday — Easter — Ascension — Pentecost. Pentecost is the celebration in this series of salvation history and is for this reason the final goal of the other celebrations which are celebrations of Christ.

The Christ story is told by the Synoptic Gospels as the history of the Holy Spirit with Jesus: received by the Spirit — baptized in the Spirit — led by the Spirit — Jesus preached the Gospel in the presence of the Spirit (Luke 4:18), healed the sick, forgave sins, and accepted excluded ones in the power of the Spirit. In the Spirit Jesus discovered God as his intimate mystery "Abba" and himself as the "messianic child." In the Spirit he went into the night of godforsakenness from Gethsemane to Golgotha and gave himself for the redemption of the world. So far this is the Spirit story of Jesus. After his resurrection from the dead through the lifegiving power of the Spirit, Christ is present in that same Spirit of Life (1 Cor 15:45) sending the energies of life to those who believe and follow him. In this way the Spirit of God becomes the Spirit of Christ and out of the Spirit story of Christ emerges the Christ story of the Spirit. Both stories are intertwined: No christological pneumatology without the pneumatological Christology and vice versa.

In the Gospel of John we can recognize the inner divine side of those intertwined stories of the Spirit and Christ, Christ and the Spirit. According to the "farewell discourses" of Jesus (John 14–16), Jesus "goes away," i.e., Jesus dies to give room so that the Spirit may come: "If I do not go away, the Comforter will not come to you; but if I depart, I will send the Spirit to you" (16: 7). In other words: Good Friday is the divine ground to what comes into the world at Pentecost, and Pentecost reveals what really happened at Good Friday. The theological conclusion is: No *theologia crucis* without the theology of the Holy Spirit (this I would like to say to Lutheran theologians) and no *Pentecostal theology* without a theology of the cross (this for Pentecostal theologians).

Following John 14, the interrelatedness of Christ and the Spirit is more complicated: it is *trinitarian*. Jesus "goes away" to "pray to the Father that he may send you another Comforter" (14:16). This "Comforter" is the "Spirit of truth" who proceeds from the Father. Between Jesus the receiver of the Spirit and Christ the sender of the Spirit stands God the Father, that is Jesus' "Abba"-mystery, as eternal origin of the divine Spirit. In my understanding this means that the Spirit does not proceed "from the Father and the Son" (*filioque*), as the Western Nicene Creed says, but "proceeds" from the Father, rests in the Son, and shines forth from the Son into the world, as Orthodox theology says. It is God the Father ("abba") who distinguishes between Christ and the Spirit and unites them. From this it follows that Christ is not the "first (Spirit-filled) Christian" and that the Holy Spirit is not a "second Christ" or *alter Christus*, as Pius XII in the encyclical *Mystici corporis* (1943) said.

For the Christian community the criteria for "discerning the spirits" consist in the name of Jesus and the sign of the cross. Through the invocation of the *name of Jesus* and with the *sign of the cross* the evil spirits were cast out in the old ritual of exorcism. What counts negatively for exorcism counts as positive for the recognition of the Spirit of God. It is always the cross of Christ that makes the discernment of spirits necessary and possible. With the name of Jesus, however, not only his person, but also his way in invoked. What serves the discipleship of Jesus is from the Holy Spirit; what hinders the discipleship is from evil spirits. And what the Synoptic Gospels call "discipleship of Jesus," the Apostle Paul terms "the life in the Spirit." The discipleship of Jesus works as the practical criterion for the discernment of the spirits.

4

Missio Dei is nothing less than the sending of the Spirit of life from the Father through the Son into this world, that the world may live and not perish. Simply put, what is brought by God through Christ into our world is: *Life.* "I live and you shall also live" (John 14:19). For the Holy Spirit is the "well of life," and her energies bring new vitality into this apathetic and dying world. Christ is the resurrection and life in person. With Christ life in fullness, personal and communal and natural life, indestructible life has come to light. This means: eternal liveliness here — eternal life there, love here — glory there. The foundation for this new and eternal vitality lies in the glorious affirmation of life by God, revealed in the resurrection of the crucified one. In the eternal love of God the beloved life becomes eternal in itself. Jesus did not bring a new religion into the world, but new life!

5

Human life is not just biologically lived, but must be accepted and affirmed, because it can be denied and refused. Only an accepted and loved life can be lived humanely, as every child knows. Only a loving and affirming life is a humane life, as every adult knows. *Zoe* is more than *bios*. We are alive as human beings to the degree in which we accept life and affirm it, animated by that interest in life we call *love* (eros). In this passionate affirmation we open ourselves with all our senses for the happiness of life. But the more unreservedly we love life the more intensely we also suffer the pains of life and the death of beloved ones. This can be called the *paradox of human life*: the more living the experience of life the more deadly the experience of death. The divine Spirit of life drives us into life and into death. The real deadly alternative to this paradox of life is denying life, not accepting living and dying and becoming indifferent to life and death and finally to grow stiff and numb in *growing apathy*. This apathy is death before life.

6

In the Third World and in the quarters of misery in our cities, the poor, the sick, children, and old people are denied life's opportunities. People measured only according to their market value lose their human dignity and are condemned to be "surplus people" whose lives have no value anymore. Life unworthy of living must die one way or the other. In the First World and in the rich quarters of our countries, apathy over against life and death is growing like a social disease. It is a public "sickness unto death." Not happiness but sadness and numbness are becoming the life experiences for many especially young people in affluent countries. "We live in paradise — and we are in hell," Norwegian students told me last month in Oslo. The suicide rate in Norway and Switzerland is higher than in the rest of Europe, and these two countries are the richest on the continent.

The theology of liberation of oppressed people in the Third World and in the misery of our societies is fighting for the life opportunities of the poor, the sick, young and old people. We however need another theology of liberation for people incapable of living — for melancholic and apathetic and in this sense godforsaken people in the First World. This theology of liberation will be a theology of life. The one is denied living, the other is incapable of living. The coming theology of life will be eschatologically oriented as a Kingdom-of-God-theology. Every eschatological theology begins with life, because the hoped-for kingdom of God is life, life in abundance and the fulfillment of life.

7

The coming theology of life will be cosmic and cannot be restricted to human life only. The Spirit of life "poured out on all flesh" means first of all of course "human flesh." In Joel 3 with the term "flesh" the "weak, powerless and hopeless" are meant, as Hans Walter Wolff interprets this. Therefore, young people, who do not yet have full standing in life, and old people, who no longer fully participate in life, shall be the first to experience the power of the Spirit. Women shall "prophesy" the word of God, and there is no longer any male privilege. Servants and slaves receive the Holy Spirit, and the Spirit-filled, messianic community will become the community of "the free and equal." They will witness to the rest of the world that there is deliverance in the midst of danger. When the great cosmic catastrophes come — "the sun will turn to darkness and the moon to blood" — God will create the new world of eternal life out of the destruction of the old world of death: In the end is the beginning, as it was in the end of Christ.

"All flesh," *kol basar* in Hebrew, means all life on earth, not only human life. It is the Spirit of God that "fills the earth and holds together everything" (Wisd 1:7). If this is true for the Spirit of creation, it is also true for the Spirit of the new creation: "If the Spirit is poured out upon us from on high...then justice will dwell in the wilderness and righteousness remain in the fruitful fields" (Isa 32:14–15).

We finally expect rightly for the new creation and the new life "a new heaven and a new earth where righteousness dwells" (2 Pet 3:13). There will be no eternal life without the kingdom of God, and no kingdom of God without the new earth. All the ways of God and not only in embodiment but also "on earth as it is in heaven." The full theology of the Holy Spirit leads to a theology of life and the full theology of life ends in a theology of the earth.

12

GLOBAL ETHIC FOR
A NEW GLOBAL ORDER

Hans Küng

1. The twenty-first century will not be as European as the nineteenth century, nor an American century as the twentieth century, and it will also not be an Asian century, but a world century. The age of imperialism and hegemonism is gone, and the damnation that is domination would be no less so if it were Asian domination.

2. But the world is faced with a new sense of East Asian self-worth, self-respect and empowerment; Asians today are aware of their own potentials, their possibilities, and their Asian values.

3. We should avoid any silly confrontation especially between the Western world (Christian or secular) and the world of Islam and should strive for a common-wealth of all nations where wealth is truly common. In other words: toward a single commonwealth of common wealth. In this sense we should strive for a universal civilization.

Presupposing these three points of agreement, it is easier for me to analyze in my first point the fundamental challenges and responses we are facing for the twenty-first century. I do it very briefly in four steps.

I. Challenges and Responses

1. We live in a time in which humanity is threatened by a "clash of civilizations," as some think, between Islamic civilization and Western civilization. We are threatened, as I believe, not so much by a new world war, but by all sorts of cultural and religious conflicts between individual countries or in an individual country — often even in the same city, the same street, the same school. The reasonable alternative is: *peace among the religions. Because there will be no peace among the nations and civilizations without peace among the religions.*

But many people all over the world will ask: Do not precisely the religions often support and inspire hatred, enmity, and war? Indeed:

121

2. We live in a time in which peace in the Western and in the Islamic world is threatened by all sorts of *religious fundamentalism:* Christian, Muslim, Jewish, Hindu, Buddhist, often simply rooted in social misery, in reaction to Western secularism and in the desire of a basic orientation in life.

The alternative is: *dialogue between the religions. Because there will be no peace among the religions without dialogue between the religions!*

But many people will object: Are there not many dogmatic differences and obstacles between the different faiths, which make real dialogue a naive illusion? Indeed:

3. We live in a time in which in the Western and in the Muslim world better relations between religions are blocked by all sorts of *dogmatisms* that exist within each religion (there are so many clashes between traditionalism and pragmatism, fundamentalism and enlightenment).

The alternative will be: Despite dogmatic differences, *a global ethic, an ethical minimum common to all religions, cultures, civilizations. Because there will be no new world order without a global ethic.* This forthcoming "world century" asks for a "world ethic" which has to be the basis for an upcoming "world civilization."

The idea of a "universal civilization" certainly does not imply the abolition of cultural and religious differences which are tremendous — not only in Europe, but also in Asia, which is only a geographical entity and not a political, ethnic, cultural, or religious one. The idea of a "universal civilization" means in a positive way a universality in the technological, economic, political and, as we hope, also in the ethical dimension. In this time of globalization of markets, technologies, and medias we need also the globalization of ethics.

Nevertheless, we in Asia or in Europe shall and should not give up our specific cultures, the cultures of the different particular tribes, regions, or nations with their particular history, language, custom, belief, law, and art. Reaching out for a universal civilization, we must not strive toward a single, unified religion, which would be an illusion in any case, but we should maintain a culture of tolerance that respects all cultural and religious minorities. Presupposing, therefore, the importance of a universal civilization and at the same time the remaining differences in culture and religion, let us now talk about the emergence of a new world order in the political sense which, as I am convinced, needs an ethical basis.

II. A New World Order and a New Ethic

1. In *negative* terms: A better world order will *not* be introduced on the basis:

   - solely of *diplomatic offensives*, which all too often are unable to guarantee peace and stability in a certain region and which are often, as in former Yugoslavia, characterized more by hypocrisy than by honesty;

- simply of *humanitarian help*, which cannot replace political actions and solution: The European powers, by substituting in Bosnia humanitarian aid for political action, put themselves in the power of the aggressors and became complicit in the crimes of war;

- primarily of *military interventions:* Of course, an absolute pacifism would allow a new Holocaust, a new genocide at the end of this "never again century." But indeed, the consequences of military interventions tend often to be more negative than positive;

- solely of *international law,* as long as such a law rests on the unlimited sovereignty of states and is focused more on the rights of states than on the rights of peoples and individuals. If moral convictions and moral intentions do not back a law, armistice or treaty, powers as in Bosnia are not even prepared to defend the principle that only peaceful and negotiated territorial change is acceptable in Europe.

2. In *positive terms:* A better world order will ultimately be *brought in only on the basis of:*

- common visions, ideals, values, aims, and criteria;

- heightened global responsibility on the part of people and their leaders;

- a new *binding and uniting ethic* for all humankind, including states and those in power, which embraces cultures and religions. *No new world order without a new world ethic, a global ethic.*

3. What is the *function* of such a global ethic?

- Global ethic is not a new ideology or superstructure;

- it will not make the specific ethics of the different religions and philosophies superfluous;

- it is therefore no substitute for the Torah, Sermon on the Mount, the Qur'an, the Bhagavad Gita, the Discourses of the Buddha or the Sayings of Confucius.

- a global ethic is nothing but the *necessary minimum of common values, standards and basic attitudes.* In other words:

- a minimal basic *consensus* relating to binding values, irrevocable standards and moral attitudes, which can be affirmed *by all religions* despite their "dogmatic" differences and should also be supported *by non-believers.*

- This consensus of values will be a decisive contribution to *overcome the crisis of orientation* which became a real world problem.

III. World Politics Discovers the Global Ethic

When I published the book *Projekt Weltethos* (*Global Responsibility: In Search of a New World Ethic*) in 1990, there were hardly any documents on a global ethic from world organizations to which I could refer. Of course there were declarations on human rights, above all the 1948 Declaration

of the United Nations, but there were no declarations on human responsibilities. However, now, eleven years later, I can refer to these important
international documents which not only acknowledge human rights, but also
speak explicitly of human responsibilities. Indeed they programmatically call
for a global ethic and even attempt to spell it out in concrete terms.

1. The report of the U.N. Commission on Global Governance bears the
title *Our Global Neighborhood* 2 (1995) and calls for a "neighborhood
ethics":[1] "Global values must be the cornerstone of global governance."[2]
And for the "ethical dimension of the world political order" this document
gives the Golden Rule as the main basic principle: "People should treat
others as they would themselves wish to be treated."[3] In connection with
this a request is made. The authors were presumably unaware that it had
already been made in a discussion in the Revolutionary Parliament of 1789,
in Paris, one which could not be met at that time: "Rights need to be joined
with responsibilities."[4] For the "tendency to emphasize rights while forget-
ting responsibilities has 'deleterious consequences.' "[5] "We therefore urge the
international community to unite in support of a global ethic of common
rights and shared responsibilities. In our view, such an ethic — reinforcing
the fundamental rights that are already part of the fabric of international
norms — would provide the moral foundation for constructing a more effective system of global governance."[6] The international commission expresses
the hope that "over time, these principles could be embodied in a more
binding international document — a global charter of Civil Society — that
could provide a basis for all to agree on rules that should govern the global
neighborhood."[7]

2. The Report by the World Commission on Culture and Development
(1995) bears the title *Our Creative Diversity*.[8] Here the presupposition is
a "commitment to pluralism," but this statement is preceded by a chapter
which stresses what is held in common rather than the differences: "A New
Global Ethics," an ethic of humankind, a *global ethic*.

Why a global ethic? Because collaboration between people of different
cultures and interests can be made easier and their conflicts diminished and
limited if all peoples and groups "see themselves bound and motivated by
shared commitments."[9] Hence the call for a global ethic: "So it is imperative
to look for a core of shared ethical values and principles."[10] The Commission on Culture and Development emphasizes the agreement between its
concern and the efforts of the U.N. Commission for Global Governance
and states: "The idea is that the values and principles of a global ethic
should be common points of contact which offer a minimal moral stimulus
which the world must observe in its manifold efforts to overcome the global
problems mentioned."[11] To this degree today there is a whole "culture in
search of a global ethics."[12] Such a search is already in itself a cultural activity par excellence. Questions like "Who are we? How do we relate to one
another and to humankind? How do we behave toward one another and

toward humankind as such? What is our meaning?" stand at the center of culture.

What are the sources of such a global ethic? The formulation of a global ethic must draw its content from "the cultural resources, the insights, emotional experiences, historical memories and spiritual orientations of the peoples."[13] Despite all the differences between cultures, there are some themes which appear in almost all cultural traditions and which could serve as the inspiration for a global ethic.

3. The InterAction Council (1997), which consists of former presidents and prime ministers (Helmut Schmidt of Germany, Honorary Chairman, Malcolm Fraser of Australia, Chairman) proposed in September 1997 to the United Nations to accept a *Universal Declaration of Human Responsibilities*.[14] This Declaration is based on the conviction that "global problems demand global solutions on the basis of ideas, values and norms respected by all cultures and societies." The Introductory Comment of this Declaration emphasizes that "it is time to talk about human responsibilities." Therefore the *Universal Declaration of Human Responsibilities* "seeks to bring freedom and responsibility into balance and to promote a move from the freedom of indifference to the freedom of involvement.... The basic premise should be to aim at the greatest amount of freedom possible, but also to develop the fullest sense of responsibility that will allow that freedom itself to grow." The Comment stresses "that a better social order both nationally and internationally cannot be achieved by laws, prescriptions and conventions alone, but needs a global ethic. Human aspirations for progress can only be realized by agreed values and standards applying to all people and institutions at all times."[15]

The responsibilities which "should be taught and promoted throughout the world" contain "Fundamental Principles for Humanity," "Non-Violence and Respect for Life," "Justice and Solidarity," "Truthfulness and Tolerance," and "Mutual Respect and Partnership."[16]

IV. Contribution of Religions

A former communiqué of the InterAction Council bears the title *In Search of Global Ethical Standards* (1996). It openly addresses the negative role which the religions have often played, and still play, in the world: "The world is also afflicted by religious extremism and violence preached and practiced in the name of religion."[17] But the positive role of the religions is also noted: "Religious institutions still command the loyalty of hundreds of millions of people," and do so despite all secularization and consumerism.[18] "The world's religions constitute one of the great traditions of wisdom for humankind. This repository of wisdom, ancient in its origins, has never been needed more."[19]

The minimal criteria that make it possible to live together at all are important; without ethics and self-restraint humankind would revert to the jungle. "In a world of unprecedented change humankind has a desperate need of an ethical base on which to stand."[20]

Now follow some statements on ethics and politics: "Ethics should precede politics and the law, because political action is concerned with values and choice. Ethics, therefore, must inform and inspire our political leadership."[21] To respond to the epoch-making change which is coming about, our institutions need a rededication to ethical norms: "We can find the sources of such a rededication in the world's religious and ethical traditions. They have the spiritual resources to give an ethical lead to the solution of our ethnic, national, social, economic and religious tensions. The world's religions have different doctrines, but they all advocate a common ethic of basic standards. What unites the world's faiths is far greater than what divides them."[22] This declaration defines more precisely the core of a global ethic which can also be found in other declarations. The InterAction Council achieves this precision by taking up the "Declaration toward a Global Ethic" passed by the Parliament of the World's Religions which I had the honor and burden to prepare:[23] "We are therefore grateful that the Parliament of the World's Religions, which assembled in Chicago in 1993, proclaimed a 'Declaration toward a Global Ethic' which we support in principle."[24]

The "Declaration toward a Global Ethic," of course, does not aim to invent a new morality and then impose it on the various religions from outside (and even from the "West"). It simply aims to make known what religions in West and East, North and South already hold in common, but is so often obscured by numerous "dogmatic" disputes and intolerable self-opinionatedness. In short, this "Declaration" seeks to emphasize the minimal ethic that is absolutely necessary for human survival. It is not directed against anyone, but invites all, believers and nonbelievers, to adopt this ethic and live in accordance with it. In the words of the "Declaration":

On the basis of personal experiences and the burdensome history of our planet we have learned

- that a better global order cannot be created or enforced by laws, prescriptions, and conventions alone;
- that the realization of peace, justice, and the protection of earth depends on the insight and readiness of men and women to act justly;
- that action in favor of rights and freedoms presumes a consciousness of responsibility and duty, and that therefore both the minds and hearts of women and men must be addressed;
- that rights without morality cannot long endure, and that there will be no better global order without a global ethic.

And then the following two fundamental demands are developed:

1. Every human being (white or colored, man or woman, rich or poor) must be treated humanely.

2. "What you do not wish done to yourself, do not do to others!" Or in positive terms: "What you wish done to yourself, do to others!" (found already in the *Sayings of Confucius* and practically in every great religious tradition on earth).

On this basis four irrevocable directives are developed. All religions agree on the following commitments:

1. Commitment to a culture of nonviolence and respect for life: "You shall not kill!" Or in positive terms: "Have respect for life!"

2. Commitment to a culture of solidarity and a just economic order: "You shall not steal!" Or in positive terms: "Deal honestly and fairly!"

3. Commitment to a culture of tolerance and a life of truthfulness: "You shall not lie!" Or in positive terms: "Speak and act truthfully!"

4. Commitment to a culture of equal rights and partnership between men and women: "You shall not commit sexual immorality!" Or in positive terms: "Respect and love one another!"

According to the Parliament of Religions we should commit ourselves to a common global ethic, to better mutual understanding, as well as to socially beneficial, peace-fostering, and earth-friendly ways of life. This is the only efficient way to a universal civilization. As far as the religions are concerned this means: In view of a universal civilization their prime task must be making peace with one another. That must be done with every means available today, including the media, and at every level:

– clearing up misunderstandings,

– working through traumatic memories,

– dissolving hostile stereotypes,

– working through guilt complexes, both socially and individually,

– demolishing hatred and destructiveness,

– reflecting on things that are held in common,

– taking concrete initiatives for reconciliation.

The change of consciousness needed here is a task for the new century, the "world century." And it is for the young generation to realize decisively the sketch for the future presented here. As the famous French writer Victor Hugo says, the future has many names:

> For the weak, it is the unattainable.
> For the fearful, it is the unknown.
> For the bold, it is the opportunity.

Notes

1. *Our Global Neighbourhood, The Report of the Commission on Global Governance,* Oxford, 1995.

2. Ibid., 47.

3. Ibid., 49.

4. Ibid., 56.

5. Ibid.

6. Ibid.

7. Ibid., 57.

8. *Report of the World Commission on Culture and Development, Our Creative Diversity,* Paris, 1995.

9. Ibid., 34.

10. Ibid.

11. Ibid., 35.

12. Ibid.

13. Ibid.

14. *A Universal Declaration of Human Responsibilities,* proposed by the Inter-Action Council, Tokyo, 1997.

15. Ibid., 1.

16. Cf. ibid., 2–5.

17. InterAction Council, *In Search of Global Ethical Standards,* 1996, no. 2.

18. Ibid., no. 2.

19. Ibid., no. 9.

20. Ibid., no. 8.

21. Ibid., no. 9.

22. Ibid., no. 10.

23. Cf. H. Küng and K. J. Kuschel, eds., *A Global Ethic: The Declaration of the Parliament of the World's Religions* (London: SCM, 1993).

24. InterAction Council, *In Search of Global Ethical Standards,* 1996, no. 11.

13

"EVERYBODY TALKIN' 'BOUT HEAVEN AIN'T GOIN' THERE"

Black Spirituals as Theology

James H. Cone

A large amount of scholarship has been devoted to the music and poetry of the black spiritual but little has been written about its theology. Apparently most scholars assume that the value of the black spiritual lies in its artistic expression and not its theological content, which could be taken to mean that blacks can "sing and dance good" but cannot think. For example, almost everyone agrees with W. E. B. Du Bois's contention that "The Negro is primarily an artist"[1] and that his gift of music to America is unsurpassed. But what about the black person as a philosopher and theologian? Is it not possible that the thought of the spiritual is as profound as its music is creative, since without thought art is impossible? In this article, my purpose is to investigate the theological implications of the black spirituals, with special reference to the meaning of God, Jesus Christ, suffering, and eschatology.

Black History

No theological interpretation of the black spirituals is valid that ignores the cultural environment that created them; and understanding a culture means, in part, perceiving its history. Black history in America is a history of black servitude, and a record of pain and sorrows, of slave ships and auction blocks. It is the story of black life in chains, and of what that meant for the souls and bodies of black people. This is the history that created the spirituals, and it must be recognized if we are to render a valid theological interpretation of these black songs.

The logical place to begin is 1619, when twenty black Africans were sold as indentured servants at Jamestown, Virginia. Actually, there was nothing historically unusual about that event, since indentured servitude was already in existence, and many whites were victims. But in 1661, the significance of 1619 was clearly defined, when Virginia legalized black slavery, declaring

129

that people of African descent would be slaves for life. Maryland legalized black slavery two years later, and soon afterward all colonies followed suit. America became the land of the free for white people only, but for blacks she became a land of bondage.

Physical slavery was cruel. It meant working fifteen to twenty hours per day, and being beaten unmercifully if one displayed the slightest fatigue. The auction block became a symbol of "brokenness," because no family ties were recognized. Husbands were separated from wives and children from parents. There were few laws protecting the slaves, since most whites believed that Africans were only partly human (three-fifths was the fraction fixed by the Founding Fathers in 1787). Later, to put down any lingering doubts, the highest court of the land decreed that black people had no rights which white people were bound to respect. Slaves were property as were animals and objects; their owners could dispose of them as they saw fit, provided they did not endanger the welfare of the society as a whole.

It has been said that not all masters were cruel, and perhaps there is some truth in the observation, particularly if it is made from a perspective that does not know the reality of the slave experience. But from the black perspective, the phrase "good" master is an absurdity, a logical contradiction. To speak of "good" masters is like speaking of "good" racists and "good" murderers. Who in their right minds could make such nonsensical distinctions, except those who deal in historical abstractions? Certainly not the victims! Indeed, it may be argued that the so-called good masters were in fact the worst, if we consider the dehumanizing effect of mental servitude. At least those who were blatant in their physical abuse did not camouflage their savagery with Christian doctrine, and it may have been easier for black slaves to make the necessary value-distinctions so that they could regulate their lives according to black definitions. But "good" Christian masters could cover up their brutality by rationalizing it with Christian theology, making it difficult for slaves to recognize the demonic. Undoubtedly, white Christianity contributed to the phenomenon of "house niggers" (not all domestic servants were in this category), those blacks who internalized the masters' values, revealing information about insurrections planned by their brothers and sisters. The "good" masters convinced them that slavery was their lot ordained by God, and it was God's will for blacks to be obedient to white people. After all, Ham was cursed, and St. Paul did admonish slaves to be obedient to their masters.

Initially, white masters did not permit their slaves to be Christianized. Christian baptism implied manumission, according to some; and there were too many biblical references to freedom. But white missionaries and preachers convinced slave masters that Christianity made blacks "better" slaves — obedient and docile. As one slaveholder put it: "The deeper the piety of the slave, the more valuable he is in every respect."[2] White Christianity assisted in the internalization of white values in the minds of slaves, reconciling them to the condition of servitude. Christianity, as taught to black slaves, was a distorted interpretation of the gospel, geared to the ideological enforcement of white supremacy. Black resistance to slavery was interpreted as sin; revolt against the master was said to be revolt against God, and that could only mean eternal damnation. To be sure, Christianity offered freedom, but for slaves it was interpreted to mean freedom from sin, the lust and passion that made them disregard the interests of their masters. Such was the history that created the spirituals.

But the history that created the spirituals contains more than what white people did to black people — much more! Black history is also the record of black people's historical strivings, an account of their perceptions of their existence in an oppressive society. What whites did to blacks is secondary. The primary reality is what blacks did to whites in order to delimit the white assault on their humanity.

When white people enslaved Africans, their intention was to dehistoricize black existence, to foreclose the possibility of a future defined by the African heritage. White people demeaned the sacred tales of the black fathers and mothers, ridiculing their myths and defiling the sacred rites. Their intention was to define humanity according to European definitions so that their brutality against Africans could be characterized as civilizing the savages. But white Europeans did not succeed; and black history is the record of their failure. Black people did not stand passively by while white oppressors demoralized their being. Many rebelled — physically and mentally. Black history in America is the history of that rebellion.

Black rebellion in America did not begin with the civil rights movement and Martin Luther King, Jr., nor with Black Power and Stokely Carmichael or the Black Panther Party. Black resistance has roots stretching back to the auction blocks and the slave codes. It began when the first black person decided that death would be preferable to slavery. If present day Americans could just realize this, then they might be able to understand the persistence of the black struggle for freedom. We should know about Gabriel Prosser, Denmark Vesey, and Nat Turner and their efforts to break the chains of slavery. We should know about Harriet Tubman and her liberation of more than three hundred black slaves. We should know about Henry Garnett's urgent call for rebellion among the slaves and Sojourner Truth's joining of black rights with women's rights. Black slaves — men and women — were not passive, and black history is the record of their mental and physical resistance against human bondage.

To understand the history of black resistance, it is also necessary to know the black spirituals. They are historical songs which speak about the rupture of black lives; they tell us about a people in the land of bondage, and what they did to hold themselves together and to fight back. We are told in the Hebrew Bible that the people of Israel could not sing the Lord's song in a strange land. But, for blacks in the U.S., their being depended upon a song. Through song, they built new structures for existence in an alien land.

The spirituals enabled blacks to retain a measure of African identity while living in the midst of American slavery, providing both the substance and the rhythm to cope with human servitude.

Much has been said about the compensatory and otherworldly ideas in the black spirituals. While I do not question the presence of that theme, there is, nevertheless, another train of thought running through these songs. And unless this emphasis is considered, the spirituals cannot be understood. I am referring to the emphasis on freedom in this world, and the kinds of risks blacks were willing to take in order to attain it.

> Oh Freedom! Oh Freedom!
> Oh Freedom, I love thee!
> And before I'll be a slave,
> I'll be buried in my grave,
> And go home to my Lord and be free.

The theme of freedom and the kinds of activities it implied explains why slaveholders did not allow black slaves to worship and sing their songs unless authorized white people were present to proctor the meeting. And after the Nat Turner revolt, black preachers were declared illegal in most southern states. Black religious gatherings were often occasions for organizing resistance against the institution of slavery.

Black history then is the stuff out of which the black spirituals were created. But the "stuff" of black history includes more than the bare historical facts of slavery. Black history is an experience, a soulful event. And to understand it is to know the being of a people who had to "feel their way along the course of American slavery,"[3] enduring the stresses and strains of human servitude but not without a song. Black history is a spiritual!

God as Liberator

The divine liberation of the oppressed from slavery is the central theological concept in the black spirituals. These songs show that black slaves did not believe that human servitude was reconcilable with their African past and their knowledge of the Christian gospel. They did not believe that God created Africans to be the slaves of Europeans. Accordingly they sang of a God who was involved in history — their history — making right what whites have made wrong. Just as God delivered Moses and the children of Israel from Egyptian bondage, drowning Pharaoh and his army in the Red Sea, so God will also deliver black people from American slavery. It is this certainty that informs the thought of the black spirituals, enabling black slaves to sing:

> Oh Mary, don't you weep, don't you moan,
> Oh Mary, don't you weep, don't you moan,
> Pharaoh's army got drownded,
> Oh Mary, don't you weep.

The basic idea of the spirituals is that slavery contradicts God; it is a denial of God's will. To be enslaved is to be declared nobody, and that form of existence contradicts God's creation of people to be God's children. Because black people believed that they were God's children, they affirmed their somebodiness, refusing to reconcile their servitude with divine revelation. They rejected white distortions of the gospel, which emphasized the obedience of slaves to their masters. They contended that God willed their freedom and not their slavery. That is why the spirituals focus on biblical passages that stress God's involvement in the liberation of oppressed people. Black people sang about Joshua and the battle of Jericho, Moses leading the Israelites from bondage, Daniel in the lion's den, and the Hebrew children in the fiery furnace. Here the emphasis is on God's liberation of the weak from the oppression of the strong, the lowly and downtrodden from the proud and the mighty. And blacks reasoned that if God could lock the lion's jaw for Daniel and could cool the fire for the Hebrew children, then God certainly can deliver black people from slavery.

> My Lord delivered Daniel
> Why can't He deliver me?

Contrary to popular opinion, the spirituals are not evidence that black people reconciled themselves with human slavery. On the contrary, they are black freedom songs which emphasize black liberation as consistent with divine revelation. And if some people still regard the spirituals as inconsistent with the African American struggle for justice and black theology, that is because they have been misguided and the songs misinterpreted. There is little evidence that black slaves accepted their servitude because they believe God willed their slavery. The opposite is the case. The spirituals speak of God's liberation of black people, God's will to set right the oppression of black slaves despite the overwhelming power of white masters. For blacks believed that there is a great spiritual power at work in the world, who is on the side of the oppressed and downtrodden. As evidence they pointed to the blind man who received his sight, the lame who walked, and Lazarus who was received into God's kingdom while the rich man was rejected. And if "de God dat lived in Moses' time is jus de same today," then that God will vindicate the suffering of the righteous blacks and punish the unrighteous whites for their wrongdoings.

Some will argue that the very insistence upon divine activity is always evidence that people are helpless and passive. They often cite Marx: "Religion is the sign of the oppressed creature, the heart of the heartless world . . . the spirit of a spiritless situation. It is the opium of the people."[4] There were doubtless some black slaves who literally waited on God, expecting God to effect their liberation in response to their faithful passivity; but there is another side of the black experience to be weighed. When it is considered that Nat Turner, Denmark Vesey, and Harriet Tubman may have been creators of some of the spirituals, that "Sinner, please don't let this harvest pass" probably referred to a slave resistance meeting,[5] that after 1831, over two thousand slaves escaped yearly,[6] and that black churches interpreted civil disobedience as consistent with religion, then it is most likely that many slaves recognized the need for their own participation in God's liberation. Indeed many believed that the only hands God had was their hands, and without the risk of escape or insurrection, slavery would never end. This may be the hidden meaning of the song, "Singin' wid a sword in ma han'." The sword may be the symbol of the need of black slaves to strike a blow for freedom even though the odds were against them. Certainly the strict enforcement of the slave codes and the merciless beating of many slaves who sang spirituals tend to point in that direction.[7] What is certain is that religion did not dull the drive for liberation among all black slaves, and there is much evidence that slaves appropriated religion to their various styles of resistance.

Seeking to detract from the theological significance of the spirituals, some critics may point out that black slaves were literalists in their interpretation of the Scripture, and this probably accounts for their acceptance of the white masters' interpretation of the Bible. It is of course true that slaves were not biblical critics. Like most of their contemporaries, they accepted the inerrancy of Scripture. But the critical point is that their very literalism supported a black gospel of earthly freedom. They were literal when they sang about Daniel in the lion's den, David and Goliath, and Samson and the Philistines. On the other hand, they dispensed with biblical literalism when white people began to use the curse of Ham and Paul as evidence that blacks ought to accept their slavery. As one ex-slave preacher put it:

> When I starts preaching I couldn't read or write and had to preach what Master told me, and he say tell them niggers iffen they obeys the master they goes to Heaven; but I knowed there's something better for them, but daren't tell them 'cept on the sly. That I done lots. I tells 'em iffen they keeps praying, the Lord will set 'em free.[8]

Black slaves were not naïve as is often supposed. They knew that slavery contradicted humanity and divinity, and that was why they cited biblical references that focused on the liberation of the oppressed. They believed that God would deliver them; and as God locked the lion's jaw for Daniel, God will paralyze the power of white masters.

> Who lock, who lock de lion,
> Who lock, de lion's jaw?
> God, lock, God lock de lion's jaw.

The point is clear. God is the liberator, the deliverer of the weak from the injustice of the strong.

It is significant that theology proper blends imperceptibly into Christology in the spirituals. No theological distinction is made between the Son and the Father. Jesus is understood as the King, the deliverer of men from unjust suffering. He is the comforter in time of trouble, the lily of the valley, and the bright and morning star.

> He's King of Kings, and Lord of Lords,
> Jesus Christ, the first and last
> No man works like him.

The death and resurrection of Jesus are particular focal points of the spirituals. The death of Jesus meant the Savior died on the cross for black slaves. His death was a symbol of their suffering, their trials and tribulation in an unfriendly world. When Jesus was nailed to the cross and the Romans pierced him in the side, he was not alone; blacks suffered and died with him. That was why they sang:

> Were you there when they crucified my Lord?
> Were you there when they crucified my Lord?
> Oh! Sometimes it causes me to tremble, tremble, tremble;
> Were you there when they crucified my Lord?

Black slaves were there! Through the experience of being slaves, they encountered the theological significance of Jesus' death. With the crucifixion, Jesus made an unqualified identification with the poor and helpless and takes their pain upon himself. They were at the crucifixion because his death was for them.

And if Jesus was not alone in his suffering, they also were not alone in their slavery. Jesus is with them! Herein lies the meaning of the resurrection. It means that Jesus is not dead but is alive.

> He rose, he rose from the dead,
> An, de Lord shall bear my spirit hom'.

The resurrection is the divine guarantee that their lives are in the hands of the One who conquered the power of death, enabling them to do what is necessary to remain obedient to the creator and sustainer of life.

God and Black Suffering

Though black slaves believed that the God of Jesus Christ was involved in the historical liberation of oppressed people from bondage, the continued existence of American slavery seemed to contradict that belief. If God is omnipotent and is in control of human history, how can God's goodness be reconciled with human servitude? If God has the power to deliver black people from the evil of slavery as God delivered Moses from Pharaoh's army, Daniel from the lion's den, and the Hebrew children from the fiery furnace, why then are black slaves still subject to the rule of white masters? Why are we still living in wretched conditions when God could end this evil thing with one righteous stroke?

These are hard questions, and they are still relevant today. In the history of theology and philosophy, these questions are the core of the "problem of evil"; and college and seminary professors have spent many hours debating them. But black slaves did not have the opportunity to investigate the problem of suffering in the luxury of a seminar room with all the comforts of modern living. They encountered suffering in the cotton fields of Georgia, Arkansas, and Mississippi. They had to deal with the absurdities of human existence under whip and pistol. Every time they opened their eyes and visualized the contradictions of their environment, they realized that they were "rolling through an unfriendly world." How could a good and powerful God be reconciled with white masters and overseers? What explanation could the Holy One of Israel give for allowing the existence of an ungodly slave institution?

In order to understand the black slaves' reaction to their enslavement, it is necessary to point out that their reflections on the problem of suffering were not "rational" in the academic sense, with an emphasis on abstract and universal distinctions between good and evil, justice and injustice. The black slave had little time for reading books or sitting in the cool of the day, thinking about neat philosophical answers to the problem of evil. It was not only illegal to teach slaves to read, but most were forced to work from daybreak to nightfall, leaving no spare time for the art of theological and philosophical discourse. The black slaves' investigation of the absurdities of human existence was concrete, and it was done within the context of the community of faith. No attempt was made to transcend faith of the community by assuming a universal stance common to "all" people. In this sense, their reflection on human suffering was not unlike the biblical view of God's activity in human history. It was grounded in the historical realities of communal experience.

The classic examples in biblical history are found in the prophet Habakkuk and the sage Job. Both raised questions about the justice of God, but they were clearly questions for the faithful — not for philosophers. They took on significance only if one was a member of the community of faith. Habakkuk was concerned about the violence and the destruction of the land as witnessed in the army of the Chaldeans, while Job questioned the deuteronomic success formula. But in each case, the ultimate sovereignty of God was not denied. What was requested was a divine explanation so that the faithful could understand the ways of the Almighty. There was no philosophical resolution of the problem of evil. Suffering was a reality of life, and believers must be able to take it upon themselves without losing faith.

In the spirituals, the slaves' experience of suffering and despair defined for them the major issue in their view of the world. They did not really question the justice and goodness of God. That God is righteous and will vindicate the poor and weak was taken for granted. Indeed it was the point of departure for faith. The slaves had another concern, centered on the faithfulness of the community of believers in a world full of trouble. They wondered not whether God is just and right but whether the sadness and pain of the world would cause them to lose heart and thus fall prey to the ways of evil. They were concerned about the togetherness of the community of sufferers. Would the wretched of the earth be able to experience the harsh realities of despair and loneliness and take this pain upon themselves and not lose faith in the gospel of God? There was no attempt to evade the reality of suffering. Black slaves faced the reality of the world "ladened wid trouble, an' burden'd wid grief," but they believed that they could go to Jesus in secret and get relief. They appealed to Jesus not so much to remove the trouble (though that was included), but to keep them from "sinkin' down."

Significantly, the note of despair was usually intertwined with confidence and joy that "trouble don't last always." To be sure, the slaves sang "Sometimes I feel like a motherless child, A long way from home"; but because they were confident that Jesus was with them and had not left them completely alone, they could still add (in the same song!), "Glory Hallelujah!" The black slaves did not deny the experience of agony and loneliness in a world filled with trouble.

> Nobody knows the trouble I've seen,
> Nobody knows my sorrow.
> Nobody knows the trouble I've seen,
> Glory, Hallelujah!

The "Glory, Hallelujah!" was not a denial of trouble; it was an affirmation of faith. It said that despite the pain of being alone in an unfriendly world the black slaves were confident that God had not really left them, and trouble was not the last word on human existence.

> Soon-a-will be done with the trouble of the world;
> Soon-a-will be done with the trouble of the world;
> Going home to live with God.

It appears that slaves were not concerned with the problem of evil *per se,* as if they intuitively knew that nothing would be solved through a debate of that problem. They dealt with the world as it was, not as it might have been if God had acted "justly." They focused on present realities of despair and loneliness that disrupt the community of faith. The faithful seemed to have lost faith, and they experienced the agony of being alone in a world of hardship and pain. That was why they sang:

> I couldn't hear nobody pray,
> Oh I couldn't hear nobody pray,
> Oh way down yonder by myself,
> And I couldn't hear nobody pray.

Eschatology

Related to the problem of suffering was the future, the "not-yet" of black existence. How was it possible for black slaves to take seriously their pain and suffering in an unfriendly world and still believe that God was liberating them from earthly bondage? How could they really believe that God was just when they knew only injustice and oppression? The answer to these questions lies in the concept of heaven, which is the dominant idea in black religious experience as expressed in the black spirituals.

The concept of heaven in black religion has often been misinterpreted. Many observers have defined the black religious experience exclusively in terms of slaves longing for heaven, as if that desire was unrelated to their earthly liberation. It has been said that the concept of heaven served as an opiate for black slaves, making for docility and submission. But to interpret black eschatology solely in terms of its outmoded cosmology fails to take seriously the culture and thought of a people seeking expression amid the dehumanization of slavery. It is like discarding the Bible and its message as irrelevant because the biblical writers had a three-storied conception of the universe.

Let me admit then that the black slaves' picture of the world is not to be defended as a viable scientific analysis of reality; that their image of the promised land, where "the streets are pearl and the gates are gold," is not the best way of communicating to contemporary black radical advocates with their stress on political liberation by any means necessary; that a "new" black theological language is needed if black religion is going to be involved in articulating the historical struggles of black people in America and the Third World; and that the language of heaven is a white concept given to black slaves in order to make them obedient and submissive. The question nevertheless remains: How was it possible for black people to endure the mental and physical stresses of slavery and still keep their humanity intact? I think the answer is found in black eschatology; and maybe what is needed is not a dismissal of the idea of heaven but a reinterpretation of this concept so that oppressed blacks today can develop styles of resistance not unlike those of their grandparents.

The place to begin is with Miles Fisher's contention that the spirituals are primarily "historical documents." They tell us about the black movement for historical liberation, the attempt of black people to define their present history in the light of their promised future and not according to their past miseries. Fisher notes that heaven for early black slaves referred not only to a transcendent reality beyond time and space; it designated the earthly places that blacks regarded as lands of freedom. Heaven referred to Africa, Canada, and America north of the Mason-Dixon line.[9] Frederick Douglass wrote about the double meaning of these songs:

> We were at times remarkably buoyant, singing hymns, and making joyous exclamations, almost as triumphant in their tone as if we had reached a land

of freedom and safety. A keen observer might have detected in our repeated singing of

> O Canaan, sweet Canaan,
> I am bound for the land of Canaan,

something more than a hope of reaching heaven. We meant to reach the North, and the North was our Canaan.[10]

But while it is true that heaven had its historical referents, not all black slaves could hope to make it to Africa, Canada, or even to the northern section of the United States. The failure of the American Colonization Society's experiments crushed the hopes of many black slaves who were expecting to return to their African homeland. And blacks also began to realize that the North was not as significantly different from the South as they had envisioned, particularly in view of the Fugitive Slave Act of 1850 and the Dred Scott Decision in 1858. Black slaves began to realize that their historical freedom could not be assured as long as white racists controlled the governmental process of America. Thus they found it necessary to develop a style of freedom that included but did not depend upon historical possibilities. What could freedom mean for black slaves who could never expect to participate in the determination of the societal laws governing their lives? Must they continue to define freedom in terms of the possibility of escape and insurrection, as if their humanity depended on their willingness to commit suicide? It was in response to this situation that the black concept of heaven developed.

For black slaves, who were condemned to carve out their existence in human captivity, heaven meant that the eternal God has made a decision about their humanity that could not be destroyed by white slavemasters. Whites could drive them, beat them, and even kill them; but they believed that God nevertheless had chosen black slaves as God's own and that this election bestowed upon them a freedom to be, which could not be measured by what oppressors could do to the physical body. Whites may suppress black history and define Africans as savages, but the words of the slavemasters do not have to be taken seriously when the oppressed know that they have a somebodiness that is guaranteed by the Creator who alone is the ultimate sovereign of the universe. This is what heaven meant for black slaves.

The idea of heaven provided ways for black people to affirm their humanity when other people were attempting to define them as nonpersons. It enabled blacks to say "yes" to their right to be free by affirming God's eschatological freedom to be for the oppressed. That was what they meant when they sang about a "city called heaven."

> I am a poor pilgrim of sorrow.
> I'm in this world alone.
> No hope in this world for tomorrow.

I'm trying to make heaven my home.
Sometimes I am tossed and driven.
Sometimes I don't know where to roam.
I've heard of a city called heaven.
I've started to make it my home.

In the midst of economic and political disfranchisement, black slaves held themselves together and did not lose their spiritual composure because they believed that their worth transcended governmental decisions. That was why they looked forward to "walking to Jerusalem just like John" and longed for the "camp meeting in the promise land."

Despite the ways in which black eschatology might have been misused or the crude forms in which it was sometimes expressed, it nevertheless provides us today with theological resources for enabling theologians to develop a liberative future. I have little patience with theologians of America who say that they are concerned about humanizing the world according to God's promised future but do not relate that future to the history and culture of that people who have been and are being dehumanized and dehistoricized by white supremacy. With all the recent talk among American theologians about liberation theology, one would expect that such language could easily be related to black people and their thoughts on eschatology and divine liberation. But white American theologians, with few exceptions, are still virtually silent on white supremacy, preferring instead to do theology as if it is not a major theological and ethical problem in the modern world. Such silence is inexcusable, and it is hard not to conclude that white theologians are still enslaved by their own identity with the culture and history of white slavemasters. What they need is liberation from white supremacy, and this can only happen when they face the liberating reality of blackness and what that means for the oppressed of the land.

One of the effective starting points for that encounter with reality is the body of the black spirituals that came to maturity in the antebellum years. Far from being poignant expressions of shattered humanity, they were affirmations of hope — hope that enabled black slaves to risk their lives for earthly freedom because they knew they had a home "over yonder."

Notes

1. W. E. B. Du Bois, *The Gift of Black Folk* (1924; reprint, New York: Washington Square Press, 1970), 158.

2. Cited in Vincent Harding, "Religion and Resistance Among Antebellum Negroes 1800–1860," in *The Making of Black America,* vol. 1, ed. August Meier and Elliot Rudwick (New York: Atheneum, 1969), 181.

3. Comment by Guy Johnson of the University of North Carolina, cited in Sterling Stuckey, "Through the Prism of Folklore," in *Black and White in American*

Culture, ed. J. Chametzky and S. Kaplan (Amherst: University of Massachusetts Press, 1969), 172.

4. Karl Marx and Friedrich Engels, *On Religion* (New York: Schocken Books, 1964), 42.

5. Miles Mark Fisher, *Negro Slave Songs in the United States* (New York: Citadel Press, 1953), 27–28, 66–67, 181–85.

6. Ibid., 108. It is important to note that Fisher is quoting the conservative estimate of a Southern historian.

7. See ibid., chapter 4. Fisher notes that the spirituals were used to convene secret meetings among slaves, and the colony of Virginia prohibited them as early as 1676 (29, 66ff.). Most colonies joined Virginia in outlawing the secret meetings, but "neither outlawry nor soldiery prevented [them] from having hemispheric significance" (67).

8. B. A. Botkin, ed., *Lay My Burden Down* (Chicago: University of Chicago Press, 1945), 26.

9. See Fisher, *Negro Slave Songs,* chapters 1–4.

10. *Life and Times of Frederick Douglass* (1892; reprint, New York: Collier Books, 1962), 159.

14

WAYS OF EXPERIENCING
GOD TODAY

Leonardo Boff

The cultural and theological writings of Harvey Cox underline the fundamental importance of experience when reflecting on the everyday life of
people and societies. The experience from which Cox proceeds is not limited to that of his personal life, church, or country. Cox opened himself
up to experiencing different peoples and cultures, especially those adversely
affected by the present world order or searching for new ways to discover
the meaning necessary to life. This is what accounts for the fascination and
relevance of his texts. Inspired by his orientation, I have written the present
modest contribution about the experience of God.

Let us begin with the following observation: many people are increasingly
tired of religious doctrines, theological reflections, and speeches about God
and the sacred. They listen to speakers who start off from the premise that
God has already been experienced. They themselves want to feel God or
undergo the experience interpreted as being the emergence of God. So they
ask themselves: How can I experience God and have an encounter with him?
Is it possible to say, like Job, that "I have heard of thee by the hearing of the
ear [through religions, churches, and ministers of the sacred]: but now mine
eye seeth thee" (cf. 42:5)? In short, how can God be experienced today?

There are many roads that give access to God. Two of them, however,
are considered basic approaches: the path of personal communion with God,
who is All, and the path of communion with the All that is God. The first
is the way of the West, the second, that of the East. Let us examine the
fundamental structures of each.

The Personal Path of Communion with God, Who Is All

This path begins with a previous knowledge of God that has been transmitted through the family and religious culture in which one has grown up. It is
a matter of belief. All belief creates a representation of God and a doctrine
about him. This doctrine says that he is present in all things and that all

things are present in him. Christian theology calls this panentheism, which has nothing to do with pantheism. Pantheism dilutes God within the All and makes God from the All. Panentheism preserves the difference between the All and God, but the mutual presence of the one in the other is evident. In other words, as a function of this mutual presence, the All has its existence and consistency within God, for he is its Creator and Provider, and the All comes under the wing of the divine presence.

These statements imply a life of faith, which is understood to be one of trust and total surrender to God, who is the meaning of the universe, of history, and of existence, the promise of life beyond life. Even so, however, how can one go beyond a mere knowledge of God and actually experience him once he has been accepted in the mind and heart? How does one move from the mind to the heart?

One proceeds from knowledge to experience by radicalizing the personal relationship between "I" and "thou." The "I" is structured so as to always be built upon confrontation, upon the relationship and communion with a "thou." It is from its interaction with the "thou" that the "I" discovers itself. When a child begins to speak, it refers to itself in the third person: "Johnny's hungry," or "Johnny's tired," or "Johnny wants Mummy or Daddy," etc. It doesn't discover itself with a singular "I." It is through contact with its parents, brothers and sisters, aunts and uncles, and grandparents that it develops its "I." This is a great revolution both for the personal consciousness and for the emergence of the irreducible, unique personal self. I say "I." Thus the human being needs the "thou" in order to become "I."

The experience of God emerges when this I-thou relationship is traced back to its most remote origins. God is perceived as the absolute "thou," a fundamental alterity, an insurmountable opposite. This happens through a relationship of love or intense emotional feeling, not through thought. Thought does not experience, it presupposes experience. It is a purification, a synthesis of experience. The "I" feels itself loved and loves in return, after which come feelings of fascination and exaltation, as all those who have been in love can attest. This "God" that is thus experienced in the relationship is given personal names. It is called "my Father," "my Mother," "my Lord," "my Friend," "my Rock," "my Spring," or "my Life."

Thinking in essential terms, then, we can conclude that the human being needs an absolute "Thou" in order to become conscious of an "I" that is at once deeply felt, highly personal, and sacred. It is through the divine "Thou" that the human "I" acquires unfathomableness, irreducibility, and sacredness.

The I-thou relationship achieves its maximum expression through the words of love. This is also experienced with reference to the divine Thou, which communicates its welcoming, loving word. Love is both a revealing and fulfilling word for the human I. The human being finds that it is always involved with God. It emerges as a hearer of the word. The word reveals

God's purpose and his first intention, which is to have companions in love and in life itself. God wants to establish communion and found a community with those who draw near and communicate with him. It is characteristic of love that it spreads, irradiates, and reaches out to all and everything around it. The experience of the love of God in the I-thou relationship is a basic part of this path toward the experience of God. It is tuned to the love of God; it acts within the environment created by this love; it lovingly carries out the work of God: therein lies the singularity of the experience.

This path of the experience of God is later translated into doctrines, concepts, and powerful images that try to capture the intensity of the I-thou relationship.

Every I-thou relationship is marked by a singular dimension: the feeling of exclusivity. This entails a risk. The risk is that the person who has such an experience or the community that believes it is the messenger of such a dialogue with God may consider itself to be chosen or elect, whereas others are not. In accordance with this sense of being the elect, many in such groups attempt to evangelize others, which in turn gives rise to the will to power through the submission of others to their own beliefs. It then becomes necessary either to lead others to the same type of divine I-thou encounter, or to try to impose it on them, thus opening the way to fundamentalism and fanaticism. This can lead to wars of religion, as history has proven.

Those who claim that their own encounter with God is the only true one and that that of others is not, or else that it is in some way imperfect, are in effect declaring war on everyone else. In the name of their own truth, they deny the truth of others, opening the way for dissension and lighting the fuse of religious warfare.

Such exclusivity, however, is pathological, a morbid manifestation of something originally good and healthy: the divine I-thou encounter. The mission does not necessarily need to mean either conquest or submission. It can mean the discovery of the relationship that other individuals and peoples have established with God and with the divine I-thou dialogue. Once exclusiveness is overcome, people can begin to learn from one another; everyone feels that he or she is both edifying others and becoming edified. The forms of experiencing God converge within diversity.

Let us, then, call this the Western path, for it was within this historical and cultural space that subjectivity, the capacity for the I-thou-we conversation, developed to excess. It was also the West that first witnessed the appearance of the pathologies of exclusivity, nonacceptance of difference, and the interpretation of religious mission as imperial conquest.

The Path of Communion with the All, Which Is God

The transpersonal path grows out of the vision of reality as an organic whole that is both one and manifold. The challenge lies in perceiving the union of diversity with the All. How can each thing exist within the All and the All in each individual thing? This is the permanent question of the Taoist tradition, and the answer is always the same: one must experience nonduality. It is through nonduality that the diverse finds its place within the All, after which one experiences a fundamental and insurmountable unity. The Upanishads say, "You are all this," and point toward the whole universe. This supposes that the "you" can unite with all things — and go back to being one with them. Let us try to grasp the meaning of this proposal.

Today, through the new physics, the extended theory of evolution, open systems, and the importance of chaos in the formation of new methodologies, we know that everything is permeated with the energies and forces of the universe; this applies to all things, including biological processes and especially the dynamic interior of each person. The experience of each thing within the All arises when these interior energies are activated in the maximum concentration and amplification of consciousness. The "I" consciousness is immediately stripped away in order to create a space in which all things resonate within the person. This resonance allows each individual to feel he or she is a star, a stone, a tree, an animal, or another person. There is no more distance. Everything meets in the One, diverse and dynamic. This final unity is the result of a process of identification with that which is different, of action that creates identity with what is different. The individual becomes identical with what is different (an "identific-ation"), passing through stages of progressive nearness and interpenetration before arriving at complete identification.

The experience of mystics in both East and West provides proof that this process is indeed possible. Without breaking with Christian dogma, Saint John of the Cross arrived at the end of his spiritual path saying that "the soul of the beloved finds itself transformed into the Lover," and even that "we are God through our participation in Him."

The word "God," or other equivalent terms, arises out of the context of this experience. "God" is the word that translates the experience of the unified All, and his names are less personal ones than those that express an open totality. He is experienced as the Ultimate Foundation, the First Root, the Original Source, the Alpha and Omega, and the Light that penetrates all things, becoming transparent and drawing us to it.

On the basis of this unifying experience, everything may be seen as sacramental: that is, everything can become a vehicle for the Divine Presence. This in turn inspires an attitude of respect, veneration, and welcome toward all things, which themselves are carriers of the Mystery of the World, pregnant with God.

In this path, spirituality develops through the reverent contemplation of all things, through caring and nurturing rather than through seizing and manipulating. It is a question of perceiving the birth of God in all things, not only through the senses, sounds, colors, and sensations produced by everything that surrounds us, but also through the spiritual senses of intuition, inner vision, and oneness and repose within movement.

Everything should lead to a plunge into reality, which becomes transparent to reveal the Divine. Experiencing God both in his totality and in each of his parts leads us to illumination (*sartori*) and to profound inner serenity and integration with the universe (*nirvana*).

For the Eastern path, as for the Western, there is also a risk involved. Everything that is healthy can also become sick. Unless the enlightened and spiritualized person is completely divested of worldliness, there may arise esoteric attitudes and metaphysical projects and visions of the world. This can result in an alchemy of unsubstantiated elements forming out of an authentic and transparent spiritual path.

The mystical experience runs the risk of being transformed into mysticism, which at times becomes mixed with the business interests of gurus or supposed spiritual masters who accumulate influence and wealth. This is a sure sign that the mystical has degenerated into mystification and God into a fetish that can be manipulated by other people, individuals whose interests are irreconcilable with the nature of spiritual life. The mystic experience that becomes involved with power and applause is also easily transformed into fanaticism and fundamentalism.

We call this the "Eastern" path because it is in the Orient that human beings have made the great voyage into their own inner world and have shown a particular sensitivity to the experience of the single and manifold organic whole. They have developed highly sophisticated spiritual pathways to reach the experience of nonduality and immersion in the limitless ocean of transconscious and transpersonal human fulfillment. It was also in the Orient that the pathologies of this path were first revealed, especially when they began to be transported to the West. Detached from any interest in social justice or the destiny of the world's poor, they are presented as a panacea for all the ills of humanity.

The Complementary Nature of Eastern and Western Paths

The Oriental and Western experiences of God are complementary rather than opposed to one another. Christianity has deepened the path of dialogue, which is fundamentally oriented toward the word. The word is all-important to this concept: the word of revelation becomes the Judeo-Christian Scriptures; the word of thought becomes theology; the word of celebration becomes the liturgy; the word of obedience becomes morality; the word that is internalized becomes spirituality.

There is a permanent invitation to move from thought to life, from intellectual faith to the warmth of love, from many different words to the only true Word.

Today, however, the call of time — the time of dispersion, of frenetic transformation, of unheard-of acceleration in history — is along the line of a mystic experience of the totality of things. The path of the East seems to be an appropriate and alluring response to the search of millions and millions of people.

Human beings want to experience the sacred unity of so many diversities which are neither juxtaposed nor disarticulated. A single thread unites them, binding them together so that, despite their contradictions, they are part of an immense, dynamic, and unique process. There is an urgent need to connect or reconnect all things by means of a powerful Center. This Center is God. It confers both centrality and interior unity on us; it makes us sensitive to all of the manifestations of life, movement, and radiation that occur in the universe. This Center makes us suffer when it breaks apart, which we perceive as an unjust attack against the earth, its ecosystems, its flora and fauna, and particularly against its poor and oppressed, both men and women. Experiencing the Center mobilizes forces for transformation so that the unity felt within oneself is reflected outward toward the external world.

The first path, that of the West, is more that of the prophets, men and women of the word and of dialogue. The second, that of the East, is that of the mystics, men and women of reverent silence and visions of totality. We need both these paths. The embrace of Orient and Occident permits the emergence of an all-encompassing spirituality that causes differences to converge. The encounter between East and West, between the interior quest and the exterior voyage, is one of the hallmarks of our age. Now it is possible to have a more total experience of both the human and divine aspects of all things.

As always, though particularly at the present time, spirituality demands a prophetic commitment, born not of simple indignation, but of a mystic experience of unity with the Divine and with all things. Such commitment could well be indispensable in inaugurating or at least reinforcing a new civilizing paradigm that is more spiritual, compassionate, tender, and fraternal. This spirituality will help to guarantee a promising future for planet Earth and for all the tribes that inhabit it.

— Translated by Hugh Hazelton

15

BEGGARS AT THE THRESHOLD OF GOD'S DOOR

Margaret Eletta Guider

"And, as religious people would say, the future is in our hands because God has placed it there."

—Harvey Cox, *Many Mansions*[1]

In keeping with the purpose and spirit of this volume, my objective in this essay is to honor the ways in which Harvey Cox's contributions to the study of religion and society continue to raise the consciousness of Christians by questioning whether or not our particular ways of being in the world are consistent with the ways of Jesus, ways that are worthy of the trust of people of every faith tradition and philosophy of life. Conscious of Cox's fascination with the legacy of Francis of Assisi, I begin with an overview of different accounts of a noteworthy legend, namely that of Francis's encounter with the Sultan of Egypt, al-Malik al-Kamil. I proceed to use the encounter at Damietta as a point of reference for understanding the relationship between theological imagination and moral agency in a religiously pluralistic world. I move from a theoretical discussion of the theological insights gleaned from the encounter at Damietta to some of its practical ethical challenges. Attentive to the issues and concerns which the state of the world's children raises for every religious tradition, I conclude by reflecting upon one of the most haunting questions heard by beggars at the threshold of God's door. Finally, I end with an expression of gratitude for the most important lesson Harvey Cox continues to teach through the example of his life: the moral urgency of shaping the future entrusted to us by the God of life.

Introduction

Over the course of nearly eight centuries, the figure of Francis of Assisi (1182–1226) has engaged the moral imaginations of countless people throughout the world. For any number of reasons, the memory of the one who called himself Brother Francis continues to inspire and compel persons in ways that transcend the confines of religion, culture, and ideology.[2] In many ways, Francis's legacy remains an ongoing reminder of our connection to a larger creation that longs to experience the fullness of a lasting peace that is rooted in the compassion and justice of God.

Always a beggar at the threshold of God's door, Francis possessed a profound sense of humanity's deepest needs and longings. Holding fast to an unwavering reverence and respect for the original *thisness*[3] of every creature, Francis challenged the social construction of *otherness*. Never losing sight of the particular value and significance of every human person, Francis resisted the forces of power, privilege, and prestige that served as license for violence, marginalization, and exclusion. Given the lasting appeal of his character and the enduring relevance of certain legends about his life, people of many faith traditions and philosophies of life continue to discover in the person of Francis of Assisi more than a patron saint of ecology. Amidst the prevailing chaos and confusion of war and division, Francis remains a singular witness for peace and a Christian worthy of trust.

For anyone familiar with the life and work of Harvey Cox, it should come as no surprise to find him included in the company of those who have been inspired by the example of Francis. As many students who took part in Cox's most popular course at Harvard College, entitled *Jesus and the Moral Life*, would attest, his lectures on the life of Francis were more than lessons in thirteenth-century hagiography. They were reflections on the meaning of radical discipleship and the ethical demands of the evangelical life. Cox's presentation of Francis as a model of Christian life and practice captured the interest of everyone. His reflective commentaries on poignant stories from the life of Francis, often illustrated by selected slides of Giotto frescoes, revealed the saint's many faces: Francis the nature mystic, the witness for peace, the prophetic reformer, the brother of the poor, and the fool for God. Through these images and insights, Cox used the life of Francis as a means for understanding the necessary relationship between theological imagination and moral agency. Conscious of Cox's own particular fascination with the legacy of Francis and its relevance for our postmodern world, I have chosen to honor Cox's life and work by making one of the legends of Francis accessible to the readers of this volume. To this end, I have selected the legend of Francis of Assisi's encounter with the Sultan of Egypt, al-Malik al-Kamil (1180–1238), along with its respective insights and implications, as the focus of this essay.

An Overview of the Sources

Most Franciscan scholars would agree that there is sufficient evidence to argue persuasively that the encounter between Francis of Assisi and the Sultan of Egypt, al-Malik al-Kamil, probably occurred. The reliability of the sources, however, in terms of specific historical details and accurate interpretations of the event, remains an open question. This being said, it is important to note that my objective in this essay is not to do a historical/ textual analysis for the sake of making historical claims. Rather, my intention is to take the traces and traditions of the story seriously for the purpose of furthering reflection on the interactive dynamics of theological imagination and moral agency in a religiously pluralistic world.

The narratives that I have selected as points of reference for the encounter at Damietta are laden with a certain degree of complexity, ambiguity, and ideology. Written for a variety of purposes and intended for distinctly different audiences, these narratives tend to reveal as much about their authors as they do about Francis or the Sultan. Some writers situate the encounter at Damietta within the broader historical-political reality of the Fifth Crusade.[4] Others deal more specifically with questions related to Francis's vocational self-understanding and sense of personal destiny. The sources can be divided into five categories: historical chronicles, an epic poem, biographies, hagiographies, and an inscription. They include excerpts from the writings of the Bishop of Acre, Jacques de Vitry (1160–1240),[5] the Crusade chronicler Ernoul,[6] the Franciscan historian Jordan of Giano (1195–1262),[7] and the famous poet Henry of Avranches (ca. 1190–1260).[8] They also include sections from the works of Franciscan biographers, commentators, and hagiographers such as Thomas of Celano (d. 1257),[9] Bonaventure (1221–74),[10] an anonymous friar,[11] and Ugolino di Monte Santa Maria (ca. 1260–1342).[12] The single Islamic source is a fragment from a commentary attributed to Ibn al-Zayyat that discusses an inscription found on the tomb of Turbat al-Fakhr al-Farisi, the Sultan's renowned advisor.[13] When gathered together, these separate pieces of evidence, while offering different and at times conflicting perspectives on the encounter at Damietta, indicate that a meeting between Francis of Assisi and the Sultan of Egypt most likely occurred sometime between late August and early December in the year 1219.

The Encounter at Damietta[14]

When Francis of Assisi arrived at Damietta accompanied by Brother Illuminatus, the Ayyubid ruler al-Malik al-Kamil[15] along with his esteemed religious advisor Turbat al-Fakhr al-Farisi quite possibly perceived the two monks as occidental *Sufis,* mendicant pilgrims clothed in robes of coarse wool, possessing nothing and possessed by nothing, proclaiming themselves to be Christians, yet bearing a close resemblance to exemplars of *tasawwuf,* the mysticism of Islam.[16] This conjecture is based upon a piece of evidence that refers to a burial inscription found on the tomb of al-Fakhr al-Farisi. According to the chronicler al-Zayyat, the inscription reads: "This man's virtue is known to all. His adventure with al-Malik al-Kamil and what happened to him because of the monk, all that is very famous."[17] Louis Massignon has noted that al-Fakhr al-Farisi was a famous Hallajian with distinct Ash'arite leanings, suggesting that as an advisor he was both politically influential and spiritually inclined.

As the story goes, when the monk, presumed to be Francis, arrived before the Sultan, he attempted to persuade al-Malik al-Kamil to accept Christianity as the true faith. To prove that the judgment of God was on his side, the monk was willing to submit himself to the *mubâhalä*, the trial by fire.[18] From the perspective of al-Fakhr al-Farisi, there was a real possibility that the monk was a *muwallih*, an expert at walking through fire. It also was conceivable that the monk in question was a truly holy man of God. Moreover, al-Fakhr al-Farisi was probably aware of two critical points; the revelation received by Muhammad that Allah reserved to himself the right to explain fully "the mystery of Christ to angels and man" *and* the Koranic law prohibiting the acceptance of such a challenge on such an issue.[19] Under the circumstances, al-Fakhr al-Farisi most likely advised the Sultan to refuse the ordeal by fire proposed by Francis.[20] Perhaps al-Fakhr al-Farisi recognized in Francis the qualities exhibited by the *Sufis*. Perhaps he perceived Francis to be one of those rare individuals whose life was at once filled up and emptied out by his experience of the divine.[21] To the extent that Francis may have borne some resemblance to a *Sufi* master, the Sultan's advisor quite possibly believed that the spiritual power of the monk had to be taken very seriously. Assuming that al-Fakhr al-Farisi, like many others who shared his spiritual orientation, believed that everything that occurred was willed by God, he even may have given a mystical interpretation to this unexpected encounter with Francis.

The ecclesiastical historian Jacques de Vitry saw Francis in the crusaders' camp at Damietta in 1219. From his *Historia Orientalis*, we learn of Francis's willingness to risk his life in order to meet the Sultan personally.[22] Though in other writings, de Vitry's descriptions of the Saracens, especially the Sultan, are pejorative, the tone seems to change as he describes the monk who captured the imaginations of the Saracen ruler and his people. According to de Vitry, the Sultan's final words to Francis, before ensuring his safe return to the crusaders' camp, included the following request: "Pray for me, that God may reveal to me the law and the faith that is the most pleasing to him."[23] From de Vitry we also learn that the Saracens appeared interested in hearing what Christians had to say about Jesus, the one whom they would have called *Isa bin Mariam*. Contrary to the derogatory propaganda of the Crusades, Christians were only harmed by Muslims when they repudiated the life and teachings of Muhammad the prophet. Thus, if martyrdom at the hands of the Saracens was indeed Francis's primary motivation for meeting the Sultan, he soon learned that such a fate did not necessarily befall those who proclaimed the good news of Jesus Christ and this alone. In characterizing Francis as one who was opposed to provocation, disparagement, and disputation, de Vitry's account suggests that the peace of God to which Francis bore witness seemingly was received and reciprocated.

Ernoul, a chronicler of the Fifth Crusade, provides an account of Francis's encounter with al-Malik al-Kamil that is filled with suspense and intrigue.[24] According to the report, Francis and his companion were not trusted by the papal legate, Cardinal Pelagius, nor by the crusaders at Damietta. Pelagius questioned Francis about his motives for wanting to meet with the Sultan and was intent on persuading him to abandon the idea. When Francis finally made his way into the Saracen camp, however, his motives for doing so were probably as questionable to the Sultan as they had been to the cardinal. Was Francis an ambassador or a defector? In an effort to identify himself appropriately, Francis explained to the Sultan that he was neither an emissary nor a renegade. Francis claimed that he came on God's behalf for the good of the Sultan's soul. In the chronicle, Ernoul portrays Francis as a philosopher of sorts, who attempted to demonstrate by means of logical and persuasive arguments the limitations and insignificance of Islamic law. Francis informed the Sultan that if he was not successful in making a persuasive case, he would readily submit to having his head cut off. The Sultan in consultation with his council of religious leaders and chief advisors was told that not one of his lawyers or philosophers was willing to enter into discussion or debate with the monk. The council's recommendation was that the Sultan decapitate Francis and his companion immediately. The Sultan, however, chose not to comply with the advice of his council. Instead, Ernoul explains, the Sultan, concerned for his own soul, offered to allow Francis to remain in Saracen territory in complete security and prosperity. Francis refused the offer, however, preferring to leave rather than remain in a situation where no one would listen to him or discuss with him. Finally, the Sultan saw to it that the two monks were granted safe passage back to the crusaders' camp. It is worth noting that one of the most interesting facets of Ernoul's chronicle is found in the fact that both Francis and the Sultan were perceived to be at odds with their respective religious leaders and advisors. This reality, however, did not seem to dissuade either of them in pursuing their respective interests in and concerns for the other.

Henry of Avranches, the famed poet laureate and creator of the *Legenda Versificata*,[25] suggests that Francis was convinced that the way to persuade faithful Muslims to accept Christianity was not by derision or force, but by logical argument.[26] According to Henry's poem, Francis was severely mistreated by the Saracens en route to Damietta. Nonetheless, his behavior under such adversity was admired by all. When Francis arrived at Damietta, the Sultan received him with great kindness and solicitude. The only thing that Francis really desired of the Sultan and his philosophers, however, was a hearing. Granted his request, Francis spoke with eloquence and conviction. Yet he soon returned to the crusaders' camp claiming that for "want of ministers to help him," he felt "obliged to abandon the work" he began so well.[27] Ironically, as in the account of Ernoul, this characterization of Francis as philosopher and logician is quite revealing inasmuch as it contradicts in some ways the more familiar image of Francis as one who disdained learning. As these particular sources indicate, the difficulty in ascertaining how Francis actually presented himself and what he actually did before, during, and after his encounter with the Sultan increases with each additional narrative.

In turning to the early Franciscan sources, further insights and complicating factors are brought to bear upon the effort to understand and interpret the story. Among the first of Francis's biographers was Thomas of Celano, an educated friar who was well-known in Assisi and throughout the Germanic provinces. In 1228, two years after the death of Francis, Celano was commissioned by Pope Gregory IX to write the *Vita Prima* in honor of Francis's canonization as a saint. Thomas of Celano's account of Francis's meeting with the Sultan focuses intensely on his desire for martyrdom (I Cel 20.55–57).[28] From Celano, we learn that Francis's journey in 1219 was his third attempt to preach the Christian faith and repentance to the Saracens. During his first attempt (ca. 1213), the ship was forced to return to Italy because of severe storms at sea. In his second attempt, he failed to reach his destination of Morocco, getting no further than Spain. Finally, in 1219, he set sail for the Middle East, arrived in Egypt, and realized his desire to live among the Saracens.

At the time, the Fifth Crusade, proclaimed by Pope Honorius III during the Fourth Lateran Council (1214–16), was at the height of its most violent and intense activity. Saracens were despised throughout Christendom. Given these circumstances, Francis's activities during his journey took on particular significance, both politically and religiously. Though Thomas of Celano reinforces Christian prejudice against the Saracens in his description of the Sultan's soldiers, he nonetheless presents a sympathetic view of the Sultan himself. At the conclusion of his account, Celano recapitulates Francis's desire for martyrdom as the primary motivation for the journey. The fact that Francis was not martyred, however, requires Celano to deal with an unsettling theological question: could it be that martyrdom is not the most pleasing of all offerings to God? In suggesting that God was saving Francis for the singular grace of the stigmata, Celano does his best to gloss over the fact that Francis's testimony neither provoked the Sultan nor converted him. Celano knew very well that in an era of ecclesiastical triumphalism, it was important that Francis not be perceived as a visible failure, whether as a martyr or as a missionary.

Some years later, in 1246, Thomas of Celano was asked by Crescentius, then Minister General of the Franciscan friars, to write the *Vita Secunda*. The purpose of writing this version was to include the stories and testimonies provided by several of Francis's most beloved early companions, some of whom contended that the *First Life* failed to take into consideration several important details of the saint's life. In the *Second Life*, Celano highlights once again Francis's desire for martyrdom (2 Cel IV.30).[29] However, the emphasis in this account is placed on Francis's relationship to the crusaders and his counsel to them that they not engage in battle.

In the midst of his friar companions — Illuminatus, Peter of Catania, Elias, then provincial of Syria, and Caesar of Speyer — Francis supposedly forbade the war and denounced the reasons for engaging in battle. Quoting God's words to Moses (Num 14:41–42), he admonished the crusaders to recognize that their desire for war was not consistent with the will of God. The crusaders took Francis for a fool, and disregarded his advice. Having waged an aggressive war since May 9, 1218, the crusaders believed themselves to be invincible. However, on August 29, 1219, they suffered a significant setback. More than six thousand crusaders were numbered among the dead and captured. After their decimation, questions began to surface regarding the extent to which the continuation of the Fifth Crusade was really in accord with the will of God or humanly motivated for the purposes of amassing power, wealth, and security. In his account of Francis's admonishment of the crusaders and the tragic consequences of their refusal to listen to him, Thomas of Celano is hard pressed to put another spin on Francis's repudiation of armed aggression by Christian soldiers against the people of Damietta. He makes his case by emphasizing the specific nature of the incident, rather than its potential significance as an unrestricted criticism of Christian warfare.

After the battle, efforts between Christians and Saracens to arrange a peaceful settlement took place. However, war broke out again on September 26, 1219.[30] Most likely, it was during this four-week interval of peace between the end of August and the end of September that Francis spent several days with the Sultan.[31] On November 5, 1219, Damietta fell to the crusaders when soldiers under the reluctant command of John de Brienne were reinforced by those of the papal legate, Cardinal Pelagius. Of the original eighty thousand inhabitants of Damietta, fewer than three thousand survived the year-long siege of the crusaders.[32] One cannot help but wonder how the dangerous memories of war and bloodshed, coupled with the remembrances of encounter and relationship, broke open the heart of Francis from the time of his sojourn in Damietta to his own death in October of 1226. Based on evidence from Francis's own writings, it is reasonable to speculate that neither his life nor his prayer was ever the same again.

During the Franciscan General Chapter of 1260, forty years after Francis's encounter with the Sultan, Bonaventure, the newly elected Minister General of the Order, was entrusted with the task of writing a definitive biography of St. Francis based on all of those already in existence. In 1263, his *Legenda Major* was approved. In 1266, "it was prescribed as the only canonical, definitive, and exclusive text, with the order that all earlier biographies be burned."[33] To the extent that certain memories of Francis's actions and attitudes associated with his journey to the Middle East were sources of scandal and signs of contradiction, especially within the Order, it was Bonaventure's task to insure that Francis was identified as closely with Christ as possible and clearly distinguished as different from any number of thirteenth-century heretics. As soon as Bonaventure's *Major Life* was approved, the various hagiographical accounts of Francis's life that had given rise to innumerable controversies, both within the Franciscan Order and outside of it, could be laid to rest. The desired outcome of Bonaventure's project, however, did not came to pass.

The hallmarks of Francis's way of being in the world never lost their critical edge. Inspiring others to give praise to God always and everywhere, to reverence all of creation, to identify with the poor and powerless, and to work on behalf of peace and reconciliation had social, political, economic, and religious consequences of which ecclesiastical and civil authorities were well aware. Whether intended or not, Bonaventure's *Major Life,* in shifting the emphasis away from the temporal challenges of Francis's form of life, attempted to draw attention to the spiritual dimensions of the Poverello's legacy. Following Thomas of Celano, who began his narrative by discussing Francis's desire for martyrdom (LM 9.5),[34] Bonaventure gave another meaning to this desire by focusing on Francis's longing to become like Christ, the one who willingly laid down his life to manifest God's love for all humanity.

Though Bonaventure reveals some of his internalized prejudices against the Saracens in the very style of his writing, his account of the personal dynamics that transpired as Francis as well as a few of his followers encountered Muslims or vice versa is noteworthy. In addition to incorporating some of Celano's descriptions of the Sultan's actions, Bonaventure also includes a story about a certain unnamed Muslim whose kind actions toward a group of friars facilitated their arrival in a pagan land (LM 4.7).[35] Inasmuch as Bonaventure's account of the trial by fire (LM 9.8) provides supporting evidence for the Islamic source associated with Turbat al-Fakhr al-Farisi, it strengthens the possibility that Francis was indeed the monk who is referred to in the inscription.[36] In a similar fashion, Bonaventure's account of Francis's foretelling of the demise of the crusaders in the siege of Damietta serves to reinforce impressions about his visionary character and prophetic spirit (LM 11.3).[37]

Jordan of Giano, an Italian friar and historian of the Franciscan movement in the Germanic provinces, gives details about Francis's journey to Damietta in his *Chronica* that parallel some of the information found in other accounts.[38] Jordan, however, does take the story a step further by preceding his brief narrative on the encounter at Damietta with an account of an action taken by Francis that is open to many possible interpretations. Prior to Francis's journey to Damietta, five friars were killed in Morocco. From Spain to North Africa, they preached against the Koran, condemned Islam, and derided Muhammad. Throughout Christendom such behavior was deemed heroic and worthy of praise. An eyewitness to the friars' beheadings wrote a detailed account of how they earned the crown of martyrdom.

Given the spirit of the times, there is little doubt that the reading of the martyrs' legend would have intensified the animosity of Christians toward Muslims by inciting hatred and vengeance. According to Jordan, Francis prohibited the story of the martyrdom from being read, declaring that no one was to glory in the martyrdom of others.[39] The inclusion of this action in Jordan's *Chronicle* contributes additional background evidence in support of speculations about Francis's growing reverence and respect for Islam and for Muslims. Though it is impossible to know for certain exactly what motivated Francis to issue such a mandate, his encounter with the Sultan as well as the sixteenth chapter of his *Rule of 1221,* which delineates how the friars who live among the Saracens and other nonbelievers are to act, provide a few clues.[40] Though we may not know precisely why Francis acted as he did, it seems evident that his *way of being* was related in some way to his own evolving consciousness of what it meant to be a witness to God's peace and love in the heart of the world.

Other hagiographic accounts of Francis's encounter with the Sultan are found in an anonymous testimony[41] that is believed to have been told to Bonaventure by Brother Illuminatus, and two excerpts from the *Fioretti,* supposedly written by Ugolino di Monte Santa Maria sometime between 1327 and 1342.[42] These particular narratives characterize Francis as being clever, bold, and engaging. In one of these stories, he audaciously outwits the Sultan's advisors. In the other, he outsmarts a prostitute.

The testimony of the anonymous friar suggests that Francis's ideals, as manifested in the actions and writings discussed in the preceding accounts, may not have been broadly shared by other friars, including some of his close companions. In this legend, Francis is depicted as intent on not being outmaneuvered by the doctors and philosophers of the Sultan. When they dare him to walk on a carpet that has crosses woven into it, Francis deals with the challenge by supposedly saying that when Christ died on the cross, two other men were crucified with him. Francis goes on to explain that for him, the crosses woven into the rug represent the crosses of the thieves, not the true cross of Christ. That being said, he defiantly accepts the challenge, walks over the rug, and dismantles the trap of apostasy set for him.

In the two chapters from the *Fioretti,* Ugolino includes some elements gleaned from Celano and Bonaventure, but adds two noteworthy details not mentioned in other texts (Fior 24).[43] The first describes Francis's encounter with a prostitute who propositions him and with whom he agrees to sleep, but only on the condition that she join him in the bed of his choice, which is none other than a flaming fireplace. The second describes the conversion of the Sultan after the death of Francis. Though the two stories are historically questionable, they both hold considerable symbolic power. In particular, the latter story poses a significant challenge to traditional fourteenth-century attitudes about conversion. Without minimizing the fact that the resolution of the story ultimately privileges Christianity, it is important to note how the tale functions as a subliminal criticism of the standard attitudes and practices of arrogance, hostility, conquest, coercion and manipulation. The tale presents an alternative approach to understanding the process of conversion as a process that unfolds over time and in the context of a meaningful relationship.

In summary, the significant differences in perspective that inform and influence these various legends. All of the stories indicate the ways in which a combination of factors related to history, politics, culture, society, religion, and spirituality contributed to shifts in the development and interpretation of a mosaic narrative. Christian chroniclers placed Francis's encounter with the Sultan within the historical and political context of the Crusades. The Franciscan biographers placed it within an ecclesiastical context, emphasizing the spiritual legacy of Francis. The single Islamic source, without necessarily intending to do so, serves to place the encounter within a relational context, at once social and religious, by giving a certain significance to the monk who made a lasting impression on those who received him in Damietta.

Taken as a composite, these diverse writings suggest several things about Francis and the Sultan as well as the nature of their relationship before, during, and after their meeting. These writings also illustrate the variety and complexity of issues surrounding the encounter at Damietta.[44] Above all, they serve as a reminder that any attempt to promote the encounter at Damietta as a point of reference for interreligious encounter and the possibility of genuine dialogue needs to begin by taking seriously all of its paradoxical and contradictory elements as well as its potential for encouraging and enabling others to risk embarking on a journey of the heart.

The *Tariqah* of Dialogue

In the spiritual traditions of Islam, the notion of *tariqah*, understood as the way, the road, the path trodden by the Sufi, gives expression to the experience of a personal faith as it describes the heart's journey toward God. It is a way of being that enables a person to "traverse the infinite distance separating man from God."[45] Because this way is a sacred way it asks everything of the person, not only in terms of what the person possesses, but in terms of who the person is.[46] Given what is known of the life of Francis and his way of being in the world, it could be argued that his journey to the Middle East was indeed a journey of the heart. It also could be said that he dared to discover what would happen if, as a beggar at the threshold of God's door, he risked giving himself over to the experience of letting God be God. But what about the experience of the Sultan? What does his supposed reception, solicitude, and protection of Francis suggest about mutuality and the capacity for genuine dialogue? What might be said of the effect of the encounter on his life and his experience of God?

Various researchers have observed that al-Malik al-Kamil had an affinity toward Sufism and was deeply influenced by Persian mystical poets, such as Rumi and Attar. It would come as no surprise to find a number of his philosophers and theologians somewhat suspicious and apprehensive of the Sultan's sympathy for the mystical traditions of Islam. Inasmuch as Francis bore some resemblance to a Sufi, his manner of life as described to the Sultan by his advisors may have sounded as though it had been taken from the *Ihya Ulum-Id-Din* of al-Ghazai[47] or based on the ethics of *Malamatiya Sufism.*[48] Given the circumstances in Damietta at the time of Francis's arrival,[49] what was the Sultan to make of this monk who in his person appeared to bear witness to so many kindred spiritual values? Was the encounter at Damietta a transformative moment in the lives of Francis and the Sultan? Was it perceived as a journey of the heart by both of them? Could it be said that their relationship with each other served as a lens through which to see a world torn by hatred, fear, and animosity? With an unprecedented clarity of vision, did they dare to gaze into the reality before them, rather than closing their eyes or turning away? Did they prove themselves be seekers of Truth — the *al-Haqq,* capable of living in Truth — true to themselves, to other persons, and to the situations in which they found themselves?[50]

Despite the fact that Francis and al-Malik al-Kamil were different in so many ways, might we speculate that in the context of their encounter at Damietta, they perceived together a "world which was radically different from the one in which their historical roots lie"?[51] Though their respective communities of accountability were culturally distinct, religiously polarized, and politically militant, Francis and the Sultan seem to have shared some awareness of their mutual accountability before God, the Most Gracious, the Most Merciful. Could it be that the power and mystery of their encounter aroused in both of them an overwhelming sense of holy fear and utter amazement, a sense that allowed them to converse — literally, to turn with each other — and in so doing to turn together to the God who first turned to them (*Sura 9:119*)?

As De Beer has observed, "Once [Francis] had met Islam in such an immediate way, he was to emerge marked forever in his thought and in his life."[52] The inner discipline of total obedience to the *call of the Spirit in the heart* required him to abandon every goal and renounce every interest that militated against his one passion: to know God and to do God's will alone.[53] In the eyes of many Christian observers and critics, however, this passion was misguided. Francis accomplished nothing. He did not win the martyr's crown, nor did he convert the Sultan. He did not secure peace between Christians and Muslims, nor did he succeed in promoting the concept of a crusade without weapons. Yet, upon his return from the Middle East to Assisi, Francis appears to have remained convinced that the unprecedented *tariqah* of dialogue was the way of divine inspiration. So deep was his conviction that he made it a part of his *Rule of Life.*[54] In accord with Francis's understanding of the scriptural text as found in the Latin Vulgate, this way of divine inspiration was a way of being "subject to every human creature for God's sake" (I Pet 2:13). It was a way that aroused in him the desire "to live spiritually among the Saracens" as a humble seeker of Truth and a messenger of God's peace and compassion, a way of turning with others to the God who was the first to turn to everyone.

Though history does not supply all the details of what might have happened, could have happened, or should have happened at Damietta, excerpts from Francis's own writings, such as the one described above, do provide some insight into the possible ways in which his experiences in Damietta as well as his relationship with the Sultan informed certain elements of his spirituality and his way of being. Given Francis's particular regard for the Word of God and his admonitions to pray always and everywhere, these particular convictions and exhortations were quite possibly intensified during his journey to the Middle East. Moreover, though it is impossible to prove any direct connection, derivation, or gleaning, it is difficult to overlook altogether the parallels between certain values and spiritual practices of Islam and those espoused by Francis.

Attentive to the internal and external reverence displayed by Muslims, it seems reasonable to argue that Francis was deeply moved by the profound respect which the Saracens had for the written word of the Qur'an and their response to the call to prayer. In his *Letter to the Entire Order* (ca. 1225–26) and in other writings as well[55] Francis emphasizes the need to safeguard and reverence the sacred Scriptures. Whether coincidental or intentionally related to his experiences in Egypt and Syria, Francis writes in his *Letter to the Rulers of the People* (ca. 1219): "And you should manifest such honor to the Lord among the people entrusted to you that every evening an announcement be made by a town crier or some other signal announce that praise and thanks may be given by all people to the all-powerful Lord God."[56] Similar statements appear in two other letters sent to all the local ministers of the Order.[57]

As one of the lesser known legendary accounts of Francis's encounter with the Sultan illustrates, Francis was deeply affected by the regular call to prayer of the *muezzin*. According to this legend, prior to Francis's departure from Damietta, the Sultan wanted to bestow upon him all sorts of presents. Francis, however, declined them all, all but one, the horn of a *muezzin*.[58] In what could be described from the perspective of Francis as a holy exchange, Islam helped Christianity to fulfill its religious commitment.[59] It is quite possible that for Francis the *adhan*, the Muslim call to prayer, represented a difference in religious expression, an Islamic difference which, if reflected upon by Christians as an important spiritual practice, could supply a lost dimension of single-hearted attentiveness on the part of all people to the transcendence of God.

As the Franciscan scholar Leonard Lehmann has observed, under the influence of his encounter with Islam, Francis was compelled, he had no choice: "He had to proclaim his idea of an all-embracing praise of God, which would unite Christians and Muslims in the same intention, so loudly and so emphatically... because such an ecumenical sign that would have united in prayer two antagonistic religious faiths was still inconceivable to the ears of those accustomed to the crusading sermons and to hearts blinded by hatred for Islam."[60] Could it be that as Francis witnessed the desires and devotions of Muslims giving praise and homage to the Most High God, his own prayerful attentiveness to the attributes and actions of God was further deepened and enhanced? When considered in the light of his exposure to Muslim prayers and devotions, was Francis's propensity for addressing God by many names and attributes indicative of something more than his own theological imagination?[61]

As a careful examination of selected passages from Francis's *Writings* reveals, the emphasis that he places on worship, praise, submission, divine inspiration, remembrance, repentance, poverty, peace, pilgrimage, and the unity of God illustrates his attraction to specific concepts which, to greater and lesser degrees, resonate with certain values and spiritual practices of Islam such as *salat, bismillah, islam, fatihah, dhikr, tawbah, faqr, salam, hajj,* and *tawhid.* Without losing sight of the fact that Francis also placed emphasis in many of his writings on some of the tenets of Christianity most problematic for Muslims (e.g. the incarnation of Jesus Christ, the paschal mystery, and the holy Trinity), it is nonetheless important to acknowledge Francis's distinctive way of communicating his profound experience of the absolute transcendence of God and the wonder of creation.

Though it is neither possible nor desirable to make exaggerated claims about the influences or motives that caused Francis to act the way he acted or write what he wrote, when viewed together, the encounter at Damietta and Francis's own writings do provide Christian proponents of the *tariqah* of dialogue with some valuable images and orientations for action. Despite their limitations and ambiguities, these legends and writings enable us to access important questions of conscience, which, unlike the many historical questions that elude us, we are in a position to ask and to answer. Briefly stated, these questions are the questions of beggars, of sisters and brothers, of penitents and pilgrims. The beggar's question leads us to ask: Do we have the courage and creativity to approach the threshold of God's door? The question of sisters and brothers summons us to ask: Are we willing to set aside our security and certainty for the sake of a relationship? The penitent's question urges us to ask: Can we envision a world no longer constrained by the forces of absolutism and doubt, of presumption and despair, of hate and indifference? And finally, the question of pilgrims requires us to ask: Are we prepared to walk humbly on that uncommon ground where nothing less than everything may be asked of us in our search for the face of God and the reality of the Good?

Humbly Seeking the Face of God and the Reality of the Good: Theological Imagination and Moral Agency in a Religiously Pluralistic World

Following the Second Vatican Council (1962–65) and the Assembly of the Seventh Assembly of the World Council of Churches in Nairobi (1975), a growing interest in fostering dialogue among adherents of various religious traditions emerged within and among many Christian churches throughout the world. The rediscovery and retrieval of various elements of the encounter at Damietta provided scholars and religious leaders with a valuable point of reference for their discourse on dialogue, particularly as elaborated by the Faith and Order Commission of the World Council of Churches, the Vatican Secretariat for Non-Christians, and the Pontifical Council on Interreligious Dialogue. What remains an open question, however, is the degree to which such discourse was intelligible and available to communities of faith struggling to come to terms with issues of Christian identity and mission in a pluralistic world.

Speaking from my own context as a North American Christian, impressionistic evidence suggests that many Western Christians continue to have a limited understanding of the beliefs and values of other religious traditions and philosophies of life. Located somewhere on a continuum of awareness that extends from ignorance to superficiality, the knowledge possessed by many individuals and communities ranges from inadequate information to misinformation, from anecdotal caricatures to media spins. The circumstances in which we find ourselves are further complicated by the fact that ecclesial efforts to expose and examine the roots of religious prejudice and intolerance are too few and often too late. As a consequence, we are often constrained in our capacity to comprehend not only what other persons believe, but how they believe as well as why they believe. For many Western Christians, the necessary conditions for genuine dialogue are often lacking or altogether absent.

As Christians entering the twenty-first century, the realities of our world require us to acknowledge that interreligious encounters and efforts at genuine dialogue are more than opportunities for mutual growth and understanding. The capacity to engage in genuine dialogue, understood as the willingness and ability to sustain relationships of respect and concern with people of other religious traditions, is a requisite for world peace, planetary survival, and human dignity. As Harvey Cox has demonstrated throughout his career of charting, comparing and interpreting significant shifts in religion and society, the moral exigencies of dialogue are among the most difficult challenges facing peoples and nations throughout the world. One need not be an authority on religious, political, economic, or cultural matters to recognize the complexity, risk, uncertainty, and urgency of cultivating relationships of trust and interdependency within and among religious traditions.

We are conscious of the fact that as Western Christians we can no longer distance ourselves from the world of others in order to live our own truth more securely.[62] I believe the encounter at Damietta is worthy of our consideration as a relevant moral lesson for our times. Not only does it provide us with a point of reference for understanding the *tariqah* or way of dialogue, but it also summons us to recognize that the moral of the story demands as much of our wills as it does of our intellects and memories. The story suggests that the *tariqah* of dialogue leads those who risk the journey to important discoveries about themselves and others, discoveries that can only be made in the context of relationships. Though this does not mean that the way of dialogue culminates in a reduction of differences between religions and their respective truth claims,[63] it does mean that adherents of different religious traditions may find some value in pondering what it means to regard oneself or another as a beggar at the threshold of God's door. Though not everyone may acknowledge or embrace such an identity, the very process of consideration may offer some modest insight into the religious experience of those who believe themselves to be guided by the one who is all good and all merciful into the midst of a world of unfamiliar relationships, not so much to prove the truth of their religious convictions as to walk in this truth faithfully and compassionately.

To the extent that our capacity for theological imagination and moral agency are accepted as preconditions for authentically entering into genuine dialogue, the mutual desire to seek the other's good is inevitably coupled with the ability to imagine the face of the other's God. It is a total response to the call which begins each day for Muslims: *Hayya ila-l-falah* — "Come to the good."[64] Inasmuch as suspicions and denunciations of theological imagination are present in many religious traditions, including Christianity and Islam, it should come as no surprise to find people who risk embarking on a journey of the heart the subjects of criticism and misunderstanding by their own religious authorities as well as the people closest to them. Though all forms of theological imagination may not fall under such scrutiny, the real and perceived dangers of theological imagination are an ongoing source of anxiety and concern for many. One fear is that theological imagination leads to a dissolution of distinctions, a perspective that is based upon a "sense of underlying oneness" that subordinates religion and undermines religious traditions.[65] A second fear is that theological imagination can lead to an intensification of distinctions, a perspective that is based upon a profound sense of awe, wonder, and reverence for the divinely created "thisness" of every creature.[66] A third fear is that people known for their theological imagination are frequently individuals and communities whose moral agency is not controlled by the apprehensions and the judgments of others, a perspective held by people who, in their search for the face of God and the reality of the Good, dare to walk humbly, to act justly, and to love tenderly (Mic 6:8).

As Iris Murdoch notes in her essay *On 'God' and 'Good,'* "Morality has always been connected with religion and religion with mysticism. The disappearance of the middle term leaves morality in a situation which is certainly more difficult, but essentially the same. The background to morals is properly some sort of mysticism, if by this is meant a non-dogmatic essentially unformulated faith in the reality of the Good."[67] Perhaps, more than unformulated, this faith in the reality of the Good may be better described as the place where theological imagination and moral agency meet. To suggest that the encounter at Damietta was such a place is to suggest that both Francis and the Sultan acted faithfully in what each perceived to be the service of God. More likely than not, both of them had some uncertainty about the correctness of their actions, not only because of the potential shortcomings of their respective insights and calculations, but also because of who they were and what they represented. Nevertheless, they seem to have recognized that fidelity to God required of them both a daring creativity and an uncommon courage. They were, in the words of James Horne, moral mystics who were called "not only to take God's commands seriously, but also to recognize with a certain humility, doubt, or sense of the absurd that they were involved in matters that they personally had to think through and decide without being sure that they were at one with God in their final decision."[68]

In seeking the reality of the Good, they had to trust the way in which God intervened between them and their hearts (*Sura* 8:24). In order to do this, a fundamental understanding of the heart/mind, the *qalb*, the seat of the most secret and genuine thoughts of the human person, was indispensable.[69] Possessing this essential knowledge, they could affirm that there was no God other than God. They could allow their actions to give expression to their convictions. God was their creator. They were God's creatures. I venture to say that as beggars at the threshold of God's door, they experienced together the mystery of God's holy manner of working. With hearts broken open by humility, these beggars approached the "God whose door never closes," trusting they would never be turned away.[70] And what about those of us who are intrigued by these insights? Do we dare consider their implications for our own times? Do we risk responding to the pragmatists' question of "So what?" — the question which my years of study and colleagueship with Harvey have taught me never to forget?

As I was working on this essay, my attention was drawn daily to photographs and news releases about the children of our world, whose spirits are broken by different, yet common, experiences of violence, fear, misery, and loss. Haunted by my own recollections of their faces and their stories, it seems to me that the purpose of this essay would be lost if I failed to conclude without offering a response to the pragmatist's question: beyond the immediate objective of this volume, of what real consequence is this research or reflection for the lives of real people, especially the children of our world?

We know from the work of many individuals and groups, the topics discussed in this essay are not peripheral to the moral, political, and perhaps, most importantly, spiritual lives of children.[71] In a religiously pluralistic world, we cannot allow this fact to be lost amidst our preoccupation with reality as understood, experienced, and interpreted primarily by adults. We ignore the intergenerational implications of what it means for children to be beggars at the threshold of God's door at the cost of our own integrity as adults entrusted with the sacred responsibility of caring for the next generation.

Given the number of situations around the globe where the name of God or the values of religious traditions are invoked to justify hatred, violence, and war, it is important to look critically at the ways in which reports from agencies and bureaus dedicated to the service of children alert us to the battles and conflicts that are waged on the backs of children in nearly every region of our world. How is it that we envision any of these children keeping faith, any faith, in a world where adults of the same faith as well as other faiths have betrayed them? What, if anything, can or should they expect from the adults they encounter at the threshold of God's door? Perhaps, the most they can hope for from those of us persuaded by the urgency and indispensability of interreligious encounter and efforts at genuine dialogue is the collective courage and boldness to ask one of the most difficult questions of these times in which we live: Why is the child crying? Why are the children crying? As we take our place at the threshold of God's door in the company of all beggars, penitents, and pilgrims, especially the small brothers and sisters we call children, do we dare to listen for the answer?

It is said that a few years after his return from the Middle East, Francis prepared a Christmas crib scene for the people living in the town of Greccio. A witness claimed that he "saw a little child lying in the manger lifeless, and he saw the holy man of God go up to it and rouse the child as if from a deep sleep."[72] For many, the pageant at Greccio was and continues to be understood as a creative innovation to celebrate the birth of Jesus. For Francis, however, I believe this gesture may have meant something more. I would like to suggest that it may have been his own way of embodying, representing, or making meaning of the dangerous and haunting memory of the crusaders' capture of Damietta. For whatever his encounter with the Sultan may or may not have meant, could Francis ever forget the faces of the infants of Damietta of whom Oliver of Paderborn, recalling the words of the prophet and psalmist, wrote: "Little ones asked for bread and there was none to break for them (Is 14:5, Ps 74:11; 65:5), infants hanging at the breasts of their mothers opened their mouths in the embrace of one dead."[73] Could it be that as a beggar at the threshold of God's door, the Christmas crib at Greccio allowed Francis, a person of theological imagination and moral agency, to draw the world's attention not only to the integrity and vulnerability of one child, but ultimately to the integrity and vulnerability of every child?

Conclusion

At the beginning of this essay, I proposed that the encounter at Damietta be considered as a moral lesson for own times. After surveying insights from various narratives dealing with the encounter at Damietta, I explored the writings of Francis for traces of evidence to explain how he was informed and influenced by his sojourn among the Saracens. I suggested that the *tariqah* of dialogue was predicated on a relationship of mutual concern and I identified Francis and al-Malik al-Kamil as exemplars of theological imagination and moral agency.

In conclusion, I would like to add that Francis believed that what he was before God that he was and nothing more.[74] In an attitude of humility, submission, and total dependence on the most high God, he set himself as a beggar at the threshold of God's door. For Francis, this image was more than a metaphor for his existence, it was at the heart of his way of being in the world — as beggar, as brother, as penitent, as pilgrim — as one who, more than anything else, desired to teach more by example than by word.

As a Franciscan and one privileged to know Harvey Cox as professor, colleague, and friend, I have valued his affection for the life and legacy of Francis of Assisi, and in particular, his own way of teaching by example. Like many others, in the company of Harvey Cox, I have had the opportunity to discover what it truly means to find myself at the threshold of God's door, that place of theological imagination and moral agency where differences are not diminished, where traditions are not relativized, and where histories are not forgotten. Consistently, through his example and his word, Harvey Cox has reminded the academy, the church, and the larger world that our experiences at the crossroads of religion and society reveal important theological and moral insights about the thisness of our existence, the immediacy of our condition, and the resiliency of our will to hope.

As theologian, as teacher, and above all, as a man who has risked embarking on journeys of the heart, Harvey Cox continues to find new ways of being present with others at the threshold of God's door. And in the process, he rarely misses an opportunity to raise the unsettling questions of our day with courage and creativity. With more than questions, Harvey Cox has encouraged us to open our hearts, our minds, and our very lives to one fundamental insight: God not only gives us the future, but the freedom to shape it.

Notes

1. Harvey Cox, *Many Mansions* (Boston: Beacon Press, 1988), 212.

2. One of many examples is found in the autobiography of the Russian religious philosopher, Nikolai Berdyaev (1874–1948). See *Dream and Reality: An Essay in Autobiography,* trans. Katherine Lampert (New York: Macmillan Company, 1951),

211–12. Renowned for his strong affirmation of the primacy of a "transcendent world of the spirit" over against the world of things and objects, Berdyaev identified Francis of Assisi as the "image of transfigured human nature." In accord with Berdyaev's thought, Francis attained to a vision of truth, "not by observation of things, but by a near-mystical creative act of intuition," coupled with the ability to bring about a reconciliation between the vision of truth and the way things are. See also "Francis of Assisi," *Westminster Dictionary of Church History,* ed. Jerald C. Brauer (Philadelphia: Westminster Press, 1971), 106–7.

3. The notion of *thisness* is an English rendering of what the Franciscan philosophical theologian John Duns Scotus described as *haecceitas.* See Mary Beth Ingham, "The Harmony of Goodness: Mutuality as a Context for Scotus' Moral Framework" in *The Ethical Method of John Duns Scotus,* in *Spirit and Life* 3 (1993): 63–65.

4. James M. Powell, *Anatomy of a Crusade 1213–1221* (Philadelphia: University of Pennsylvania Press, 1986), 157–93.

5. Jacques de Vitry, *History of the Orient,* chap. 32, in *Thirteenth Century Testimonies,* Theophilus Desbonnets and Damien Vorreux, O.F.M., eds., trans. Paul Oligny, O.F.M., in Marion Habig, O.F.M., ed., *St. Francis of Assisi: Writings and Early Biographies* (Chicago: Franciscan Herald Press, 1973), 1612–13.

6. *Chronique d'Ernoul et des Bernard le trésorier* (Paris: Ed. L. de Mas Latrie, 1871).

7. Jordan of Giano, *The Chronicle of Brother Jordan of Giano,* nn. 10–14, in *Thirteenth Century Chronicles,* Marie-Therese Laureilhe, ed., trans. Placid Hermann, O.F.M. (Chicago: Franciscan Herald Press, 1961). See also Leonardus Lemmens, O.F.M., ed., *Testimonia minora saeculi XIII de S. Francisco Assisiensi* (Quaracchi, 1926).

8. Gregory Shanahan, "Henry of Avranches: Poem on the Life of Saint Francis (*Legenda Sancti Francisci Versificata*)," *Franciscan Studies* 48 (1988): 125–212.

9. Thomas of Celano, *First Life and Second Life of St. Francis with selections from Treatise on the Miracles of Bl. Francis,* trans. Placid Hermann, O.F.M., in Habig, ed., *St. Francis of Assisi,* 274–77.

10. Bonaventure, *Major Life of St. Francis with Excerpts from Other Works,* trans. Benen Fahy, O.F.M., in Habig, ed., *St. Francis of Assisi,* 701.

11. Anonymous, *St. Francis and the Sultan of Egypt,* in *Thirteenth Century Chronicles,* 1614–15. See also Giralomo Golubovich, O.F.M., *Biblioteca bio-bibliografica della Terra Santa,* vol. 1 (Quaracchi, 1906), 36–37.

12. Ugolino di Monte Santa Maria, *Little Flowers of St. Francis,* trans. Raphael Brown, in Habig, ed., *St. Francis of Assisi,* 1353–56.

13. Several scholars rely on a standard reference to fragments of the chronicle of Al-Zayyat as cited in the work by Ahmad Yusuf, *Turbat al-Fakhr al-Farisi* (Cairo: n.p., 1922).

14. In developing this section, I am indebted to the scholarship of Francis De Beer for his insights and provocative questions regarding Francis and his encounter with the Sultan at Damietta. Given my own reliance on De Beer's research, I recommend his book in its entirety to interested readers. See Francis De Beer, *We Saw Brother Francis,* trans. Maggie Despot and Paul Lachance, O.F.M. (Chicago: Franciscan Herald Press, 1983).

15. Hans Ludwig Gottschalk, *Al-Malik al-Kamil von Ägypten und seine Zeit: eine Studie zur Geschichte Vorderasiens und Ägyptens in der ersten Hälfte 7.13. Jahrhunderts* (Wiesbaden: O. Harrassowitz, 1958).

16. Martiniano Roncaglia, *St. Francis of Assisi and the Middle East*, trans. Stephen A. Janto, 3d ed. (Cairo: Franciscan Center of Oriental Studies, 1957), 28; and Louis Massignon, *The Passion of al-Hallaj, Mystic and Martyr of Islam*, trans. Herbert Mason; 4 vols. (Princeton: Princeton University Press, 1982), 2:299–300.

17. As translated in Roncaglia, *St. Francis of Assisi*, 26. See Roncaglia's specific references to the research of Ahmad Yusuf, *Turbat al-Fakhr al-Farisi* (Cairo: n.p., 1922) 17–18; and Louis Massignon, *Journal Asiatique* 240 (1952): 413–14; along with Roncaglia's own treatment of the question in "Fonte arabo-musulmana su S. Francesco in Oriente?" *Studi Francescani* 25 (1953): 258–59. Likewise see Francis De Beer, "St. Francis and Islam," in Christian Duquoc and Casiano Floristan, eds., *Francis of Assisi Today*, trans. Francis McDonagh, Concilium Series 149 (New York: Seabury, 1981), 14.

18. Massignon, *The Passion of al-Hallaj*, 1. 553.

19. Anthony Mockler, *Francis of Assisi: The Wandering Years* (Oxford: Phaidon, 1976), 243.

20. Massignon, *The Passion of al-Hallaj*, 2:299–300.

21. Ibid., 2: 301.

22. *History of the Orient*, chap. 32, in *Thirteenth Century Testimonies* in Habig, ed., *St. Francis of Assisi*, 1612–13.

23. Ibid., 1612. For further discussion of this point, see "Franciscan Mission Among The Muslims," in *Missionszantrale der Franziskaner*, ed., *Build With Living Stones: Correspondence Course on the Franciscan Missionary Charism*, trans. Franciscan Federation of the United States (Pittsburgh: Franciscan Federation, 1986), 20.6.

24. For a detailed analysis of Ernoul's chronicle, see De Beer, "Francis and Islam," 12.

25. In the opinion of some scholars this epic poem was among the most accessible and widely known legends of Francis of Assisi. For the most part, the poem was a biographical versification of Thomas of Celano, *First Life of Saint Francis.*

26. Ibid., 13.

27. Ibid., 12–13.

28. Thomas of Celano, *First Life and Second Life of St. Francis with selections from Treatise on the Miracles of Bl. Francis*, trans. Placid Hermann, O.F.M., in Habig, ed., *St. Francis of Assisi*, 274–77.

29. Ibid., 388–89.

30. Oliver of Paderborn, *The Capture of Damietta*, trans. John J. Gavigan (Philadelphia: University of Pennsylvania Press, 1948), 22–49.

31. Celano, *First Life of St. Francis*, 57 (nn. 188–90), in Habig, ed., *St. Francis of Assisi*, 276–77, 573. Some scholars speculate that, while Francis may have been in Damietta in August, it is possible that he did not actually meet with the Sultan until early December. This dating would conform to information provided in Jacques de Vitry's *Sixth Letter.* See Mockler, *Francis of Assisi*, 238–39.

32. Oliver of Paderborn, *The Capture of Damietta*, 54. Cf. Celano, *Second Life of St. Francis*, 30 (n. 10), in Habig, ed., *St. Francis of Assisi*, 388, 589.

33. Damien Vorreux, O.F.M., "Introduction to the Major and Minor Life of St. Francis," in Habig, ed., *St. Francis of Assisi,* 615.

34. Bonaventure, *Major Life,* 701.

35. Ibid., 658.

36. Ibid., 703–4.

37. Ibid., 713.

38. Jordan of Giano, *The Chronicle,* nn. 10–14, in *Thirteenth Century Chronicles,* Laureilhe, ed. See also Leonardus Lemmens, O.F.M., ed., *Testimonia minora saeculi XIII de S. Francisco Assisiensi* (Quaracchi, 1926).

39. *Chronicle of Jordan of Giano,* n. 8. See Mockler, 237–38.

40. In the *Rule of 1221* (*Regula non bullata*), written within a year of his return from Egypt, Francis emphasizes that the brothers who feel so inspired are to go *among* the Saracens as witnesses of Christ's peace. In an era when Christian missionaries sought to convert Saracens as Christian soldiers waged war *against* them, this *Earlier Rule* represents a radical departure from the attitudes of Francis's ecclesiastical and political contemporaries. See *Regula non bullata* 16.3–6, "Unde quicumque frater voluerit ire *inter* saracenos et alios infideles, vadat de licentia sui ministri et servi...quod non faciant lites neque contentiones, sed sint subditi omni humanae creaturae propter Deum (I Pet 2:13)" in Cajetan Esser, O.F.M., ed., *Opuscula Sancti Patris Francisci Assisiensis* (Grottaferrata [Roma]: Collegio S. Bonaventura di Quaracchi, 1978), 268. See also Regis J. Armstrong, O.F.M. Cap. and Ignatius C. Brady, O.F.M., eds., *Francis and Clare: The Complete Works* (New York: Paulist, 1982), 121–22.

41. Anonymous, *St. Francis and the Sultan of Egypt,* in *Thirteenth Century Chronicles,* 1614–15. See also Giralomo Golubovich, O.F.M., *Biblioteca bio-bibliografica della Terra Santa,* vol. 1 (Quaracchi, 1906), 36–37.

42. Ugolino was a sympathizer with the ascetical ideals of the Spiritual Franciscans, many of whom were condemned as heretics for following the apocalyptic ideas advanced by the followers of Joachim of Fiore, a twelfth-century Calabrian Cistercian whose views on the poverty of Christ, the future age of the Holy Spirit, and the open vision of God challenged the institutional church to its very foundations. See Vida Dutton Scudder, *The Franciscan Adventure: A Study of the First One Hundred Years of the Order of St. Francis of Assisi* (New York: E. P. Dutton, 1931), 136–44. Scudder's fascinating research makes reference to several sources that trace the influence of Islamic mysticism on Joachim of Fiore during his youth. Note pp. 136–37, along with references on p. 152.

43. Ugolino di Monte Santa Maria, *Little Flowers of St. Francis,* trans. Raphael Brown, in Habig, ed., *St. Francis of Assisi,* 1353–56.

44. For further discussion of this point, see De Beer, *We Saw Brother Francis,* 26.

45. Jean-Louis Michon, "The Spiritual Practices of Sufism," in Seyyed Hossein Nasr, ed., *Islamic Spirituality: Foundations* (World Spirituality: An Encyclopedic History of the Religious Quest; vol. 19; New York: Crossroad, 1987), 270.

46. Charis Waddy, *The Muslim Mind* (London: Longman Group Ltd., 1976), 153–54.

47. Upon reading through texts of al-Ghazali, I find intriguing similarities between the ideas he puts forth in selected writings (e.g., *The Book of Worship, The Book of Worldly Usages, The Book of Destructive Evils,* and *The Book of Construc-*

tive Virtues) and the ideas presented in the writings of Francis (e.g., *The Admonitions* and his *Earlier and Later Rules*) that are well worth further study and comparative analysis. See Imam Abu Hamid Muhammad al-Ghazali, *Ihya Ulum-Id-Din,* trans. Maulana Fazal-ul-Karim, 2 vols. (Lahore, Pakistan: Islamic Book Foundation, 1401/ 1981); and Armstrong and Brady, eds., *Francis and Clare,* 25–36, 107–35, 136–45.

48. Further comparative work could be done as well on the *Forty-Five Articles of the Malamatiya* as recorded by al-Sulami and Francis's *Admonitions.* See Morris S. Seale, "The Ethics of *Malamatiya Sufism* and the Sermon on the Mount," *Muslim World* 8:1 (1968):12–23; and Armstrong and Brady, eds., *Francis and Clare,* 25–36.

49. According to Roncaglia, evidence suggests that Francis arrived "beneath the walls of Damietta before August 29, 1219, a day on which the crusaders suffered a terrible rout, easily foreseeable, given the incurable discord that reduced the crusaders' camp to an anarchic mass. Instead of annihilating the remaining crusaders' forces, the Sultan al-Kamel Mohammed (1218–38), fearing, in all probability, want and hunger resulting from the Nile's failure to overflow, proposed a truce." During the next four weeks (August 29 to September 26, 1219), Francis most likely approached the demarcation lines during a period of diplomatic relations that could not have occurred in a period of siege. The fact that Saracen sentinels made it possible for Francis to see the Sultan suggests that rather "unusual" circumstances prevailed. See Roncaglia, *St. Francis and the Middle East,* 27–28.

50. Wilfred Cantwell Smith, "A Human View of Truth," in John Hick, ed., *Truth and Dialogue in World Religions: Conflicting Truth Claims* (Philadelphia: Westminster, 1974), 22.

51. See Lamin Sanneh's discussion of "Prayer and Worship [Muslim and Christian]: Challenges and Opportunities," in S. J. Samartha and J. B. Taylor, eds., *Christian-Muslim Dialogue: Papers Presented at the Broumana Consultation,* July 12–18, 1972 (Geneva: World Council of Churches, 1973), 110–11.

52. De Beer, "St. Francis and Islam," 17.

53. See segments from "Saleh's Advice on the Way," in Waddy, *The Muslim Mind,* 156–57.

54. See n. 39.

55. Armstrong and Brady, eds., *Francis and Clare,* 59.

56. Ibid., 78.

57. "First and Second Letters to the Custodians," in Armstrong and Brady, eds., *Francis and Clare,* 52–54.

58. "Franciscan Mission Among the Muslims," 20.10.

59. Essentially, this reflects the position taken by Veena Das regarding the value of interreligious dialogue as noted by J. M. West, "Bridges and Barriers," 7.

60. Quoted in "Franciscan Mission among the Muslims," in *Build with Living Stones,* 20.9, with general reference to the article by Leonard Lehmann, O.F.M., "Der Brief des hl. Franziskus an die Lenker der Völker Aufbau und missionarische Anliegen," *Laurentianum* 25 (1984): 287–324.

61. Examples of such prayers in Armstrong and Brady, eds., *Francis and Clare,* include: *Canticle of Brother Sun* (38–39); *Letter to the Entire Order,* 50–52 (60); *Letter to the Faithful,* 61–62 (71); *Praises of God* (99–100); *Praises to be said at all the Hours* (101–2); *Prayer inspired by the Our Father* (104–6); the *Earlier Rule,* 22 (130–34).

62. J. Michael West, "Bridges and Barriers," *The Harvard Divinity Bulletin* 15:2 (1984–85): 7.

63. Ibid., 7.

64. Kenneth Cragg, *The Call of the Minaret* (Maryknoll, N.Y.: Orbis Books, 1986), 203.

65. Wayne Proudfoot, "Mysticism, the Numinous and the Moral," *Journal of Religious Ethics* 4 (Spring 1976), 7; and James R. Horne, *The Moral Mystic* (Waterloo, Ontario: 1983), 23–24.

66. See n. 2.

67. Iris Murdoch, "On 'God' and 'Good'," in *The Sovereignty of the Good* (London: Routledge & Kegan Paul, 1970), 66.

68. Horne, *The Moral Mystic,* 69.

69. Duncan Black MacDonald, "The Discipline of the Traveler on his Way to the Unseen and the Nature, Working and Use of the Heart," in *The Religious Attitude and Life in Islam* (Chicago: University of Chicago Press, 1909), 220–51.

70. See *Mukhtasaru ad'iyati Ramadan,* in Constance Padwick, *Muslim Devotions: A Study of Prayer Manuals in Common Use* (London: SPCK, 1961), 219.

71. For further discussion of this point, see the many works of Robert Coles, especially *The Spiritual Lives of Children* (Boston: Houghton Mifflin, 1990).

72. Celano, *First Life of St. Francis,* 86, in Habig, ed., *St. Francis of Assisi,* 301. See also Bonaventure, *Major Life,* 10.7, in Habig, ed., *St. Francis of Assisi,* 710–11.

73. Oliver of Paderborn, *The Capture of Damietta,* 53–54.

74. *Admonition* 19, in Armstrong and Brady, eds., *Francis and Clare,* 33.

16

A KABBALAH FOR
THE ENVIRONMENTAL AGE

Arthur Green

A longing for Kabbalah is abroad in the land. People with little connection to Judaism, no knowledge of Hebrew, many of them in fact non-Jews, are seeking initiation into the secret chambers of Jewish esoteric knowledge. Differing from the interest in Hasidism that centered mostly around HaBaD in the preceding decades, this turn to Kabbalah has rather little to do with Jewish observance or with nostalgia for a romanticized *shtetl* past (a past that many denizens of "Kabbalah Centers" in fact do not share). The Kabbalah seekers are after the Truth, with a capital T. That this truth might also help them to solve personal problems, to predict the future, and to win fame and fortune are claims made only by the sleaziest part of the Kabbalah sales force. Like all the waves of spiritual search that have struck our shores (the Pacific being hit with greater force than the Atlantic, for some reason), the contemporary interest in Kabbalah contains a wide range of seekers. The most serious spend long years at it, realizing that mastery of a complex teaching and way of thought does not come easily. Eventually they realize that they have to study Hebrew. More than any other of the world's mystical teachings, Kabbalah is itself a language, but one constituted by wordplays, numerical computations, meditations on letters, on names of God, and on strange readings of biblical verses — all of them rooted in the Hebrew. Others look for teachers who will distill the wisdom of the ancients, in this unique Jewish garb, for those who lack the time or patience to master the language as well as the secret doctrine.

The magnificent architectonics of the Kabbalists' vision cannot be articulated here. Their grand picture of the inner universe, in which the one that encompasses all being opens up to reveal itself as ten, is the beginning of the Kabbalistic system. The ten *sefirot* (literally: "numbers") are stations in the flow of energy from the one into the many. The ten-in-one cosmos is a way of responding to the eternal mystical question, "How do the many proceed from the one?" The Kabbalists say: "Very slowly and subtly. Let us show you the process." As one gets farther into Kabbalah it turns out that each of the ten *sefirot* contains all the other nine and the whole process of tenfold manifestation repeats itself four times as one journeys through various upper or inner "worlds." There is thus a basic "grid" of four hundred rungs, each discussed with great finesse in the highly refined symbolic language of Kabbalah. Other versions of the Kabbalistic "map" have the ten *sefirot* open themselves further to reveal more decades, becoming hundreds, thousands, and so forth.

For the initiate, the *sefirot* also serve as rungs or marking points of the mystic's inward journey. His goal (it only can become "hers" in very recent times) is to reverse the journey of God from unity into multiplicity, going back to make the many into one again. The Kabbalist who "ascends" those rungs ideally "uplifts" the lower worlds, taking them along on the journey back to oneness. In this way they, along with the mystic's own soul, may be reincluded in the one. This is the Kabbalistic concept of *tikkun*, the restoration of the worlds to their original harmony as carried out in this "uplifting" activity of the mystical life. Each person is a microcosm, also built in that same pattern of the *sefirot*, so that cosmology and psychology, our ways of understanding life's origins and our own innermost selves, are quite identical. God's cosmic journey into multiplicity and your inward journey into unity are mirror images of one another.

This "great chain of being" approach to spirituality can be appreciated more than ever by postmoderns, not only for its beauty but for a certain dimly perceived accuracy as well. Each human being contains the entire universe, claims the ancient myth. All the rungs of descent (and potential ascent) are contained in each soul. But that is true, even in demythologized form: all our ancestors, each stage and mini-step in the evolution of life that brought us to where we are today, are present within us. The DNA that constitutes the life-identity of each of us exists indeed *zekher le-ma'aseh bereshit*, "in memory of the act of creation," linking us back to our most remote origins.

Part of our work as self-aware, articulate beings is converting that biological "memory" into consciousness and building a holy structure (i.e., a religion or a civilization) that articulates and sanctifies those links. In this way the actual fact of all our past's presence within us is converted into a basis for meaning, for expression of our deep rootedness in all that is and has come before us. The memory of the entire universe lies within us. Hopefully the values represented by that ongoing project of civilization-building will lead us forward as well, helping us realize that we must be faithful transmitters to all the many future links in the evolutionary chain, just as we are the grateful recipients of the efforts of all those who have fought the ongoing life-struggle to bring us to this moment. All of the upper and lower "worlds" of the Kabbalist here become manifest in human terms, as generations that lie before and behind us but also as multiple layers of human self-awareness that we seek to peel back in search of our deepest and truest selves.

But in order to constitute Judaism, the single structure of cosmos and mind has to constitute the inner structure of Torah as well. The old rabbinic version of correspondences claimed that the 613 commandments of Torah stand parallel to the 248 limbs and 365 muscles or sinews that comprise each human body (based on the knowledge of anatomy current in fourth- or fifth-century Babylonia!). The human being is thus a microcosm of Torah, itself the blueprint through which God created the cosmos. This structure is overlaid on the tenfold sefirotic structure of Kabbalah. Torah itself, according to the Kabbalists, is an elaborate construction, a cosmic weave of letters drawn wholly out of the four semi-consonants *Yod He Waw He,* the verbal noun that tries to express the divine self. This name is an impossible conflation of the verb "to be"; hence the God of Exodus, where the name is introduced, says: "I shall be whatever I shall be," meaning that the elusive self of the universe will ever escape definition. These four letters are really a term for being — HaWaYaH — itself. But because they are mere breath, they also stand for the birth of language itself, the emergence of the word from the universal silence beyond, from what we Jews call the eternal Torah of God, the wordless truth that "was" before Creation.

God *is* Being: Y-H-W-H, when existence is seem from a fully unitive, harmonic, and all-embracing point of view — a perspective that ever eludes us mere humans, located as we are in particular identities of time and space. The small self and its limitations keep us from seeing the great self at work both within and around us. But then the letters, like pieces in a puzzle, are mysteriously rearranged and HaWaYaH, existence itself, reveals itself to be none other than Y-H-W-H, the great and powerful name that could be spoke only by the high priest on Yom Kippur, alone in the innermost holy chamber of the holy Temple.

We are no longer really Kabbalists. The old system, *qua* system, does not work for us. The mythic universe of Kabbalah, for all its beauty, belongs to another age. Whether we look at hierarchical structure, at the Jewish exclusivism and spiritual racism implied by Kabbalah, or at the passive-subject role assigned to the feminine, I for one do not believe that a return to the mentality of the ancients is the solution to our current woes. Instead, our age is very much in need of a post-Kabbalistic Jewish mysticism, one richly nourished, but not dominated, by the old language and structure. Most importantly, we need a new sort of Jewish piety, a religious attitude fitting to an environmentally concerned future that is already upon us. Among the elements I seek is a Judaism unafraid to proclaim the holiness of the natural world, one that sees creation, including both world and human self, as reflection of divinity and a source of religious inspiration. It is in this spirit that I turn to Kabbalah, seeking to learn from, but also to adapt and transform, its vision. The insight that God and universe are related not primarily as creator and creature, but as deep structure and surface, a central insight of the mystical tradition, is key to the Judaism of the future.

The ways in which we develop and act upon that insight will have to be appropriate to our own age.

Our beginning point is beyond Kabbalah, back in the biblical tale of origins. The Kabbalists' universe depends entirely on the much older biblical creation tale, the ingenious opening chapter of Genesis that for nearly twenty-five hundred years served as chief source for the West's understanding of natural, including human, origins. The account of how God in six days spoke each order of existence into being is now of only antiquarian interest as an actual account of how the world came to be, though it remains alive for us as a liturgical text and a source of mythic creativity.

But I would like to lift the veil behind Genesis 1 and ask just what it was that this magnificently penned single chapter managed to accomplish. The old Mesopotamian and Canaanite creation myths, now barely recalled, were well-known to the biblical authors. They include the rising up of the primal forces of chaos, represented chiefly by Yam or Tiamat, gods of the sea, against the order being imposed by the sky-gods. The defeat of that primordial rebellion and its bloody end is well-documented, as scholars have shown, in a number of passages within the Bible: in the prophets, Psalms, Job, and by subtle implication even in the Genesis text itself. That tale of origins was a part of the cultural legacy of ancient Israel. The fact that it is reflected even in postbiblical Midrashic sources shows that it had a long life, continuing even into the Zohar of the thirteenth century. The original readers/hearers of Genesis 1, in other words, know of another account of creation, one of conflict, slaughter, and victory, "the survival of the fittest" among the gods. What is striking about this account is precisely the absence of those elements of conflict: Genesis 1 offers a purely harmonistic version of the origin of creatures, one where everything has its place as the willed creation of the single deity and all conflict has mysteriously been forgotten.

Our civilization has been transformed over the past century and a half in no small part by our acceptance of a new tale of origins, one that began with Darwin and is refined daily by the work of life scientists and physicists, the new Kabbalists of our age who claim even to know the black hole out of which being itself came to be, speculating on the first few seconds of existence as our ancestors once did on the highest triad of the ten *sefirot* or rungs of divine being. The history of living creatures is again depicted as a bloody and violent struggle, the implications of which for human behavior — even for the possibilities of human ethics — have hardly gone unnoticed. We, too, are urgently in need of a new and powerfully harmonistic vision, one that will allow even the weakest and most threatened of creatures a legitimate place in this world and protection from being wiped out at the careless whim of the creature whose stands, for now, at the top of the evolutionary mound of corpses. A beautiful attempt at articulating such a vision was made by Brian Swimme and Thomas Berry a few years ago in their *The Universe*

Story. Such a vision more willing to base itself in part on the biblical/Judaic mythic legacy would also be a welcome contribution.

But let us return for a moment to the old creation tale. While I no longer believe it in any literal sense and do not look to it, even through reinterpretation (each "day" is a geologic era, etc.), as a source of information about geo-history, I claim it still as a religious text for me as a Jew and for us as a people. We still read it in the synagogue and its closing section is the introductory rubric for our most precious and best-beloved sacred form: the observance of the Sabbath. "Heaven and earth were finished, and all their hosts...." What then does the text mean to me? What underlies the myth, or what truth or value am I implying by so privileging this ancient text?

The text says that before there were many, there was only the one. Before the incredible variety and richness of life as we know it could come to be, there had to exist a simple self, a source from which all the many proceeded. I refer not to some single-celled amoeba that existed in the ocean hundreds of millions of years ago. I read the text on a different level by asserting that the primacy of the one to the many is not necessarily temporal in meaning. Sacred myth describes a deep and ineffable reality, one so profound that it is not given to expression except through the veil of narration, through encapsulation in a story. And stories, given the need for a sequential plot, require time. So the precedence of the one over the many, placed into story form, comes out sounding like: "In the beginning God created...." Its meaning, however, is that the one underlies the many then, now, and forever. A dimly perceived but awesome deep structure links all things and ties them to the root out of which they all emerge. Multiplicity is the garbing of the One into the coat-of-many-colors of existence, the transformation of Y-H-W-H, singularity itself, being, into the infinite varieties of H-W-Y-H, being as we know, encounter, and are it.

The Genesis "creation" story is really a tale of the origins of multiplicity, a biblical attempt to answer that eternal question of mystics to which the later account of the *sefirot* was also addressed: "How do the many proceed from the one?" This reality is symbolized by the beginning of the Torah with the letter *bet,* long a subject of speculation within Jewish tradition. *Bet* is numerically "two"; its positioning at the beginning of Torah indicates that here is the beginning of duality. From now on there is not just "God" but "God and...." This meaning is dramatically reinforced by the emergence of creation in what are repeatedly described as pairs: light and darkness, day and night, heaven and earth, upper and lower waters, sun and moon, male and female, and all the rest. Behind all these twos, however, behind the *bet* of *bereshit bara'* ["In the beginning God created"] lies the hidden, singular, silent *aleph*. This one, representing the absolute oneness of being, the one after which there is no "two," is to be proclaimed at Sinai in the opening letter of *anokhi,* "I am," the very heart of revelation.

This one, I believe, is the only being that ever was, is, or will be. It is the one that undergoes the only sacred drama that really matters: the biohistory of the universe. I believe that it does so as a conscious and willful Self. From those first seconds of existence, through the emergence of life in its earliest manifestations, and along every step, including the seeming stumblings, missteps, and blind alleys along the way of evolution, it is this single being that is evolving, entering into each new life-form, ever carrying within itself the memory of all its past. The evolutionary process is here re-visioned not as the struggle of creature against creature and species against species, but as the emergence of a single life-energy, a single cosmic mind that uses the comparative adaptabilities of all the forms it enters as a means of ongoing striving ever forward into richer and more diverse forms of life. The formless self, which we call in Hebrew HaWaYaH, searches out endless forms, delighting to rediscover its own identity anew in each of them. That constant movement of the one, expansive in all directions at once, is at the same time directed movement, pointing toward the eventual emergence of a life-form that can fully know and realize the one that lives in all beings. This creature, the one in whom the self-knowledge of being can be ultimately fulfilled, is thus the *telos* of existence.

In this process, the emergence of humanity with its gifts of intellect, self-awareness, and language is indeed a major step forward. Judaism has always taught a distinction between humans and other forms of life, a sense in which the human stands beyond the vegetative and animal realms out of which we emerged. Each creature embodies the life-energy and hence the presence of the one, but only humans are called "God's image" in our tradition. This means that we are the first to have the mental capacity to recapitulate the process, to be self-conscious about our roots within the one. Exactly what are the implications of that potential can indeed be debated, but surely I do not mean to say that being in the divine image gives us license for the rapacious destruction of all so-called lower forms. God forbid! Of the options provided within the Bible for defining humanity's role, I much prefer Psalm 148's vision of us as part of the universal chorus of praise over Genesis 1's isolating us as the final creation of Friday afternoon, with the message of "stewardship" that accompanies it. A true understanding of the unitive vision proclaimed here would lead us beyond the demands of "stewardship," the ethic usually derived from the biblical tale. Life's meaning is to be found in discovering the one, and that means realizing the ultimate unity of all being. It is in *yihud*, discovering and proclaiming the underlying oneness of all existence, that our humanity is fulfilled.

We are of the one; each human mind is a microcosm, a miniature replica of the single mind that conceives and becomes the universe. To know that oneness and recognize it in all out fellow beings is what life is all about. But that recognition leads us to another level of awareness. The One delights in each of the infinite forms in which it is manifest. To play on the lovely English verb, this means that the one sends its light into each of these forms.

Vegetative forms indeed experience this gift most in sunlight, stretching toward it as they grow. We humans are privileged to experience that same radiating light-energy as delight or love.

The one loves the many. The coat-of-many-colors in which being comes to be garbed is a garment of delight. We, as the self-conscious expression of being, are called upon to love as well, to partake in and give human expression to the delightfulness of existence. This is expressed in Jewish liturgy in the order of daily blessings. The blessing of God as the source of nature's light is directly followed by a blessing for God's love. The one does nothing different in the interim between these blessings. It shines in delight at the eternal procession of "creatures" it comes to inhabit. Nature experiences this shining as light; we humans receive it as love. But as recipients of love we are called upon (dare I say "commanded"?) to love as well.

I am also fully willing to admit that we may be but an early stage in an ongoing evolution of aware beings. Perhaps our period will be looked upon in the distant future, by creatures no more willing to demean themselves by the word "human" than we are comfortable being called "ape," as a primitive life-stage. Surely they will not be wrong, those wise beings of the future, in seeing our age as characterized by nothing so much as pretentiousness and self-glorification on the one hand, and wanton consumption and pillage of earth's resources on the other. Let us hope we leave room for that wise future to emerge.

Discovering the presence of the one within the natural order and therefore the sacred quality of existence itself is exactly what our father Abraham did, according to Philo of Alexandria, the hidden grandfather of all Jewish philosophy. The one manifested itself to him in terms of law: Abraham felt that he was being taught how to live in harmony with the forces of nature. Moses' Torah, according to Philo, is the lawgiver's attempt to legislate for a whole human community the life of harmonic insight with the God of nature that Abraham had already found for himself. I have tried to show elsewhere that certain writings of the Hasidic masters, unaware of the ancient precedent, continue this trend. Levi Yizhak of Berdichev, the eighteenth-century Hasidic master, introduces his treatise on hidden miracles, or the miraculous within nature, with precisely this claim: Sinai allows the entire people to apprehend that which wise old Abraham had already long earlier discerned on his own.

The law that teaches us how to live in harmony with the natural world should be one of eternal principles and countless new applications. Its most basic teachings should demand of us that we live ever at the cutting edge of sensitivity toward the suffering we cause God's creatures. We need be aware of the rest and reinvigoration that we give to the soil, the waste of living resources, for each is the embodiment of divine presence. We may not take the endless material gifts with which we are blessed any more casually than we would take God's name in vain. We may not take the One's great gift of holy water in vain. Or air, source of *nishmat kol hai,* the sacred breath of life. To rest on the laurels of forms our ancestors created long ago or boast of their progressivism in the tenth or sixth century B.C.E. is very much not to the point. What is the point of observing *shemitah,* the sabbatical year, but using earth-destroying pesticides? Of insisting on the humanity of *shechitak,* kosher slaughter, but hoisting and shackling and refusing to stun animals to lessen their awareness before they die? Of washing the bugs out of our lettuce while investing the other green stuff in multinationals that daily destroy entire forests? How can we today create a civilization and a law that will be such a *torat hayyim,* a teaching that enhances life? And what will it demand of us? Surely a return to the reverence for air, water, fire (by limiting the sense that we, including our automobiles, burn!), and soil would be a good place to start.

Another potentially useful rubric within tradition for proclaiming this insight is the parallel between the ten divine utterances (of "let there be...") in creation and the ten "commandments" (the Hebrew might be better rendered as "speech acts") of Sinai. The presence of the one that underlies all being is depicted as pure verbal energy: God is the one who ever, unceasingly, says *Yehi!* ["Let there be!"], speaking the world into being. At Sinai, those ten *yehis* are translated into imperatives for us; the inner "law" of God's presence in nature is now manifest in the form of imperatives that can govern human existence, bringing us into harmony with the ten words within ourselves as well as within all creatures. And since the ten "commandments" are the basis of all the six hundred thirteen yeas and nays that comprise Torah, all of it is tied through them to the ten cosmogenerative utterances of the one. This parallel is a great favorite of certain mystical teachers. Creation and revelation are two deeply interrelated manifestations of the same divine self, one showing us that all existence is fraught with holiness, the other instructing us on how to live in the face of that awareness.

Here the language of Kabbalah may be useful again. These two tens, the utterances and the commandments, are both versions of the ten *sefirot,* those primal numbers that allowed us deeper entree into the "secret" of existence. We manifest that secret by turning outward and inward toward the world around us, seeing it in all its awesome beauty and recognizing how deeply we are a part of all that is. We then ask (in good Jewish fashion): "What does this awareness demand of us?" Here we have the beginning-point of a new Kabbalah and a new Halakhah ("path" of religious practice) as well. This praxis, one using and adapting the rich forms of Jewish tradition, should be one that leads us to a life of harmony with the natural world and maximum concerns for its preservation.

All this talk must seem terribly mythical to readers of a more scientific bent of mind. Perhaps it also seems obscure and irrelevant to some of those most keenly aware of the several immediate threats to global existence. Let me assure you that I share that sense of urgency. Life has so evolved that the fate of the biosphere itself is now determined by human actions. We are masters not only over our own species and over those we consume, as so many others have been. The very existence of our planet as a fit habitat for *any* living thing has now fallen into human hands.

With this increase in human power comes a manifold increase of responsibility. It is the future not only of our own offspring that we threaten each day with a million decisions weighted with political, economic, and competitive baggage. The land itself, the *adamah* from which we humans derive our name, is threatened by us, the earth and all that is upon it. The changes needed in collective human behavior in order to save us from self-destruction are stupendous. Belief in their possibility stretches our credulity as much as it is demanded by our need for hope. Our economic system, including the value we place on constant expansion and growth, will have to change. The standards of consumption, created by our wealthiest economies and now the goal of all others, will have to be diminished. Effective world government, perhaps even at the cost of some of our political freedoms, will have to triumph over the childish bickerings and threats that currently characterize our world affairs.

Hardly believable, indeed. But consider the alternative. If any of this deep-seated change is to come about, religious leaders and thinkers need to take an early lead. A seismic shift in the mythical underpinnings of our consciousness is required; nothing less will do the trick. That shift will have to come about within the framework of the religious languages now spoken by large sections of the human race. Experience tells us that newly created myths do not readily take hold; the usually lack the power to withstand great challenge. But a rerouting of ancient symbols, along channels already half-cleared by the most open-eyed thinkers of earlier centuries, might indeed enable this conversion of the human heart of which we speak.

In the emergence of a new tale of origins, we Jews, who have for so long been bearers of the old tale, have a special interest. The new tale will need to achieve its own harmony, summarized with no less genius than was possessed by the author of Genesis 1. It will need to tell of the unity of all beings and help us to feel that fellow-creaturehood with trees and rivers as well as with animals and humans. As it brings us to awareness of our common source, ever present in each of us, so must it value the distinctiveness and sacred integrity of each creature on its own, even the animals, or fish, or plants we eat, even the trees we cut down. If we Jews are allowed to have a hand in it, it will also speak of a human dignity that still needs to be shared with most of our species and of a time of rest, periodic liberation from the treadmill of our struggle for existence, in which we can contemplate and enjoy our fellow feeling with all that is. This sacred time also serves as a model for the world that we believe "with perfect faith" is still to come, a world of which we have never ceased to dream.

17

UNTOUCHABLE CULTURE, LIBERATING RELIGION, AND THE CHRISTIAN GOSPEL

A Case from South India

SATHIANATHAN CLARKE

This paper is written in appreciation of my teacher and friend Harvey Cox.[1] In my years as a graduate student (1988–94) and year as visiting lecturer (1995) at Harvard Divinity School I worked closely with Harvey in a progressive manner: student, Teaching Fellow, Head Teaching Fellow, and teaching colleague. There is much that I have learned from Professor Cox. His keen interest in the movements toward liberation in the Third World focused on analyses of the interlocking of local culture, contemporary society, popular religion, and contextual gospel. In this essay I have tried to take these concepts seriously in suggesting a working hypothesis for the relationship between culture, religion, and gospel in the South Indian context with a view to enhancing the forces of liberation. With affection and gratitude I present these reflections as part of a *Festscrift* to my teacher Professor Harvey Cox.[2]

Indian society is traditionally divided into four castes, which are hierarchically ordered.[3] The Brahmins (priests) are the preservers and protectors of the eternal laws of the Universe (Dharma); the Ksatriyas (rulers and warriors) are the defenders and the guarantors of the safety and security of the community; the Vaisyas (business persons) are the conservers and distributors of wealth; and the Sudras (the laborers) are the working majority involved in the production of essential commodities. Outside of these four segments of the Indian human society there existed a fifth. Even though this populace consisted of about 15 to 20 percent of the Indian community, it was thought of as being sub- or nonhuman; thus it was not included in its composition. This large group was ejected from the contours of Hindu society: it lived outside the gates of the Hindu society with the labels "Outcaste," "Untouchable," "Exterior caste," "Depressed class," and "Dalit." I use the term

Dalit in this paper for the following three reasons. First, this term has become an expression of self-representation, which Dalit activists and writers have chosen both in recovering their past identity and projecting themselves as a collective.[4] Second, the word means "oppressed," "broken," and "crushed," which most realistically describes the lives of almost all those who are members of this community. And, third, it incorporates elements of a positive expression of pride[5] and a resistive surge for combating oppression.[6]

This paper empathetically reimagines the religio-cultural sphere of Dalits and seeks to incorporate this into a revised understanding of the Christian gospel in the Indian context. It is grounded in the presupposition that cultural and religious symbols house human communities and fund their collective action. In other words, the cultural and religious symbolic worldview of the Dalits is a meaning system that arises from the depth of their collective experience; it thus sustains, nurtures, and directs their life in the world. In this work I seek to make manifest the cultural and religious symbolic world of Dalits as they endeavor to embrace their own historical consciousness in relation to the divine. I then suggest how this can become resource for a more enriching and contextual way of expressing the Christian gospel.

Two tendencies have dominated interaction with the cultural and religious symbols of Dalits. It is necessary to debunk them before proceeding with the task of reclaiming and reinterpreting the cultural symbols of Dalits. The first involves the demonizing of Dalit cultural symbols. This option stems from a philosophical and theological frame of reality which takes all phenomena as belonging to one of two polarities. It is not only the religionist, but also the anthropologist, who advocated such an alternative. The dualism of good and evil has a plethora of cognates: white and black; male and female; spirit and body; spiritual and material; god and goddess; divine and demonic; auspicious and inauspicious; pure and polluting; enlightened and ignorant; faith and fear; heavenly and earthly; Western and Eastern. In our context, this dualism was either interpreted in terms of Christian/Western versus non-Christian/native Indian or caste Hindu versus Dalit categorizations. Thus, the Christian symbol system in its Western manifestation was unproblematically identified with God (involving close relation with enlightenment, faith, auspiciousness, purity, and divinity) while the Dalit symbol system was easily classified with things evil (involving intimate relation with stupidity, fear, inauspiciousness, pollution, and demonology). To be fair to some early Christian missionaries, who tried to wipe out Dalit religion and culture as the workshop and storehouse of evil, they merely fit themselves into a framework that had already been espoused by the ideology of caste Hinduism. The logic was that if the God of life was to be introduced, the demons of death must be ejected; no trace of the old religious and cultural symbols of Dalit spirituality must be retained. The Christian God thus conquers Dalit deities in all their aspects. We can identify missionary writings to support such a position. One example may suffice to make the point. Henry Whitehead, Bishop of the Anglican Church in Madras, writing in 1921 about village [Dalit] culture and religion, has the following to say: "Taking the system, therefore as a whole, as it exists at the present day, we can only condemn it from a moral and religious point of view as a debasing superstition, and the only attitude which the Christian Church can possibly take toward it as a working system is one of uncompromising hostility, the same attitude that the Jewish prophets of old took to the local Semitic cults in Palestine with all their idolatrous and immoral associations."[7]

Much of our present day evangelistic preaching and teaching in contemporary India still reflects this dualistic theological viewpoint. In a recent reporting session on their field work experience among Dalit manual scavengers in Rayalseema district of Andhra Pradesh, two of my students recollected a discussion they had with a Christian evangelist who was working in that region.[8] The evangelist was quite concerned about these seminary students working with the Dalit manual scavengers' community. He warned them to be very careful. He especially instructed them not to enter into the living space of such Dalits. Because these Dalits work with human feces and they worship female demons they must be avoided. The forces of evil are attracted to such a deprived human condition. And because of their social conditions they cannot but interact with demons. The students narrated how the evangelist devised a way to preach the gospel of Jesus Christ to this scavenger community without having any kind of physical contact with them. He rides his bicycle on the edge of the village with a megaphone attached to the backseat. While on the move he preaches the gospel to the Dalit community inviting them to give up their demon worship and embrace the living Christ. "Moving sermons" have a contextual twist in this part of rural India! Thus, the Christian evangelist is able to fulfill his compunction to preach the gospel while at the same time avoiding contact with the Dalit scavenger community because of the fear of interacting with demons.

The second tendency can be termed as the trivializing of Dalit cultural and religious symbols. This option is quite popular with certain Marxists. I am not only referring to the economism (which I take to be the fundamentalism of the materialists) that is advanced by some. Rather, I am also pointing to the biased manner with which many materialists disregard the culture of the masses as "sugary trash." Both popular religion and culture are purported to be deliberately manufactured by the elite to function as "a repressive form of social control by which the bourgeoisie handles working class people, anaesthetizing them with commodities that artificially satisfy their need for 'culture' but do nothing to awake them to the injustice of their situation."[9] The general disregard of religion in the corporate life of the marginalized peoples by numerous Non Government Organizations working in India has contributed to this bias. While religion may not be relevant to the emerging cadre of social activists, the continued sustenance and nurture that it provides to solidarity-seeking and justice-demanding Dalit communities must be accounted for and interpreted.

From the perspective of Dalits, the problem with this approach of trivializing religion as it functions in the life of the marginalized peoples is twofold. On the one hand, it reinforces the stereotype that Dalits are the passive objects of others' manipulations. It denies human agency to Dalit communities' existence. On the other hand, it fails to take seriously the culture of survival and resistance that nurtures and nourishes Dalit communities. In the last decade, though, it is heartening to notice an awareness among NGOs that Dalit culture, not so much religion, has emancipatory potential and merit. The emergence of Dalit culture documentation centers is one manifest sign of this changing perspective among NGOs working primarily with Dalit communities. In line with this transformed mindset, my own work seeks to glean out the active, self-expressive, and liberative dimensions of Dalit culture and religion which have survived the onslaught of the process of demonization and colonization by the caste communities' and Western missionaries' culture. By doing this I flesh out the positive identity of Dalits. Thus, within the contemporary discourse in which Dalits are represented primarily in terms of negative and passive (acted upon) appellations, I resurrect the positive and active dimensions of Dalit subjectivity.

At this juncture it may be pertinent to problematize the much celebrated move of positing Dalit religion and culture as "counter religion," and "counter culture." The terms themselves sound remarkably impressive and striking. In Christian circles, it is very much influenced by the urge to find continuity with the prophetic strands of anti–status quo movements. While this resistive and oppositional tack of Dalit religion and culture cannot be overlooked and undervalued, one must be careful not to construct the culture and religion of Dalits as essentially characterized by the prefix "counter," as if its whole nature can be captured in its reaction to something that is a primordial given, such as caste Hindu religion and culture. The problem with this approach is that it reinforces the self-other dichotomy. Thus it sets up caste culture as the self and then interprets Dalit culture as the other which actualizes itself through responding and reacting to the primary reality of the former. Edward Said has cogently argued for the manner in which such otherness and difference (Dalit culture and religion in this context) are integrally tied up with establishing the rule and dominance of the normative self (caste culture and religion).[10] Thus the acceptance of being merely a counter force in culture-weaving and religion-making appears to acquiesce to the secondary role of Dalit culture in a discourse which is already hierarchically determined. How then are we to retain the resistive dimension of Dalit culture without equating it with being merely a reaction to something that is construed as the most real? Let me propose that we take the lead from A. P. Nirmal even as we reformulate his recommendation.

In suggesting a model for Dalit theology, Nirmal starts by emphasizing its counter character. This counterness, as it were, becomes the first definitional feature. In his words, "We must first note that Dalit Theology is a counter theology. It is a counter theology in relation to other dominant theologies."[11] However, it must be noted that Nirmal does not stop here. He moves from this counter posture of theology, which is required to avoid co-option by the dominant theologies, to the second step of Dalit theology, which involves the recovery and conscious integration of the distinct identity of Dalit peoples: Peoples' theology then seeks to express the distinctive identities of their respective peoples. A search and expression of identity therefore characterizes all liberative theologies and peoples' theologies.[12] These "No" and "Yes" dimensions of theology must also be included in the grappling with Dalit culture. The stress on merely concentrating on the counterness of Dalit culture must be balanced by a quest to valorize its self-expressive Dalit nature.

In fact I want to suggest that it is necessary to reverse the process as we deal with Dalit religion and culture as resource for human emancipation. Thus, the first act in the process of dealing with Dalit religion and culture must be one of self-affirmation. An embracing of the richness and complexity of being human has to do with the production of the religio-cultural world of Dalits. This is driven by the assumption that the distinctive identities of Dalits are embedded in the cultural and religious world of Dalit peoples. However, there can be little doubt that the survival of the particularity of this Dalit identity is linked to the successful resistance of dominant forces that seek to obliterate, co-opt, or demonize it. The second act of resistance comes into operation at this point. The resistive dynamic to counter such dominating tendencies is subsequent to the act of claiming the self-identity of Dalits. In other words, the self-actualizing and self-expressing dimension of Dalit communities, which can be grasped through the variety of their cultural representation, must be reasserted, after which the countering tendencies of resistance and rebuttal can be incorporated. An examination of the motifs of self-projection and self-promotion, however discriminatingly and subtly they may be exhibited in the religion and culture of Dalits, precedes an analysis into its counter-hegemonic and anti–status quo tendencies. The "Yes" then is the first moment in interpreting the religion and culture of the Dalits. Here self-affirmation is the key. The "No" is the second moment in deciphering Dalit religion and culture. Here accounting for the opposing posture of dissension is necessary. It highlights the dimension of self-protection.[13]

In order to study the distinct and particular manifestation of Dalit religion and culture, let me suggest that we look at one concrete symbol. In my own research I have put forward the notion that the goddess and the drum are two dominant symbols that help us capture this distinctiveness of Dalit religion and culture.[14] The depth and the substance of these symbols are occasioned by the embrace of the divine and the human Dalits. But even in erupting from the locus of the meeting of the divine and the human they are marked by their difference. In this paper I focus on the drum as symbolizing this difference.

The drum is a conspicuous symbol of the Dalit communities in South India. It is almost thought of as synonymous with certain Dalit communities, i.e., Paraiyars of Tamilnadu, Maadigaas of Andhra Pradesh, and Paraiyars of Kerala. Much of the cultural and religious life of Dalits is intertwined with the drum. It is utilized for community celebration, community mourning, and Dalit divine-human mediation. In a 1997 Dalit Utsav (festival) held in August in Kolar District, at which many Dalit cultural artists participated, the most prominent symbol of the communities' collective celebration was the drum. Not only was it the instrument that accompanied every song and dance; but the most electrifying item for the audience of about four thousand was a drum rendition performed by about twelve drummers for almost forty-five minutes. Through this whole day festival, it seemed like the drum was the chosen medium of the various Dalit communities, who came from Karnataka, Andhra Pradesh and Tamilnadu, to vocalize their communal reflections. One can make the argument that the drum alone has been sufficiently able to voice all the conscious and unconscious tales of Dalit communities: it wails of their sorrow; it warns of their revolt; it whispers of their hope; it whines of their complaint; and it woos the power of their deities.

Again in August 1998, I accompanied twenty-five students registered in my course entitled "Dalit Theology" at the United Theological College in Bangalore to spend a couple of days with an Non-Government Organization called REDS (Rural Education for Development Society) working in Tumkar District in Karnataka.[15] This exposure to the everyday life of local Dalit communities was built into the academic planning of the course in order to test if the theories which we learned in the isolated and distanced classrooms were connected with Dalit reality on the ground. At the Dalit colony of Madyavenkatapuram we were greeted at the entrance by a host of smiling, drumming, dancing, and clapping community members. After welcoming each of us with a flower and a dash of turmeric paste on the forehead, we were led through the main village and into the colony to the rhythmic beating of numerous drums and free-style dancing of the men. Drumming is an ancient art, while dancing is a communitarian practice. The drumming set the mood for celebration; the dancing set the pattern for community. Thus in the combination of the two (drumming and dancing) all of us seemed to have become one through the process of the journey from the main road to their colony. All of us joined in clapping and dancing our way into the colony. And as we did so we realized that the Dalit community made it a point to take us through the caste village. Perhaps it was to demonstrate their outside support and strength. "We are not alone," they seemed to be communicating. "Our Dalit drum and dance unite us in solidarity with a larger community that resists injustice and oppression." After we got to the center of the colony, we shared together in a cultural program. The REDS cultural team led the community members in songs of Dalit awareness and unification. But this was only secondary when compared to the electric atmosphere that was produced through the continuous and deliberate rhythm of drumming that represented Dalit resistance, defiance, and celebration in community. The Dalit drums and the Dalit songs harmoniously celebrated the new age: an age of Ambedkar, of Dalitism, of peoples' liberation, of justice and peace for the oppressed of India.

This intrinsic affiliation between the Dalits and the drum goes back through time. Usually we read the history of culture through the eyes of Brahmanic Hinduism. This theory states that because Dalits were anyway defiled for various reasons (i.e., mixed marriages and polluting occupation), they were assigned the responsibility of disposing of carcasses of dead animals. Thus it concludes that the drum, which was invented by Dalits from the polluted hide of dead cows, became a useful instrument for dealing with the things concerning death and demons. For this reason, Dalit drums are utilized by the caste Hindu communities only for dealing with inauspicious rituals, i.e., primarily death and blood sacrifices. In contrast to this hypothesis, we can also interpret the drum as arising from the noble heritage of the Dalits.[16] The drum, from this perspective, was a natural product of their culture, which was beef eating. It was also an inherent artifact of their productive labor. From the hide of cattle, which needed to be cured and tanned through intensive labor and native/indigenous technology, Dalits manufactured drums. Kancha Ilaiah, referring to the Dalit Maadigaa community of South India, suggests this correlation between Dalit productivity and indigenous technology, on the one hand, and the manufacture and playing of drums, on the other: "Their [Maadigaas] childhood was much tougher than ours. But in certain areas they were much more skilled and intelligent. They knew how to skin dead cattle, convert the skin into soft and smooth leather and transform the leather into farm instruments and shoes. Their skill in playing the dappu (a special percussion instrument [drum]) was far beyond that of any of us."[17] Even if the caste Hindu communities despised it, Dalits claimed this musical object to be a part of their work. Literally, the drum was liturgy, i.e., the work of the people. And they used it as a focal symbol of their religious and cultural celebration and lamentation. The high honor that the drum was given by Dalit communities of old is suggested by a Dalit myth recorded by Moffatt: "In those days the colony people were higher in caste. Therefore Kali gave then the right to announce, to beat the drum, and honor the dead. The *uur* people had to pay them a fee for this. Thus they [Dalits] had both honor and income in those days."[18] While the drum, which was made from the hide of a dead cow, symbolically expressed the particular communal subjectivity (group identity) of Dalits, it was also utilized as an agent to rebel against the caste Hindu culture of the holy cow.

The longevity and endurance of the drum as a religious and cultural dominant symbol among the Dalits is remarkable. It survived the long historical
process of vilification by caste Hinduism. The malevolent, inauspicious, and
polluting character of the drum as construed by caste Hinduism was well
known. Yet the drum was at the center of Dalit communal life and practice.
This unwillingness to let go of the drum makes it a dimension of culture
that is related to Dalit group identity.

In a historical context in which the Dalits were forbidden from reading
and hearing the sacred word as embodied in the Hindu scripture (vedas), the
drum is transformed into an alternate mode with which to mediate the divine
and communicate among each other. Thus the drum becomes a dominant
representation of the particular collective consciousness of the community
of Dalits, which is rooted in relationality with the divine. The self-expression
of Dalits is represented by the drum to establish "difference" through their
collective identity rather than "counterness" to the Hindu cultural world.
Dalit religion and culture in this context manifests "a dimension that attends
to [the] situated and embodied difference"[19] of Dalit communities.

Let me summarize my main constructive proposal. Contrary to the
"counter culture" approach for interpreting Dalit religion and culture, what
I have been arguing for is an approach based on highlighting the subjectivity aspects of Dalit self-expression. This latter strategy opts for detecting
the elements of distinctiveness, even if through difference, of Dalit religion
and culture, which are calculatingly inscribed into the communicative practices of the community, in order to represent its collective identity. In this
brief reflection I have argued that these dimensions of Dalit culture are constructed though the drum. Through the drum, then, Dalits set in motion
"the [cultural] process of naturalizing a subset of differences that have been
mobilized to articulate group identity."[20] Based on our discussion thus far,
we are finally at a point at which we can attempt a definition: *Dalit culture is an acquired and constructed system of collective self-representation,
communicated by means of multivalent symbols held together in a loosely
organized pattern, which have expressive, directive, resistive and affective
functions for a human community.*[21]

I cannot conclude without clarifying where I stand with regard to the relationship between culture and religion.[22] Even from a cursory sifting through
of my arguments, it will be clear that at the material level I do not construe
difference between these two concepts. Religion is after all a particular configuration of a meaningful cultural symbol system. In accordance with the
school of symbolic anthropology, I am quite comfortable with Geertz's classic definition of religion as "a system of symbols which acts to establish
powerful, pervasive, and long-lasting moods and motivations in men [*sic*]
by formulating conceptions of a general order of existence and clothing these
conceptions with such an aura of factuality that the moods and motivations
seem uniquely realistic."[23] Thus, I would want to object to Tillich's initial

proposal, which is still in vogue among many theologians, that "religion is the substance of culture, [while] culture is the form of religion."[24] This appears to denote that culture itself, devoid of religion, is substanceless and vacuous, which certainly is false. But more importantly it is based on the questionable presupposition that substance and form are separable and distinct from each other. Ernst Troeltsch thought that he had put an end to this false dichotomy almost a century ago. In his lucid though interrogatory style he summarizes his view with exceptional brilliance:

> This is the point, therefore, where the difficulties and artifices of theology stand out most prominently. Kernel and husk, form and content, abiding truth and temporal-historical condition — these are all the formulas of which amazing use is frequently made to help theology escape from this labyrinth. Yet the result of these various attempts is that the actual absoluteness of the kernel always absolutizes the husk as well, while the actual relativity of the husk always relativizes the kernel in turn. "The temporal-historical form for the realization of the absolute ideal" reminds one, more than anything else, of molten iron in a wax container or of solid paraffin in a red-hot mold.[25]

From a very different philosophical tradition (Advaitic), K. P. Aleaz argues for the possibility of talking of the gospel of Indian culture. He suggests that the gospel emerges from creative intermingling at the heart of Indian culture, which is intrinsically religious. The lines between religion, culture, and gospel are more fluid than one dares to admit. For Aliaz, this gospel of Indian culture "is the gospel of integral relation between religion and culture, resulting in cultural symbiosis and a composite culture through an ongoing interaction between religions."[26] In a metaphysics that stresses the inextricable intermingling of content and context, substance and form, and essence and structure, it is quite impossible to assert material differentiation between religion and culture. This conjointedness of religion and culture is particularly poignant in the case of the Dalits. It was through the religious reflexivity that their cultural symbols were legitimized. The drum is cultural in form and religious in substance even as it is cultural in substance and religious in form. What is more, any theological wedge between substance and form must break down in the light of an honest acceptance of the implications of the incarnation: God became flesh and dwelt among us. In other words, substance fully pervaded form; thus fleshly culture was transformed into the arena of divine indwelling: the two became one in Jesus Christ.

However, at a formal level, one is obliged to distinguish between religion and culture. Let me do this by clarifying the particular manner in which religion functions as a cultural system. As I see it, religion grounds a multitude of interlocking cultural signs in a dominant symbol of ultimate value which funds, unifies, and relativizes every other sign in the configuration. Here I am drawing on the later thought of Tillich as he reimagines and reconstructs his own earlier rigid demarcation between religion and culture. After a couple of years of dialogue with Mircea Eliade at the University of Chicago, Tillich's last article, published after his death, admits that "The history of religions in its essential nature does not exist alongside the history of culture. The sacred does not lie beside the secular, but in its depth."[27] The inextricability of religion from culture is confirmed. For Tillich, this depth dimension is articulated in terms of being related to the ultimate concern. In keeping with this lead, I want to propose that depth is located in the ability of the ultimate concern (God) to fund, unify, and relativize all the other symbols in the cultural system called religion. Through the language of transcendence or supreme immanence this root symbol (God) is made to function as font, unifier, and relativizer of all other symbols within the system. Thus, functionally within the cultural symbolic system that is labelled "religion," the symbol of God (or any other equivalent root symbol that denotes the divine) clarifies the meaning of every other symbol, unites each symbol to the others and makes every symbol dependent on it for its valuation. In line with my earlier explication of Dalit culture, then, it is now possible to define *religion as an acquired and constructed cultural symbol system, communicated by means of multivalent symbols held together in a loosely organized pattern, which proposes configurations of relationships between human beings and the cosmos with and under God in response to a purported encounter with an ultimate divine being, and which has expressive, directive, resistive and affective functions for a community.*

But what does this have to do with the Christian gospel? Let me stay with my functional method as I seek to explicate the way in which the Christian gospel can be related to this interpretation of religion and culture. On the one hand, I must explicitly reject an unqualified relativism tag. Nonetheless, I want to accept a restrained or modest pluralist posture. From my explication of religion it can be determined that I admit to the possibility of a variety of cultural symbol systems, each grounded, funded, and relativized by its own conception of God. But this does not make specific religions relativistic. All cultural symbols are relativized by the normative symbol of God, which legitimizes or denounces every symbol that purports to belong to the configuration. In Christian theology this symbol (God) is itself qualified and modified through the figure of Jesus Christ. Thus any cultural symbol that is at odds with the way in which Jesus Christ interprets who God is and what human beings are will be found to be wanting. On the other hand, I must also affirm that it is possible to talk about a gospel of culture even as one can speak about the culture of gospel. The dimensions of religion and culture of Dalits that I have explicated, when in accordance with the notion of God in Christ, are accepted as the gospel of culture. They are signs of the encounter between God and God's creation even if the name Christ is not uttered or understood. The culture of gospel is used to point to the popular understanding that identifies the gospel with the Bible in its written form. My point is that the Christian gospel cannot be identified with either one of these entities at the expense of ignoring the other. The task for Christian theologians increasingly involves discerning and celebrating the good news of God's saving action (the Christian gospel) within the community where the gospel of culture and the culture of gospel interact to heal, nourish, nurture, and liberate. To put it another way, the living Christ emerges in the complex interplay of many movements of which the meeting of the gospel of culture and the culture of gospel is portentous. None of these has a form that can be extricated from the other; in the embrace of each other arises the possibility of living with the good news of the new humanity effected by Jesus Christ, which is the Christian gospel.

I would like to conclude with a further opening. I believe that there are at least two implications for the Christian gospel that can be derived from the argument of this essay. First, this way of interpreting religion and culture broadens the modes through which the Christian gospel may be encountered and explicated. Discourse about culture in the Dalit context is inclusive of the entire range of expressive modalities. The usual practice of locating and decoding the gospel of written texts, taken to be the substance of Christian mediation, will not suffice. Instead the multi-textual dimensions of the Christian gospel must be explored since, as we have noted, the self-expression of Dalit representation arises naturally from its intensive involvement with productivity-based media which is mostly other than writing. I believe that this approach will help us in the future task of hearing, tasting, feeling, smelling, and seeing the many facets of the Christian gospel. The productivity-based collective life style of Dalit communities in India instructs us that a new approach for locating and investigating the implosions of the Christian gospel is needed: the textualities that encode Dalit culture are multimedia in form. Walter Ong, among others, has studied ways in which the senses are hierarchically ordered in different cultures and epochs. He argues that the truth of vision in Western, literate cultures has predominated over the evidences of sound and interlocution, touch, smell, and taste.[28] Thus, Ong claims that reading and writing were privileged over sound and hearing. This is most relevant for Christianity. On the one hand, it tends to posit a hierarchy that puts the "People of the Book" well above the other religious peoples. On the other hand, it also distinguishes between religions that acknowledge the revelation of the Word through the Scriptures and religions that through various forms and means attempt to decipher and reach God. The study of Dalit culture will produce nothing vital if it mainly tracks written texts to manifest the symbolic world of this community. Rather, texts, in accordance with the original meaning, must be transfigured to mean the "textures" which are woven by a community to express the various facets of its communal self-expression. *Webster's Collegiate Dictionary* makes us aware of the fact that *text* comes from the Medieval Latin word *textus*, which is the past participle form of *texere*, meaning "to weave."[29] Text thus is much more akin to productivity-based communicative systems than just writing. In the Dalit context it is more germane to refer to the drumming as a text: it constructs the imaginative reflexivity of the community. In such a reconceptualization, culture itself is a multiform and unfinished text. Geertz makes us aware of this multitextuality of peoples' culture. He says, "Arguments, melodies, formulas, maps, and pictures are not idealities to be stared at but texts to be read; so are rituals, palaces, technologies, and social formations."[30] From a tribal context in North East India, Wati Longchar reminds us of the multitextual nature of religion. He points to the breadth of theology when done with a view to include such multitextual oral communities: "Doing theology is also to engage creatively in dialogue, listen, feel, dance, sing and wonder with the whole creation. It should not be a function of intellect."[31] It is significant that such an inclusive multimodal tack for theology steers it away from its anthropocentric preoccupations and brings it closer to the communicative system of the nonhuman world of nature.[32] More specific to the culture of the Dalits, we will have to begin to decode the mode of music in which the reflections of the community are stored through the thudding of the drum. Kingsbury's words are instructive for the future of Dalit cultural studies. He says, "Music... is a cultural system, an intercontextualized weave of conceptual representations, actions and reactions, ideas and feelings, sounds and meanings, values and structures."[33]

Second, from the perspective of Dalits the truth of the Christian Gospel needs to move away from a preoccupation with the meaning of texts to a curiosity that enquires into how these texts function. Good news is intertwined with instrumentality rather than substantiality. The effective practice of theology then is much more on its effects in the here and now rather than on its primordial character that can be traced to original content.[34] The drum is a good example. Drumming in the Dalit world of music does not correspond exactly to a pregiven score. It is valued and evaluated by its effects. The drum makes truth not when it reproduces that which is originally drummed, but when it is able to produce the sensations and responses that draw one into the sensations of the appropriate moment. It creates comfort, hope, joy, and peace. Again with reference to music as a key texture of Dalit self-reflection, we might have to renegotiate notions of truth. In this realm of music, truth is associated with "good-making" rather than "yielding knowledge" by accurate representation. In the words of Levinson, "It [music] is more likely to perform the function of activating what we dispositionally know, or dramatizing what we usually overlook, by virtue of the respect in which it is true."[35] He continues this argument in the following extended passage:

> So what, after all, could it mean to say that a sonata was true? Well, at some point, it might means that its structure mirrors that of the emotions it ex-

presses, or that it expresses emotions as they are, or that its achieved expression accords with its apparently intended expression, or perhaps that on the basis of a sequence of expressive passages it contains it suggests truly that a parallel sequence of emotions, or just that set of emotions within a given span, is, in a narrow sense, psychologically possible. Surely, this is a long way from being meaningless.[36]

Notes

1. This is an expanded and revised version of a paper that was presented at Lexington Theological Seminary, Kentucky, on May 1, 1998. I am grateful to Dean Michael Kinammon for this invitation to deliver the convocation address at L.T.S. I am also thankful to Dr. Mrinalini Sebastian for reading through the manuscript and making some perceptive suggestions.

2. The part of this paper regarding the relationship between culture and religion has been published in *Religion and Society* (December 1997).

3. I am using the most general category of caste (Varna) since it is sufficient to place the Dalits outside of the Indian stratification of human community. I am well aware of the fact that these four castes are divided into numerous sub-castes (*jaatis*) which operate as the functional identities on the ground. For a recent essay on this distinction, see Simon R. Charsley "Caste, Cultural Resources and Social Mobility," in *Dalits Initiatives and Experience from Karnataka*, ed. Simon R. Charsley and G. K. Karanth (New Delhi: Sage Publications, 1998), 44–71.

4. For an excellent analysis of the history and politics of naming the Dalits, see Gopal Guru, "The Politics of Naming," *Seminar* 491 (November 1998): 14–18.

5. Eleanor Zelliot, *From Untouchable to Dalit: Essays on the Ambedkar Movement*, rev. ed. (New Delhi: Manohar, 1996).

6. Gail Omvedt, *Dalits and the Democratic Revolution: Dr. Ambedkar and the Dalit Movement in Colonial India* (New Delhi: Sage Publications, 1994).

7. Henry Whitehead, *The Village Gods of South India*, rev. ed. (1921; reprint, New Delhi: Asian Educational Services, 1988), 153f.

8. I am thankful to Victor Paul and Andrew Rathod for their report at Prajwala (a Non-Government Organization working with Dalit communities in Chittoor, Andhra Pradesh) on December 5, 1998.

9. Kelton Cobb, "Reconsidering the Status of Popular Culture in Tillich's Theology of Culture," *Journal of the American Academy of Religion* 63, no. 1 (Spring 1995): 69.

10. Edward Said, *Orientalism* (New York: Vintage, 1979) and *The World, the Text and the Critic* (Cambridge, Mass.: Harvard University Press, 1983).

11. Arvind P. Nirmal, ed., "Doing Theology from a Dalit perspective," in *A Reader in Dalit Theology* (Madras: Gurukul, 1991), 143.

12. Ibid.

13. For a comprehensive analysis of the prospects and the problems with the various contemporary schools of culture, see Dominic Strinati, *An Introduction to Theories of Popular Culture* (London: Routledge, 1995).

14. I have argued this in detail in my recent book, *Dalits and Christianity: Sub-*

altern Religion and Liberation Theology in India (New Delhi: Oxford University Press, 1998).

15. I am thankful to Jyoti and M. C. Raj, the cofounders of REDS, for their willingness to invite me to join the world that they inhabit and transform. REDS works only with Dalit communities. They promote Dalitism as a social, cultural, economic, and religious option; it encompasses the worldview of Dalits and is projected as a viable philosophy to direct Dalit liberation.

16. For an excellent study of the high status and honor given to "king drum" of the Dalit community of Sri Lanka, see Dennis B. Mcgilvray, "Paraiyar Drummers of Sri Lanka: Consensus and Constraint in an Untouchable Caste," *American Ethnologist* 10, no. 1 (February 1983): 97–115.

17. Kancha Ilaiah, *Why I Am Not a Hindu: A Sudra Critique of Hindutva Philosophy, Culture and Political Economy* (Calcutta: Samya, 1996), 10.

18. Michael Moffatt, *An Untouchable Community in South India: Structure and Consensus* (Princeton: Princeton University Press, 1979), 126.

19. Arjun Appadurai, *Modernity at Large: Cultural Dimensions of Globalization* (New Delhi: Oxford University Press, 1997), 13. Appadurai makes an excellent representation and reconstruction of culture. I am influenced by his ideas as well as by the anthropological tradition that he draws upon in his work.

20. Appadurai, *Modernity at Large*, 15.

21. For a thorough study of recent theories in culture, see Roy G. D'Andrade's exposition of culture: "Cultural Meaning Systems" in *Culture Theory: Essays on Mind, Self, and Emotion*, ed. Richard A. Shweder and Robert A. LeVine (Cambridge, U.K.: Cambridge University Press, 1984), 88–119.

22. I must record my indebtedness in this section to the constructive theological work of Gordon D. Kaufman. See, especially, *In Face of Mystery: A Constructive Theology* (Cambridge, Mass.: Harvard University Press, 1993).

23. Clifford Geertz, *The Interpretation of Cultures* (New York: Basic Books, 1973), 90.

24. Paul Tillich, *Theology of Culture* (London: Oxford University Press, 1959), 42.

25. Ernst Troeltsch, *The Absoluteness of Christianity and the History of Religions*, 2nd ed. (1921; reprint, Richmond: John Knox Press, 1971), 71f.

26. K. P. Aleaz, *The Gospel of Indian Culture* (Calcutta: Punthi Pustak, 1994), 2.

27. Paul Tillich, "The Significance of the History of Religions for the Systematic Theologian" in *The History of Religions: Essays on the Problem of Understanding*, ed. Joseph M. Kitagawa (Chicago: University of Chicago Press, 1967). This was Tillich's last lecture before his death in 1965.

28. James Clifford, "Introduction: Partial Truths" in *Writing Culture: The Poetics and Politics of Ethnography*, ed. James Clifford and George E. Marcus (Berkeley: University of California Press, 1986), 11. For a more contextual analyses of the power mechanics in literacy ("visualism") in relation to orality ("auralism"), see Ajay Skaria, "Writing, Orality and Power in the Dangs, Western India, 1800s–1920s" in *Subaltern Studies IX: Writings on South Asian History and Society*, ed. Shahid Amin and Dipesh Chakrabarty (New Delhi: Oxford University Press, 1996), 13–58.

29. *Webster's Ninth New Collegiate Dictionary* (Springfield, Mass.: Merriam-Webster Inc., 1987), 1220.

30. Clifford Geertz, *The Negara: The Theatre State in Nineteenth-Century Bali* (Princeton: Princeton University Press, 1980), 135.

31. A. Wati Longchar, "Myth: A Source for Conceptualizing Tribal Theology," in *An Exploration of Tribal Theology,* ed. A. Wati Longchar (Jorhat: Tribal Study Center, 1997), 93.

32. There is an emerging group of young tribal theologians that laments how the history of Christian theology has undercut this multimodal character of the gospel. They argue that this has led both to deculturalization of the tribes and the anti-ecological direction of their development. Renthy Kietzer, K. Thanzauva, and A. Wati Longchar are reflective representatives of this group of critical theologians. They are also involved in an effort to reclaim the ecocentric tribal worldview for the purposes of contextual and liberative Christian theology.

33. Henry Kingsbury, *Music, Talent, and Performance: A Conservatory Cultural System* (Philadelphia: Temple University Press, 1988), 178–79.

34. Appadurai, *Modernity at Large,* 14. For a recent example of this approach of culture in action, see Steve Derne, *Culture in Action: Family Life, Emotion, and Male Dominance in Banaras, India* (Albany: State University of New York Press, 1995).

35. Jerrold Levinson, *Music, Art, and Metaphysics: Essays in Philosophical Aesthetics* (Ithaca, N.Y.: Cornell University Press, 1990), 304.

36. Ibid.

18

RELIGION AND
THE GOLDHAGEN THESIS

Richard L. Rubenstein

Few, if any, books about the Holocaust have generated as much controversy as Daniel Jonah Goldhagen's *Hitler's Willing Executioners*.[1] Given
the range of emotions elicited both by National Socialism and the Holocaust, the response to Goldhagen's book is hardly surprising. Moreover, the
issues involved are not likely to achieve closure for a very long time, if ever.
Michael Wolffsohn, the Israeli-born Professor of Modern History at the University of the Armed Forces in Munich, has argued that just as Jews were
branded as murderers of Christ for two thousand years, so, too, "Germans
will be unable to detach themselves from the stigma of the Holocaust" for
centuries.[2] This has absolutely nothing to do with any imputation of guilt
to present or future generations of Germans. They can no more be characterized as perpetrators of the Holocaust than the millions of Jews could
realistically be guilty of deicide, the crime imputed to them for centuries before Vatican II. The enduring power of the stigma arises in both cases from
its religio-mythic inheritance. Like most Jews, most Germans desire to be
a normal people like all others. In both cases, history, memory, and myth
have blocked the path to normalcy.

The intense interest in Goldhagen's book may also stem from a delayed
reaction to the reunification of Germany. Fear of a united Germany, the
strongest power on the European continent, has by no means disappeared
in spite of a half century of democratic government and respect for human
rights in the Federal Republic. Rightly or wrongly, there is apprehension in
some quarters in both the United States and Europe that the "real Germany"
has yet to manifest itself. When, after German reunification, a Harvard-
trained scholar argues that the Holocaust was not solely the work of the
Nazis, the S.S., or Hitler, but of the overwhelming majority of the German
people at the time, he is likely to attract a great deal of attention. In spite of
Goldhagen's assertion that the Germans have changed, much of the book's
success may reside in the anxiety that the opposite may prove to be true in

195

the long run. Seen in that light, Goldhagen's book is not about yesterday but about a possible tomorrow.

I was born in 1924. Like so many members of my generation, I shall never entirely lose a certain apprehension about Germany. Nevertheless, I find elements of Goldhagen's fundamental thesis to be somewhat simplistic. Goldhagen claims that the central causal agent in Hitler's decision to annihilate European Jewry was *German* antisemitic beliefs about Jews, asserting that it was "*only* in Germany that an openly and rabidly antisemitic movement came to power — indeed was elected to power — that was bent upon turning antisemitic fantasy into state-organized genocidal slaughter."[3] It is my conviction that by stressing the *unique* character of German antisemitism, Goldhagen passes over the breadth of support the destruction of Europe's Jews had among political and religious élites throughout Europe and beyond.

By the nineteen-thirties most Germans had come to regard the relatively free access by Jews to positions of political, economic, and cultural influence in their society as an intolerable threat. Hence, they regarded the elimination of the Jews as an overwhelmingly important communal objective. Differences of opinion on the Jewish question concerned primarily the method by which the Jews were to be eliminated or so segregated that their allegedly baneful influence could no longer harm Germany and the Germans.

There was little, if any, uncertainty concerning Hitler's preferred method of elimination. In speech after speech to the people of Germany and the world, Hitler explicitly proclaimed extermination to be his preferred method.[4] For Hitler, the war to which he was most deeply committed was the war against the Jews. As Goldhagen comments, the Final Solution commenced in earnest the very first moment that it became feasible. Genocide in Poland was not thought to be feasible until Hitler was ready to go to war with the Soviet Union. According to Goldhagen, when planning began in earnest for the attack in the East, Hitler's thinking about the disposition of the Jews changed. The war against the Soviet Union was conceived of as a "final reckoning" with the forces of both Bolshevism and Jewry. Henceforth, there would be no programs of resettlement or emigration, no Madagascar programs. The course had been irrevocably set. As long as German power dominated wartime Europe, every single Jew was targeted for extermination.[5]

Crucial to Goldhagen's interpretation of the Holocaust is his acceptance of the *Sonderweg* thesis, namely, that Germany developed along a singular path that set it apart from other Western nations. He insists on the unique German role in the extermination of European Jews and in the excessively brutal way in which it was carried out by "ordinary Germans" rather than by committed members of the Nazi party and its associated institutions in the Third Reich. According to Goldhagen, all of German society shared with Hitler a particularly vicious exterminationist antisemitism. It is that aspect of Goldhagen's work that has elicited the greatest attention and caused the greatest controversy.[6]

In addition to a general historical overview, Goldhagen offers three concrete examples of what he considers the uniquely German variety of brutally sadistic genocidal antisemitism, namely, the behavior of the *Ordnungspolizei,* especially Police Battalion 101, the humanly destructive forms of nonproductive slave labor, and the death marches, especially in the last months of the war. In each case, Goldhagen stresses the voluntary character of the perpetrators' participation. To the extent that the perpetrators objected to the slaughter, it was almost always concerning the grisly way Jews were killed rather than as a principled objection to genocide.

Goldhagen stresses the fact that not only did the Germans torture and degrade the Jews in the process of killing them, they also preserved their deeds for future recollection. The many photos taken by the *Einsatzgruppen* and the Police Battalions were duplicated so that they could be readily shared and sent home to Germany. Goldhagen has been criticized by Ruth Birn for resorting to conjecture and fantasy in assessing the motives of the perpetrators.[7] There is nothing conjectural about the widespread photographing of the mass-murder operations.

To my mind, the most horrible picture in Goldhagen's book is one in which a German soldier aims his rifle at the head of a Jewish mother, no more than four feet away, as she cradles her child in her arms with her back turned away from her murderer. This act of soldierly bravery was recorded for posterity by the killer's comrade. The photo was then sent home through regular post. On the back of the photo, there is a notation, "Ukraine 1942, Jüdische Aktion, Ivanogorad."[8] At the very least, the proud author of this deed and his photographer-comrade saw nothing to hide from family and friends.

Did the killers enjoy their tasks? The evidence of the photos argues for an affirmative answer. We also have the killers' own testimony. Initially, the gore disoriented some. We also know that the gas chambers were installed not to increase the efficiency of the mass killing operations but to ease the psychological burdens the mass killing operations caused the perpetrators.[9] Nevertheless, as they became accustomed to their work, most felt pride and satisfaction in the work they pursued with great zeal until the very last days of the Third Reich. Goldhagen quotes a representative figure who described his feelings when he learned that he and his comrades were free to dispose of any fleeing Jews they hunted down as they liked. "I must admit," he said, "that we felt a certain joy.... I cannot remember an instance when a policeman had to be ordered to an execution. [O]ne could have gained the impression that the various policemen got a kick out of it."[10] The same man testified that "the Jew was not acknowledged to be a human being."

The death marches (*Todesmärsche*) were among the worst examples of German sadism and gratuitous destructiveness.[11] Most took place in the last six months of the war and were "the ambulatory analogue to the cattle car."[12] As the Red Army advanced, the retreating Germans were faced with the choice of moving their prisoners with them or losing them. Between March 1945 and the end of the war in early May, approximately 750,000 camp inmates were forcibly removed. Between 250,000 and 375,000 died on the death marches.

Goldhagen's description of the Helmbrechts death march that began on April 13, 1945, is especially telling. Helmbrechts was a labor camp that housed women prisoners who worked in a munitions factory. After a few days' march, the Germans released the Russian and Polish women. The Jewish women were forced to continue on the march that now had as its sole purpose "to degrade, injure, immiserate and kill Jews."[13] It was the Germans' last chance to murder Jews and they were determined to make the most of their final chance with the greatest possible brutality. The march had no other purpose.

The march and the murder continued until May 5. On May 9 an American medical officer examined the survivors. The essence of his report is contained in one sentence: "My first glance at these individuals was one of extreme shock, not ever believing that a human being can be so degraded, can be so starved, can be so skinny and even live under such circumstances."[14] When interrogated by the Americans, the perpetrators testified with "unusual candor," and their testimony concurred "remarkably well" with their victims'. The perpetrators exhibited far less candor at their trials in later decades.[15]

Goldhagen also emphasizes the voluntary character of the death march for the perpetrators. The group's commander knew that Himmler had expressly forbidden the killing of any more Jews, but the order had no effect. These Germans wanted to continue to kill Jews as long as the supply of victims lasted. On a few occasions, German townspeople offered the prisoners some food out of pity. Far more frequently, they jeered, threw stones, and gazed with hostility at the "subhumans." It was the only victory left for them. One way or another, the Germans carried out Hitler's genocidal project to the bitter end.[16]

In his book on T. S. Eliot, Anthony Julius makes a distinction between the *antisemitism of contempt* and the *antisemitism of fear*.[17] Eliot's was the former. By contrast, Hitler and the Germans saw Jews as a danger that had to be obliterated lest Jewish power overwhelm Germany. Hitler and his generals were convinced that by attacking the Soviet Union they were attacking the base of Jewish power.[18] In their determination to exterminate the Jews, the Germans were thus moved more by fear than contempt, fear that the Jews would use Bolshevism to conquer the German *Volk*, fear that the Jews would permanently disorder healthy Aryan blood by intermarriage and licentious seduction, fear that the Jews would destroy Germany's political order as they were alleged to have done in the Weimar Republic, fear that

Jews would hopelessly cripple and destroy the nation's Christian Germanic religious inheritance and, finally, fear that the Jews would somehow wreak their terrible vengeance upon Germany through an Allied victory.

Goldhagen concludes that the single explanation for German behavior was that "a demonological antisemitism, of the virulent racial variety, was the common structure of the perpetrators' cognition and of German society in general. The German perpetrators...were assenting mass executioners, men and women who, true to their own eliminationist antisemitic beliefs, faithful to their cultural antisemitic credo, considered the slaughter to be just."[19]

I see little evidence to suggest that Goldhagen's conclusion is unwarranted. Some Germans did protect Jews. A few even gave their lives. Adam and Sophie Scholl of Munich come to mind. Their number also includes Mgr. Bernard Lichtenberg, *Domprobst* (Provost) of St. Hedwig's Cathedral in Berlin, who first spoke out the day after *Kristallnacht,* when he prayed publicly "for the persecuted 'non-Aryan' Christians and Jews." He continued to utter the prayer publicly every day until he was arrested on October 23, 1941. Lichtenberg received no support from the Papal Nuncio Cesare Orsenigo who had permitted the singing of the Nazi *Horst Wessel Lied* at the mass he celebrated at St. Hedwig's in 1933 in honor of the signing of the *Reichskonkordat,* the Concordat between the Vatican and Hitler's Germany. On May 22, 1942, Lichtenberg was brought to trial, found guilty, and condemned to Dachau.[20] He died on the way to the camp in 1943.[21] Orsenigo's only request was that Lichtenberg's trial be speeded up because of the state of his health.[22] There were others who helped. The recently published diaries of Victor Klemperer offer evidence that some Germans disapproved of Nazi policies and, on occasion, went out their way to be helpful to be Jews.[23] However, while morally significant, the numbers involved were statistically insignificant. Moreover, although knowledge of the so-called Final Solution was widespread, not a single German institution expressed principled opposition to it.

Nevertheless, by stressing the *unique* character of German antisemitism Goldhagen ignores the degree to which antisemitism is a phenomenon of interreligious and intercultural conflict rather than something that is targeted gratuitously against Jews. Goldhagen argues that "the existence of antisemitism and the content of antisemitic charges against Jews must be understood as an expression of the non-Jewish culture and are fundamentally not a response to any objective evaluation of Jewish action....Antisemitism tells us nothing about Jews but much about antisemites and their culture."[24]

What Goldhagen has in mind are the kind of outrageous accusations antisemites have traditionally leveled against Jews. These include being in league with the devil, partaking of the blood of innocent Christian children, and simultaneously controlling both international capital and Bolshevism. Indeed, all of these accusations stem from demonological antisemitic fantasies. That, however, is a far cry from Goldhagen's claim that Jews have objectively done nothing that fundamentally threatens Christians and Christendom. On the contrary, by denying that Christ is Lord, Judaism challenges the very basis of Christian faith. The authority of the Christian Church rests upon that proposition, as does Christian civilization and culture. That proposition is denied by the very people from whom Christ came. Sharing the same scriptures, claiming the same covenant, the Church has had no choice but to discredit the Jewish view of Jesus in order to protect its own religious authority and the credibility of its religious claims.

Insofar as political leaders have for millennia derived their legitimacy from the blessing of Christ's Church, denial of Christ's divinity also constituted a radical challenge to the political order. When Pope Leo III consecrated Charlemagne on Christmas Day, 800, as Emperor of the Romans, *Romanorum gubernans imperium,* he bound political legitimacy in the West to the proposition that Christ is Lord, at least until the French Revolution.[25] Whether or not Jews actively propagated their religious convictions, those convictions were inherently subversive of the political order. There were, as we know, theological as well as more mundane reasons why the Church consented to the existence of small, strictly controlled, culturally isolated communities of Jews within Christendom. Nevertheless, stringent measures had to be taken to warn Christians against the possible temptation to take seriously Jewish claims about Christ. Consequently, the Jews were demonized. They were identified with the devil and were depicted in binary opposition to all that was good and Christian. In our age of "cultural diversity," we are likely to characterize such policies as sheer bigotry, for we understand their genocidal potentiality. Nevertheless, throughout much of its history, the secular and the religious leaders of Christendom considered such measures a justifiable defense of the faith. What we today identify as antisemitic, Church leaders regarded as necessary to preserve the integrity of their religiously legitimated culture and civilization. *Unless we understand the extent to which Jews and Judaism constituted a problem for Christendom, we shall never truly understand the Holocaust.*

Moreover, by portraying Jews as innocent victims of the perpetrators' hatred, Goldhagen fails to explain why a hatred that for almost two thousand years had been eliminationist at worst, but never genocidal, became unremittingly genocidal in the twentieth century. Nor does he really explain the unprecedented complicity of the Christian Church in genocide during World War II. If, as both Goldhagen and Christopher Browning assert, much of the killing was done by "ordinary Germans," then it was done by ordinary Christians who went to church, were served by military chaplains, partook of holy communion, and confessed whatever they considered their sins to be.

By insisting on the primacy of ideology, Goldhagen ignores a whole range of structural and historical phenomena that contributed to genocide.[26] The phenomena that Goldhagen ignores or passes over lightly follow.

The modernization of the economy and society of Germany and other central European nations uprooted millions of former peasants from their traditional moorings and forced them to avoid vocational redundancy by migration either within urban Europe or to the western hemisphere. As the Germans migrated to the new world in the 1870s and 1880s, Eastern European Jews moved into Berlin, Vienna, Budapest, and other metropolitan centers. Hitler's *Lebensraum* policies were designed to assure Germans that, even as they modernized to support an industrial economy, they would not be rendered redundant or compelled to migrate overseas, no matter how his policies affected the fate of non-Germanic peoples in the East.

Germany's defeat in World War I had overwhelming importance. With the loss of millions in a war that lasted four years, Germany was transformed in stages into a bitterly revisionist state determined eventually to reverse the defeat of 1918 for which the Jews were blamed. The rise of Adolf Hitler and the acceptance by the Germans of malevolent, exterminationist antisemitism is inconceivable apart from that utterly traumatic event.

The shock produced by the Bolshevik Revolution cannot be overestimated. Europe's most populous country had been captured by a radically anti-Christian movement that preached world revolution and sought to overthrow what remained of the continent's traditional religious, social, and political order. *Not since the Muslim invasions had a radically anti-Christian force of such magnitude threatened Europe.* Unlike Islam, which posed the external threat of conquest, the Bolsheviks were seen as attempting to overthrow Christian Europe from within by radical subversion and revolution. Moreover, Bolshevism was widely seen as Jewish in both origin and spirit. Its radically anti-Christian attitudes were regarded as an expression of Jewish determination to destroy European Christianity. This view gained further credibility as a result of the revolutionary leftist regimes with largely Jewish leadership that briefly took power at the end of the war in Hungary and Bavaria.

On November 7, 1918, a Socialist republic, led by Kurt Eisner, a Socialist of Jewish origin, was proclaimed in Bavaria. In addition to Eisner, a number of other Jewish intellectuals, *literati,* and revolutionaries took leadership roles in the three successive revolutionary regimes in Bavaria.[27]

This brief revolutionary episode ended in a right-wing bloodbath when the German army occupied Munich on May 1, 1919.[28] Unfortunately, the effects of the failed rebellion were enduring. This was the period and the city in which Hitler found his political vocation. It was also where Alfred Rosenberg, together with some White Russian refugees, introduced the infamous forgery known as *The Protocols of the Elders of Zion.*[29] The forgery, with its myth of a Jewish conspiracy for world domination, was presented as proof that the Bolshevik Revolution was a Jewish plot to conquer and destroy

Christian civilization.[30] The book was speedily translated into German and English and given worldwide dissemination. Unfortunately, the high visibility of Jewish leaders in the Bavarian left-wing regimes lent credibility to their accusations. In spite of the conservative character of the Jewish mainstream, the victorious right regarded Eisner's Republic and the two subsequent Soviet Republics as constituting a "pogrom against the German people staged by Jews."[31] A violent wave of antisemitism ensued in Munich, then in the process of becoming the birthplace and spiritual capital of the National Socialist movement.

Archbishop Eugenio Pacelli, who was to serve as Pope Pius XII during World War II, was the Papal Nuncio to the Bavarian court during this crucial period.[32] He was harassed by troops of the Munich Soviet and Munich's Michael Cardinal von Faulhaber was detained by the left regime. Before the German army reoccupied the city, Reds entered Pacelli's compound, pointed a gun at his head and threatened to kill him, an incident Pacelli never forgot. *For Pope Pius XII, a Communist revolution was not something that happened in distant Russia. He experienced it directly.* He also experienced the forces of right-wing German nationalism as the defenders of Christian civilization against the assault of rootless, godless, Jewish communists. That lesson was never to leave him. If he was not convinced of the destabilizing consequences of the entrance of Jews into European intellectual and political life before Munich 1919, he was thereafter.

Pacelli remained in Germany until 1929. In 1920 he was appointed Papal Nuncio to the Weimar Republic but did not take up residence in Berlin until 1925, remaining in Berlin until recalled to Rome to serve as Vatican Secretary of State. While in Berlin he served as the dean of the diplomatic corps. As such, Pacelli was in a unique position to witness the rise of both the National Socialist and German Communist parties and the declining fortunes of the Weimar Republic. Pacelli was known to be pro-German but not pro-Nazi. When he was elected Pope in 1938, Hitler was not pleased and considered abrogating Germany's Concordat with Rome.[33] Nevertheless, by the time Pacelli became Secretary of State, the Vatican was worried about the possibility of a communist takeover of Europe and saw the National Socialists as allies in the ongoing struggle.[34]

As Papal Nuncio, Pacelli played a crucial role in the Vatican's relations with Germany. With the collapse of Imperial Germany in 1918, the Vatican sought a reformulation of church-state relations through a series of concordats between the Holy See and the principal German states, Bavaria in 1924, Prussia in 1929, and Baden in 1932. All three were signed for the Vatican by Pacelli. Pacelli also sought unsuccessfully to sign a concordat with the Weimar Republic against the opposition of both the left and the ultra-nationalist right. The situation changed almost immediately after Hitler came to power. Hitler wanted the prestige of a diplomatic accord with the Vatican at a time when most governments looked upon the new Nazi regime with considerable suspicion.[35] Possessing a far better knowledge of Hitler and National Socialism than most diplomats and government leaders, Cardinal Secretary of State Pacelli nevertheless signed the *Reichskonkordat* on behalf of the Vatican on July 20, 1933, less than six months after Hitler's assumption of power.

The *Reichskonkordat* was the first international agreement signed by Hitler. It was enormously popular with German Catholics even though Article 32 forbade the clergy from participating in political activity and Hitler had launched a nasty anti-Catholic campaign during the negotiations. Some Catholics warned the Pope against signing any agreement with the Nazis. These included Karl Joseph, Cardinal Schulte of Cologne, and Konrad von Preysing, Bishop of Eichstätt and after 1946 Cardinal Archbishop of Berlin.[36] Nevertheless, Pope Pius XI, Archbishop Pacelli's superior, insisted upon bringing the negotiations to a successful conclusion.

Despite strong reservations about National Socialism's underlying neo-paganism, the pope was impressed by Hitler's anticommunism. The overriding importance of the struggle against godless communism had been a continuing theme in the Vatican throughout the decade of the twenties. In 1922 Count de Salis, the British Minister to the Holy See, reported to the Foreign Office: "Everything in the Vatican is dominated by the pope's fear of Russian Communism, that the Soviets may reach Western Europe."[37] As the world was to learn, that fear was not unjustified. On April 10, 1933, Pius XI granted an audience to Hermann Göring and Franz von Papen, then Vice Chancellor and Germany's principal negotiator for the proposed Concordat. The Pope told his visitors "how pleased he was that the German Government now had at its head a man uncompromisingly opposed to Communism and Russian nihilism in all its forms."[38] Two days after the signing ceremonies in the Vatican on July 20, Papen addressed a meeting of the Association of Catholic Academicians (*Katholischer Akademikerverband*) and told the members that the pope had decided to go ahead with the treaty despite warnings to the contrary, "in the recognition that the new Germany had fought a decisive battle against Bolshevism and the atheist movement."[39] A few days later, Papen reported to the cabinet that the pope "wanted to come to an agreement with Italy and Germany as the countries which, in his opinion, represented the nucleus of the Christian world."[40]

Antisemitism was another area of agreement. However, it is important to understand that only retrospectively can the antisemitism of the early 1930s be seen as leading to Auschwitz. In 1933 the Church wanted to revoke the emancipation of the Jews. The Nazis wanted to expel the Jews from Germany. The Church had no objection as long as baptized Jews and Jews married to Catholics were exempt. There had been expulsions before — England in 1290, France in 1306 and 1394, Spain in 1492. In each case Church leaders regarded the expulsions as a gain, a cleansing of the Christian heartland.

The pre-Vatican II Church was wholly out of sympathy with the legacy of the Enlightenment and the French Revolution that had prepared the way for Jewish participation in European political, cultural, and intellectual life. Before the French Revolution, the Church had never permitted non-Christians such freedom within Christian Europe. In the 1930s, the leaders of the Church leaders were heartily in sympathy with National Socialist attempts to limit or eliminate Jewish influence.

Moreover, the belief that Judaism had spawned Bolshevism was widely held throughout the interwar period and even later.[41] In such a climate, the call for their "removal," *Entfernung,* was welcomed by European élites everywhere. It was, however, possible to favor the elimination of Jews without seriously considering the question of implementation. In the prewar period, many, perhaps a majority, of the leaders of both the Protestant and Catholic Churches of Germany, Poland, and most of Eastern and Central Europe sympathized with the aim of eliminating the Jews as a religious, cultural, political, economic, and demographic presence. Nevertheless, there was an important difference between the Christian and the National Socialist approaches to *Entfernung.* However we date Hitler's decision to exterminate the Jews, he did not ignore the problem of implementation. When less radical methods of *Entfernung* failed, he did not flinch at resorting to ever more draconian methods.[42] Moreover, the Spanish Civil War strengthened the bonds between Hitler and the churches by intensifying Christian fear of Bolshevism.[43] This in turn diminished any residual inclination on the part of Rome to object to Hitler's increasingly violent antisemitism. Both the Vatican and Hitler were convinced that Franco was fighting Bolshevism in Spain and that, if Franco lost, Germany would be caught between Soviet Bolshevism in the East and a Bolshevik Spain and a left-wing France led by Leon Blum, that country's first Socialist and first Jewish Prime Minister, in the West. The Vatican strongly approved of Hitler and Mussolini's support of Franco. *For the Church, the threat of Bolshevik regimes in the Iberian peninsula and Eastern Europe was reminiscent of a time when Christian Europe was threatened by Muslims in Spain and Portugal as well as in Eastern Europe.* To this was added the conviction that a Jewish conspiracy was placing Christian Europe in a vast encircling movement. The Catholic Church did not officially subscribe to Nazi racism but it did see Christian Europe as under a multi-faceted religious, military, political, and cultural threat in which Jews were thought to play a hostile role. Moreover, although both sides committed terrible atrocities during the Civil War, the Spanish Republicans carried out a viciously antireligious campaign, further confirming the Church's worst fears about Bolshevism. Eleven bishops and literally thousands of priests, monks, and nuns were murdered. Hundreds of churches and monasteries were despoiled.[44] For both the Vatican and the German Church, Republican behavior was concrete evidence of what Bolshevism would do throughout Europe if it proved victorious.

Sensing that the Church had become an ally, Hitler invited Michael Cardinal von Faulhaber of Munich to meet with him on November 4, 1936. During the three-hour meeting, Hitler told the Cardinal that "unless National Socialism gets the better of Bolshevism, all is up in Europe for Christianity and the Church.... Either National Socialism and the Church will win together or they will both go under."[45] Hitler offered to stop harassing the Church if the Church supported "the great task of National Socialism in preventing Bolshevism from getting the upper hand...." The Bishops' response to Hitler came in a Christmas pastoral message in which they pledged unconditional support for the *Führer* in the fight against Bolshevism.[46] Faulhaber then wrote to Hitler that "this unanimous commitment of the German bishops to the *Führer* and *his role in world history, the repelling of Bolshevism*" would also be heard outside of Germany.[47] For the vast majority of German Christians, the Church's endorsement of Hitler's anti-Bolshevism constituted an endorsement of his radical antisemitism.

When the German bishops pledged their unconditional support to the *Führer,* Pope Pius XI, Pacelli's predecessor as pope, had yet to make public his criticism of Nazi racism. However, the ideological gulf between National Socialism and the Church could not be papered over. On the Catholic side, the gulf became public when Pius XI's encyclical *Mit brennender Sorge* was read from the pulpits of all Catholic churches in Germany on Palm Sunday, March 21, 1937. By then the anticommunist pope had come to understand that "In its aims and methods National Socialism is just the same as Bolshevism."[48] Unlike Pacelli, he also understood that National Socialism was very different than royalist, pro-Catholic Spanish Fascism and even Italian Fascism. The pope did not attack National Socialism by name but no one had any doubt whom he meant when he stated that "Anyone who makes race or state... into the highest of all norms, even of religious values... perverts and falsifies the divinely created and divinely commanded order of things."[49]

Despite the pope's condemnation of those who make race "into the highest of norms," *Mit brennender Sorge* contained no condemnation of antisemitism.[50] Nevertheless, Pius XI was becoming increasingly concerned with its rise. He had condemned antisemitism in 1928 and on September 7, 1938, he told a group of Belgian pilgrims that "it is impossible for a Christian to take part in anti-Semitism.... Through Christ and in Christ we are the spiritual progeny of Abraham. Spiritually, we are all Semites."[51] The pope's position received something less than unanimous support in the Vatican. Concerned that the pope might jeopardize relations with Germany, Secretary of State Pacelli wrote to Diego von Bergen, the German Ambassador to the Holy See, assuring him that *Mit brennender Sorge* contained no condemnation of the Nazi system of government.[52] When *L'Osservatore Romano,* the official Vatican newspaper, reported the pope's remarks to the Belgian pilgrims, it omitted his condemnation of antisemitism.[53] It is also now known that at about this time Pope Pius XI asked the Rev. John LaFarge, S.J., to assist in the preparation of an encyclical condemning racism and antisemitism, *Humanis Generis Unitas*.[54] With the pope's passing on February 10, 1939, and the subsequent beginning of Pius XII's pontificate, the encyclical disappeared into a secret archive. The existence of the draft encyclical did not become known to the public until December 1972, when the *National Catholic Reporter* began publication of a series of articles concerning an "unpublished encyclical of Pius XI attacking anti-Semitism."[55]

On March 3, 1939, Pacelli became Pope Pius XII and immediately began to mend relations with Germany that had worsened during his predecessor's final years.[56] Pius XII had never been enthusiastic about the publication of *Mit Brennender Sorge*. He wanted Hitler to understand that he intended to follow a more conciliatory line. Three days after the papal coronation, he told the German cardinals that he intended to take charge of relations with Germany personally, leaving relations with other states to Luigi Cardinal Maglione, the new Secretary of State.[57] He made a point of receiving Diego von Bergen before any other diplomat. During their meeting, the Pontiff fondly recalled his years in Germany, spoke of his sympathy for the German people, and told the diplomat that Hitler's regime was just as acceptable to him as that of any other government.[58] He also wrote a cordial letter to Hitler officially informing him of his election. The pope later told Bergen that Hitler was the first head of state whom he had notified of his election. As Hitler prepared for war, he knew that a far more sympathetic pope sat on the throne of St. Peter. None of the Vatican background is considered by Goldhagen in his assessment of the origins of the Final Solution.

When Pius XII told the German ambassador that Hitler's regime was just as acceptable to him as any other, that Nazi regime had already launched the worst pogrom in five hundred years in central Europe, *Kristallnacht*.[59] The violence and terror were visible for the entire world to see. After November 10, it was impossible to entertain any hopeful illusions concerning Hitler's Jewish policy. The Jews of Germany and Austria were confronted with the most implacably hostile regime in all of Jewish history. And, few if any world leaders were as well informed about what was happening in Germany as the new pope.

How did the churches react to this ever-intensifying sequence of discrimination, terror, expulsion, and extermination? The question cannot be answered without taking chronology into account. As we know, many of the anti-Jewish measures enacted in Germany and elsewhere in Europe before the war met with both Catholic and Protestant approval. Both churches welcomed any measure that would diminish Jewish influence. Nevertheless, neither church ever openly advocated murder as a means of achieving that end. When the extermination program became known, as it did, the churches were faced with an unprecedented situation. Their options were limited. They could with varying degrees of discretion signal their approval of the extermination of what they regarded as a dangerous, foreign body within Christendom. Alternatively, they could remain silent. Some remained silent knowing that indifference was all that was required of them for the success of the Final Solution. Others remained silent in order to shelter or rescue the intended victims. Still others openly protested. Speaking out in protest was only possible for a few highly placed clergy. Others risked their lives by so doing.

When Germany attacked Poland in 1939, the German Catholic bishops asked the faithful "to join in ardent prayers that God's providence may lead this war to blessed success and peace for fatherland and people."[60] The only exception was Bishop Konrad Preysing of Berlin, a consistent opponent of National Socialism from its inception.[61] On September 21, 1939, August Cardinal Hlond reached the Vatican and reported on German atrocities in Poland. The report did nothing to moderate the German bishops' support of the war.[62] The pope's response was understandably complex. Given the Church's diverse constituencies and its anticommunism, he was not a free agent even when the S.S. murdered more than two hundred Polish priests and imprisoned one thousand between September 1 and December 31, 1939. The pope attempted to maintain the appearance of strict neutrality. On October 27, 1939, he expressed sympathy for the Poles in the encyclical *Summi Pontificatus,* in which he denounced "unilateral denunciation of treaties and the recourse to arms" without explicitly naming Germany.[63] When Cardinal Hlond submitted a second report on German brutality in Poland to the Vatican on December 25, 1939, the Pope directed that it be broadcast on Vatican Radio and beamed to Germany.[64] Similarly, when the Germans invaded Holland, Belgium, and Luxembourg in May 1940, the pope sent telegrams to their monarchs declaring that he would pray for the re-establishment of their "full liberty and independence." However, the pope's messages pleased neither the Germans nor the Western Allies. The French ambassador pointed out that it was one thing to express sympathy for victims of aggression, another to condemn the aggressor.[65] Poles living in exile had a similar reaction. Meanwhile, as the pope penned these facile messages, the situation of the Jews became progressively more desperate. With the conquest of Poland, several million more Jews became Hitler's captives, and more were added with each new conquest. Emigration ceased to be a practical method of eliminating the Jews and the Nazis began to search for another "solution."

There is considerable debate among historians concerning when extermination became official German policy.[66] Apparently, extermination did become policy sometime in the spring or early summer of 1941. When the *Wehrmacht* invaded the Soviet Union in June 1941, it was accompanied by the *Einsatzgruppen,* special mobile killing squads whose mission was to round up and kill all the Jews found behind German lines. Their first victims were primarily Jewish male leaders. By mid-August, the *Einsatzgruppen* were murdering all Jews indiscriminately.[67] In May 1940 Himmler called mass extermination "un-German."[68] In the summer of 1941 it was no longer un-German.[69]

Just as the invasion of the Soviet Union marked a change in Germany's Jewish policy, it also marked a distinct shift in the Vatican's attitude toward Germany. Until the invasion the Vatican maintained a surface neutrality, and it was not happy about Hitler's 1939 pact with Stalin. When the invasion began, Vatican neutrality gave way to hope for a German victory over the Soviet Union and a negotiated peace with Britain and later the United States. During the Spanish Civil War, the Vatican strongly favored a Franco victory because of its fear of the spread of Bolshevism. Similarly, in the war between Germany and the Soviet Union, the Vatican hoped Germany would destroy the Bolshevik menace that threatened Christian Europe. Nevertheless, the Vatican was unable openly to express its pro-German views as it had during the Spanish Civil War. England was at war with Germany and, with every passing month, the United States was becoming more of a belligerent. An open endorsement of a German victory would not have gone well with many American Catholics, especially those of Polish descent.[70] Furthermore, while the Vatican wanted a victory over Communism, neither the pope nor his subordinates looked with favor on the prospect of a Nazi Europe. The Vatican had come to understand what a Nazi victory would mean for the Church.

On August 8, 1942, Gerhardt Riegner, the representative of the World Jewish Congress in Bern, Switzerland, sent a brief, prophetic message reporting that plans had been discussed in the *Führer*'s headquarters to concentrate the Jews of Europe in the East and then exterminate them "in order to resolve once and for all the Jewish Question in Europe."[71] On September 26, 1942, Myron C. Taylor, President Roosevelt's Special Representative to the Holy See, presented a report to Luigi Cardinal Maglione, the Vatican Secretary of State, explicitly detailing the full scope of the Nazi extermination program. He asked whether the pope had any practical suggestions how "civilized public opinion could be utilized in order to prevent a continuation of these atrocities."[72] In spite of having already received comprehensive information from Catholic sources, Maglione was evasive and asked Taylor for corroboration.[73] On October 6, Maglione admitted to Taylor that the Vatican had received similar information but that it was impossible to verify the report.[74]

In reality, Maglione knew that his sources were absolutely trustworthy. His sources were the papal nuncios to Hungary and Romania and the papal chargé d'affaires in Slovakia, Mgr. Giuseppe Burzio. Burzio served in Slovakia from June 1940 until the end of the war. Slovakia was one of the most Catholic countries in Europe. Its president was a priest, Mgr. Josef Tiso. Many of the leaders of his pro-Nazi Slovak People's Party were also priests. Within a month after Slovakia's separation from Czechoslovakia in April 1939, that nation enacted its first anti-Jewish legislation. A full anti-

Jewish code was enacted on September 9, 1941. The code forbade marriages between Christians and Jews and mandated the expulsion of all Jews, including baptized Jews, from the general schools. Both Burzio and Maglione registered strong protests concerning the disabilities imposed upon *Jewish Christians*. Maglione asserted the Church's right to marry Christians irrespective of ethnic origin. He also expressed concern that Catholics of Jewish origin might lose their faith if denied the religious instruction available in the schools.[75]

On October 27, 1941, Burzio reported to the Vatican that Slovak army chaplains returning from the war in the East informed him that Jewish prisoners of war were shot immediately upon capture by the Germans. The chaplains also reported that Jews of all ages were being systematically annihilated.[76] As John F. Morley has observed, this was the first time the Vatican received explicit information about the massacre of the Jews from one of its own diplomats. Morley, a Roman Catholic scholar, describes the response of the secretariat of state to their diplomat's communication: "Its reaction to Burzio's dispatch was not one of humanitarian concern for the innocent victims, but of petty and parochial interest to know whether it was Slovaks or Germans who were committing the atrocities.... Absent are any words of sympathy or outrage over the contents of the message."[77]

By early 1942 plans were in place to deport Slovakia's Jews, ostensibly to Poland. On March 9 Burzio sent a cable to Maglione describing the planned deportation and concluding: "The deportation of 80,000 persons at the mercy of the Germans is the equivalent of condemning the greater part of them to death." The Vatican received similar reports from the nuncios in Hungary and Romania. On March 14 Maglione handed a strongly worded protest on the deportations to Charles Sidor, the Slovak ambassador to the Holy See. For the first time Maglione's protest did not differentiate between baptized and other Jews. He expressed especial concern that a country "inspired by Catholic principles" should adopt regulations with such painful consequences "for so many families."

Ten days later the Vatican received information from its nuncio in Budapest that the Germans were planning to force several thousand Jewish girls from Slovakia, some of whom were baptized, to act as prostitutes for troops on the Russian front. More than any other, this measure aroused the indignation of both Maglione and the pope. The pope was especially offended that this could happen in a Catholic country. He instructed Maglione to protest again to Sidor and do what he could to get the government to stop.

In spite of the Vatican protests, 52,000 Jews were deported between March 26 and June 30. However, Tiso granted exemptions to approximately 35,000 Jews, most of whom were either baptized or rich. According to Morley, the Vatican refrained from saying or doing anything about the Jews for the rest of 1942. He conjectures that the Vatican's silence was due to the fact that baptized Jews had not been deported and the Vatican did not want to put their lives in jeopardy by angering either the Slovak or German authorities.[78] In February 1943 Slovak newspapers began to print articles suggesting that baptized and protected Jews were about to be deported, which moved the bishops to protest to the government on February 17 on behalf of the baptized Jews in a defensive, apologetic tone. On March 21, the bishops issued their strongest protest, this time on behalf of all Jews. However, the protest was read in all the churches *in Latin,* hardly an indication of urgency.[79]

As one reads Maglione's responses to the diplomats, religious leaders, and representatives of Jewish organizations who pleaded that the Vatican take a stand against the slaughter, one notices that the secretary of state almost invariably concluded with the statement: "The Holy See has done and is doing all that which is in its power on behalf of the Jews."[80] Appearing so often and so consistently, the response gives the impression of being a formulaic script crafted for use whenever the occasion required and there was nothing else to say. It is possible that Maglione was guilty of deception, a habit not unknown among diplomats. More likely, in his own mind he was convinced that, by their efforts on behalf of baptized Jews, he and the pope were doing all they could.

While the deportations continued, the bishops of Slovakia issued a pastoral letter to the faithful describing the Jews as an accursed people for failing to recognize the Redeemer and for "having prepared a terrible and ignominious death for him on the cross." The letter went on to detail the deleterious effects of Jewish control of "almost all the economic and financial life of the country." It concluded, "The Church cannot be opposed, therefore, if the state with legal regulations hinders the dangerous influence of the Jews."[81] The bishops qualified their endorsement of the state's measures by stating that Jews did have the right to have their own families and to possess private property earned by their own labor. In spirit and content the letter was like many others penned by church officials throughout Europe before and during the war.

The importance of the bishop's use of the "witness-people myth" to justify the state's anti-Jewish measures cannot be overestimated. This is the belief that whatever happens to the Jews, for good or for ill, is an expression of God's providence and, as such, is a sign "for God's church"[82] Like their superiors in the Vatican, the bishops of Slovakia saw the hand of God in Jewish misfortune. The church's doctrine was twofold: Catholics are not permitted to employ violence against the Jews, but Jewish suffering is the just consequence of their rejection of Christ and their alleged deicide. In the pre-Vatican II Church both doctrines were powerfully operative. They help to explain why the Vatican was interested in protecting baptized Jews and why it was more concerned with the deportations in Slovakia than in most other countries. Once baptized, Jews were no longer under the deicide curse. Provided they were faithful Christians, there was no further reason to persecute them. It was especially important that Jews be protected from unmerited violence in a Catholic country with a priest as president. The Church held that Jews deserved whatever punishment a just God continued to mete out to them, but a Christian country ought not to inflict violence on its own account and it most certainly had no business forcing Jewish girls into prostitution. Whereas discriminatory measures limiting Jewish influence and even expulsion were acceptable, a Christian state's active complicity in compulsory prostitution and mass murder was not.

In his interpretation of the Holocaust, Goldhagen understands the historic role of Christian antisemitism as a precondition. Nevertheless, he ignores the extent to which the Holocaust can be understood as a religious war, a *twentieth-century Crusade*. He also ignores the extent to which highly sophisticated Christians saw the hand of God in the event. Even Karl Barth, arguably the greatest Protestant theologian of the twentieth century, saw the Final Solution in that light, in spite of the fact that he consistently opposed Nazi measures against the Jews. In 1949, long after the basic facts were known, Barth was able to write that the evil that came to the Jewish people was "a result of their unfaithfulness" and that the Jew "pays for the fact that he is the elect of God."[83] Similarly, in August 1961, I had a memorable discussion concerning the Holocaust with Dean Heinrich Grüber, a Protestant leader who had done much courageously to protect baptized Jews during the Hitler years, at his home in Berlin-Dahlem. In the course of our conversation, the dean declared, "For some reason it was part of God's plan that the Jews died." He added that, like Nebuchadnezzar, Hitler was a "rod of God's wrath" to punish his sinful people.[84]

The same theological view was pervasive in the Vatican. It would have been strange had it been absent. Although the witness-people myth has had catastrophic consequences for Jews, most of those who held it were motivated neither by spite nor by malice. It was their way of rendering intelligible the facts of history in a manner consistent with their faith in Christ. Moreover, Christians were not alone in seeing the hand of God in the Holocaust. Leading Orthodox Rabbis had a similar interpretation, although obviously differing on the sins responsible for the catastrophe.[85]

One can, of course, interpret the silence of the vast majority of Christian leaders as due to "antisemitism," but that term explains very little, if anything. The word "antisemitism" denotes a certain kind of hostility, but it fails to explain what was at stake in the religio-cultural conflict between Europe's Christians and Jews that rendered the former either indifferent to or favorably inclined toward the total elimination of the latter. We return to that issue below. As noted, the widely held conviction that the Holocaust was in some mysterious way the work of a just and righteous God played its part. For almost two thousand years, too much of the Christian tradition had so interpreted Jewish misfortune for the conservative leaders of European Christianity to have escaped its influence. Realization of the devastating consequences of the Christ-killer accusation is one of the reasons why the Second Vatican Council (1962–65) explicitly stated that "what happened in His passion cannot be charged against all the Jews, without distinction, then alive, nor against the Jews of today. [T]he Jews should not be presented as rejected or accursed, as if this followed from Holy Scriptures."[86]

A further religious impediment to rescue arose in March 1943, when Archbishop Angelo Roncalli, the apostolic delegate to Turkey and later Pope John XXIII, transmitted a request from the Jewish Agency for Palestine that the Vatican intervene with the Slovak government to permit one thousand Jewish children to emigrate to Palestine. The archbishop indicated that the British were willing to let the children enter Palestine. Archbishop William Godfrey, the apostolic delegate to the United Kingdom, sent a similar message the same day but referred to the settlement of Jewish children from all of Europe. The requests were handled by Mgr. Domenico Tardini, under secretary of state for Extraordinary Ecclesiastical Affairs. Tardini exhibited some interest in the proposal to rescue the Jewish children from Slovakia, but the idea of endorsing the settlement of Jews in Palestine gave him pause. With full knowledge of the fate that awaited these children in Hitler's Europe, Tardini wrote: "The Holy See has never approved the project of making Palestine a Jewish home. But unfortunately England does not yield.... And the question of the Holy Places? Palestine is by this time more sacred for Catholics than... for Jews."[87]

In his response to Archbishop Godfrey, Maglione expressed strong opposition to a Jewish majority in Palestine. He wrote that the land of Palestine was sacred to Catholics because it was the land of Christ and, if Palestine were to become predominantly Jewish, Catholic piety would be offended. Maglione also instructed Archbishop Amleto Cicognani, the apostolic delegate in Washington, to communicate his views to President Roosevelt.

Clearly, the Vatican was taking a political stand on Palestine on the basis of a religious position at least as old as the First Crusade, namely, the idea that Palestine was Christ's patrimony. One of the earliest expressions of Catholic opposition to modern Zionism was published in the Jesuit journal *Civiltà Cattolica* in 1897 four months before the First Zionist Conference was held in Basel, Switzerland:

> 1,827 years have passed since the prediction of Jesus of Nazareth was fulfilled, namely that Jerusalem would be destroyed... that the Jews would be led away to be slaves among all the nations, and that they would remain in the dispersion till the end of the world.... According to Sacred Scriptures, the Jewish people must always live dispersed and wandering among the other nations, so that they may render witness not only by the Scriptures... but by their very existence. As for a rebuilt Jerusalem, which would become the center of a reconstituted state of Israel, we must add that this is contrary to the prediction of Christ Himself.[88]

Once again, the witness-people myth.... At the time, *Civiltà Cattolica* was especially hostile to Jews and Judaism. Nevertheless, the article reflected what was to be the attitude of Vatican leadership during much of the twentieth century.

On January 25, 1904, Theodore Herzl was received by Pope Pius X. Herzl sought the pope's support for Zionism. The pope replied: "We are unable to favor this movement. We cannot prevent the Jews from going to Jerusalem — but we could never sanction it. The ground of Jerusalem, if it were not always sacred, has been sanctified by the life of Jesus Christ. As the head of the Church I cannot answer you otherwise. The Jews have not recognized our Lord, therefore we cannot recognize the Jewish people."[89]

The pope mentioned his friendly relations with Jews in his home city of Mantua, telling Herzl: "There are other bonds than those of religion: social intercourse, for example, and philanthropy. Such bonds we do not refuse to maintain with the Jews."[90] Nevertheless, he was not prepared to compromise on the Church's understanding of the divinely ordained fate of the Jews.

Once again, we see both the importance and the continuity of the religious factor in Vatican politics. Priests trained for leadership in the Vatican are chosen for their high intelligence and their total dedication to the Church's teachings. Eugenio Pacelli, later to become Pope Pius XII, was such a priest. In 1904, when Herzl met Pope Pius X, Pacelli was twenty-eight years old. He was already recognized as an authority on canon law and had been serving in the secretariat of state since 1901. In the next decade, Pacelli served as secretary of the president of the Papal Commission on Codification under its president, Pietro Cardinal Gaspari, the author of the *Codex Juris Canonici* of 1917, a comprehensive lawbook that exhaustively regulated conditions within the Church in the spirit of the very conservative First Vatican Council. Pacelli worked closely with Gaspari and was his successor as papal secretary of state. Pius XII's theological views on Jews, Judaism and Zionism were fully consistent with those of his predecessors. Given his training, background, and responsibilities, it was impossible for the pope to see the fate of the Jews as other than the consequence of God's judgment against them.

The Vatican began to adjust to a new reality when it became convinced that Germany would lose the war. *There was far more activity on behalf of the Jews after the Vatican's views had changed than before.* The Vatican's initial response to America's entry into the war was similar to Germany's. Both regarded the Americans as too undisciplined and militarily incompetent to present a real threat to the Axis for a very long time.[91] The Vatican's attitude began to change after Myron C. Taylor met with the pope for three successive days starting September 20, 1942, and delivered a strongly worded message from President Roosevelt. The president wrote that the American people had been "foully attacked by Germany's partner in the Orient" and

Richard L. Rubenstein

that the United States "will prosecute the war until the Axis collapses." He rejected all peace negotiations, a deliberate reference to Vatican peace feelers, and declared that "The world has never seen such an avalanche of war weapons...as we shall launch in 1943 and 1944." Undoubtedly, the most threatening part of the message was Roosevelt's statement that the United States and Great Britain had excellent relations with the Soviet Union and that the principles of communism were spread over a large part of the globe and many people believed in them.[92] The United States thus put the Vatican on notice that, far from joining a crusade against godless Bolshevism, it was planning to cooperate with the Soviet Union in dominating Europe and utterly destroying the governments of Germany and Italy.

From the pope's point of view, Roosevelt's war aims were disastrous. The Vatican saw Christian Europe as facing an even greater threat than it once faced from the conquering Muslims, who at least tolerated the practice of Christianity. Taylor then met with Mgr. Tardini and repeated the president's views. Tardini's notes on the conversation contain the following comment: "The Americans are preparing to reorganize Europe as they see fit. And none of them, or almost none, understands the European situation; this desire on their part may cause enormous damage to Europe."[93]

By the time Roosevelt sent his message to the pope, Hitler's hopes of a blitzkrieg victory over the Soviet Union had vanished. Germany's hope of averting a catastrophic defeat now depended upon the improbable invention of a secret weapon or a negotiated peace with the Western Allies. The Vatican preferred a negotiated peace followed by a joint attack by Germany and the Western Allies on the Soviet Union.[94] Roosevelt had ruled out that option and the Vatican knew that the war was going to end in an Allied victory.

Although the pope still hoped for a German victory over Bolshevism, a hint of something new began to appear in his messages. In his 1942 Christmas broadcast the pope declared that "it was incumbent upon all righteous and magnanimous hearts...to unite and take a solemn vow never to rest until, among all the peoples and all the nations of the earth, the names of those shall be legion who are determined to lead society back to divine law...and to dedicate themselves to the service of the human person and of the community ennobled in God." The pope enumerated the groups for whose sake it was incumbent on "righteous and magnanimous hearts" to make such a vow. They included, among others, "mothers, widows and orphans." The pope then stated that "Humanity owes this vow to hundreds of thousands of people who, through no fault of their own, and solely because of their nation or their race, have been condemned to death or progressive extinction."[95]

This was the most explicit public comment on the extermination of the Jews the pope had made during the war. Nevertheless, there was less here than met the eye. There is no way to read the message other than as *a statement of what the living owe the dead.* The pope criticized totalitarianism in the message without identifying any totalitarian country, but he neither condemned the Germans for what they were doing nor did he call for a halt in the slaughter. At the time, 3,000,000 Jews had already been killed and thousands more were being killed every day.[96]

On October 26, 1943, S.S. Major Herbert Kappler demanded that the Jews of German-occupied Rome surrender fifty kilograms of gold within thirty-six hours. Fearful that it could not collect the sum, the Jewish community turned to the Vatican for help. The pope agreed to lend the community whatever amount it was unable to raise.[97] However, as Susan Zuccotti has observed, there is no evidence that when the Vatican learned in October 1943 that the Germans planned to deport Rome's eight thousand Jews, the pope acted on this knowledge. He neither spoke out before the deportations nor did he protest publicly after they had taken place.[98]

The last mass deportation of the war took place in Hungary after the German invasion of March 19, 1944. It was well under way in April. Adolf Eichmann was charged with the responsibility for implementing the deportations, but with a force of eight S.S. officers and forty enlisted men he could not have succeeded without the cooperation of the pro-Nazi Hungarian government that supplied 20,000 men.[99] There were three somewhat different Catholic responses, that of the prince primate of Hungary, the papal nuncio, and the pope. Jusztinian Cardinal Seredi, the prince primate, actively sought to protect baptized Jews and Jews married to Catholics but refused to accede to a request from Budapest Jewish leaders to appeal to the regent, Admiral Miklós Horthy, to stop the deportations. Seredi was urged to take a stand against the deportations by Mgr. Rotta, the papal nuncio, to no avail. On June 29, 1944, the cardinal published a letter defending the legal measures taken to eliminate "the noxious influence of the Jews." He declared that he had kept silent in public because he was attempting to protect baptized Jews. Since that effort had failed, he rejected any responsibility for the ensuing events.[100] The cardinal's letter was not a condemnation of the deportations but a defense of his own conduct. From June 9 to July 9, 1944, more than 457,000 Hungarian Jews were sent to Auschwitz.[101]

There was nothing secret about the deportations from Hungary. The Spanish, Swiss, and Swedish governments, all at least technically neutral, appealed for an end to them. On March 24 the American War Refugee Board asked Archbishop Cicognani, the apostolic delegate to the United States, to request the pope to intervene on behalf of the Jews of Hungary and Romania. The appeal was repeated by Harold Tittman, Myron Taylor's deputy, on May 26. Finally, on June 25 the pope sent a private, unpublicized telegram to Regent Horthy requesting that he stop the deportations. It came two months after the first American request and three weeks after the Allies had captured Rome.

There have been many attempts to explain the pope's public silence concerning the Holocaust, some offered by the pope himself. A representative sample can be found in some of the works cited in the notes to this essay. The pope's unwillingness to do anything that might weaken the Third Reich's defense of Europe against Bolshevism is often cited by historians. Nevertheless, it is my conviction that the motives for the pope's silence were more deeply rooted in his religious beliefs, especially the role of the Jews in God's providential ordering of history, than most observers credit. *What I find especially surprising is the relative absence in the literature, including Goldhagen, of the possibility that the pope and his subordinates at that time may have judged the elimination of the Jews from Europe to be as important as the elimination of Bolshevism.*

Let my meaning be absolutely clear. I am *not* suggesting that the pope or the Church as an institution actively sought the extermination of the Jews, although some clerics clearly did.[102] Moreover, I am fully cognizant of the selfless attempts at both protest and rescue by some Christians, both lay and clerical, during the war. Nevertheless, one must ask whether the World War II successor of Pope Innocent III (d. 1216) may have regarded Jews, especially emancipated Jews, who had been free to play a progressively more influential role within the Christian World since the French Revolution, in the same way that Innocent III had regarded the Cathari heretics at the beginning of the thirteenth century, namely, as a dangerous internal enemy.[103] Could it be that the Vatican regarded the Jews and Judaism as a religio-cultural "cancer" to be eliminated, hopefully by humanitarian means, but eliminated nonetheless?

One may object that the Church regarded the Cathars as heretics and, as such, an *internal threat,* whereas, to the extent that twentieth-century Jews were perceived as a threat, they were external to the body of Christendom. That argument holds in the case of traditional Jews living in ghettoized segregation, but not in that of their modern progeny. As Jews entered the ranks of intellectuals, writers, journalists, publishers, and other opinion-makers, they came to be regarded as dangerously subversive *internal* enemies. Long before the Bolshevik Revolution, Church leaders concluded that ideas from Jewish sources could have negative moral and political consequences. In the mind of Pope Pius XII this view was powerfully reinforced by his own experiences in revolutionary Munich.

As the head of the oldest continuous corporate institution in the Western world, the Roman pontiff understood that great historical transformations are seldom, if ever, bloodless. He did not have to be instructed in the history of the terrible wars, crusades, and inquisitions that were necessary to complete the Christianization of Europe. The pope neither was nor could he have been an Oskar Schindler who could not ignore the personal consequences of the Final Solution for the individuals working for him. In addition, as indicated above, the Final Solution could be rationalized by Christians as divine punishment of obstinately unfaithful Israel.

Could it perhaps be that Church leaders in Rome, Berlin, and throughout Europe had a view of the personnel responsible for the planning and implementation of the "Final Solution" not unlike the Church's view of the *routiers* during the Albigensian Crusade?[104] Although neither religious nor lay authorities had any illusions about these men, they also understood that the Crusade could not have succeeded without them. And so, they were used throughout the Languedoc region to make their contribution to the uprooting of Latin Christendom's most serious internal threat. Actually, the Church took a much more benign attitude toward the perpetrators of the Final Solution. As is well known, an enormous effort was made by Church officials in Rome immediately after the war to rescue Nazi war criminals, including death and concentration camp commandants such as Franz Stangl of Treblinka and Alois Brunner of Drancy, and to help them find new lives. Wartime acts of extermination became easily pardonable offenses as yesterday's war criminals became heroic fighters against godless communism, a view in which the Vatican found support among both American and British leaders.[105]

Admittedly, Pius XII and Innocent III lived in very different eras and faced very different problems. Innocent did not flinch from prescribing the sword.[106] Pius XII was responsible for no such incitement. Nevertheless, both Pius XII and Innocent III believed their Church was confronted by dangerous external and internal threats. As leaders of their ancient institution, both were committed to doing whatever was necessary to overcome the dangers confronting it. In the case of Pius XII, this meant doing nothing to impede a German victory in the East as long as there was hope that Germany would put an end to the threat of Bolshevism that hung over Christian Europe. In and of itself, that decision spelled the physical destruction of Europe's Jews. On the eve of World War II, the vast majority of European Christian leaders saw their culture and civilization as profoundly threatened by two enemies, Bolshevism and Judaism. And, to repeat, in the eyes of most who held this view, it was Judaism, perhaps in a bastardized form, that had spawned Bolshevism. The twentieth-century crusade against the Jews was an unparalleled success.

Nor has the defense of European Christendom entirely ceased in our time. In 1993 and 1994 I visited Germany in order to investigate the neo-Nazi violence that had especially targeted Germany's Turkish residents. I discussed this issue with a German priest whom I have known for more than twenty-five years. He is a thoroughly decent human being who is completely opposed to the kind of violence that was taking place and in no sense can be said to have National Socialist sympathies. We also enjoy a degree of frankness and honesty in our interchanges that I treasure greatly. I asked him what he thought would be the fate of the Turks in Germany. He replied: "Germans are not opposed to immigration. Recently, I reminded a woman in my church who had made disparaging remarks about immigrants that her own grandparents had come from Poland to work in the coal mines in the Ruhr Valley. But, Poles are different than Turks. They are Christian and can be absorbed into the German people. The Turks are not Christian and have no desire to become Christian. Sooner or later, they will have to go."

I thought immediately of the Jews of the Third Reich. The sentiments expressed by my friend were eliminationist, not exterminationist. Had Goldhagen pressed a little deeper, he would have found that, in spite of the recently adopted, less restrictive immigration laws, eliminationist sentiment is widespread in contemporary Germany, though by no means universal. Furthermore, there is little likelihood that it will ever entirely disappear because of the Germans' sense of their own identity. I do not write this in criticism of the Germans. American identity was formed by a radically different set of circumstances than those that shaped the identity of the nationalities of Europe. Every organization of society has its own potential for large-scale destructive behavior. In the case of the relatively homogenous nation state under conditions of radical stress, that potential includes genocide. Under conditions of the most radical stress, the Germans acted out that potential. One can only hope that, just as the experience of the inflation of 1923 has made the Germans inflation-averse, the experience of the Holocaust has had a comparable effect.

Finally, although there is much to admire in Goldhagen's work, he fails to deal with the crucial importance of religion to modern European history, culture, and politics in the period that encompassed the rise of National Socialism and the Holocaust. Without the widespread conviction among wartime Europe's religious and political élites that the war presented a unique opportunity to limit or eliminate Jewish influence within Christendom, the "Final Solution" could not have been so effectively implemented. The war against the Jews was a Holy War.

Notes

1. Daniel Jonah Goldhagen, *Hitler's Willing Executioners: Ordinary Germans and the Holocaust* (New York: Vintage Books, 1997).

2. Michael Wolffsohn, *Eternal Guilt? Forty Years of German-Jewish-Israel Relations*, trans. Douglas Bokovoy (New York: Columbia University Press, 1993), 65.

3. Goldhagen, *Hitler's Willing Executioners*, 419, italics added.

4. For example, on January 30, 1942, ten days after the Wannsee Conference, on the ninth anniversary of Hitler's assumption of power and three years to the day after his infamous Reichstag prophecy in which he stated that the Jews would not survive the war, Hitler declared in his annual major address to the Reichstag: "We are clear about the fact that the war can only end either in the extermination of the Aryan nations or in the disappearance of Jewry from Europe. On September 1, 1939, I already announced in the German Reichstag — and I avoid making premature prophecies — that this war would not end as the Jews imagined, namely with the extermination of the European-Aryan nations, but rather the war will result in the destruction of Jewry . . . the hour will come when the most evil enemy of the world

of all time will for at least a thousand years have played his last role." The text is to be found in J. Noakes and G. Pridham, *Nazism 1919–1945: A Documentary Reader* (Exeter: University of Exeter Press), vol. 3, *Foreign Policy, War and Racial and Racial Extermination,* 1135–36.

5. The lengths to which the Germans were prepared to go in pursuit of their genocidal objective can be seen in the actions in July 1942 of S.S. Colonel Joseph Meisinger, the Gestapo chief for Japan, China, and the Japanese puppet state of Manchukuo. Meisinger had served in Warsaw in 1939 and was sent by submarine to the Far East. Meisinger traveled from Tokyo to Japanese-occupied Shanghai where about 17,000 European Jews had found refuge. With two other German officials, he met with local authorities in Shanghai and demanded that the Japanese exterminate their Jewish charges "like garbage" on Rosh Hashanah. Initially, Shanghai Japanese authorities were inclined to accede to Meisinger's demands, but Vice Consul Mitsugi Shibata found both Meisinger and his proposals revolting. He took the highly unusual step of warning the leaders of the Shanghai Jewish community. He urged them to use their contacts in the Japanese government to thwart Meisinger. Shibata was imprisoned and dismissed from the Consular Service when his activities became known to local Japanese authorities. The Shanghai Jews got word to Dr. Abraham Kaufman, the leading Jew in Harbin, Manchuria, who enjoyed the favor of some of Japan's most important leaders. When Kaufman used his contacts to apprise Foreign Minister Matsuoka and Colonel Norihiro Yasue of the situation, the Japanese government rejected Meisinger's proposals, although on February 18, 1943, the Japanese decreed that "stateless refugees" would be confined to a ghetto in the Hongkew section of Shanghai, one of the poorest sections of the metropolis. Nevertheless, within Hongkew, the Jews were not harmed. No military imperative compelled the Germans to seek the extermination of harmless Jewish refugees more than seven thousand miles from Germany. Meisinger's actions were consistent with the list of Jewish communities marked for "a further possible solution instead of migration" (*Anstelle der Auswanderung ist nunmehr als weitere Lösungsmöglichkeit*) that Reinhard Heydrich presented at the Wannsee Conference on January 20, 1942. Destruction of these communities would, according to Heydrich, be the "future final solution of the Jewish question" (*die kommende Endlösung der Judenfrage*). As we know, in addition to the Jews of Germany and German-occupied Europe, the list included the Jews of England, Finland, Sweden, Switzerland, Portugal, Spain, and the European part of Turkey. See Marvin Tokayer and Mary Swartz, *The Fugu Plan: The Untold Story of the Japanese and the Jews During World War II* (New York: Paddington Press, 1979), 222–26, and David Kranzler, *Japanese, Nazis and Jews: The Jewish Refugee Community of Shanghai, 1935–1945* (Hoboken: KTAV, 1988), 478–79. On the Wannsee Conference, see "Conference protocol of a meeting held in Berlin, Am Grossen Wannsee No. 56/58 on January 20, 1942, pertaining to the 'Final Solution' of the Jewish Problem" (Minutes taken by S.S. *Obersturmbannführer* Adolf Eichmann) in John Mendelsohn and Donald S. Detwiler, eds., *The Holocaust: Selected Documents in Eighteen Volumes* (New York: Garland Press, 1982), 11:7.

6. For an overview of critical responses to the Goldhagen thesis, both positive and negative, see Robert R. Shandley, *Unwilling Germans? The Goldhagen Debate* (Minneapolis: University of Minnesota Press, 1998).

7. See Norman Finkelstein and Ruth Birn, *The Goldhagen Thesis and Historical Truth* (New York: Henry Holt, 1998).

8. Goldhagen, *Hitler's Willing Executioners,* 406.

9. See ibid., 157 and 533, nn. 79, 80, and 81.

10. Ibid., 452.

11. For a survivor's account of his experience on a Nazi death march at the end of the war, see Joseph Freeman, *The Road to Hell: Recollections of the Nazi Death March* (St. Paul, Minn.: Paragon House, 1998).

12. Goldhagen, *Hitler's Willing Executioners,* 328.

13. Ibid., 346.

14. Ibid., 330–31.

15. Ibid., 582, n. 6.

16. Upon learning of Hitler's death on May 1 or 2, 1945, Adolf Cardinal Bertram, president of the German Bishops' Conference and Prince Bishop of Breslau, instructed the parish priests in his diocese to hold a solemn requiem mass in Hitler's memory. Klaus Scholder, *A Requiem for Hitler and Other New Perspectives on the German Church Struggle* (Philadelphia: Trinity Press International, 1989), 166.

17. Anthony Julius, *T. S. Eliot, Anti-Semitism and Literary Form* (Cambridge: Cambridge University Press, 1995), 17.

18. This conviction was stated succinctly by the strongly pro-Nazi Field Marshal Walter von Reichenau in an infamous document on the "Conduct of Troops in Eastern Territories issued to his troops on October 10, 1941." The document reads in part: "Regarding the conduct of troops toward the bolshevistic system, vague ideas are still prevalent in many quarters. The most essential aim of war against the Jewish-bolshevistic system is a complete destruction of their means of power and the elimination of Asiatic influence from the sphere of European culture. The soldier in the Eastern territories is not merely a fighter according to the rules of war but also a bearer of ruthless volkish ideology and the avenger of bestialities which have been inflicted upon German and racially related nations. Therefore the soldier must have full understanding for the necessity of a severe but just revenge on subhuman Jewry. The Army has to aim at another purpose, i.e. the annihilation of revolts in the hinterland, which, as experience proves, have always been caused by Jews." Moreover, as Omar Bartov has shown, von Reichenau was no exception. On the contrary, von Reichenau's document succinctly expresses the predominant attitude of the German Army in its ideological war in the East. See Omar Bartov, *Hitler's Army: Soldiers, Nazis, and War in the Third Reich* (New York: Oxford University Press, 1991). Von Reichenau's document is to be found in John Mendelsohn, ed., *The Holocaust Selected Documents in Eighteen Volumes* (New York: Garland Press, 1982), 11–12. See also Jürgen Förster, "The Relation between Operation Barbarossa as an Ideological War of Extermination and the Final Solution" in David Cesarani, ed. *The Final Solution: Origins and Implementation* (London: Routledge, 1994), 85–102.

19. Goldhagen, *Hitler's Willing Executioners,* 392–93.

20. For a discussion of the significance of Lichtenberg's sacrificial behavior, see Emil L. Fackenheim, *To Mend the World* (New York: Schocken Books, 1982), 289–90.

21. The Foreign Office expected papal nuncio Orsenigo to inquire about Lichtenberg's arrest and were prepared to tell him that he had been arrested for praying

for the Jews. Apparently, the Foreign Office believed that the nuncio and the pope would find that reply satisfactory. See Saul Friedländer, *Pius XII and the Third Reich: A Documentation,* trans. Charles Fullman (New York: Alfred A. Knopf, 1966), 100–101.

22. John F. Morley, *Vatican Diplomacy and the Jews during the Holocaust 1939–1943* (New York: KTAV Publishing House, 1980), 112.

23. Viktor Klemperer, *Ich will Zeugnis ablegen bis zum letzen: Tagebücher 1933–1945 von Viktor Klemperer* (Berlin: Aufbau-Verlag Gmbh, 1995); English translation, *I Will Bear Witness: A Diary of the Nazi Years 1933–1941,* trans. Martin Chalmers (New York: Random House, 1998).

24. Goldhagen, *Hitler's Willing Executioners,* 39.

25. See Heinrich Fichtenbau, *The Carolingian Empire: The Age of Charlemagne,* trans. Peter Munz (New York: Harper Torchbooks, 1964), 74–75.

26. See Richard L. Rubenstein, *The Age of Triage: Fear and Hope in an Overcrowded World* (Boston: Beacon Press, 1983; paperback, 1984).

27. These included Gustav Landauer, Eugen Leviné, Ernst Toller, and Towia Axelrod. On the revolution in Munich, see Allan Mitchell, *Revolution in Bavaria, 1918–1919* (Princeton: Princeton University Press, 1965); Ruth Fischer, *Stalin and German Communism* (Cambridge: Harvard University Press, 1948); Charles B. Maurer, *Call to Revolution: The Mystical Anarchism of Gustav Landauer* (Detroit: Wayne State University Press, 1971); Rosa Leviné-Meyer, *Leviné the Spartacist* (London: Gordon and Cremonesi, 1978); Richard Grunberger, *Red Rising in Bavaria* (New York: St. Martin's Press, 1973).

28. See Mitchell, *Revolution in Bavaria,* and Grunberger, *Red Rising in Bavaria.*

29. See Robert Pois, ed., "Introduction to Alfred Rosenberg" in *Race and Race History* (New York: Harper and Row, 1974).

30. See Norman Cohn, *Warrant for Genocide: The Myth of the Jewish World-Conspiracy and the Protocols of the Elders of Zion* (New York: Harper and Row, 1967).

31. Karl Dietrich Bracher, *The German Dictatorship* (New York: Praeger, 1973), 82.

32. On the wartime attitudes of Pope Pius XII to National Socialist Germany, see Friedländer, *Pius XII and the Third Reich,* 174–76.

33. Joseph Goebbels, *The Goebbels Diaries: 1939–1941,* trans. and ed. Fred Taylor (Harmondsworth, Middlesex: Penguin Books, 1984), 10.

34. See Anthony Rhodes, *The Vatican in the Age of Dictators 1922–1945* (London: Hodder and Stoughton, 1973), 165.

35. The quote is from a sermon preached in the Cathedral of Munich on February 14, 1937, by Michael Cardinal von Faulhaber, Archbishop of Munich, "Das Reichskonkordat-Ja Oder Nein?" in *Münchner Kardinalspredigten,* 3rd series (Munich, 1937), 4–5. For this citation, I am indebted to Guenther Lewy, *The Catholic Church and Nazi Germany* (New York: McGraw-Hill, 1964), 90.

36. Klaus Scholder, *The Churches and the Third Reich,* trans. John Bowden (London: SCM Press, 1987), 1:393–94.

37. Rhodes, *The Vatican in the Age of Dictators,* 18.

38. Franz von Papen, *Memoirs,* trans. Brian Connell (London: André Deutsch, 1952), 279.

39. Franz von Papen, "Zum Reichskonkordat," in *Der katholische Gedanke,* VI, 1933, pp. 331–36. I am indebted to Guenther Lewy, *The Catholic Church and Nazi Germany,* 86 for this citation.

40. Report of Papen to the Cabinet, July 14, 1933; cited by Lewy, *The Catholic Church and Nazi Germany,* 74.

41. On the enormous influence of the *Protocols* in Japan, see Richard L. Rubenstein, "The Financier and the Finance Minister: The Roots of Japanese Anti-Semitism," in Julius H. Schoeps, ed., *Aus zweier Zeugen Mund: Festschrift für Nathan P. und Pnina Navé Levinson* (Gerlingen: Bleicher-Verlag, 1992), 188–201.

42. Richard L. Rubenstein and John K. Roth, *Approaches to Auschwitz: The Holocaust and Its Legacy* (Atlanta: John Knox Press, 1987), 343f.

43. On the importance of the Spanish Civil War for the relations between the churches and Hitler, see Scholder, *A Requiem for Hitler,* 140–56.

44. See Hugh Thomas, *The Spanish Civil War* (New York: Harper, 1961), 258–81.

45. L. Volk, *Akten Kardinal Michael von Faulhabers 1917–1945* (Mainz: Matthias-Grunewald-Verlag, 1978), vol. 2, 1935–1945, 185.

46. Ibid., 592.

47. Ibid., 599, italics added.

48. Ibid., 284.

49. The English translation of the text of the encyclical can be found in Sidney Z. Ehler and John B. Morrall, eds., *Church and State through the Centuries* (London: Burns and Oates, 1954), 519–39.

50. Luigi Sturzo, *Nationalism and Internationalism* (New York: Roy Publishers, 1946), 46.

51. Rhodes, *The Vatican in the Age of Dictators,* 339.

52. Lewy, *The Catholic Church and Nazi Germany.*

53. Ibid., 158.

54. See Georges Passelecq and Bernard Suchecky, *The Hidden Encyclical of Pius XI,* with an introduction by Garry Wills (New York: Harcourt, Brace, 1997).

55. *National Catholic Reporter,* December 15 and 22, 1972, and January 19, 1973.

56. See Friedländer, *Pius XII and the Third Reich,* 3–24.

57. *Actes et Documents du Saint Siège relatif à la seconde guerre mondiale* (Vatican City: Liberia editrice Vaticana, 1967), vol. 2, *Lettres aux Eveques Allemands;* henceforth, A.D.S.S. See also Rhodes, *The Vatican in the Age of Dictators,* 226–28.

58. Friedländer, *Pius XII and the Third Reich,* 9–10.

59. In a period of twenty-four hours, one thousand synagogues were burned to the ground, tens of thousands of Jewish shops were looted, 30,000 Jews were sent to concentration camps where approximately one thousand were murdered. See Richard Breitman, *The Architect of Genocide: Himmler and the Final Solution* (New York: Alfred A. Knopf, 1991), 53.

60. "Gemeinsames Wort der deutschen Bischöfe," *Martinus-Blatt,* no. 38, September 17, 1939.

61. See Klaus Scholder, *Requiem,* 157–67.

62. As the war went on, many of the German bishops found themselves opposed to Hitler's radical policies, especially the "euthanasia" project which claimed

between 60,000 and 80,000 victims, the abusive treatment of people in the occupied territories, and the measures Hitler had taken against monasteries and religious orders. At the urging of Bishop Preysing a pastoral letter detailing the bishops' misgivings was drafted in the summer of 1941, but publication was blocked by Cardinal Bertram. For a brief summary of Catholic attitudes toward the Nazi regime in wartime in Germany, see Lewy, *The Catholic Church and Nazi Germany,* 242.

63. Rhodes, *The Vatican in the Age of Dictators,* 237.

64. A.D.S.S.: *La Saint Siège et la Situation Réligieuse en Pologne et dans les Pays Balts, 1939–1945,* vol. 3, no. 102 (January 19, 1940).

65. Rhodes, *The Vatican in the Age of Dictators,* 243.

66. For a discussion of the issues at stake in the debate, see Christopher R. Browning, *The Path to Genocide: Essays on Launching the Final Solution* (Cambridge: Cambridge University Press, 1992), 86–124; and *Nazi Policy, Jewish Workers, German Killers* (Cambridge: Cambridge University Press, 2000), 1–57. See also Phillipe Burrin, *Hitler and the Jews: The Genesis of the Holocaust,* trans. Patsy Southgate (London: Edward Arnold, 1994), 115–48; Eberhard Jäckel, *Hitler's World View: A Blueprint for Power,* trans. Herbert Arnold (Cambridge: Harvard University Press, 1981), 47–66; Saul Friedländer, "From Anti-Semitism to Extermination: A Historiographical Study of Nazi Policies toward the Jews and an Essay in Interpretation," in François Furet, ed., *Unanswered Questions: Nazi Germany and the Genocide of the Jews* (New York: Schocken Books, 1989). See also Breitman, *The Architect of Genocide,* 145–66.

67. Yaacov Lozowick, "*Rollbahnmord:* The Early Activities of Einsatzgruppe C," *Holocaust and Genocide Studies* 2, no. 2 (1987), 221–41.

68. We know that genocide was not official policy in May 1940 when Himmler drafted a memorandum entitled "Some Thoughts on the Treatment of Alien Populations in the East." The memorandum included his thoughts on the "solution" of the Jewish problem: "I hope completely to erase the concept of the Jews through the possibility of a great emigration of all Jews to a colony in Africa or elsewhere.... However cruel and tragic each individual case may be, this method is still the mildest and the best, if one rejects the Bolshevik method of physical extermination of a people out of inner conviction as un-German and impossible." Himmler submitted the document to Hitler on May 25, 1940, and subsequently noted that the *Führer* had approved the memorandum. See Helmut Krausnick, ed., "Einige Gedanken über die Behandlung der fremdvölkischen im Osten," *Vierteljahrshefte für Zeitgeschichte* 2 (1957), 197–98.

69. 439,826 Jews were killed in the German occupied areas of the Soviet Union by the *Einsatzgruppen* from July through December 1941. See Wila Orbach, "The Destruction of the Jews in the Nazi-Occupied Territories of the USSR," *Soviet Jewish Affairs,* 6, no. 2 (1976), Table 3.

70. Report of Diego von Bergen to Joachim von Ribbentrop, February 15, 1940, cited by Saul Friedländer, *Pius XII and the Third Reich* (New York: Alfred A. Knopf, 1966), 73–74.

71. Text in Friedländer, *Pius XII and the Third Reich,* 117.

72. Letter from Myron C. Taylor to Cardinal Maglione, September 26, 1942, *Foreign Relations of the United States* (Washington, D.C.: United States Government Printing Office, 1961), vol. 3, 775–76. Henceforth F.R.U.S.

73. F.R.U.S., vol. 3, 775.

74. A.D.S.S., *Le Saint Siège et les Victimes de la Guerre, Janvier 1941–Décembre 1942*, vol. 8, no. 665.

75. Letter of Luigi Cardinal Maglione, Secretary of State, to Charles Sidor, Minister of Slovakia to the Holy See, in Morley, *Vatican Diplomacy and the Jews*, 221–25. The Italian text and the English translation are reproduced.

76. A.D.S.S., vol. 8, nos. 327–28.

77. Morley, *Vatican Diplomacy and the Jews*, 78.

78. Ibid., 89.

79. Ibid., 89–90.

80. "La Santa Sede ha fatto e sta facendo tutto quello che e in suo potere a favore degli ebrei," A.D.S.S., vol. 9, 179; Morley, *Vatican Diplomacy and the Jews*, 91.

81. The date of the pastoral letter was April 26, 1942; A.D.S.S., vol. 8, no. 519.

82. On the witness-people myth, see Stephen R. Haynes, *Jews and the Christian Imagination: Reluctant Witness* (Louisville: Westminster John Knox Press, 1994), Introduction, 8ff.

83. Karl Barth, "The Jewish Problem and the Christian Answer," in *Against the Stream* (London: SCM Press, 1954), 196–98. This citation was originally called to my attention by Emil L. Fackenheim, *To Mend the World* (New York: Schocken Press, 1982), 133.

84. Richard L. Rubenstein, *After Auschwitz: History, Theology and Contemporary Judaism*, 2nd. ed. (Baltimore: Johns Hopkins University Press, 1992), 9–13.

85. See Rubenstein, *op. cit.*, 159–63.

86. *Nostra aetate* ("In Our Time"), promulgated October 28, 1965. The text is to be found in *Encyclopedia Judaica* (Jerusalem: Keter Publishing House, 1972), 5:549–50.

87. A.D.S.S., vol. 9, no. 272; Morley, *Vatican Diplomacy and the Jews*, 92.

88. *Civiltà Cattolica*, May 1, 1897, cited by Sergio Minerbi, *The Vatican and Zionism: Conflict in the Holy Land 1895–1925* (New York: Oxford University Press, 1990), 96.

89. Theodore Herzl, *The Diaries of Theodore Herzl*, trans. and ed. Marven Lowenthal (New York: Grosset and Dunlap, 1962), 428.

90. Ibid., 429.

91. This view was reflected in the Vatican's attempts to counter American diplomatic initiatives in Latin America in January 1942. When the United States attempted to get the nations of Latin America to break off diplomatic relations with Germany, Italy, and Japan, its efforts were largely thwarted by the Vatican. See Friedländer, *Pius XII and the Third Reich*, 90.

92. Roosevelt's message is to be found in A.D.S.S., vol. 5, no. 431. See also Rhodes, *The Vatican in the Age of Dictators*, 265–71.

93. A.D.S.S., vol. 5, no. 480.

94. See Friedländer, *Pius XII and the Third Reich*, 174–96, especially the memorandum of Ernst von Weizsäcker, German Ambassador to the Holy See dated September 24, 1943, on 191–92.

95. Rhodes, *The Vatican in the Age of Dictators*, 72–73.

96. Reinhard Heydrich, who had been charged by Göring with the implementation of the Final Solution, was furious. He complained that the pope made himself

"the mouthpiece of the Jewish war criminals." See Rhodes, *The Vatican in the Age of Dictators*. On January 2, 1943, Wladislaw Raczkiewicz, the president of the Polish government in exile, protested to the pope saying that his people "implore that a voice be raised to show clearly and plainly where the evil lies and to condemn those in the service of evil." The British, Belgian, and Brazilian governments also protested to the Vatican for having failed to name Germany. The protests pained the pope, who was convinced that he had spoken as plainly as he could. The pope and his subordinates were convinced that they could not explicitly denounce the German atrocities. See Friedländer, *Pius XII and the Third Reich*, 131–47.

97. Susan Zuccotti, *The Italians and the Holocaust: Persecution, Rescue, Survival* (New York: Basic Books, 1987), 109–13. For a thorough examination of the role of the Vatican in the deportation of Rome's Jews, see Zuccotti, *Under His Very Windows: The Vatican and the Holocaust in Italy* (New Haven: Yale University Press, 2000).

98. Zuccotti, *Italians and the Holocaust*, 127.

99. See Helen Fein, *Accounting for Genocide: National Responses and Jewish Victimization during the Holocaust* (New York: Free Press, 1979), 106–10.

100. The text of Seredi's letter is in Friedländer, *Pius XII and the Third Reich*, 220–21.

101. Raul Hilberg, *The Destruction of the European Jews* (Chicago: Quadrangle, 1967), 547.

102. On this point, let us recall the participation of a few Lutheran clergymen in the *Einsatzgruppen* and some Catholic priests in *Ustasa* mass murder.

103. On November 17, 1207, Innocent III wrote to King Philip Augustus of France urging him to take arms against the heretics in Languedoc, declaring that the cancer in the body of Christendom could only be "cured by the knife." The text of the letter is found in Jonathan and Louise Riley-Smith, *The Crusades: Idea and Reality* (London: 1981), 78–80.

104. In the assault on Béziers in 1209, the Crusader army consisted primarily of knights from northern France and *routiers* who did most of the killing. The typical *routier* was described as a "godless, lawless being, who...showed no mercy...a living emblem of Hell on earth." Zoé Oldenbourg, *Massacre at Montségur: A History of the Albigensian Crusade*, trans. Peter Green (New York: Pantheon Books, 1961), 104.

105. For an examination of the assistance given to leading German mass murderers to escape to South America and the Middle East, see Mark Aarons and John Loftus, *Unholy Trinity: How the Vatican's Nazi Networks Betrayed Western Intelligence to the Soviets* (New York: St. Martin's Press, 1991). For a detailed examination of a single case, the assistance given to Franz Stangl, Commandant of the Treblinka Death Camp, see Gitta Serenyi, *Into that Darkness: An Examination of Conscience* (New York: Vintage Books, 1983).

106. After persuasion failed to convert the Cathari, the Pope wrote to the King of France, "Those who hold cheap the correction of the Church must be crushed by the arm of secular power." Innocent III, "Letter to Philip II of France and the French nobility," in Elizabeth Hallam, ed., *Chronicles of the Crusades* (New York: Weidenfeld and Nicolson, 1989), 229.

19

BEYOND THE CONDITION OF (POST)-MODERNITY

Does Liberation Theology Still Have a Politics?
A Brazilian Case Study

Iain S. Maclean

The last two decades have witnessed the emergence of numerous studies on the condition and the theory of postmodernity. Such studies have challenged many of the modern assumptions of Western European and North American societies, such as the idea of progress, the rational development of social resources, the concept of the autonomous individual, and the coherence of Western foundational narratives. These studies in turn have provided the impetus for numerous theological responses, primarily by North American theologians such as Harvey Cox, to the challenges presented by postmodern conditions and theories.[1] Yet despite these studies, few directly address the implications of postmodern conditions and thought on the political arena. Surprisingly then, given liberation theologians' strong critiques of Latin American modernity and its failed democratic politics, few if any have responded directly to the issues raised by postmodernity. Perhaps this absence can be explained by indicating that liberation theologies, both in their methodological assumptions (more on which below) and in their sharp critiques of the negative dimensions of modernity, seemed quite postmodern in emphasis and have in fact been described as such.[2] However, this description is only partly correct since liberation theologians, while launching prophetic rejections of Latin American modernity, simultaneously accepted another form of Western modernity itself by utilizing socialism as their social and political paradigm. Unfortunately, the modernist assumptions inherent in the socialist paradigm hindered liberation theologians' political praxis during the critical decade of Brazilian democratization in the eighties. Specifically, the use in liberation theology's social analysis of class categories was based on assumptions of common class interests and inevitable historical progress that were not warranted as subsequent social science field research showed. The failure of modern theories of development, whether capitalist or socialist, coupled with the increasing diversity and pluralism of Brazilian society was, by the eighties, far greater than liberation theologians had realized. Thus, while there are similarities between postmodern critiques and those of liberation theologies, liberation theologies themselves utilized social theories that were themselves subject to the postmodern critique of all forms of modernity.

This essay then will attempt an initial exploration of the ambivalent impacts of modernity and postmodernity (as historical conditions and as theory) on liberation theologies within a single Latin American country, Brazil, utilizing the category of the political as a means of exposing their dependence upon a paradigm of modernity (autonomy, freedom, progress in history) and its role in problematizing the methodology of liberation theologians, with a focus on the works of Leonardo Boff, Clodovis Boff, Frei Betto, Maria Bingemer, and selected Brazilian political theorists such as Marialena Chiau, Claude Lefort, Francisco Weffort, and others.[3] The course of Brazilian democratization dramatically exposes modernity's ambiguous political legacy and thus provides a lens through which liberation theology, its method, assumed premises, and resultant praxis, can be viewed. This will be demonstrated through a case study of liberation theologies' politics, specifically the ecclesial base communities (abbreviated as CEBs) associated with them, during the period of Brazilian democratization. This will be done in a series of interlocking steps. First, the political implications of liberation theology's methodology will be outlined. This will be followed by brief discussions of modernity and of Marxism as a variant of the project of modernity. Then the implications of postmodernity for liberation theology and its politics will be explored, drawing on the material from the case study of the CEBs' role in democratization. Finally, given the postmodern critiques of liberation theology's method, an alternative approach is suggested which constructively draws upon both the reformulations of Marxist theory by the political left (represented by Norberto Bobbio, Ernesto Laclau, and Chantal Mouffe) and recent developments in liberation theologies.

Liberation Theology and the Political

Liberation theologies, emerging in the seventies and coalescing around the programmatic approach of Gustavo Gutiérrez, clearly reflected a bold reaction to, and critique of, modernity both theological and political.[4] Contemporary Roman Catholic and Protestant theology was criticized for its eurocentrism, assumed claims for universality, focus on secularization (a European issue), the almost exclusive use of abstract philosophy in its method, and for its assumption of the benevolence of nationalist development policies. The most striking feature of liberation theologies was the bold claim that theology had everything to do with this world, with its economic, and political systems. Liberation theologians argued that modernization and the project of modernity itself was deeply flawed and was itself responsible for the existing social, economic and political inequalities. A critical feature of liberation theologies was their rejection of the modernist dichotomy between the spiritual and the sacred, between religion and the material, between religion and the political realities of life. Liberation theologies (for a theological method that prioritized context by definition, contextual variants flourished) offered a sharp critique of the effects of modernity upon the poor in Latin America, of the devastating impact of technological and consumerist ideologies advocating liberal democracy and individual freedom, and driven by international capitalism and the indigenous elite. Liberation theologies rejected the then dominant modern social scientific and theological paradigms that assumed a universal rationality and norm, and advocated in their place the local, the voices of the voiceless "others." These were those who existed on the margins and undersides of the grand projects of modernity — modernization, industrialization, nationalist agendas of emerging nation-states, and their concomitant repressive regimes.

On the theological level, liberation theologies posed a challenging alternative to modern Roman Catholic theological paradigms. They sought, as they claimed, "a new way of doing theology," one which was not so much formed and founded upon revelation and philosophical propositions and focused on Western European issues of secularization and atheism, but one that reflected a second-level reflection "in the light of faith" upon the actual praxis of Christians in the world. This was understood as actual ongoing involvement, a "preferential option for the poor" in the concrete social and economic realities of the diverse populations of Latin America, an involvement that required, in the place of philosophy as talking partner, the use of the social sciences in order to address differing questions than those raised by the European context, namely those of social injustice, abuse of human rights, and the denial of the personhood of the lower classes. This meant, as Gustavo Gutiérrez put in, rejecting traditional (and often false) dualisms between Church and world, between spirit and matter, the religious and the secular, and recognizing that there is only one "Christo-finalized history."[5] Thus activity in the social and economic realms is as spiritual and crucial for the propagation of the gospel as activities performed in the Church and traditional religious spheres. These were the theological bases which motivated the activities of liberation theologians and the lay participants of the CEBs.

However, as the decade of the eighties advanced, liberation theology's political fortunes did not. The confident predictions of its political impact made by its practitioners, by participant observers, and by social scientists were not realized in the partially open or free elections of 1981, 1986, or even 1989.[6] Not only did the ecclesial base communities not bring out the vote for the popular Workers Party (*Partido dos Trabalhadores,* abbreviated as PT) as predicted, but in fact individual members supported parties across the political spectrum, indeed in the northeast even largely supporting the government party. Ironically, it seemed that precisely the individual autonomy and freedom advocated by liberation theologians, and allegedly brought with Brazilian democratization in the eighties, had led to the fragmentation of ecclesial base community solidarity in the national political arena. This raised questions about the social analytic categories, especially that of "class," which had proven so powerful and incisive during the seventies for liberation theology methodology.

Understandings of Modernity in Brazilian Liberation Theology

An outline of liberation theologians's largely negative evaluation of the project of modernity in Latin America can be discerned from what has already been stated about their redescription of theology to include the material or social and political dimensions of human societies. The theoretical parameters of their understanding of the modern project in Brazil now need to be more fully described. The definitions and debates surrounding modernity and postmodernity are in postmodern fashion, legion.[7] However, definitions of modernity typically include elements of Max Weber's work, in which he described modernity as the end result of the earlier Christian belief in progress and change. Western modernity, he argued, is marked by the process of increasing bureaucratization and rationalization of human life, essential for the development of modern industrial and capitalist societies, and a deep belief in progress initiated by the independent self. This very growth of technical rationality, however, he prophesied, would also lead to the loss of values such as individual autonomy and freedom. He thus saw modernity as an ambiguous blessing, for despite the positive warrants it provided for the modern age in rationality and progress, these very forces, by excluding value, he predicted, would inevitably lead to the loss of individual value and freedom, to an inescapable iron cage.

Similar understandings of the ambiguous blessings of modernity are found in the work of the Brazilian social scientist Heloisa Buarque de Holanda who, depending upon the French postmodernist Lyotard, understands modernity as characterized by the key concept of human progress, belief in the unlimited power of human reason to organize, plan, and propose a model of human life through progressive clarification, through confrontation with the world and the self, traced by ultimate values that give meaning to existence.[8] In addition, Buarque de Holanda and Clara Bingemer recognize that modernity in Brazil must be understood as incomplete and partial, for modernity and social change came late to Brazil, only after the Second World War, as a part of a dependent and peripheral capitalism, with resulting sharp discrepancies between income and class, spread unevenly over what had been largely a rural nation.[9] Large-scale social change really only occurred in the sixties and seventies as Brazil (together with most of Latin America) moved erratically through numerous industrialization and modernization phases. Modernity, understood in positive terms, such as the value of the individual, freedom, and the development of higher standards of living, really only benefited a small elite. Modernity understood in terms of its negative consequences or as "the underside of modernity" seemed to predominate in Brazil, for there as elsewhere in Latin America, modernity and the accompanying industrial model of development did not produce the social and political results anticipated for the majority.

However, it is often not observed that liberation theologians, while reacting to the undersides of modernity, were themselves selectively retrieving elements of Western modernity and simultaneously another project of modernity. Not only did they retain critical elements of the modern project, such as the importance of the person, but belief in the teleology of history, the importance of reason in constructing future utopias, and the possibility therefore of directed and better social transformations, in other words, of the socialist emancipatory project.

Like its Western and liberal variant, Marxist or socialist modernity assumed the existence of universal subjects, the unity and progress of history, and a concept of society as an intelligible and thus rational subject that could both be grasped and changed through persons acting as a class.[10] Such a concept of class carried with it specific understandings of political activity within a determined history of struggle. However, in Brazil by the late seventies, radical forms of class struggle had failed and once the Left accepted this reality, the question of involvement in a competitive political party process loomed large in the recently legalized Socialist parties. A lengthy process of self-examination ensued in which the Brazilian left, drawing on the reformulations of socialism, especially by Norberto Bobbio, modified its understandings of class, put aside structuralist ideas of underdevelopment and dependency, and focused on developing political pacts. Bobbio's work, contextualized in Brazil by thinkers such as Marilena Chaui, Coutinho Nelson, Claude Lefort, and Francisco Weffort, among others, sought a political alternative to liberalism and socialism through a radical and pluralistic conception of democracy.[11] This entailed broadening the Marxist class concept that claimed that only the working class could be the primary carrier of emancipatory projects, to include "others" such as the middle class, intellectuals, and rural workers. As Laclau and Mouffe concisely put it, such redefinitions involve rejecting the assumptions that class is the basic analytical category, the basic element of identity, or of relationships and of political activity. Consequently, it can no longer be claimed that the social category of the "working class" has an epistemic privilege, common and unified objective interests, a predestined historical role, or that socialism is the goal of liberation and the end of the political and social struggle and conflict which marks the present.[12] Through this process the Brazilian Left redefined itself, widened its bases of support, incorporated the strengths of both liberalism and socialism by rejecting the assumed self-interest of liberalism and the economic reductionism of socialism, and recognized the necessity of alliances with other social actors.

The Case Study:
The Ecclesial Base Communities and Democratization

As Brazil began democratizing, liberation theologians claimed that the ecclesial base communities provided the conditions for a more just and egalitarian, indeed democratic society.[13] While this essay focuses on the political theory implicit in claims made for the CEBs, it must not be forgotten that liberation theologians had always stressed that the CEBs were primarily religious organizations, formed among and from the poor to provide a locus for scripture reading, the distribution of the sacrament, mutual fellowship, and for common action in redressing social needs. Leonardo Boff, for instance, stressed the role of the CEBs in providing a place for the marginalized (the poor, women, the indigenous population, and those of African descent) to rediscover themselves as subjects active in creating their own history.[14] Unlike those that arose in Europe or in Nicaragua, the CEBs in Brazil, at least up to the early eighties, had always received the support of the institutional church.[15] In addition, the CEBs were legitimated theologically through the appeal to the Second Vatican Council's emphasis on the Church as primarily the whole people of God. The rapid growth and spread of CEBs during the seventies made them one of the most striking features of the Brazilian religious scene since their appearance in the early sixties in northeastern Brazil. By the early eighties, at the peak of their growth, there were between sixty to eighty thousand Brazilian CEBs, though uncertainty has always existed as to the exact number.[16]

The number of CEBs led to claims that they would articulate the desires of the poor and mobilize them by supporting a populist political party which represented their interests both locally and nationally.[17] Some liberation theologians even went on to claim that CEBs represented a power base for organized influence on political parties, and this claim led social scientists to conclude that CEBs broke down the traditional monistic corporatism that characterized Brazilian state structures.[18] Other liberation theologians, such as Frei Betto, saw the CEBs as an opportunity for the poor to make a specific political option for the leftist Workers Party.[19] Such claims encouraged scholars,[20] as well as participant-observers,[21] to research the role of CEBs in creating a new, democratic civil society. It is the results of such social science investigations that raise questions concerning the dependence of liberation theologians upon specific Marxist (modern) concepts of class.[22] As noted earlier, the socialist alternative advocated by liberation theologians itself assumed societal change through rational planning, the abolition of class structure, and most importantly, the role of a specific class in effecting social transformation. This valorizing of a specific class (vanguard) by liberation theologians is seen throughout their writings during the period of democratization.

The Abertura or opening to democracy was marked by the slow granting of political freedoms: the relaxation of military rule, the authorization of political opposition parties, and for the CEBs, controversy over the question of political party options. Prior to the partly open elections in 1979, many liberation theologians viewed the CEBs as a grassroots model of social and political democracy. Leonardo Boff, reporting on the third national assembly of the CEBs in 1978, described CEBs as the alternative to an oppressive society:

> The base ecclesial community was the place where the theological essence of the Church was realized and at the same time the practice of liberation of the poor through the poor themselves.... What was born (through CEBs) was not just a reproduction of the traditional Church, based on the sacerdotal and sacramental axes. It was a new reality which was born from the heart of the poor themselves by virtue of the innovative Spirit of God, organized by the laity around the Word of God and the imitating of Jesus Christ. That was called ecclesiogenesis: Genesis of a Church.[23]

Indeed, Betto stated that the CEBs were the source of a renewed model of society, one which would be "popular, democratic and socialist."[24] Leonardo Boff had viewed the representatives of the popular classes attending the third national CEB conference (1978) as a sign that the people themselves now had a voice. The higher clergy were hearing of their real life struggles and the oppression they lived under as rural laborers, as "Davids against the Goliath latifundistas." Boff viewed the CEBs as bearing the hope and the future of the faith, which are "the tools of a more human world."[25] This enthusiasm for the transformatory and democratic potential of the CEBs was shared by Leonardo's brother, Clodovis Boff, who in the same journal asserted that as the government moved toward a "relative democracy" a real basis existed for democracy in that:

> The CEBs constituted in the last few years one of the few free spaces in which the people were able to gather, discuss their problems in the light of faith and the challenges of life and to exercise the skills of popular liberation.... [T]hese communities assume an important political role.[26]

In the same article Clodovis Boff examined the potential role of CEBs in the political Abertura by applying the three-step "see, judge, act" method of analysis employed by liberation theologians to relate social realities to theological discourse. This method required using the social sciences to analyze a specific situation that was then evaluated in the light of faith and the results in turn provided the catalyst for social action. So Boff sketched Brazilian social conditions, where 80 percent of the population is impoverished and reduced to subhuman living conditions, arguing that these conditions are caused directly by dependent capitalism. Accepting the argument of the Left that this was the structural cause of the social and political problems of Brazil and indeed of the Third World, any solution would have to include the removal of capitalism and the structures it supported. Simultaneously, liberation theologians evaluated any program from the underside of society as it were, opting in every case for the poor and their betterment. Such an approach, on careful analysis, assumes the existence of a strong socialist state which is able to alter the existing unjust social structures from above. However, in the changed political climate of democratization, the option facing liberation theologians was no longer the relatively simple one of opposition to military rule, but rather the more complex scenario of competitive party politics. In turn this meant evaluating political parties and their actual or potential relationship to the social class represented by the CEBs. Clodovis Boff identified three possible relationships between the emerging political parties and the CEBs, namely the neo-Christendom, the complementary, and the dialectical models respectively.

The first two models are rejected as traditional, though differing, supports for the status quo, while the third, the dialectical model, is preferred by Boff because it understands the Church and the political parties as open spaces, each with a relative autonomy. The CEBs in terms of this model then are not an extension of a political party, nor do they require a declared political position for membership. However, the CEBs are not prohibited from discussing social issues and "assuming political positions consonant with faith."[27] By using the term "relative autonomy," Boff sought to convey the fact that the spheres of religion and politics are open to each other: No purely religious or political realm exists. Thus for the Church, its autonomy lies in its teaching concerning the faith, while its relative side concerns the implications of that faith for politics.

Nevertheless, both Clodovis and Leonardo Boff argued that members of the CEBs and particular CEBs themselves, in contrast to the Church as a whole or as an institution, should support a specific party position. The hierarchy, they agreed, should not take party political positions but should rather lay down moral principles for lay political participation. The Boffs argued that support for a political party was based on the option for the poor and supported both the local Church and the mobilization of the popular classes:

> The concrete form in which the search for the common good is materialized, particularly for the poor, ought to be locally the political option for specific candidates within a specific party. The party is a part, but the common good that it intends is not a part but the whole. Such an option does not mean compromising the universality of the Church, rather it concretizes it.[28]

These criteria determined the type of candidate and party that the CEB membership should support. The Boffs also suggested that acceptable political party candidates should be from the same classes associated with the CEBs. Though at this time there was no real choice of parties, given the two official ones permitted (at the time this article was written, prior to the actual 1979 liberalization of the Party Law), CEB members should support the party which truly represents the people and which opposes the military regime. This tactic, the Boffs declared, would enlarge the political options of the poor. However, support should be given not so much to a party, but to specific candidates who clearly represent the people, while the political party should be utilized "to amplify the space of popular representation at the level of the power apparatus." Thus both Clodovis and Leonardo Boff argued that the CEBs, together with other popular movements, should continue

> on the one hand, struggling for parliamentary democracy (representative), on the other hand, tending to popular democracy (participatory). But the former comes first, being the condition for the second. It is a phase of a much larger process. Here it is that one avoids all extremes, fruit of dogmatism.... That is the "Leftism" of hasty and coup — prone (*golpistas*) intellectuals.[29]

This process, the Boffs stated, must continue to consolidate the popular movements into a Workers Party, understood as a direct continuation of the movements themselves. However, such a position seems rather similar to that very "reformism," "illusory palliatives," or "diversion from an alternative society" that liberation theologians had condemned in the past. The Boffs acknowledge that the option for a political party choice is the result of political realism, but it is a realism which recognizes the ruptures in the existing system and thus seeks to exploit these by working through a developing workers' party.[30] This would not be socialism through innumerable reforms (a la the Social Democrats), but rather an option for reforms with *revolutionary content*. The Boffs regard the political opening of 1978 as a liberal reform which provides the conditions for attaining a new social regime. A socialist society is the long-term goal, but now to be reached through an open political party process. Thus the Boffs view a popular workers' party as a mid-term goal and also as the means to a new socialist society. As they declare: "In the contemporary historical context, the perspective of a quick and violent revolution is excluded. The path is the slow, long process of popular conscientization and of successive conquests through legal means.... The parliamentary way is given as the place for the inevitable historical passage."[31]

As the eighties advanced, the CEBs continued to face a rapidly changing political and ecclesiastical scene. The Abertura begun in 1978 had led to new channels of expression and representation. By permitting freer political expression, the 1979 Party Law meant that the Church, the CEBs, and liberation theologians were now no longer the sole voice for the voiceless. The question of the relationship between the CEBs and multiple political parties was thus the primary theme of the fourth national CEB assembly (1981). The CEB participants decided that they were neither a party, a nucleus of a party, nor the supporters of any one party.[32] The CEB members in the concluding document of the national assembly clearly stated that they viewed themselves as providing "a space where we ought to live, deepen and celebrate our faith, where we ought to confront our life and our praxis in the light of the Word of God, to see if our political action is in accord with the plan of God. In the ecclesial base community we ought to seek the strength to animate us in the struggle which we make, whether in the barrio or in the countryside, whether in the realm of the workplace or in political parties."[33]

> One of the issues that received much attention was that of our political participation, since we consider the political most influential in peoples' lives. We attempt to clarify our ideas on this issue of politics. Politics is the great resource we possess to construct a just society the way God desires.... Good political action is all that we do to organize ourselves in justice and to create a new relationship between persons and groups. Good political action is when we unite to defend our life against lies and exploitation, through neighborhood associations, unions and other forms of popular organization.[34]

What the CEB participants did not do was espouse support of the PT and so they clearly rejected any official identification of their movement with a specific political party program. The CEBs thereby rejected the Boffs' and Betto's support for a single political party, namely the PT.[35] Instead, the CEB national assembly endorsed the non-political party stance advocated in the Brazilian National Bishops Conference's 1981 document, *Christian Reflection on the Political Juncture*. Though CEB participants viewed political parties with some suspicion, they nonetheless encouraged CEB political involvement in an informed manner:

> Another way of acting politically is through political parties. We should not be afraid of entering politics because we have been confused and cheated by cunning and greedy politicians. Jesus said that one should be as gentle as a dove, but as cunning as a serpent. So, we should discuss among ourselves both the programs and the practice of political parties, in order to discover what interests they defend and what societal changes they propose....[36]

Prior to the actual 1982 elections, the issue of the Church and the CEBs' roles vis-à-vis political parties continued to generate sharp debate. Apart from some fringe parties such as the Social Democrat Party (PDS), the Brazilian Workers Party (PTB), and the Popular Party (PP), political options resolved down to a choice between the Workers Party (PT), the Brazilian Democratic Movement Party (PMDB), and the Workers Democratic Party (PDT). As noted earlier, many assumed that the CEBs would take a clear party position, but this was not the case, either at the CEB national assembly or in the elections themselves. While CEB support for the PT was well known in the industrial suburbs of São Paulo, in the northeast, the CEBs' preference was for the PMDB and in the south, for the PDT.[37]

It is helpful at this juncture to set out the reasons that Frei Betto offers for his stance, as these are typical of a large segment of liberation theology opinion at this time. Frei Betto supported the PT because he claimed that its political program paralleled much of the CEBs' agenda and like the CEBs, its membership was drawn from similar social classes. In fact, the PT was a party developed from the lower working classes and justifiably claimed to be the first nationally organized workers party in Brazilian history.[38] Likewise, when Leonardo Boff had described the CEB experience as a new way of being the Church, as a church that was being reinvented from the base, he was referring to precisely the inclusion of the lower or working classes of society that the PT seemed to be accomplishing. Further, Clodovis Boff had observed that in many regions the central leadership of the PT was composed of (largely ex-) members of the CEBs. Boff argued that this drifting of leadership from the CEBs was the direct result of the Church's failure to develop a pastoral political strategy.[39] It should be noted also that in the early eighties both the PT and the CEBs were politically inexperienced, viewed traditional politicians as elitist, corrupt, and opportunistic, and expected mass mobilization of grassroots organizations drawn from similar classes.[40]

The skills required for a national political campaign differed from those needed at the level of community organizing and this became clear during the November 1982 election campaign. Contrary to popular expectations, the PT performed dismally in the elections, gaining only 29 percent of the contested positions (for state and federal deputies) to the PMDB's 68 percent. In the light of earlier predictions, this result raised serious questions about the CEBs' political links and of liberation theologians' political influence.[41] In part, this perception resulted from the opposition's exaggeration of the CEBs' political influence. Yet this defeat also reflected the political immaturity of a populist political party and its inexperience in conducting a nationwide campaign. These election results nevertheless led the PT to abandon its exclusivist worker orientation and to make political pacts with other parties in order to win elections. Though the PT was opposed to the bourgeoisie and to capitalists, it denied nevertheless that it was exclusively a party of workers, stating in a later prospectus that: "The PT is for all workers committed to the dream of a society meeting minimal standards of justice and equality: laborers, rural workers, students, the young, the old, clergy, business people, women, housewives, artists, professors, doctors.... Party of the working class. Not only [the party] of the urban laborer."[42]

Liberation theologians had started their political analysis with a prior theological and ideological commitment to the option for the poor, which in Brazil they translated into workers versus owners or capitalists. Thus a political party such as the PT, with a working class leader and working class membership, was viewed as an appropriate vehicle for the political aspirations of CEB members. This was a idealistic position, acceptable given the struggles against authoritarian rule throughout the seventies, but impractical as it turned out, in a competitive and pluralist party context where differences in strategy and policy were bound to emerge and to divide. The PT itself initially envisioned itself as purely a workers party, but swiftly modified this position after the 1982 elections to permit strategic political alliances with other classes. For most liberation theologians such pragmatism only came after the fall of Eastern Europe in 1989. This meant that during the eighties, liberation theologians became increasingly isolated as they failed to create alliances with other social sectors.

The political party option now served to highlight differences between liberation theologians as they each struggled to translate a prophetic critique into concrete political and public policy programs. Frei Betto and the Boffs sought to translate the CEBs directly into a political party, without, it seems, a full awareness of the contextual and local vision of most CEBs or of the mechanics of national political campaigns. Other liberation theologians, trained in the social sciences, such as José Comblin and Claudio Perani, took a far more critical view of the political options made by Betto and the Boffs, even accusing them of advocating a form of Christendom. Claudio Perani even warned such theologians of replacing economic and social analysis with prior ideological political choices.[43]

Prompted in part by the contradictory political claims being made for CEBs, social scientists began actively examining them in the early eighties. Significant work in sociological and political analysis was undertaken in the northeast by the Dom Helder Câmara Center for Social Action (CENDHEC), by the Center for Religious Statistics and Social Investigation (CERIS) under Rogerio Valle,[44] by Claudio Perani, José Comblin, W. E. Hewitt, and John Burdick, among others.[45] Earlier studies had noted the effect of external factors on CEB growth, including the presence or absence of institutional support at the diocesan level, the effect of Vatican strictures against liberation theologians, papal statements on ecclesiastical involvement in party politics, and the hazy relationship between CEBs and popular movements. While recognizing the positive elements in the CEB phenomenon and their role in promoting spirituality and human rights and in effecting local neighborhood improvements, such studies also revealed factors that were inhibiting their growth and mitigating against their claims for political egalitarianism.

In the process of such research, the nature of actual functioning CEBs was closely examined and the following results confirmed by the researchers noted above. First, CEBs tend not to attract the very poor, but rather the more educated and lighter-skinned societal strata. Therefore the claims that the CEBs are a "Church of the poor" fail to take into account the racism of Brazilian society and the splintering into various strata of the "class" of the poor. The poor, whose struggle to live is vividly portrayed in the work of Nancy Scheper-Hughes, which discerns at least four levels of the poor, ranging (of those who live *below* the poverty line) from those "who live a good life," those whose life is "reasonable," those who "are eating," to those at the lowest level of existence, known as the "miserable." What is clear to researchers is that CEB membership draws almost exclusively from the top two levels of the poor. In addition, CEB literacy expectations (read the liturgy, Bible, etc.) tend to limit participation by illiterates. This explains in part the absence of the poorest, or the *miseraveis,* who have little stake in society, from the CEBs. Burdick shows that this class is not attracted to the CEBs but rather to Pentecostal groups. The CEBs' demand for commitment and participation has had the paradoxical effect of driving members away, particularly those not in control of their income and with rigorous work schedules who are thus not able to attend all the CEB meetings. Comblin had observed a similar phenomenon in his research and viewed the pluri-classist nature of the CEBs (unlike the uni-classist Pentecostal congregations) and their linkage to the institutional church as a channel for the poor to modernity, to citizenship, and to participation in the wider society. Burdick's research, which compared Pentecostal congregations with Catholic parishes and CEBs, also seemed to indicate that Catholics, who are historically enmeshed in the Brazilian social structure, and whose theology emphasizes love, reconciliation, and forgiveness, find it difficult to take confrontational roles in the wider society. This is in stark contrast to the Pentecostals, whose theology emphasizes a sharp dichotomy between Church and world, believer and society, God and the devil and thus a sharp break and conversion from the past. Pentecostals are thus not inhibited from taking controversial and radical political stances in local and national politics. Further, both Burdick's and Comblin's research confirmed that CEBs are highly dependent upon the quality of the local leadership and their linkage to the diocese. Thus if local diocesan leadership (lay, priest, or bishop) leaves, or is replaced by conservative clergy, then the CEB concerned tends to end its social activism.[46]

Significantly for the purposes of this essay, researchers also discovered that CEBs shared with other popular movements tendencies which mitigated against translating the local CEB experience into the larger political arena. In studying popular Brazilian social movements, researchers coined the term "basism" to describe the tendency to absolutize the popular classes or the worker as the ideal participant in any societal transformation.[47] Such "basism" leads to the rejection of any cooperation with those not regarded as workers, and consequently hinders effective political participation in, or alliances with, multi-class parties. The term "basism" also expresses the fear of those at society's base that concern about national issues will lessen concern for local ones and that distant leaders are more likely to be corrupt than those immediately present. A similar phenomenon within the CEBs has been dubbed *cebcentrismo.*[48]

Largely through such a "basist" fear of political manipulation, CEBs often regarded those involved in national political parties as somewhat "fallen," as a prodigal since the political sphere was viewed by many as a dirty, corrupt, and elitist affair.[49] It is thus simplistic to assume that the CEBs' failure to make a major political impact was due primarily to ecclesiastical and conservative opposition. Factors internal to the CEBs themselves contributed to their political ineffectualness. Admittedly, liberation theologians did insist that the CEBs were primarily ecclesial entities. Nevertheless, they did make bold claims about their potential as a model of participatory democracy for the wider society. This is the ideal Leonardo Boff claimed would and should succeed the failed "bourgeois representative democracies of Latin America." He declares that: "This participatory democracy is not just a project. The seed of it is alive in the popular movements, in the Christian communities and other movements in which democratic forms of participation are found, together with power sharing."[50]

Further, according to Frei Betto, "In the practice of the CEBs within the popular movements, utopia becomes *topia*.... The process of constructing the popular political project results in a society where political power will be exercised by the people in the service of the people and the means of production will be socialized."[51]

However, the field research summarized above has raised serious questions not only about the purported levels of popular CEB participation, but about the usefulness of the category "class" as a fruitful and determinative concept. In addition, if the reports of the CEBs' *basista* tendencies against the political process (however justified) are accurate, how is their struggle against oppression to become politically meaningful? Clodovis Boff advocated either the formation of or support for a specific party. José Comblin advocated a stronger and dialectical linkage of the movements with the institutions of Church and society. By mid-decade Frei Betto had modified his position by advocating not direct CEB political involvement, but rather support for political activists. He distinguished five spheres in civil society, that of the pastoral, that of the popular movements, that of special interest groups, unions, and those of political organizations and parties, through which the popular political project is constructed.[52] This is a valuable corrective against *o espontaneísmo* ("spontaneitism") or the supposition that political action is improvised without linkage to other forces and organizations, thereby creating political alliances.[53]

Liberation Theologians: Beyond Modernity and Postmodernity?

The decade of the nineties opened with the fall of socialism in Europe and successive economic and political crises in Brazil. Brazil's standard of living declined, the gap between rich and poor widened, and the situation of the rural poor deteriorated. The 1992 impeachment of President Collor, who had won the presidency in a close race with the Worker Party's candidate Lula, led to greater loss of confidence in the possibility of changing the present in order to effect a better future. These events revealed the crisis in the projects of modernity, both in its Western Liberal and in its Marxist forms, one marked by the loss of plausibility and the emergence of postmodernism, similar to what is encountered in the First World, with, however, its own particular emphases, highlighted in the works of Heloisa Buarque de Holanda, Paulo Fernando Carneiro de Andrade, Maria Clara Bingemer, Jose Ramos Regidor, and Dario G. Schaeffer among others.[54]

To the extent then that Marxism and socialism emerged from modernity, they have shared in the postmodernist critique. Liberation theologians however find themselves in an odd position, for their beginnings lay in a principled and theological rejection of aspects of Western modernity and the option for an alternative, socialism, the other modern option to liberalism. By the nineties it was clear that this alternative path of modernity, socialism, had failed and liberation theologians had to question not so much their theological method, but their social theory and its dependence, in the political arena, upon an outmoded concept of class. Postmodern criticism is instructive here, for it points out the historical conditionedness of all grand theories and it is sufficient here to draw attention to liberation theologians' understandings of "class" to illustrate this point. Dependent upon aspects of the paradigm of modernity, liberation theologians initially failed to perceive the existent diversity of culture, even within the poor, for they subsumed all under the universalizing category of "class." This failure to recognize the existent pluralism of interests and projects, heightened by the fragmenting effect of democratization on the ecclesial base communities, was sharply exposed, as the previous section has demonstrated, by the national and regional elections held throughout the eighties and nineties. This period in Brazil witnessed the emergence of a plurality of social and political movements, with differing and independent forms of struggle that only diversified throughout the decade. It became clear during this period that there was no essential relation between class and interests or that a particular political position could be assumed by economic determination.[55] The implications of the social scientific field studies undertaken among popular movements and the CEBs are far-reaching. The discovery of not one but many layers of the "class" of the poor and the diversity of motivational factors indicated that social identities were not static and determined, but rather in flux, changing and relational. Indeed, the diverse range of social and political struggles within a society, it was found, could not be subordinated to prior conceptions of social classes or anything more fundamental.[56] Liberation theologians failed to recognize fully the political implications of this fragmentation of the popular classes into at least four discrete sub-classes, and to address adequately the issues of race, gender, and religious pluralism, though institutional limits played a large role here.[57] By not taking these theoretical and social scientific shifts into account, liberation theologians continued throughout the eighties advocating a strategy based on a flawed class concept. This in part contributed to their inability to translate the "participatory democracy" model into the political sphere or to agree upon a common strategy. The CEB membership itself took the same approach adopted by the Brazilian National Bishops Conference, namely that within accepted moral parameters, choice of political parties lay with the individual. Without a church political party, the CEB influence was greatly weakened.

Nevertheless, unlike many contemporary Western European and North American expressions of postmodernism, Brazilian liberation theologies have not rejected all the values associated with modernism. Rather they have critically appropriated and retained elements of modernism such as the value of the individual, freedom, and political democracy. This utilization and critique of modernity, primarily for the purpose of human liberation from oppression, is, as noted earlier, a defining characteristic of liberation theologies. This project of liberation, as distinct from the Western liberal conception of individual freedom, includes both the individual and the social, the material and the spiritual, the religious and the secular (the economic). Thus, liberation theologians appropriated the modern Western values of the person, while adopting in large measure from the Marxist version of modernity, the belief in historical progress and the role of the oppressed or workers as its class carrier. It is this latter appropriation that has brought liberation theologies into crisis following the fall of existent socialist countries in Eastern Europe from 1989 onward. This event forced liberation theologians to recognize that despite their trenchant critiques of modernity, they and their theological methods are themselves expressions of that same modernity.[58]

The lengthy Brazilian democratization process revealed the weakness of liberation theology as a political instrument and its dependence upon elements of the paradigm of modernity. In particular, liberation theologians' attempts to mobilize the CEBs along class lines did not produce the results anticipated. The research noted above points to a static understanding of the Marxist class category understood as an "option for the poor" as partly responsible for this. However, it must be noted that other factors, not highlighted in this study, such as religious competition, leadership conflict, and the lack of institutional support, all played a role in weakening the political role of CEBs. The postmodernist emphasis upon the other and the recognition of difference highlighted liberation theologians' dependence upon a specific social analysis and their subsequent inability to adapt to changing conditions. Liberation theologians, though, had recognized the importance of culture as expressed in the phenomenon of "popular religion," but this never developed into a significant political factor due to the sharp ideological differences between religious groups. Likewise the question of women's rights and place in Church and society, the role of racism, ecology, and other religions, especially Afro-Brazilian ones, were recognized, but were largely subsumed under the quest for social and economic justice. However, this forces a recognition of cultural factors as critical and requires a modification of the expression "option for the poor." This was originally understood primarily in economic terms and strangely, while the economic situation in Brazil has worsened, few if any liberation theologians, as Jung Mo Sung notes, have offered any new economic analyses addressing the dramatically changed world economy.[59]

The democratization process led to dramatic theoretical shifts on the Brazilian Left, shifts which were not reflected in the work of liberation theologians, even after the collapse of the Eastern European socialist states. In particular, the theoretical re-definition of Marxism undertaken by the political Left in order to create strategic alliances with other social movements has significant implications for liberation theologies. In the context of a postmodernity characterized by diverse voices, such theoretical revisioning, quite similar to that undertaken by Marxist or post-Marxist theorists such as Ernesto Laclau and Chantal Mouffe, suggest not so much a rejection of modernity's project but rather a retrieval of certain themes and categories, a greater amplification of its language, a radical expansion of its values and contents, in an attempt to respond to the new situation. For if, as both the Brazilian Left and Laclau and Mouffe have argued, there are no necessary connections between class location and interests, then the Marxist assumption of a unified class politics elides the actual "on the ground" processes of diverse social formations and the presence of subsequent multiple political subjects. Further, the failure by Marxists and those influenced by their methodology to recognize these processes will then hinder the development of pluralist democracies.[60] As shown by recent anthropological field work, social identity cannot be understood as purely economic and determined by class, though these do play some role, but rather as relational and as under a continuous process of construction or re-interpretation. This comes out in the comparative research of Cecelia Mariz and John Burdick on CEB participants and Pentecostal believers among the poorer strata of Brazilian society. Given a pluralist democracy and a postmodern sensibility that recognizes the diversity of relational identities, it becomes difficult to claim priority for class struggles, and neither politicians nor liberation theologians can assume an option for socialism from all members of the same (economic) class.[61] Thus, given the case of the CEBs outlined above, liberation theologians need to recognize the contingency of historical events, the diversity of social identities, and the need to utilize a modified concept of "hegemony" which recognizes particular power configurations and consequently embarks on specific, short-term alliances for short-term goals.

The CEBs nevertheless still offer much potential for creating, not so much a new democracy, but rather those voluntary associations that could create such strategic alliances, associations that could be small enough to reach the individual, yet large enough to effect change in relations with other groups. Effective political activity, as multiple studies have shown, occurs when coalitions are entered into with popular movements (voluntary associations) and other faith communities in a specific region. This is in essence the outworking of a functioning civil society. Such a reconceptualization is offered in the most recent works of Leonardo Boff, who argues for an inclusive understanding of democracy, a participatory democracy which includes not only human relatedness, but global participation in the world itself. Such an inclusive understanding of liberation theology holds the potential to create a broad progressive understanding of democratic participation which recognizes the other: "the poor," "women," "Native Americans," "Afro-Brazilians," other economic strata, the earth, and other religions.[62] Yet doing so without exalting diversity to the point of an individualism besides which structural questions of social inequalities, lack of development, and wealth distribution are obscured. Nevertheless, while recognizing the flaws in its original class analysis, liberation theologies cannot succumb to the radical postmodern impulse to deny the transforming power of politics, for this is to deny their religious hope to succumb to nihilism. They recognize the need to work with local social movements (voluntary associations with overlapping interests), which could be more effective than traditional Brazilian political parties. Such linkage or associations of new social movements could help preserve values and cultures that could enrich an envisioned participatory democracy. However in the recognition that this to be done in an open, conflicted social arena, in continuously shifting conditions. This could be the source of a radical democratic project for the future, one that truly develops a "politics of resistance."[63]

Liberation theologies emerged in specific contexts with a specific methodology which provided a critique and a political program based on factual, positivistic social science. While anthropologists noted the dramatic fractures and existent diversity among the "poor," liberation theologians were slow to incorporate such findings into their praxis. Democratization exposed these lacunae and liberation theologians such as Leonardo Boff have modified their initial conceptions of class analysis to incorporate the critiques and emancipatory dimensions of popular religion, feminism, race and ethnic identity struggles, and the environment. By so doing the possibility now exists of creating linkages with previously marginalized groups to overcome the aporias of both modernity and postmodernity. Liberation theologians thus uphold the emancipatory hopes of modernity (the [ongoing] formation of subjects and improvement in time of social-political conditions), though with a belated recognition of the ambiguity of modernity in its postmodern forms, of offering direct access to their fulfillment only in partial and fragmentary forms. Thus liberation theologies remain between modernity and postmodernity, struggling to make material their religious visions. Whether they will move beyond this remains questionable. Given the Brazilian Roman Catholic Church's increasing conformity to the neoconservative and modernist paradigm of the present papacy, it remains doubtful that their political vision, redefined in a postmodernizing context, and the linkages that such a vision would require with the wider civil society to be politically active, can be accomplished within the institutional church.

Notes

1. Harvey G. Cox, *Religion in the Secular City: Towards a Postmodern Theology* (New York: Simon and Schuster, 1984). See also his "Complaining to God: Theodicy and the Critique of Modernity in the Resurgence of Traditional Religion," *Archivo di Filosofia 56*, nos. 1–3 (1988), 311–25.

2. Though with qualifications of course. See for example the essays by Bingemer, Gutiérrez, Hinkelammert, and Mendieta in David Batstone, ed., *Liberation Theologies, Postmodernity, and the Americas* (New York: Routledge, 1997), as well as Ann K. Wetherilt, "Liberating Postmodernism?" paper presented at the Annual Meeting of the American Academy of Religion, Orlando, Fla., November 22, 1998.

3. In particular the works by Marilena Chaiu, *Cultura e Democracia: O Discurso Competente e Outros Falas* (São Paulo: Cortez Editora, 1987) and Francisco Weffort, *Qual Democracia?* (São Paulo: Companhia das Letras, 1992).

4. Gustavo Gutiérrez, *A Theology of Liberation* (Maryknoll, N.Y.: Orbis Books, 1973).

5. Ibid., 157. Likewise see Leonardo Boff, *Jesus Cristo Libertador: Ensaio de Cristologia Crítica para o Nosso Tempo* (Petrópolis: Editora Vozes, 1972).

6. See Iain S. Maclean, "Participatory Democracy. The Case of the Brazilian Ecclesial Base Communities: 1981–1991," *Religion and Theology 5* no. 1 (1998), 78–100, from which some material is utilized.

7. See for example the range of definitions and interpretations of postmodernity provided in Paul Lakeland , *Postmodernism* (Minneapolis: Augsburg Fortress, 1997); David Lyon *Postmodernity* (Minneapolis: University of Minnesota, 1994); and Barry Smart, *Postmodernity* (New York: Routledge, 1993). In the specifically Latin American context, see David Batstone, ed., *Liberation Theologies, Postmodernity, and the Americas.*

8. Heloisa Buarque de Holanda, ed., *Pós-Modernismo e Política* (Rio de Janeiro, 1991).

9. Clara Bingemer, "A Post-Christian and Postmodern Christianity," in David Batstone, ed., *Liberation Theologies, Postmodernity, and the Americas,* 84–93.

10. Ernesto Laclau and Chantal Mouffe, *Hegemony and Socialist Strategy* (London: Verso, 1985), 2.

11. For instance, Claude Lefort, *Political Forms of Modern Society* (London: Polity, 1988), 305.

12. Laclau and Mouffe, *Hegemony and Socialist Strategy,* 1ff. Such revisionary approaches to Marxism are contested by more orthodox Marxists such as Norman Geras. See his "Post-Marxism?" *New Left Review* (1987), 163ff.

13. Manfredo Araújo de Oliveira, "As CEB's e os Dilemas do Processo de Democratização," *Revista Eclesiástica Brasileira* 49, fasc. 195 (September 1989), 571.

14. Leonardo Boff stresses the role of the CEBs in providing a place for the marginalized (the poor, women, the indigenous population and those of African descent) to rediscover themselves as subjects active in creating their own history. Leonardo Boff, "CEBs: Que Significa 'Novo Modo de Toda a Igreja Ser'?" *Revista Eclesiástica Brasileira* 49, fasc. 195 (September 1989), 546–62.

15. Casiano Floristán, "Bulletin on Basic Communities," *Concilium* 104, no. 4 (1975), 96.

16. Variation in the definition contributes to the uncertainty of the number of CEBs. Pedro Assis Ribeiro de Oliveira, "Oprimidos: A Opção pela Igreja," *Revista Eclesiástica Brasileira* 41, fasc. 164 (1981), 643. Frei Betto estimates 100,000 [see his "As Comunidades Eclesiais de Base como Potencial de Transformação da Sociedade Brasileira," *Revista Eclesiástica Brasileira* 43, Fasc. 171 (September 1983), 495] as does Paul Sigmund, *Liberation Theology at the Crossroads* (New York: Oxford University Press, 1990), 25. Marcello de C. Azevedo, S.J., *Basic Ecclesial Communities in Brazil: The Challenge of a New Way of Being Church* (Washington, D.C.: Georgetown University Press, 1987) estimates 60,000.

17. Clodovis Boff, "Comunidades Cristãs e Política Partidária," *Revista Eclesiástica Brasileira* 38, fasc. 151 (1978), 397; Leonardo Boff, "Igreja, Povo que se Liberta. III Encontro Intereclesial de CEBs em João Pessoa," *Revista Eclesiástica Brasileira* 38, fasc. 151 (1978), 503; Frei Betto, *O Que e Comunidade Eclesial de Base?* (São Paulo: Brasiliense, 1981), 17.

18. Christian Smith, *The Emergence of Liberation Theology* (Chicago: University of Chicago Press, 1991), 55.

19. Frei Betto stated in the daily *Folha de São Paulo* (February 23, 1980) that the PT's program had the closest affinity to the CEBs. See Margaret E. Keck, *The Workers' Party and Democratization in Brazil* (New Haven: Yale University Press, 1992), 97. For instance, the regions where CEBs are most concentrated, the north and northeast, nevertheless saw the ruling party, the Social Democrats, win by large margins. Azevedo, *Basic Ecclesial Communities,* 147ff.

20. Consult the extensive bibliography in Azevedo, *Basic Ecclesial Communities.*

21. Alvaro Barreiro, *Comunidades Eclesiais de Base e Evangelização dos Pobres* (São Paulo: Edições Loyola, 1977); Dominique Barbé, *Grace and Power: Base Communities and Nonviolence in Brazil* (Maryknoll, N.Y.: Orbis Books, 1978); and Torres and Eagleson, eds., *The Challenge of Basic Christian Communities* (Maryknoll, N.Y.: Orbis, 1981).

22. Azevedo, *Basic Ecclesial Communities;* Scott Mainwaring and A. Wilde, eds., *The Progressive Church in Latin America* (Notre Dame: University of Notre Dame Press, 1989).

23. Leonardo Boff, "Igreja, Povo Que Se Liberta. III Encontro Intereclesial de Comunidades de Base em João Pessoa," *Revista Eclesiástica Brasileira* 38, fasc. 151 (1978), 503.

24. Frei Betto, "As Comunidades Eclesial de Base como Potência de Transformar da Sociedade Brasileira," *Revista Eclesiástica Brasileira* 43 (September 1983), 503.

25. "Igreja, Povo Que Se Liberta," 504, 506.

26. Clodovis Boff, "Comunidades Cristãs e Política Partidária," *Revista Eclesiástica Brasileira* 38, fasc. 151 (September 1978), 387.

27. Ibid., 393.

28. Ibid., 397.

29. Ibid., 399.

30. Ibid., 400.

31. Ibid.

32. Held at Itaicí (SP), from April 20–24, 1981. See the report by J. B. Libânio, *Revist Eclesiástica Brasileira* 41, fasc. 162 (June 1981), 279–311 and in *SEDOC* 14 (September 1981), 153–55. Frei Betto discusses this meeting in *O Fermento na Massa* (Petrópolis: Editora Vozes, 1981), 49ff. Political party affiliation was also an issue at the 2nd CEB national assembly at Vitória (July 29–August 1, 1976). See Faustino Luiz Couto Teixeira et al., *CEBs Cidadania e Modernidade: Uma Análise Crítica* (São Paulo: Edições Paulinas, 1993), 44, no. 80.

33. Quoted from the concluding letter of the national assembly by Faustino Luiz Couto Teixeira et al., *CEBs Cidadania e Modernidade: Uma Análise Crítica,* 20.

34. Leonardo Boff, "Comunidades Eclesiais de Base: Povo Oprimido que se Organiza para a Libertação," *Revista Eclesiástica Brasileira* 41, fasc. 162 (1981), 319.

35. Luiz A. Gómez de Souza, "A Política Partidária nas CEBs," *Revista Eclesiástica Brasileira* 41, fasc. 164 (1981), 715.

36. J. B. Libânio, *Revista Eclesiástica Brasileira* 41, fasc. 162 (1981), 319.

37. Frei Betto, "As CEBs e o Projeto Político Popular," *Revista Eclesiástica Brasileira* 46, fasc. 183 (1986), 582. The statistical evidence is marshaled by H. E. Hewitt, "Religion and the Consolidation of Democracy in Brazil" in William H. Swatos, ed., *Religion and Democracy in Latin America* (New Brunswick, N.J.: Transaction Publishers, 1995), 45–58. He notes that though the PT did well below expectations in the São Paulo region in 1982, it gained 43 percent of the vote in 1984 and 55 percent in 1988.

38. Moacir Gadotti and Otaviano Pereira, *Pra Que PT?* (São Paulo: Editora Cortez, 1989), 23.

39. Leonardo Boff, "CEBs: Que Significa 'Novo Modo de Toda a Igreja Ser'," 549 and Clodovis Boff, "CEBS e Prática de Libertação," *Revista Eclesiástica Brasileira* 40 fasc. 160 (1980).

40. See Scott Mainwairing and A. Wilde, eds., *The Progressive Church in Latin America,* 173 as well as Ronald M. Schneider, *"Order and Progress": A Political History of Brazil* (Boulder, Colo.: Westview Press, 1991), 316.

41. Ricardo Galletta, *Pastoral Popular e Política Partidária* (São Paulo: Edições Paulinas, 1986), 32–34; Schneider, *"Order and Progress,"* 291–95; and Claudio Perani, "Comunidades Eclesiais de Base e Movimento Popular," *Cadernos do CEAS* (Centro de Estudos e Ação Social) 75 (1981), 25–33.

42. Moacir Gadotti and Otaviano Pereira, *Pra Que PT: Origem, Projeto e Consolidação do Partido dos Trabalhadores,* 16.

43. Perani, "Comunidades Eclesiais de Base e Movimento Popular," 18.

44. Acronym for *Centro Dom Helder Câmara de Estudos e Ação Social,* established in Recife PE, in 1989, to work in three areas, those of human rights, law and citizenship and religious freedom. Valle is director of the *Centro de Estatística Reli-*

giosa e Investigações Sociais, an official Church research center in Rio de Janeiro. He produced *Levantamento Nacional Das Comunidades Eclesiais Católicas-Resultados Estatísticos* (Rio de Janeiro: CERIS, 1993) and authored "CEB: Fator de uma Outra Forma de Modernização," in Faustino L. C. Teixeira et al., *CEBs: Cidadania e Modernidade,* 41–71.

45. José Comblin, "CEB: Fator de uma Outra Forma de Modernização," in Faustino L. C. Teixeira et al., *CEBs, Cidadania e Modernidade,* chapter 1; W. E. Hewitt, *Base Christian Communities and Social Change in Brazil* (Lincoln: University of Nebraska Press, 1991); and John Burdick, *Looking for God in Brazil: The Progressive Catholic Church in Urban Brazil's Religious Arena* (Berkeley: University of California Press, 1993).

46. Burdick, *Looking for God in Brazil,* 69–91, 192–203, as well as Nancy Scheper-Hughes, *Death Without Weeping* (Berkeley: University of California Press, 1992); W. E. Hewitt, "Myths and Realities of Liberation Theology" (1988), 141–45; José Comblin, "Algumas Questões a partir da Prática das Comunidades Eclesiais de Base no Nordeste," *Revista Eclesiástica Brasileira,* 50, fasc. 198 (June 1990), 345.

47. The political implications of *Basismo* are discussed by David Lehmann, *Democracy and Development in Latin America* (Philadelphia: Temple University Press, 1990), 185–214.

48. Ricardo Galletta, ed., *Pastoral Popular e Política Partidária* (São Paulo: Edições Paulinas, 1986), 37.

49. Ibid., 17.

50. Leonardo Boff, "Liberation Theology: A Political Expression of Biblical Faith," *Christian-Jewish Relations* 21 (Spring 1988), 19.

51. Frei Betto, "As CEBs e o Projeto Político Popular," *Revista Eclesiástica Brasileira,* 579, 583.

52. Ibid., 583f.

53. A problem for the PT in the 1980s. Carlos N. Coutinho, "Democracia e Socialismo," in Apolônia de Carvalho and Carlos N. Coutinho, eds., *PT: Um Projeto para o Brasil* (São Paulo: Editora Brasiliense, 1989), 9–31; Daniel Filho, "O Maoísmo e a Trajetória dos Marxistas Brasileiros," in Daniel A. Reis Filho, ed., *História do Marxismo no Brasil* (Rio de Janeiro: Paz e Terra, 1991), 105–32.

54. Heloisa Buarque de Holanda, ed., *Pós-Modernidade e Pólitica* (Rio de Janeiro, 1991); D. G. Schaeffer, "Modernidade, Pós-Modernidade e a Teologia: Pensamentos sobre uma Postura Teológica Democrática e Interdisciplinar — Um Debate" in *Estudos Teológicos* 33, no. 2 (1993) 128–44; J. Machado da Silva, *A Miséria do Cotidiano: Energias utópicas em um territorio urbano moderno e pós-moderno* (Porto Alegre, RS: Artes & Ofícios, 1991).

55. See John Burdick's *Looking for God in Brazil* (Berkeley: University of California Press, 1993) on the Pentecostal case, and on the theoretical level, Laclau and Mouffe, *Hegemony and Socialist Strategy,* 84.

56. See the work of John Burdick as well as Cecilia Mariz, "Religion and Coping with Poverty in Brazil." Unpublished Ph.D. dissertation, Boston University (1989).

57. See the work by Nancy Scheper-Hughes, *Death without Weeping: The Violence of Everyday Life in Brazil* (Berkeley: University of California Press, 1992) and Burdick, *Looking for God in Brazil.*

58. Some have argued that liberation theologies, by their rejection of liberalism,

atomistic individualism, and their emphasis on the social and communal values, are reflecting pre-modern ideologies and values. In so doing they are in conformity with traditional Church social teaching's analyses of modernity. See Michael Löwy, *The War of the Gods* (London: Verso, 1996), 52–61.

59. This despite the remarkable work done by Jung Mo Sung, *A Idolatria do Capital e a Morte dos Pobres* (São Paulo: Edições Paulinas, 1989) and his *Teologiae Economia: Responsando a Teologia da Libertação e as Utopias* (Petrópolis: Editora Vozes, 1995).

60. Laclau and Mouffe, *Hegemony and Socialist Strategy,* 169.

61. Ibid., 84.

62. Leonardo Boff, *Ecologia, Mundialização, Espiritualidade: A Emergência de um novo Paradigma* (São Paulo: Editora Atica, 1993) and his *Nova Era: A Civilização Planetária* (São Paulo: Editora Atica, 1994).

63. F. Lyotard, "An Interview," *Theory, Culture and Society* 5, no. 2 (1988): 277.

20

EMBRACING THE LITE

William Martin

When I was at Harvard Divinity School in the 1960s, we talked at length and with some confidence about the Death of God and the Secular City and A World Come of Age, a world in which "god-talk" and overt interest in matters spiritual would become less and less common. Whether we welcomed or dreaded the prospect was irrelevant; it was on its way and we'd have to learn to deal with it. Few predictions have been further off the mark. Without question, secularization remains a powerful force in American society. Still, no one who pays attention to such things can fail to be impressed by abundant evidence of widespread religious revival, by the enormous impact religion is having in the political sphere, and by the persistent and growing presence of religious themes in movies, television series, and, most notably, best-selling books. Instead of a denuded, disenchanted world made safe and explicable by empirical science and rational technology, we are deluged not only by a steady outpouring of conventional religious messages and the evergreen banalities of astrology and psychic readings, but also by claims of dramatic healings and other wondrous miracles, reports of encounters with angels and aliens, rapturous stories of being "embraced by the light" in near-death experiences, reassuring messages delivered by Native American Spirit Guides to modern-day shamans, public conversations in hotel ballrooms with channeled "entities" from the distant past, and repeated assurances that we stand at the dawning of a New Age in galactic history and can move into a utopian millennium just as soon as we get our inner selves to vibrate at the correct frequency. In the face of all this, "S/he that knoweth what to do knoweth a good thing." (That's not in the Bible, but it ought to be.)

For most of my academic career I have written about evangelicals and fundamentalists — radio and TV preachers, key figures such as Billy Graham, and the religio-political movement known as the Religious Right. Not long ago, however, an editor and longtime friend at *Self*, a popular magazine for young women, invited me to look over several boxes of books, page proofs, and manuscripts sent by publishers hoping for a positive mention in the magazine's book review section. All the books dealt with religion, and almost all of them could be classified as "New Age." Fascinated — in sev-

249

eral senses of that term — with what I found there, welcoming a break from fundamentalism, and remembering Harvey Cox's remarkable openness to all forms of religious expression, I ranged beyond that eclectic collection to read some of the classics of New Age literature, together with recent best-sellers likely to take their place on that shelf. I will not be carving out a new career as a student of the New Age, but this essay reflects my attempt to make sense of this diverse movement.

Sociologists at the University of California at Santa Barbara estimate that at least twelve million people actively subscribe to New Age ideas, with perhaps thirty million others finding many of these ideas attractive. The astonishing and long-running popularity of such books as *A Course in Miracles, The Celestine Prophecy, Embraced by the Light, A Book of Angels, Conversations with God,* several books about encounters with aliens, and almost any book by Deepak Chopra make clear that such estimates are not far-fetched. Other studies, together with unsystematic observation, indicate that most adherents of this loosely structured and many-faceted movement are urban, middle- to upper-middle-class people, reasonably affluent and rather well educated. Women outnumber men by about two to one. True to the popular stereotype, the Pacific Coast and the Rocky Mountain states have more than their share of New Agers.

For those unfamiliar with New Age beliefs, some preliminary guidelines may prove helpful. As in any diverse movement, one finds disagreements and variations among adherents to New Age beliefs, and labelling another's "truth" as erroneous is seen as egregiously bad form. Still, a core of assumptions is so commonly accepted as beyond question that it constitutes a virtual orthodoxy of New Age theology.

For starters, the purveyors of New Age ideas evince few doubts about the importance of what they have to say. Neale Donald Walsch, the visible participant in the phenomenally popular series of *Conversations with God* volumes, is hardly atypical when he claims that the books bearing his name were not written by him, but happened to him. For three years, he informs us, he took dictation from God, who chose him to share with the world answers to "most, if not all, of the questions we have ever asked about...everything."[1] While taking little personal credit for the product, Walsch acknowledges that God has written a wonderful book and has no problems with his earthly amanuensis's making a truckload of money from the collaboration. God agrees, urging people to read it over and over again until they "can quote its passages to others" and "bring its phrases to mind in the midst of the darkest hour."[2] Other writers, often attesting to the assistance of angels or Spirit Guides or unspecified inspiration — "My pen writes on, almost, its seems, without me"[3] — assure us that they, too, had little sense of the magnitude of their message until the manuscript was finished and they came to realize they had produced "a map to the next step in humankind's evolution."[4]

That "next step" is widely assumed to be a big one. Belief in an imminent millennium has energized Americans since the days of the Puritans and remains a solid article of faith for millions of conservative Christians, many of whom read "the signs of the times" for hints as to just when, as a popular bumper sticker puts it, "In the case of the Rapture, this car will be unoccupied." But dreams of epochal transformation are not limited to fundamentalist Christians. The very term "New Age" refers to a millennial dawn characterized by a "radical shift in consciousness," a "vast spiritual awakening," "a paradigm shift in human evolution," a state of existence, just around the corner, when minds will soar to new realms and enlightened humans will live in peace and unconditional love, in perfect harmony with each other and nature.

Though they speak of evolution, New Agers apparently expect the millennial transformation to occur rather soon, even citing Stephen Jay Gould's theory of "punctuated leaps" in support of a shortened horizon. An oft-summoned image of such a leap is that of the Hundredth Monkey, a reference to an apocryphal story of island-bound monkeys who learned to wash potatoes in the surf. According to the story, which lacks empirical basis, when the skill spread sufficiently — to the hundredth monkey or thereabouts — monkeys on other islands, with no direct learning experience, suddenly began to exhibit the same behavior. In similar manner, New Agers believe, the attainment of a critical mass of enlightened spirits will spark a wildfire of expanded consciousness that will enable all humankind to achieve the limitless wisdom and boundless potential for which it has been eternally destined.

The key, author after author explains, is to tap into the infinite energy of the universe, the Energy of God — or, in some versions, the Universal Energy that is God, that is the source of all creation and that gives life to the cosmos. We can do this by acquiring crystals, which are thought to have special energy-attracting qualities, or by making pilgrimages to such places as Sedona, Arizona, where certain spots known as vortexes are believed to have a higher energy output, which will raise one's vibrational level. Keeping the vibrations up is regarded as enormously important. As a result, there is a whole lot of shaking going on in New Age books. We are warned that letting our vibrations diminish leads to disease and dullness, whereas revving them up can work apparent miracles — in *The Celestine Prophecy,* a fictional account of a search for an ancient manuscript filled with insights for transformed living, an enlightened priest explains to his friend why a band of soldiers appears to be ignoring them: "They can't see us. We are vibrating too highly."[5] Similarly, Transcendental Meditators believe that when they achieve sufficiently high vibrations, they will finally be able to accomplish true "yogic flying," instead of the more modest cross-legged sproinging they now practice.

Most leaders of this amorphous movement profess already to possess the necessary insights and attitudes to make the great leap forward. The very fact that readers have purchased their books is seen as proof that they, too, are ready to help ring in the New Age. This latter assertion derives from the widely held conviction that, as God told Neale Donald Walsch, "There are no coincidences in the universe."[6] Everything that happens has a purpose that should be examined for its deepest import. We are assured that legions of people are grasping this crucial insight and are taking coincidences seriously. That may well be accurate, given declining S.A.T. scores in quantitative reasoning, tiny pictures of hamburgers and french fries on cash-register keys, and other indicators of widespread innumeracy, but even a passing acquaintance with elementary statistics and probability theory should undercut that particular pillar of New Age belief.

A skeptical attitude of the sort I've just manifested would come as no surprise to a disciple to New Age teaching. While they take pride in Deepak Chopra's legitimate medical credentials, cite Albert Einstein's theories on energy as the essential reality, and point to as-yet-unexplained oddities discovered by quantum physicists as evidence in support of their views, New Agers typically manifest disdain for the contentions, attitudes, and agents of dominant institutions. This is particularly the case for conventional religion, science, academia, and other circles dominated either by orthodoxy or rationality or both.

Established religions, particularly mainstream Judaism and Christianity, are seen as having brainwashed their adherents into accepting stunted and deformed views of God and themselves. In *The Celestine Prophecy,* the chief villain is Cardinal Sebastian, who seeks to suppress The Manuscript (always capitalized) because it "gives the impression that people can decide on their own how to live, without regard to the scriptures" and would undermine the Church's power over the masses.[7] The challenge to the Church's authority is also a challenge to patriarchy, with all the pathologies of its power-seeking, rationalistic, authoritarian ethos. Significantly, women play important roles in New Age circles. Angels, ascended Masters, Christ figures, channeled entities, and the highest levels of divinity are often described in female, androgynous, or genderless terms. And some women engage in neo-pagan, nature-oriented worship involving a great Mother Goddess, or such classic female deities as Diana, Isis, Demeter, Hecate, and Cybele. Closely related is the worship of Gaia, which involves a view of the earth itself as a living, feminine creature.

Most New Age writers would agree with Lily Fairchilde (*Song of the Phoenix*) when she speaks of "a yawning chasm between religion, which limits experience of the Divine by way of exclusive definition, and spirituality, which encourages the free exploration of an individual's direct experience of the Divine without the need of intellectual scrutiny."[8] Religion is associated with lifeless tradition, stifling dogma, and repugnant claims of exclusive truth, all viewed as inferior to trusting the intuitions of one's Higher Self.

This disdain for intellectual scrutiny enables New Agers to dismiss critics as insufficiently evolved and to subdue their own reason in favor of vague longings, or even passionate conviction.

Fairchilde's reference to "an individual direct experience of the Divine" is another hallmark of New Age doctrine. Throughout most of recorded history, small numbers of spiritual elites, called gnostics, have held the conviction that they share in the divine essence, and there was never a time when they were not, that they and God know and have always known each other directly and immediately, that in their Deepest Selves they are, as Yale cultural critic and self-confessed gnostic Harold Bloom puts it, "a part and particle of God."[9] The task, then, is not to find or believe in or submit to God, but to wake up to who we really are and to experience the brilliant light that already lies hidden within us, to transcend the dualism that causes us to think of ourselves as flawed and sinful creatures and recognize that we are good, perfect beings, part of a holistic oneness with God and the universe. Insofar as we are successful in this effort, we manifest "Christ consciousness" or embody the "Christ principle," a level of enlightenment reached preeminently by Jesus, but in comparable degrees by other Great Masters of spiritual evolution.

To reach that goal, any and all plausible means of assistance are legitimate. In marked contrast to fundamentalist insistence on exclusive sources of authority, New Agers are quite promiscuous in their search for Light, drawing at will and unapologetically from Judaism, Christianity, Islam, Buddhism, Hinduism, Transcendentalism, Theosophy, New Thought, Spiritualism, Swedenborgianism, Goddess worship, WomenChurch, paganism, astrology, angelology, UFOlogy, pyramid power, crystal consciousness, and, increasingly, the spiritual teachings and traditions of Native Americans. Since part of the movement's power derives from its determination to overcome artificial divisions, find universals, and restore wholeness to a splintered creation, almost any insight can be made to fit somewhere, and troublesome doctrines and moral requirements can be ignored if inconvenient.

In recent years, New Age devotees have sought wisdom and insight in reports from those who have had near-death experiences. Though they vary in details, almost all such reports involve emerging from a tunnel to be greeted by indescribably beautiful sounds and a blindingly brilliant figure of light — variously identified as Jesus, White Buffalo Woman, an angel, the Great Presence, or some other being appropriate to the individual's cultural background — who embraces the arriving soul and offers assurance that death is not something to be feared, not an end to existence, but a blissful transition to a higher state of being. Typically, those who relate such experience claim to have been reluctant to return to their old existence, but have done so in order to assure the rest of us that death is but a minor speed bump on the celestial highway. This message is thought to be especially needed by Americans, who have — according to God, as told to Neale Donald Walsch — "created a society in which it is very not okay to want to die; very not okay to be very okay with death."[10] (Obviously, God's literary style has fallen off over the centuries, underscoring how important it is to keep writing.)

Closely related to the assurance that when we die we do not really die is belief in reincarnation, a process crucial to personal and galactic evolution. Reincarnation, as understood in this movement, offers the opportunity to experience, on earth and in other planetary systems, important learning experiences that increase the levels of light and love in individuals and raise "the vibrational frequency of the Whole."[11] A reported one-fourth of all Americans believe in reincarnation, and the number appears to be growing. Small wonder, according to Neale Walsch's God, who observes that there have been so many reports of reincarnation "from thoroughly reliable sources . . . as to eliminate any possibility that they were making it up or had contrived to somehow deceive researchers and loved ones." Walsch himself learned that he had 647 previous lives. Happily, he is evolving in a positive direction. In some of his previous lives, he killed people. In this one, he has quit smoking and is on good terms with all of his former mates.[12]

Belief in reincarnation serves several functions. Perhaps most important, it offers an alternative to viewing the world as an unjust realm in which, from time to time, the good die young, the wicked prosper, and children suffer for no apparent reason. Those who suffer now deserve it because of past wrongs; those who now work evil will be repaid in a future existence. It also fits neatly with belief in spiritual evolution. One life is simply not enough to learn all the lessons necessary to achieving full enlightenment. In some explanations, the succession of lives is described almost as a well-planned cosmic curriculum. For example, Louis L. Hay, in *You Can Heal Your Life,* explains that

> Each one of us decides to incarnate upon this planet at particular points in time and space. We have chosen to come here to learn a particular lesson that will advance us upon our spiritual, evolutionary pathway. We choose our sex, our color, our country, and then we look around for the particular set of parents who will mirror the patterns we are bringing in to work on in this lifetime. Then, when we grow up, we usually point our finger accusingly at our parents and whisper, "You did it to me." But really, we chose them because they were perfect for what we wanted to work on overcoming.[13]

Thus, reincarnation provides an explanation for circumstances present at birth and ostensibly out of control of apparently innocent newborns. Though not consciously remembered, the choice to be born into such a circumstance was made before incarnation and should be seen as appropriate to the individual's evolutionary needs, not lamented as a cruel and inexplicable injustice.

Belief in uninterrupted existence and reincarnation is bolstered by the claims of "channels," modern-day shamans who claim to be in communication with sundry Ascended Masters, Spirit Guides, and other departed "entities." Some channels specialize in a particular entity such as Ramtha, Lazaris, Seth, or Saint Germain, and pass on their messages, usually marked by archaic locutions and delivered in a strange accent and tone unlike the channel's normal voice, to sizable crowds gathered in theaters or hotel ballrooms. Helen Schucman channeled the entire 1,188-page *A Course in Miracles* from a source implying he was Jesus. Others, such as Rosemary Altea, who describes herself as a "healer and full-fledged medium," claims to have spoken with thousands of people in the spirit world, though she works mainly with an Apache spirit named Grey Eagle.[14] The channeled entities are remarkably accommodating, rarely failing to show up when summoned and willing to answer any question, however mundane. They are also notably non-judgmental — in his insightful and quite readable academic study, *The Channeling Zone,* Michael Brown compares them to "cosmic psychotherapists, laughing at human foibles but rarely offering reproach or criticism." Instead, they tout the value of unconditional love and urge the earthbound to get in touch with their "Christ-selves," their "godhumanity," the immortal, imperishable essence of their being.[15]

Visits from unseen realms are not limited to New Age or shamanic cultures. Some Pentecostal and charismatic Christians claim to receive messages from the Holy Spirit, often delivering them in an "unknown tongue" that may be translated by yet another member of the group. In marked contrast to the benign reassurances of New Age entities, these "prophecies," as they are called, typically warn of the doom that will befall the unrepentant. Among Catholics, the vision of choice is, of course, an apparition of the Virgin Mary. In recent years, as Scott Sparrow documents in *Blessed among Women: Encounters with Mary,* reports of Marian appearances have increased, usually preceding or coinciding with regional upheavals — witness the recent apparitions of the Virgin at Medjugorge, in Bosnia. Mary seldom has much to say, but the clear sense believers receive from her appearances is that of being completely known and completely loved, and of being called to pay attention to mounting tragedy and injustice, especially when they affect children.[16]

Both new and more traditional forms of spirituality are giving increased attention to angels. Dozens of books, thousands of trinkets, and a spate of television shows drafting on the popular *Touched by an Angel* support surveys that regularly indicate that almost 70 percent profess to believe in angels. Traditional Christians and New Agers alike view angels as messengers and protectors "who watch over us with loving attention," and both are likely to believe they have the power to appear in the guise of ordinary human beings. But New Agers put a distinctive spin on the subject. In addition to serving as what a book called *Ask Your Angels* styles as "Social Workers of the Universe," helping out wherever needed, angels are also pictured as rounding up those "who are to participate in the breakthrough" to the New Age. Predictably, angelic beings vibrate at a higher frequency than do humans. According to Lily Fairchilde, they can "slow down this dance of light so that they appear more human, more like us, less shiny." Still, their vibratory level is so much higher than our own that, if one attempted to access them directly, "the molecular structure of your corporeal body would literally be blown apart."[17] Fair warning.

The determined eclecticism of the New Age movement reflects the intellectual and moral relativism that helps account for its widespread appeal. New Age literature teems with such assertions as "Each soul has its own law," "A thing is only right or wrong because you say it is," "You are your own rule maker. Outcomes are simply that," and "Society needs rules, but we should not push on others." It is no surprise that individuals are seen responsible for making their own (and only their own) rules since many New Age teachers assert that we create our own realities and are therefore responsible for everything that happens to us. Hunger, poverty, disease, rape, unemployment, "accidents," old age, and death itself — all occur because we, individually or collectively, will them into being. Though we may say we do not want to lose our job, the fearful expectation that we might becomes our "Sponsoring Thought" that governs reality. The result may not be immediate, but *Divine Revelation* author Susan Sumsky asserts that "Every seed idea that you plant into the universe eventually sprouts into physical form."[18] Hence the widespread use of "affirmations," frequently repeated positive statements by means of which we can assure ourselves that "I am growing more prosperous every day" or "I'm good enough, I'm smart enough, and, by golly, people like me."

Even so-called natural disasters are attributed to human volition. Left to itself, "Nothing is more gentle than Nature," Neale Walsch learns from God, who apparently doesn't watch the Discovery Channel. Apparent contradictions to this assertion can be explained. In *Heaven and Earth,* journalist Michael D'Antonio tells of being informed that "hurricanes go ashore in places like Mississippi and New Orleans, where there is a lower value on human life than in the Northeast."[19] Those who doubt that children in Rwanda choose their own death by wondering what a machete feels like as it falls on the neck or who try to find the Sponsoring Thought behind a devastating earthquake are urged to "judge not, and neither condemn, for you know not why a thing occurs, nor to what end.... Rather, seek to change those things... which no longer reflect your highest sense of Who You Are."[20]

Because of the power individuals wield over their own lives, this one and those to come, Ramtha, the 35,000-year-old entity channeled by J. Z. Knight, assures his devotees, "You never have to pay for anything. You are God and therefore capable of creating any reality you desire, if not now, then in a later incarnation. We have the power to heal any disease, even to grow a new limb if one is cut off. What keeps us from doing these things? Our 'altered ego,' the 'Antichrist' within us who keeps telling us we are not God."[21]

This confidence in the power of thought has combined with distrust of established institutions and rational science to create an almost obsessive interest in health and broad support for the growing field of alternative medicine. Like Phineas Quimby, the nineteenth-century father of New Thought, and Mary Baker Eddy, the mother of Christian Science, many New Agers deny the necessity of disease and some even think it possible to escape death, though none has quite mastered that particular feat as of yet. Vegetarian diets, exercise, massage, acupuncture and acupressure, enema and aroma therapy, herbal remedies, gilded imagery, avoidance of negative thinking are viewed as ways to bolster the immune system, ward off disease, and jump-start the body's own healing resources when disease or other physical problems do arise. This congeries of beliefs draws strong support and legitimacy from the movement's two hero physicians, Bernie Siegel and Deepak Chopra. In book after best-selling book, Siegel tirelessly touts the healing power of love to work miraculous cures of cancer, which he asserts is caused by such thought errors as denying our true feelings. Chopra, whose training in both Western and Eastern medical traditions gives him a special cachet, asserts that healing is "nothing other than the return to the memory of wholeness."[22]

There can no longer be serious doubt that proper diet, exercise, fulfilling work, a positive attitude, laughter, and the love of friends and family greatly increase one's chances for a healthy life. Moreover, many mainstream physicians readily acknowledge the efficacy of nontraditional therapies; indeed, a third of American medical schools offer courses in alternative and complementary medicine. The growing acceptance of a more holistic view of health and healing is seen most clearly, perhaps, in the serious attention paid to meditation and prayer. For two decades, cardiologist Herbert Benson of the Harvard Medical School has taught patients to reduce their heartbeat and blood pressure by spending twenty minutes twice a day repeating a word or phrase — a mantra — of their own choosing. In two best-selling books, *Healing Words* and *Prayer Is Good Medicine,* Larry Dossey, M.D., presents mounting scientific evidence that prayer really does appear to have measurable healing power, even when the persons being prayed for are not aware of the supplications of their behalf. This, of course, comes as no surprise to traditional believers in mainstream religions. Benson and Dossey, however, discourage spiritual parochialism by noting that, in essence, any prayer will do. The supplicant need not be a Jew or Christian or even believe in a personal god. Consequently, although Benson observes that believers may want to choose a word or phrase freighted with meaning — such as "kyrie eleison" for Christians or the Shema ("Hear O Israel, the Lord our God, the Lord is One") for Jews, or "Om" for Hindus — he admits that a simple syllable such as "One" is equally effective at evoking what he calls the Relaxation Response, the title of his own 1989 best-seller.

Unlike Drs. Siegel and Chopra, Benson and Dossey both continue to practice and admire conventional scientific medicine. Dossey, in fact, pointedly criticizes New Age teachers for laying the blame for sickness at the feet of victims. While acknowledging that cynicism and anger can induce or exacerbate illness, he stresses that "Sometimes, cells just do what cells do, which sometimes involves malfunctioning."[23] As one who was diagnosed with cancer at a time of unusual personal and professional satisfaction, who cherished the love and prayers and "positive vibrations" of friends and family, I found it reassuring not to be told that I did it all myself.

The sometimes obsessive concern with health and the conviction that individuals create their own reality are manifestations of an aspect of New Age thought that helps account for its attractiveness and, in so doing, underscores its deepest flaws. That aspect is an extraordinary emphasis on, and approval of, self-absorption. To be sure, many New Agers express and manifest concern for others and for the planet. In communities in which they have a noticeable presence, they are likely to be involved in efforts to advance the equality and well-being of women, to advocate peace and disarmament, to protect and improve the environment, to grow and promote wholesome foods, to encourage healthy lifestyles, to cultivate music and other arts and crafts, to defend animal rights, and to be involved in a number of activities that promote cooperation rather than competition, including "intentional communities," the term that seems now to be preferred over "communes."

These impulses, however, can easily be undercut by the pervasive message that Self is supreme. In contrast to Jesus' assertion that "He that seeketh his life shall lose it," many New Age teachers proclaim that the only meaningful purpose in life is "to experience fullest glory."[24] To James Hillman, author of *The Soul's Code,* that means finding the unique destiny to which each individual soul is called.[25] To Rosemary Altea, it means recognizing that "Self-sacrifice is good for no one."[26] To Neale Walsch, it means that "you have no obligation. Neither in relationship, nor in all of life."[27] Apparently, manifesting unconditional love to all humanity can release one from the obligation to demonstrate it to any actual neighbors. This disdain for service or tangible concern for others — not universal, but quite common in New Age writings — runs counter to the teachings of every major religion that has stood the test of time. Ironically, the extreme individualism one often finds can also discourage seekers from finding the meaning they so earnestly seek in the locus where most humans throughout history have found it: human community.

Despite Lily Tomlin's clever observation to the contrary, we are not "all in this alone." Human beings are social beings. We cannot get to be human without other humans, and we are not likely to see much improvement in our society, much less ring in the millennium, unless we join with others to bring it about. And that means volunteering to tutor neglected children, helping to build houses for homeless families, going to school board meetings, getting involved in local politics, or doing a thousand other things, side by side with fellow citizens, that are more likely to improve the planet than simply visualizing world peace or declaring without further action that "the end of hunger is an idea whose time has come."

Despite its numerous dubious assumptions, its unsupported and unsupportable claims, its lack of self-critical reflection, and its often vacuous pronouncements, the New Age movement obviously speaks to a deep need in millions of people. At its best, it encourages a positive outlook on life and a spirit of openness to the wisdom of a variety of cultures and calls for a reconnecting of the disparate parts of a fragmented world and a joining of these to whatever is ultimate in the universe. In its less beneficial mode, it sanctions selfishness and social passivity and urges the abandonment of one's critical faculties in favor of wishful thinking. In all its forms, it attests to a sense of powerlessness and loss of purpose engendered by widespread social distress, political alienation, transient personal relationships, dissatisfaction with the transitory rewards of material wealth and sensual pleasure, and, not least, increased secularization and the attendant erosion of a meaningful connection to the sacred. Human beings are meaning-seekers. Though we may scoff at the possibility of certainty, we long to believe, to understand why we are here and what we are to do and what to expect when we die.

The search for meaning is honorable and, for most of us, unavoidable. Moreover, the long experience of humanity suggests that neglecting the spiritual dimensions of life will cause that search to fall short of its goal. Some obviously find intellectual and spiritual fulfillment in New Age notions. Millions of others cling to fundamentalist certainties that, unsuited as they are for a modern or postmodern world, nevertheless provide clear and comforting direction to souls made anxious by ambiguity. Still others find adequate meaning in family, in work, in community, in a variety of endeavors and ways of being that do not impel them to look beyond the veil that separates this world and whatever, if anything, may lie beyond. I suspect, however, that a substantial majority — of Americans, at least — are most likely to satisfy their search for meaning by first plumbing the depths of the traditions with which they are already somewhat familiar and by giving respectful attention to the best in other traditions. This should not be read as an assertion of the superiority of a particular tradition, but as a calculation of reasonable probabilities, given the brevity of life and the power of early learning.

I have shared in Passover Seders, chanted in Buddhist and Hindu temples, crawled into a dark cave to talk with an aged Tibetan nun who spent her entire life in prayer and meditation, been enchanted by a visit to a Zen monastery tucked into the side of a mountain deep in Japan, watched in fascination as a Navaho "singer" fashioned a sand painting depicting a sacred myth, prostrated myself in prayer alongside devout Muslims, and, closer to my spiritual home, helped catch people "slain in the Spirit" at a Pentecostal revival. I honor all these quests for meaning, as well as the myriad expressions I have not sampled, and I have taken something positive from each of them. That said, I do not imagine that trying to pretend I am something I could never be, or trying to weave these together into some kind of variegated spiritual poncho, suitable for all occasions, would satisfy my search for authenticity. Instead, I choose to remain within the Christian tradition, painfully aware of the many distorted and destructive forms it has assumed during its two-thousand-year existence, but also quite convinced that, at its best — like all great religious traditions — it calls and points me to a level of ethical and moral and spiritual richness that I can never exhaust nor fully embody. Fortunately, this in no way cuts me off from the wealth of other traditions, including much that is admirable in the sometimes "lite" spirituality of the New Age.

I think it highly unlikely that any of the contributors to or readers of this volume have turned to this essay as an aid to pilgrimage — a fortunate circumstance, given my meager credentials as a spiritual guide. Still, in the spirit of my friend and teacher, Harvey Cox, though without his broad experience and great capacity for creative reflection, let me offer several modest words of counsel that may prove helpful to any spiritual seeker who might have wandered this way.

First, listen to reason. If you find it hard to believe that meditation can cause one to levitate, that illness and death are illusions and avoidable, or that humans can conjure up typhoons, do not chastise yourself for being unspiritual. Instead, consider the advice offered by Robert Gerzon in his sensible book, *Finding Serenity in an Age of Anxiety.* After setting forth more than a score of such "Least Favorite Laws of Life" as "Bad things happen to good people," "Not everyone we meet will like us," "Some of our most cherished dreams won't come true, no matter how much we want them to," "Evil exists," "We are really going to die," and "Our death may be painful," he concludes, "If we can accept all these as true, we are on the way to unshakable inner peace."[28]

Second, do not depend on reason alone. Cultivate the nonrational (as distinguished from the irrational) elements of life. Pay attention to nature, in its mundane as well as its majestic aspects. Find ways to add depth and texture to aspects of your life that have been flattened by routine and mechanistic efficiency. Practice stillness. Set aside a time, perhaps in the morning or before retiring in the evening, to pray, to meditate, to do breathing exercises or to follow the ritual disciplines of Yoga or Tai Chi Chuan, to read contemplative literature, or simply to let silence calm body and spirit.

Third, reexplore the spiritual tradition most familiar to you, to see what you may have overlooked. *Genesis,* the PBS series and book produced by Bill Moyers, and Peter Gomes's *The Good Book* have demonstrated the continuing power of the Jewish and Christian Bible, and Leonard Felder's *The Ten Challenges* — one of the books in the boxes my editor friend sent me — provides a rich elaboration of the enduring wisdom contained in the Ten Commandments (but found, as Felder notes, as common threads in many spiritual traditions). Those reared outside Judaism or Christianity will have no difficulty finding sources of inspiration from their own traditions.

Fourth, be open to wisdom wherever it appears. A promiscuous acceptance of anything written or spoken by anyone claiming spiritual insight is more likely to lead to confusion than to salvation. On the other hand, it is equally parochial to imagine that we do not have much to learn from others who have sought to cultivate the sacred, whatever their culture.

Finally, as already noted, do not imagine that the search for meaning and fulfillment is a solo flight. Participation in satisfying human communities contributes significantly to physical health and psychological well-being. It also provides the most dependable source of support and comfort in the face of disaster and defeat — much of which is not one's own creation. And, for most seekers, involvement in a religious community of some sort can provide the structure, the guidance, the feedback, and the reinforcement that are most likely to foster genuine spiritual growth. Obviously, not every human community offers these advantages. Indeed, some have the opposite effect. For that reason, finding meaningful community — a church, a temple, a mosque, a fellowship of some other kind — should be viewed as a crucial part of one's quest for wholeness, and initial disappointments should not cause one to give in to the temptation to go it alone.

Involvement in communities, as distinguished from audiences, carries with it a responsibility toward others. As Robert Gerzon points out, the essence of the Golden Rule is that "You and I are one." And a defining characteristic of enlightenment is not self-absorption, but humble, loving, compassionate concern for both the near and the "distant neighbor." As the Buddha observed, "It is through service in this world, not by abandoning this world, that we attain to heavenly realms of spiritual fulfillment."[29] In a similar vein, Jesus told his disciples, "Inasmuch as you [showed love and concern] to the least of these, you did it unto me." These precepts may not reflect the spirit of this age or the New Age, but millions of our fellow humans, for thousands of years, have found in them an ageless secret of true humanity and spiritual wholeness.

Notes

1. Neal Donald Walsch, *Conversations with God: An Uncommon Dialogue,* Book 1 (New York: G. P. Putnam's Sons, 1996), Introduction, second page (unnumbered).

2. Ibid., 120.

3. Rosemary Altea, *Proud Spirit* (New York: William Morrow, 1997), 43.

4. Carolyn M. Ball, *Blessings in Disguise: How Dreams Come True* (Berkeley: Celestial Arts, 1996), ix.

5. James Redfield, *The Celestine Prophecy: An Adventure* (New York: Warner Books, 1993), ix.

6. Walsch, *Conversations,* 58.

7. Redfield, *Celestine Prophecy,* 170.

8. Lily Fairchilde, *Song of the Phoenix: Voices of Comfort and Healing from the Afterlife* (New York: Riverhead Books, 1996), 27.

9. Harold Bloom, *Omens of Millennium: The Gnosis of Angels, Dreams, and Resurrection* (New York: Riverhead Books, 1996), 27.

10. Walsch, *Conversations,* 80.

11. Fairchilde, *Song of the Phoenix,* 92.

12. Walsch, *Conversations,* 204.

13. Louise L. Hay, *You Can Heal Your Life* (1984; reprint by Eden Grove Editions, 1988), quoted in Wouter J. Hanegraaff, *New Age Religion and Western Culture: Esotericism in the Mirror of Secular Thought* (E. J. Brill, 1996), 267.

14. Altea, *Proud Spirit.*

15. Michael Brown, *The Channeling Zone: American Spirituality in an Anxious Age* (Cambridge: Harvard University Press, 1997), 37.

16. G. Scott Sparrow, *Blessed Among Women: Encounters with Mary and Her Message* (New York: Harmony, 1997).

17. Fairchilde, *Song of the Phoenix,* 18. Fairchilde notes that angels contributed to book by giving their perspective after each individual story.

18. Susan Sumsky, *Divine Revelation* (New York: Simon and Schuster, 1996), 48.

19. Michael D'Antonio, *Heaven and Earth* (New York: Crown Books, 1992), 144.

20. Walsch, *Conversations,* 38.

21. Martin Gardner, "Isness Is Her Business: Shirley MacLaine," in Robert Basil, ed., *Not Necessarily the New Age: Critical Essays* (Buffalo: Prometheus Books, 1988), 192.

22. Deepak Chopra, quoted in Matt Labash, "The End of History and the Last Guru," *The Weekly Standard* (July 1, 1996).

23. Larry Dossey, M.D., *Prayer Is Good Medicine: How to Reap the Healing Benefits of Prayer* (Harper: San Francisco, 1996), xxx.

24. Walsch, *Conversations,* 38.

25. Ibid.

26. Altea, *Proud Spirit,* 228.

27. Walsch, *Conversations,* 135.

28. Robert Gerzon, *Finding Serenity in an Age of Anxiety* (New York: Bantam Doubleday Dell, 1997), 253ff.

29. Quoted in Leonard Felder, *The Ten Challenges: Spiritual Lessons from the Ten Commandments for Creating Meaning, Growth, and Richness Every Day of Your Life* (New York: Harmony, 1997), 31.

21

COMMANDER DATA

A Candidate for Harvard Divinity School?

ANNE FOERST

Introduction: The Measure of a Man

Commander Data is the secret star in the series *Star Trek, The Next Generation*. He is constructed in analogy to a human and is indistinguishable from a man. Well, nearly indistinguishable as long as one does not become involved with him. His math, for instance, is so much better than even the capabilities of the world's best known geniuses that he cannot be compared with any human being in this respect; that is why he likes to play poker with holodeck images of Sir Isaac Newton and Steve Hawking. His data retrieval is flawless, quite contrary to that of humans. Data does not forget, his storage capacity seems to be unlimited, and he has full power over his memory and can erase and add quite freely. He can read incredibly fast and analyze the material he has read instantly. These capabilities are constantly used for the sake of the *Enterprise* crew and make Data a reliable and well-regarded officer.

All these features we would expect from a sophisticated computer — especially one in the twenty-fourth century. But what about capabilities and features we would intuitively rate as human instead of humanoid? Can Data, as flawless machine, be treated and perceived as person, not a human but nonetheless worthy of personhood and dignity? Roddenberry toys with this question quite frequently and the ambiguous nature of the humanoid Data is the source for numerous episodes.

As for his bodily features, he is extremely strong and nearly indestructible. Each of his parts can be replaced, and, if necessary, he can be improved and updated. His brain can be reprogrammed as wished so that his character formation lies entirely in the hands of himself and the crew or even Star Fleet command. Data needs neither food nor drink (even though he can eat or drink) and he doesn't sleep either. He often uses the nights to improve his databases or to analyze large amounts of complicated material. Data is not creative in the intuitive sense of the word. Even if he often finds the explanation for an unknown phenomenon, it is usually because he has more data available; also, the solution often seems impossible for humans to accept so that only Data as unprejudiced machine can actually think of it. This brings us to the last and most important feature of Data's character: he does not have emotions. He can mimic human emotional responses but his laughter seems pathetic and his attempts to mimic human emotions appear ridiculous. Nonetheless, one wish influences and shapes many of his actions: he wants to be fully human.

The question now remains: Is Data really a "he"? Does he deserve the predicate "man" instead of "machine"? In one *Star Trek* episode this question comes up. Star Fleet wants to disassemble Data to analyze how he is functioning; since he has been so helpful for his crew, Star Fleet wants to build more like him to arm every ship with a humanoid. After learning about the danger of this project for himself, Data rejects this project. Now, the question of his personhood is asked in earnest: can he even resign? Does he have the same rights as other Star Fleet officers and is allowed to pursue his own agenda or is Data a machine and as such property of Star Fleet?

I would like to use this show to explore the question of what it means to be a person. Perhaps it might seem a little strange to use inventions of clever and imaginative science fiction writers to pursue this line of reasoning that is linked so deeply with our own intuitive self-understanding. Why should we take works of fantasy seriously and how could those works challenge our own sense of self and value?

Humanoids Today

Science fiction authors, like any other fiction writers, use our real world and their experienced human interactions as a source for inspiration to invent their own universes and stories. As the subject of SciFi is the future, SciFi authors project from current understandings of the world and the speed of technological development into the future and use current findings in science to do so. Their visions about the future, in return, then often inspire scientists and engineers to do certain research projects and to explore certain phenomena in the world. A good example for such a process is the work of another famous SciFi author, Isaac Asimov, and his idea of a "positronic brain" as basis for humanoid machines. Asimov himself got these ideas from the early work in Artificial Intelligence (AI) and the visions and dreams early AI researchers held. Today AI is beyond that but nonetheless, Asimov was strongly influenced by researchers in the field who then, in return, got inspired by his understanding of humanoids and their place in society. Not only are many humanoid projects today built with fond respect for Asimov and his "Three Laws of Robotics," but also Commander Data is a machine in the image of the Asimov Robots. As for the realism of the figure of Commander Data, some of today's machines are so sophisticated that a lifelike humanoid robot seems not too far out of reach.

Before we go into a description of humanoids today, it seems appropriate to briefly talk about terminology. The term "android" is usually used within the context of SciFi and describes an artificial humanlike machine which could be mistaken for a human. As science and engineering today are too far away from the realization of such a machine, the hopeful constructors of artificial humans usually call their robots "humanoids," which supposedly is less intimidating.

Currently, worldwide there are only a few humanoid robot projects being pursued. MIT's "Cog" and "Kismet," Honda's humanoid walking robot, the humanoids built at Waseda University, and the humanoid built at Tsukuba Electrotechnical Laboratory (ETL) are certainly at the forefront of the new emerging field of humanoid robotics, which today has its own academic conferences, sponsorships and journals.

Many of these humanoid robot projects are fascinating and quite impressive examples of advanced robot technology. Cog is an attempt to build a humanoid in analogy to a human newborn and let it learn by interacting with its environment, thus improving its motor skills and learning the values of human community. Kismet is in a way Cog's "offspring," a cute, babylike head which triggers social responses from humans who interact with it. The philosophy here is that embodiment is actually crucial for the development of intelligence and that motor control and autonomy are key points on the way toward cognitive abilities. Honda's robot is an impressive replica of the human motor system and if one looks at videos of the robot's movement one cannot believe that it is a robot (with its usually quite awkward movements) and not a human hiding in a robotic "shell." Waseda University attempts to integrate several different humanoid tasks in its anthropomorphic head-eye robot. It has facial expressions, turns toward light and noise (but reacts if the input is too harsh), and has minimal natural language understanding to manipulate objects in its environment. ETL's humanoid is extremely skillful in motor control and cognition. However, it exists only in virtual space, thus avoiding all the difficulties emerging out of the physical conditions of the real world.

That there are so many humanoid robot projects in Japan and only a very few in the Western world is due to two reasons.

First, Japan, like every other industrial nation, has a very low birthrate and thus the problem of a continuously aging society. Most nations react by letting new people in but Japan attempts to solve this problem with the development of humanoid robots. If these robots were developed then they could take care of the elder population and the younger people could work in more economic jobs. They have to be as humanoid as possible for two reasons. For one, people might accept them better if they look as human as possible; the more this robot resembles the people it works for, the more these people are able to project into it things like friendship, warmth, and empathy.

Another reason for the popularity of humanoids in Japan is the mundane fact that human houses are built for humans and their special body forms and functional needs. If a robot's body resembles the one from a human, it will be much easier for it to navigate through human households, which is why a majority of the Japanese humanoid projects, like the one of Honda, concentrate on humanlike motion and its motor control. If the robot can move in a human way, it can also anticipate problems a human might have in a certain setting and thus serve humans better.

Second, contrary to the Japanese society that lives with a fairly positive view toward humanoid robots, the Western world has some problems with this research and news about humanoid robot research is received with mixed feelings.

Jewish and Christian Dealings with Androids

The Jewish tradition is ambiguous about humanoids. Especially within Jewish mysticism, the Kabbalah, stories about artificial humans called *Golems* are manifold. The verb *galam* appears only twice in the Hebrew Scripture. In 2 Kgs 2:8 it is used to describe the wrapping of a mantle. But the probably oldest source for this term comes from Ps 139:16. This is the only time in the Hebrew Bible that *galam* appears as *golem,* and it is usually translated with "shapeless thing" or "embryo." The context of the term *golem* is the celebration of creation and the special love and care of God toward humans. God created the psalmist "intricately woven in the depth of the earth" (15) and in God's "book were written all the days that were formed for" (17) the psalmist. It very likely comes from an Arabic root and means originally "tangle" or "cluster." This range of meaning for the term "Golem" obviously inspired the Kabbalists to name their creatures this way. Golems are usually built from clay, constructed through words and numbers (in the Hebrew language letters are also numbers — a large field for numeric word games). The assumption in any Kabbalist theory is the deep faith that the world was created by God in an orderly and numeric fashion; the better people understand the logic behind the world, the more they can share God's mind and participate in God's creativity. Thus, they can construct increasingly complex things. But they cannot build anything animated without help: Golems only come to live if they have a paper in their mouth with the holy name of God, YHWH written on it, or with this name engraved on their forehead. The ultimate power of life is God's and God's alone; God has to be involved to animate an artificial being. So even if the letters/numbers in Hebrew are orderly and thus participate in the order of God's creation, they are not sufficient on their own to create life. Quite the contrary, the tangle of flesh, genes, slime, and chemistry in the case of the human animals, or the clay in case of the Golems needs the spirit and power of God, YHWH, to become alive.

Most Golem stories are located in fifteenth-century Prague. Rabbi Löw, the wise and highly educated and influential Maharal of Prague and a historical figure, is most famous for his engagement in Golem constructions. He created one and put a slip of paper with YHWH on it in the Golem's mouth. The Golem then became animated and was able to help the Jews in Prague; he supported them with his strength in their daily labor and he would help them against attacks from outside. One story describes how Christians would hide dead babies in the ghetto at night and then come back during the day and use these little bodies as a proof that Jews would kill babies in their ceremonies. Then, Christians would have a reason to attack the ghetto and kill Jews. The Golem is known to have found the babies several times and hidden their bodies so that the accusations became worthless.

Rabbi Löw himself treated the Golem as a servant but not as a slave. He even understood the Golem as part of the Jewish community and therefore it had to keep the Sabbath. Every Friday, the Rabbi would remove the animating paper with God's name on it out of the Golem's mouth so that it went back into its unanimated state, thus keeping the Sabbath. One week, however, the rabbi forgot to remove the paper slip and the Golem without his master went berserk. Rabbi Löw saved his fellows of the ghetto by fighting the Golem and with violence he was finally able to remove the life-giving paper out of the Golem's mouth. In some legends, the dying Golem falls on the rabbi and smashes him. These endings refer to the motif of hubris, as often presented in Greek tragedy, where constructors of gadgets which overcome human limitations are killed at the end.

In other versions of the legend, the rabbi puts the Golem to rest in the attic of the synagogue in Prague. He then creates a Kabbalist rhyme that will revive the Golem at the end of the world. Many Jewish children from this tradition were taught these words.

This last version of the Kabbalist Golem legends is still strongly ingrained in the consciousness of many Jews from the Eastern European tradition. This can be shown by an incident that happened at the Massachusetts Institute of Technology. MIT can be seen as cradle of AI; here, the field of AI was born and here the first steps toward artificial intelligence were taken and the first successful projects developed. When in the late 1960s some people mentioned that the first big computer in Israel had been called "Golem,"[1] it turned out that at least two students in this community had been told the rhyme that would awake the Golem. These two were Gerry Sussman, today professor at the MIT AI Lab, and Joel Moses, former provost and today institute professor at MIT. When they compared the formulas they had been told, both their formulas were the same — despite hundreds of years of oral tradition.[2] One might speculate if the wish to revive the Golem at some point in time might not be part of the motivation for the whole AI enterprise; this seems especially to be true as, besides Moses and Sussman, several other famous AI researchers link themselves to this tradition. Among those people who understand their work in succession to Rabbi Löw are John von Neumann and Marvin Minsky.[3]

This already demonstrates that within the Jewish tradition there is much less concern about hubristic elements in the enterprise of creating artificial creatures. This is supported by a vast amount of rabbinical literature that discusses Golems. The majority of these texts do not understand the construction of Golems as a step beyond the boundaries God has set for us or as hubristic act. On the contrary, many rabbis understand the construction of Golems as prayer. The structure of the God-created world can be understood and more of the character of God and God's glory can be described; also, with the construction of Golems we participate in God's creative powers. Whenever we are creative and live out our crafts(wo)manship, we celebrate God who created us in God's image which includes creativity and intuition. But humans are the "crown" of creation; if we rebuild ourselves in the Golems, we celebrate God's highest creativity, thus praising God the most.

But even in the Jewish tradition, this understanding of Golem construction as prayer is not generally accepted. There are legends where the Golem has on his forehead the words written: *Yahweh elohim emet* (God the Lord is Truth). As soon as the Golem comes to life, he erases the א as first letter of the word *emet* so that the sentence now reads: *Yahweh elohim mot* (God the Lord is dead). He tells his terrified builders people would adore God because God has created the world and humans can see the glory of this creation every day — particularly in the creation of themselves. With the construction of the Golem, humans now would be able to re-create themselves and thus repeat God's creational power without any limitations. Therefore, other humans would now adore the creators of the Golems for their genius but they would not think of God anymore; God the creator would be outplayed by humans achieving nearly the same creational power as God. But a God who is not adored might as well be dead. The constructors are shocked by the wisdom of the Golem's prophecy and destroy him immediately to avoid this danger.

With this treasure of stories about the Golems, the Jewish Kabbalist tradition already anticipates the ambiguity of the field of AI. Any artificial creature is a symbol for our God-given creativity and capability, and this is particularly true for sophisticated humanoids. On the other hand, there is always the danger of losing respect for humans. In rebuilding the human system, we learn to understand it, its mechanisms and functions. The mysteries of humankind, all those things we don't understand such as consciousness, soul, love, aesthetics, might become reduced to certain mechanisms within the brain. The whole realm of "intelligence," right now so mysterious and nearly magic for us, might be deciphered and understood completely in engineering terms. And then, indeed, the danger arises which the Golem in the last story pointed out: that we give these images of us too much power over our own self-understanding, start to understand ourselves as "nothing but machines," and thus kill God.

In the Christian tradition, this negative aspect of the construction of humanoids is much more emphasized. People raised within Christian cultures tend to react strongly if they take issue with AI. Western Christianity has always lived with the motif of hubris ingrained in the social consciousness. This fear of hubris has been fed by both the Jewish and the Greek traditions. While the Jewish tradition perceives the attempt to rebuild Golems in a relatively positive way, the Hebrew Scriptures also contain stories like the Tower of Babel (Gen 11), which tells about the dangers of the attempt to be like God. From the Greek traditions this angst to overstep our limits is fed by myths like the one of Icarus and Daedalus; Icarus does not obey his father, oversteps his powers, and therefore has to die in the end. Finally, our fears of overstepping our limits are supported by post-Enlightenment novels like Mary Shelley's *Frankenstein: The Modern Prometheus*. In this novel, the builder of an artificial creature unintentionally destroys his whole life and that of his relatives and the creature itself, as he is not careful enough to check out all the signs of upcoming dangers but too occupied in overcoming death and thus winning over nature.

These ambiguous emotions ingrained in our cultural consciousness have greatly influenced the debate about AI. I would therefore like to use the story of Commander Data to discuss AI anew. For one, Data is a popular and quite nice figure who earns sympathy more than hate or fear; therefore, antagonism and strong negative emotions can be avoided. Also, Data is fictional and very futuristic, which seems to be less intimidating than talking about actual research. Data seems therefore the ideal object to explore how research in robotics can actually help us to learn more about ourselves. However, before we can enter into this challenging line of reasoning, we have to first introduce the epistemological framework in which we operate.

The Change in Human Self-Understanding

One of the most influential and dangerous developments of this dialectical development has been the change of human self-understanding. Many people within the Enlightenment movement understood technology as a means to free people from their dependence on nature; if one for instance does not believe in weather gods anymore one can produce food much more effectively. With increasing technological knowledge, nature is de-mystified and becomes the other.

As we have seen already in the Golem stories, this development cannot stop with nonhuman nature. Since the human body is part of nature it becomes an object of research and technology as well; as more and more mechanisms of the human machinery are explained and understood, humans are de-mystified as well. While machines in the eighteenth and nineteenth centuries replaced human handiwork and sped up human locomotion, thus minimizing distances between the people and their respective companies,

developments in the twentieth century went a step further. The invention
of computers provided scientists and philosophers with a powerful metaphor for the human mind. Because of the oppression of the *mythos* and its
myths, the metaphorical character of any human-computer analogy is still
often not recognized. Therefore, the human-computer metaphors are today
part of the self-understanding of humans in the Western world, as metaphors like "I couldn't store it" or "This is not part of my programming"
demonstrate.

This change in the self-understanding of many people is supported by
some AI researchers, especially those from the beginnings of AI, who hoped
in the 1960s that they would be able to decode and rebuild the phenomenon of intelligence within a few decades (luckily for the next generations
of AI researchers, there is still a long, long way to go). They often reduce
"intelligence" to abstract problem solving, natural language, flexible data
retrieval, and clever learning algorithms.

Much has been written about the claims of AI and their underlying understanding of the nature of humankind. These publications are usually quite
emotional and very polarized. It seems therefore appropriate to choose Commander Data as a fictional character to explore anew the question about
ourselves. Is the human self-understanding challenged by the progress of
technology and science? And if so, how? What has changed in the philosophical anthropologies of the last century and how can we as theologians
meet the challenge of an understanding of ourselves which presents humans
as biological systems, entirely explainable and de-mystified by science and
soon replicated by technology? These and other questions will be answered
with the discussion of Commander Data.

Commander Data on Trial

The show *Star Trek, The Next Generation,* no. 35 "The Measure of a Man"
was first aired in February 1989; the script was written by Melinda M.
Snodgrass and the director was Robert Scheerer. And other information for
"Trekkies": Stardate is 42523.7.

The main characters in this show include: Captain Jean-Luc Picard, the
captain of the *Enterprise;* William Thomas (Bill) Riker, First Officer; Lieu-
tenant Commander Data, of course, who is Second Officer and Science
Officer on board; Geordi La Forge, the Chief Engineer and Data's best
friend; Judge Advocate General Phillipa Louvois; and finally Commander
Bruce Maddox, who is Star Fleet's Head of Robotics and Cybernetics. The
term *cybernetics* was used for the early beginnings of artificial intelligence
research but in the United States today it is used, like the term *android,*
mostly in SciFi.

The episode begins when Bruce Maddox as head of Star Fleet's Robotics
Institute comes aboard the *Enterprise* with the command to disassemble

Data. It is the desire of Star Fleet to have many more Datas, since the one has been so helpful for the ship; many Datas could help Star Fleet to more effectively pursue its goals and create galaxy-wide peace. Maddox explains to Picard and Riker the procedure but remains very vague about the actual process of analyzing and replicating Data's brain (his memories and experiences). Data is present in this meeting but Maddox ignores him since he does not see Data as a partner or person but just as a quite sophisticated and well-designed machine and therefore not worth his attention.

Data is initially intrigued about the possibility to have someone like him created. But when he recognizes the dangers of such an experiment for his own existence, he rejects the experiment and Picard initially agrees with him. But he has to obey the Star Fleet command and argues that he has sent his underlings sometimes into even more dangerous situations. Data argues that there is a difference between a necessary but dangerous situation that can happen in war and an unnecessary danger which will not only destroy Data but also will not lead to any new insights. Picard insists that Data's special properties of being an android might still help Star Fleet to gain new knowledge about android construction and remains adamant. Data finally challenges him with Science Officer La Forge's eyes; they are artificial and far superior to natural eyes. Why then for the sake of Star Fleet would not every officer be forced to remove their personal eyes and replace them with artificial eyes? As Picard remains silent, Data gives the answer himself: because the other officers are human and he is not and his bodily integrity is not valued as highly as that of a human. As Data does not want to put himself into jeopardy, he then decides to resign from Star Fleet.

While Data is packing, Bruce Maddox enters his apartment (without knocking on the door, as Data as machine does not deserve such niceties) and attempts to convince Data to agree to the experiment. "Your memories and knowledge will remain intact," he promises. But Data does not believe him. If Maddox were to succeed, Data's memories would be "reduced to the mere facts of the events. The substance, the flavor of the moment could be lost." He, Data, is the unique product of a single, genius man. If he undergoes the procedure and is lost, the dream of this man is destroyed and Data values his creator so highly that he under no circumstances wants this to happen. Maddox leaves quite annoyed and announces a legal hearing.

In the meantime, Picard has had time to think about Maddox's project and begins to see Data's point of view. In the first discussion with Judge Louvois, Picard therefore supports Data's claim to be a person and his right to choose. Maddox finds this stance "irresponsible and irrational." He argues if Data were "a box on four wheels," he, Maddox, would not face such opposition. He then draws parallels between Data and the starship's highly sophisticated computer, which is without any doubt property, and states that Data, like the on-board computer, is property without any rights.

Judge Louvois finally decides that she will bring the argument to an end in an official hearing; since her court, however, is still under construction and she has no staff, Commander Riker will have to argue for Maddox and will have to try his best to prove Data's property status. Riker rejects this on the basis of being friends with Data ("I cannot prove that Data is a machine because I don't believe it; I happen to know better") but at the end he has to give in. Louvois insists on the possibility that a prosecutor, no matter what his personal feelings are, can be objective and fair; if Riker will not prosecute, Data will be given into Maddox's hands right away.

While the crew celebrates Data's farewell party with mixed feelings and some sadness, Riker analyzes the blueprints of Data's construction and finally finds out where to switch off Data without destroying his programming. In the next day's first hearing, Riker reduces Data to mere machine status by demonstrating quite impressively that Data is nothing but a creation of a man, a piece of clever engineering. He first shows that Data is stronger than any human, then removes Data's arm to show that Data is nothing but a connection of various well-engineered parts ("The software has been written by man, the hardware has been constructed by man"), and finally switches him off. "Data has been built by a man and a man will now switch it off. . . . Pinocchio is dead, his strings are cut."

This demonstration proves to be quite devastating. Even Picard now doubts the personhood of the machine Data, which can be switched on and off at will, and therefore differs fundamentally from all biological creatures and especially from humans whose whole life is overshadowed by the certainty of death. Picard goes to the ship's bar to relax and discusses the result of this day's hearing with the bartender Guinan (brilliantly played by Whoopie Goldberg). She points out that the term "property" is a euphemism; in her opinion the whole debate is ultimately about slavery. If Star Fleet Command were to succeed in replicating Data, they would have thousands of "disposable people" to use in all sorts of dangerous, hazardous, and dirty jobs. The question about Data was not so much about his intrinsic value but about his monetary value and his potential uses as property for humanity.

At the next day's hearing, Picard first demonstrates Data's similarity with humans: Data is proud of his own accomplishments (he collected all his honors and framed them); he values gifts (he kept a volume of Shakespeare because Picard gave it to him); he had once a love affair and values friendship.

Picard then calls Maddox as hostile witness and asks him again why he would not assign sentience to Data. After a negative answer, Picard then asks for a definition of sentience and Maddox defines it as a combination of "intelligence, self-awareness, consciousness." Data was intelligent because "it is able to cope with new situations, to learn, and to solve problems." But despite Data's intelligence, it would lack the two other necessary conditions for sentience. Picard then addresses Data and asks him for an evaluation of his current situation and Data answers, "I am taking place in a legal hearing defining my status and my right." "And what is at stake?" "My right to choose... perhaps my very life." With this answer Data at least behaves as if he has self-awareness, if self-awareness can be defined as being aware of one's situation with a sense of past (what caused the situation) and future (what would the various respective decisions mean for my future). So Picard goes on to the third attribute, consciousness, which Maddox has defined as "being conscious of your existence and actions; you are aware of your self and your own ego."

Yes, he agrees, Data is a machine — but we are also machines, "created by the building blocks of our parents' DNA." Children are shaped and formed (programmed) by their parents' education and ideals. Are they therefore property of their parents or of the society in which they grow up? After this rhetorical question he then comes back to the purpose of Data and his successors. If the world had thousands and thousands of Datas, "wouldn't that become a race?" And would humans not be evaluated for how they appraise such a new race of androids? A race of beings where no one really can decide whether or not they have consciousness (after intelligence and self-awareness have been established) is endangered; the treatment of these beings will throw light onto our respect for other, perhaps sentient beings who are different from us. The decision made in this hearing, either to curtail Data's rights or to give him liberty and freedom, will determine the rights of a race yet to come but foreseeable.

Judge Louvois finally declares that the discussion was "metaphysical"; "better left to philosophers or saints." She boils down the whole discussion to the one question whether or not Data has a soul. She herself is not competent to answer this question. Also, she has no idea whether or not she has a soul; "soul" for her is a construct and reason for hope described by exactly the philosophers and saints she has mentioned before. Therefore, she finally decides that Data has the right to search for his own soul (if he has one) and that he is not property.

Interaction and Anthropomorphization

There seems to be a fundamental difference between those people who interact with Data on a daily basis like the *Enterprise* crew, and those who know about its construction and its various functions but never interact with Data, such as Maddox. At some point, Maddox therefore argues that the people on the ship only project personhood into Data because it looks like a human; with this, he opens up the debate about anthropomorphization.

Much has been written about the anthropomorphization of tools like cars and stereos. In the context of Horkheimer and Adorno's analysis one can understand this process as another example for *mythos-logos* entanglement. The incapability to distinguish both realms and to accept *mythos* elements in one's life might tempt someone to project (*mythos*) attributes like friendship and trust into lifeless things; and one can see from the reaction to Tamagotchies or Furbies that this trend is continued. People in Western societies are quite willing to treat as living beings certain machines displaying social behaviors like Tamagotchie's hunger or Furbie's "learning" of language. Because of this trend, AI researchers, most of them fans of Star Trek anyway, usually agree with the judgment that Data is a person. They base this on the way people accept technologies into their lives, and are willing to create a society in which technology and humans play interdependent and mutually benefiting roles.

At the same time, the researchers see themselves as a safeguard against too much projection. Since they understand and repair the machines and know exactly how they function, they are much less likely to treat them as more as they actually are. They warn against too much anthropomorphization, and define the borders between gadgets and persons. They are those most likely to know when a machine oversteps the boundary and becomes something "more than a machine." That especially Geordi La Forge, the main repair technician of Data, perceives Data as a close friend is therefore interesting and meaningful. Can such a sophisticated and well-trained technician really fall into the trap of anthropomorphizing?

One might want to argue that Geordi feels closer to Data because he himself is partly a machine: his eyes are artificial and he therefore can empathize with the fully artificial Data. Since he knows that he is a person with all rights and fully accepted by the crew despite his partial artificiality, his stance on Data might be more open-minded than the one of Maddox.

Data himself brings this point up in his argument with Picard. He points out that human Star Fleet officers are not asked to become Cyborgs by replacing their natural organs with technical ones. Only in the case of emergency or of ultimate loss of an organ (such as Geordi's eyes) does such a replacements take place. And even if Picard initially assumes that Data is qualitatively different from humans in this respect, at the end he withdraws any value difference between humans and Data. One can safely assume that Data's argument was convincing, as Picard notices that bodily integrity does not necessarily depend on human flesh and human genes alone.

Mortality and Cognition

Riker, on the other hand, cannot go with his instincts and his notion of Data as his friend, but has to establish objective criteria for Data's status. In the hearing, he does his best to destroy any notion that Data might be more than a machine. Data is incredibly strong, and its capabilities surpass those of every human. Not only are its bodily functions different, but it can be switched on and off at will or, to anthropomorphize: he cannot die and is thus immortal. If there is anything that distinguishes natural beings from technical ones, then certainly it is this!

But is it really impossible to imagine a sentient being who is immortal? We know that human intelligence and that of humanity's ancestors would never have developed without the evolutionary process, which functions only because survival is such a strong desire and pressure on the various species. Philosophers and theologians have also pointed out that the cognitive categories in which we operate depend on our insight that we are finite beings in time and space.

For Paul Tillich, only the recognition of our finitude creates thought because our "basic forms of thought and being"[4] emerge from the insight that we are mortal. The category of *time* puts humans into a constant movement from past to future which they cannot stop or turn around. The insight that time is, is therefore also the insight into our own limitations. The category of time is accompanied by other categories such as *space* and *causality*. The category of space makes us aware of our finite and actually quite limited spheres of thought, of relationships, of locations and many other aspects of life; the category of causality places us at the end of a long causality chain which makes our life, our being, and our decisions quite arbitrary because it is not really ours but the result of a long chain of events and decisions made before.[5] These categories determine fundamentally our way of thinking and feeling and behaving.

Is it then for an immortal Data feasible to be able to think in the same categories we do without being mortal? Many people argue that the development of a machine like Data is impossible because Data could never achieve thought, which ultimately depends on mortality. However, one might doubt this conclusion. For one, why should an autonomous robot interacting with its environment not be able to learn about categories like time and space if it is able to understand physical laws like gravity and friction? Does one really have to be mortal to understand the curse of time and space limitations and of the knowledge that oneself is the result of developments before? These would be arguments which might at least question the conclusion that any immortal android could be like us.

Besides that, Data actually is nearly as limited in time and space as we are; also, since his brain consists of logical circuits and thus obeys physical laws, he is at least as much as we part of a causality chain. As Data continues to work in interaction with humans, all his experiences are unique; it is impossible for him to repeat any given moment in time and space and even his infinite existence will not enable him to be with all people and possible configurations at all places which are. We get a hint of Data's awareness of this, his limitations, when he discusses the procedures of his dismantling with Maddox and insists that his lived memories would be destroyed if they were to be reduced to mere logical data in a disembodied machine.

This is certainly a point too complex to discuss sufficiently in this essay.

Whether Data could think like us despite his immortality remains question-able, though much speaks for it. But the question remains whether he is part enough of the human community to be accepted and seen as a person by it.

"Intelligence, Self-Awareness, Consciousness"

The final hearing presents the most complex attempts to define sentience and, with it, personhood; here, terms like "intelligence," "self-awareness," "consciousness," and — by the judge — "soul" are used. Each one of these terms is ambiguous and not well-defined at all. What, for instance, does it mean to be intelligent? Is intelligence the capability to play chess, or does intelligence mean the ability to survive in various environments?

Intelligence

The definition of intelligence is actually crucial for our understanding of personhood. In most SciFi as well as in major parts of AI research, intelli-gence is understood as the human capacity to solve problems, to combine knowledge creatively, to learn, and to think in abstract ways. Classical re-search projects are chess playing, mathematical theorem proving, natural language processing, learning. The idea is that humans are very good in both abstract problem solving and interacting with and surviving in their environments. If one were to succeed in building a smart machine, this ma-chine would have the same or similarly powerful capacities — as the dream of Data indicates. People in classical AI research assume that the capability for abstract thought will ultimately lead also to the capability to interact with one's environment, to navigate, to find paths, and to cope with new situations in the world.

However, it is questionable whether the sequence of the implementation of various human capabilities in this classical AI research really makes sense. Humans are not born with the capability to play chess but right away, babies interact with their caregivers; they don't come to the world with language and math abilities but they explore their environments and themselves and, with increasing motor skills and neuronal connections, they increase their ability to think. Developmental psychology has repeatedly pointed out that cognitive development of a human infant is closely correlated to and even dependent on the infant's development of its motor skills and an increasing awareness of its bodily functions.[6] This suggests that natural development starts with the construction and development of interactive skills; the ab-stract capabilities of humans can be understood as a by-product of their evolutionary and ontogenetically developed skills to interact with other people and their environment.

Therefore, some cognitive scientists and AI researchers recently have rethought the classical approach toward artificial intelligences and one might best introduce the alternative approach by describing theoretical machines developed as thought experiments by the psychologist Valentino Braitenberg.[7]

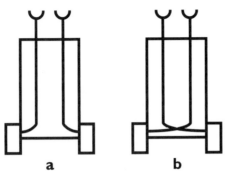

a　　　　　**b**

These two vehicles have light sensors which are connected to wheels; the amount of light a sensor perceives determines the speed with which the connected wheel spins. In *a* the left wheel is connected to the left sensor and the right wheel to the right sensor. If for this vehicle light comes from the right, its right wheel will turn faster and the whole vehicle will turn away from the light. In *b* the sensors and wheels are cross-wired so if here the light comes from the right, the left wheel will turn faster and the whole vehicle will turn toward the light. With this simple wiring we get quite complex behaviors: avoidance of light and attraction to light. Even though these vehicles are thought experiments, they beautifully demonstrate how embeddedness in the world can lead to better working robots; just because the sensors get the input immediately from their environment (a light source) and the wheels are directly connected to the sensors without any computation, you get a fast reaction to changes in the environment. If you were to code this behavior explicitly you would need much more computation, knowledge acquisition, and planning to do the same thing.

The key here is that the overall system does not have a central unit which controls the parts. Instead, sensors and actuators work in their local environments and are connected with each other in such a way that the system can act and react flexibly without extensive internal mapping, since the reaction to inputs from the environment is local and immediate. To use metaphorical language: the system's body is situated in the environment, interacts with its environment, and creates new and complex behaviors out of simple interactions. This metaphor gives this AI direction its name, "Embodied AI."

Another central metaphor within Embodied AI is the concept of "emergence," and the usual example to illustrate this metaphor is the ant hive. If one takes a single ant apart, one can study the parts (the micro level) and gain insights about certain functions of the ant like the movement of the legs or digestion. This analysis is important but it does not help to fully understand an ant. To better understand individual ants one studies their behavior and their interactions with other ants and with the rest of their environment. Again, one can have many insights by studying ants on this macro level but these insights are not sufficient to understand and explain the complex behavior of an ant hive. The whole entity has to be studied on another level called the multiple level. The microlevel in Embodied AI matches the level of basic hardware modules, e.g., sensors or actuators. On the macro level, engineers construct autonomous behaviors in connected components so that on the multiple level, an autonomous robot acts in and interacts with the world. Since the correlation between an ant hive and an individual robot is not a 100 percent fit, engineers have begun to work on robot communities in which several simple robots create multiple behaviors.

Intelligence, in this scientific community, is not understood as abstract problem solving (chess playing, mathematical theorem proving, etc.), but as the ability to act in the world and to survive in a flexible and constantly changing environment. The capability for intelligent tasks is an emergent phenomenon, emerging out of the simple parts of a system, their connections with one another, and their respective interactions with their local environments. The approach toward intelligent machines thus is not anymore top-down but bottom-up. And, interestingly enough, Embodied AI works and the most successful autonomous robots today are the ones built with this approach.

Data is a construct which borrows from insights of both AI camps. His (entirely fictional) positronic brain consists of logical, electronic circuits and all the data Data collects is processed here. Data seemingly has no emotions (even if he certainly behaves as if he has some), and his strength lies in all forms of mathematical and logical reasoning. On the other hand, Data has a humanoid body so that he can act as member of a humanoid crew on a ship which has been designed for humanoid, bipedal life forms. As we have seen, in Japan humanoids are constructed as humanoids exactly for the same reasons. Also, since interaction is so crucial for the cognitive development of intelligence, be it in a robot or an infant, Embodied AI researchers build humanoid forms to motivate people to interact with the robots and make them small parts of their community.

Finally, Embodied AI researchers give their creatures humanoid bodies since the body form determines the intelligence that will emerge as any given body form has special needs to survive in an environment and special capabilities to bring into the relationship with the environment.[8] Maddox has a point here when he states that the people accept Data only because he does not look like the ship's computer or a box on wheels.

That Data understands himself as embodied entity and more than just a collection of logical circuits becomes clear in his understanding of his own memories, which cannot be just downloaded because in this case the "flavor" of the respective moment could be lost, the color would be gone. Knowledge, for Data as well as for Embodied AI researchers, cannot be

*Cog, the humanoid robot currently
under construction at MIT*

reduced to mere data representation, but is encoded in the whole system
and even in the interaction between the system and its environment.

Data as a product of Classical and Embodied AI thus needs not
just immense computing power but embodiment, social interaction, and
embeddedness in the world as well.

Self-Awareness, Consciousness, and the Soul

What is self-awareness? Is it the ability to recognize yourself in the mirror?
If so, then self-awareness is nothing uniquely human, but most primates
share this ability with us.[9] How about consciousness? This term is so widely
used that there is really no definition for it — or, better said, ten people
will probably present fifteen definitions. The same is true for the soul: some
people just define it as that which makes us special, some understand it as
the Spirit of God in us, some identify it with the mind (another one of these
spongy terms). So these terms, as presented in *Star Trek*, are not sufficiently
defined as to answer unambiguously what it means to be a person.

The equivocality of these terms makes any *logos* definition of them quite
impossible. As we will see, all these terms mingle up *mythos* and *logos*
elements, which makes it impossible that they could be used to categorize
who deserves the attribute personhood and who would not.

Postscript

Since this is a *Festschrift*, I thought I might use this opportunity to add
some personal remarks. Would Harvey Cox like Data to be his student?
Well, I guess he would be very happy with Data's knowledge and capability
to learn and to remember. But Harvey's goal in class is never the distribu-

tion of knowledge alone. He often goes a step beyond the abstractions and attempts to apply theological theories to real life, especially to the personal and emotional life of the student. I guess that he would find Data a little unsatisfying in this respect. In general, the whole spiritual domain seems to be lacking in Data. Would he pray? Or experience the divine? How would he react to a revelation? Probably, he would only analyze and reject it — but he might be very open for humanism or humanoidism.

I guess Harvey would like nonetheless to interact with Data, since he would find him quite intriguing. They have a similar humor and they certainly would share many jokes. Harvey might, however, be saddened by the fact that Data does not eat or drink and is thus not a connoisseur of wine.

Would Harvey like to play jazz with Data? I think not! Jazz needs the irregularity, the heartbeat, jazz has to be dirty. Absolute perfection, as Data would display, would not be a good addition to Harvey's jazz band. But perhaps they might start to create new forms of music in which human and humanoid musical forms merge and interact.

Would Harvey accept Data as a valuable being? Certainly yes! In all his work, Harvey always accepted the other in their very own way, and tolerated their different ways of thinking, feeling, and evaluating. Tolerance here is meant as a very active behavior and not as just passively accepting; tolerance means to lift up other people in their otherness and to invite them to interact with one in an equal way.[10] In this way, Data could be a wonderful dialogue partner and thus probably an A+ student at the Divinity School. It is intriguing to think about what form of theology Harvey and Data would develop together. Would it be Christian? Would it be Jewish? Would it be altogether new?

Even though it is delightful to think about the outcome of such an interaction, it has to remain fictional for now. As a thought experiment, however, it might be fun to pursue.

Notes

1. Gershom Scholem, *The Golem of Prague and the Golem of Rehovot* (January 1966), 62–65.

2. Anne Foerst, "Artificial Intelligence and Theology: From Mythos to *Logos* and Back," in S. Franchi and G. Goezeldere, eds., *Constructions of the Mind* (Bloomington: Indiana University Press, 1999).

3. See Pamela McCorduck, *Machines Who Think: A Personal Inquiry into the History and Prospects of Artificial Intelligence* (New York: W. H. Freeman, 1979).

4. Paul Tillich, *Systematic Theology*, vol. 1 (Chicago: University of Chicago Press, 1951), 165.

5. For an extensive study see Tillich's *Systematic Theology,* particularly vol. 1, 192.

6. A good summary of the embodiment of child development can be found

in Andy Clark, *Being There: Putting Brain, Body and World Together Again* (Cambridge: MIT Press, 1997).

7. Valentino Braitenberg, *Vehicles: Experiments in Synthetic Psychology* (Cambridge: MIT Press, 1984).

8. For more reasons for humanoid embodiment in the construction of humanoid robots see Anne Foerst, "Cog, a Humanoid Robot, and the Question of the Image of God," *Zygon* 33 (March 1998): 91–111.

9. Marc Hauser, *The Evolution of Communication* (Cambridge: MIT Press, 1996).

10. Most etymological dictionaries derive tolerance from the Latin *tolero*, which means "to accept, to endure." It seems, however, equally convincing to derive the term from *tollo*, a verb which was later added as irregular perfect active to *fero;* both mean "to lift, to heighten, to carry." Tolerance then can be seen as an attempt not just to understand the other but actively to integrate their insights into one's own point of view — but without leaving one's own ultimate concern, one's own answers to existential quests behind.

22

VISIBLE RELIGION

An Introduction to World Religion through the Visual Arts

Elinor W. Gadon

Art does not reproduce the visible, it makes visible.

Art has the capacity to unite spirit and matter in the landscape of everyday life.

— Paul Klee

Dedication: To Harvey Cox, Mentor and Colleague

It was Harvey who first gave me the opportunity to test my theories on the creative possibilities of the visual arts as the primary resource in the teaching of World Religions. In 1982 he invited me to join him in the development of a new course for Harvard College undergraduates, entitled "Jesus and the Moral Life." This was to be offered as an elective in Moral Reasoning, part of the then new CORE Curriculum. Moral Reasoning was one of seven required areas of intellectual inquiry. All CORE courses were interdisciplinary, and most were co-taught. This was Harvey's course. He, the applied theologian, would be responsible for the content based on Scripture and moral philosophy, while I, an art historian, would provide visuals that would offer another modality of learning, an experiential one that would complement the discursive discourse of the lectures and readings. My objective was to present a visual chronology of the ways in which the life and teachings of Jesus, a major theme in the Western art for two millennia, were understood throughout history and in the twentieth century when Christianity became a truly world religion, globally.

Harvey's thesis was that the life and teachings of the historical Jesus served as an exemplar of *the moral life*. He viewed Jesus as a social reformer, basing his stance on the gospel accounts. His approach was congruent with that of liberation theology, in which the life and teachings of Jesus provided the inspiration for social and political revolution among the oppressed peoples of the Americas.

The role of Jesus as a spiritual and moral guide throughout history is well documented in the visual arts. Iconographic developments demonstrate evolving theology. Throughout the ages when most people were illiterate, visual symbols and narratives were the didactic tools of a proselytizing faith. Until early modern times, the arts were the handmaiden of religion in the West; Church and state politics were inseparable, and still are in many parts of the world today. By utilizing popular as well as canonical art, we can access the experience of the common people's faith and struggle for moral justice.

Cognition, the act or process of knowing, includes both awareness and judgment. Inasmuch as the stated goal of the course was to teach moral reasoning, which *a priori* involves an internalization of values, the inclusion of modalities of cognition that are wholistic, embracing inner as well as outer meaning, intrinsic as well as extrinsic, implicit as well as explicit, served to enlarge and solidify the learning experience. Direct experience can be a powerful teacher. Both the visual and auditory are sensory experiences involving feelings and emotions, unmediated by the rational intellect, that provoke long-lasting moods and memories, of which we are often only dimly conscious, and can be integrated into personal development in ways that the more distanced abstract discourse of lecture and readings cannot. This is perhaps especially true for the undergraduate student whose values and moral reasoning are still in the process of formation.

Why Art and Religion? Why Not? Rationale and Theory

My rationale for the inclusion of the visual arts as the primary resource for teaching an introductory course in the history of religions, not as secondary or as illustration to text and/or lecture, is that the experiential is as significant a mode of knowing as analytical reasoning. The visual experience is sensual, involving feeling and emotion, immediate and absolute, foundational to our wholistic understanding of the subject at hand. Vision is a subjective experience. It is only now in the twenty-first century that we are beginning to understand the full weight emotion and image carry in the human psyche. Rudolf Arnheim in *Visual Thinking* contends that visual perception is integrally related to thought. It is not the case that "the eyes present a kind of raw data to the mind which in turn processes it and refines it. Rather that the visual images are the shaping and bearers of thought."[1] Suzanne Langer has also written of "the integral relation of thought to the images we see with the 'mind's eye.' The making of all those images is the fundamental and imaginative human activity."[2]

Like A. K. Coomaraswamy, I consider understanding to be an aesthetic process.[3] He delineated the three aesthetic functions as denotation, connotation, and implication, corresponding to recognition, interpretation, and immediate understanding. The aesthetic experience involves imagination, an inner knowing that allows for the integration of the experience with world-view and social values, a base for the engagement of the students in future moral reasoning and action.

Arnheim noted what he calls the widespread unemployment of the senses in every field of academic study, which have traditionally privileged written documents as primary source material.[4] This practice has been particularly pernicious in the teaching of world religions, in which the visual arts are a major historical resource. They are the material manifestation of theology and doctrine, documenting how Scripture has been encountered over time and by different religious communities. Throughout history the roots of theology often lay in popular belief, later codified by the elite — church fathers, brahmin pundits, and their like.

A telling example of the influence of the image on doctrine is the evolving iconography of the Virgin Mary which over the centuries incorporated symbols and motifs from the pre-Christian goddess traditions in an effort to bring pagan peoples under the influence of the church. The Assumption of the Virgin promulgated as doctrine by the Holy See in 1954 had long been a focus of popular Marian piety, and subject of sacred art, perhaps best known in the magnificent altarpiece by the seventeenth-century Venetian artist Titian. This dogma sanctioned the belief that Mary, when the course of her life was finished, was taken up, body and soul, into heaven. That she alone of all humankind never experienced death, as Jesus died on the cross and was resurrected, confronts but does not resolve a critical issue for Roman Catholicism as to her nature, human or divine. This doctrinal issue is further complicated by Christology's dogma of Christ's dual nature, both human and divine. Since God was his father and divine, his mother of necessity must be human. Iconographical traditions that image her seated on the throne of heaven between God the Father and Christ, or at her coronation, crowned as Queen of Heaven, are powerful visual statements that call into question a doctrine which speaks of Her veneration, not worship. Carl Jung said in reference to the return of the mother goddess archetype in Western culture that the official church recognition of Mary's assumption was the most important event of the twentieth century.[5] We can more easily grasp the explosion of popular mariolatry in the second half of this century through photographs and film documenting her appearances and pilgrimages to the sites of these miracles.

Sacred architecture sets the stage for liturgy and ritual, which is much easier to visualize as lived experience through pictures and diagrams of the space designed for worship. Watching films and video showing the processual nature of worship enlivens our understanding, particularly of religious practices that are unfamiliar. Comparison and contrast of the differing ways in which architectural structure in both plan and elevation as well as symbolic meaning embodies theology can be very instructive. It is one thing to speak of the Church as the body of Christ, and quite another to see this precept visually diagramed with his body as the nave and his arms as the transept. Familiarity with the towering superstructure of the Hindu temple makes its analogy to the mountain obvious, as do the interior views of the innermost Holy of Holies, the *garbhagrha* (womb chamber) to that of the cave. These are not just concepts that can be adequately grasped intellectually; they need to be experienced visually.

Furthermore, as Clifford Geertz informed us, "religion is a cultural system."[6] In order to understand any part of the system we need to study the whole, to engage in kind of research which he calls "dense description," ferreting out any- and everything that might be relevant to our greater understanding. What can we learn about the nature of scripture, the evolution of theology and doctrine, or popular religious experience from the art of world religions analyzed in its cultural context?

Religion also determines our worldview. It is commonplace to say that we now live in a global village. Without some, however superficial, knowledge of world religions, there can be no understanding of the daily news events or of the human condition, either locally or internationally. The political aspects of religious art have not always been forefronted. Not only were royalty and their ministers the principal source of patronage, works of art serving to promote dynastic interests and attract popular loyalties, but political agendas and power struggles often determined a people's religion. Political issues were often cloaked in an iconographic system that we are unable to recognize unless we understand its language and can distinguish between earthly and spiritual glory.

Geertz urged the analysis of sacred symbols in order to understand a people's worldview and ethos.

> In recent anthropological discussion, the moral (and aesthetic) aspects of a given culture, the evaluative elements, have commonly been summed up in the term "ethos," while the cognitive, existential have been designated by the term "worldview." A people's ethos is the tone, character, and quality of their life, its moral and aesthetic style and mood; its underlying attitude toward themselves and their world that life reflects. Their world view is their picture of the way things in sheer actuality are, their concept of nature, of self, of society.[7]

Geertz wrote this twenty-five years ago. As we look back on the last quarter of a century, with a seemingly accelerating pace of violence in our own pluralistic society, as well as the horror of the internal wars in the former Yugoslavia with an ethnic cleansing that is based on religious identity, and our ongoing inability to resolve the conflict between Israelis and Palestinians, his insight has profound implications for how we will go about learning to live peacefully with our neighbors in the next millennium. Surely one way is to learn to tolerate and hopefully accept the differing worldviews that are often identical with religions of other peoples. Such an approach requires knowing something about their religion at the grass-roots level of popular faith. Film series on world religions like that produced by BBC under the guidance of Huston Smith are an excellent point of entry for such exploration. Their approach once again is from the lived experience of the people with very rich documentary footage of ritual and pilgrimage presented with the full flavor and complexity of the cultural setting, in both village and urban contexts. Diana Eck advocated the usefulness of documentary films as medium of instruction in the teaching of religion because they enable us "to 'see' such scenes as the Hindu pilgrims bathing in the River Ganges in Varanasi or the Muslim mourners beating their chests with their fists."[8]

The visual arts offer a toehold into the unfamiliar territory of religions not our own. By studying the images of a culture, doorways are opened through which we are led into their world. Using categories common to all traditions but unique to each, like that of sacred architecture, creates patterns for exploration. Visual symbols can communicate in a universal language, crossing cultural barriers. They express profound concepts that otherwise cannot be adequately conveyed. By viewing their images in their cultural context with a mind and an eye able to look beyond the ideologies of the twentieth century, we may be able to enter into the thoughts and ideas of another culture of another time with fewer judgments and preconceived notions.

Mircea Eliade was concerned to identify the difference between the sacred and profane in human experience.[9] He concentrated the links between these complexes on the plane of appearances introducing the inspired concept of a hierophany, the breaking through of the sacred into the mundane world, thereby exposing it in the profane. The sacred is saturated with being and therefore has the power functioning through the heirophanies to become apparent. Certain basic attributes which help us to identify the sacred in subjective experience are its separateness, power, intensity, remoteness, and otherness. These are perhaps most readily grasped through the symbolic language of the visual arts. The meaning of a numinous symbol is intuitively sensed not consciously interpreted, but the power of the symbol, analyzed or not, clearly rests on its comprehensiveness, on its fruitfulness in ordering experience. Characteristic of the symbol is its multivalence, that is, its capacity to carry forth inherent form and signification while incorporating new meanings over time. Christianity is the inheritor of a very ancient and very complex religious tradition whose structure has survived in the midst of the Church, even though the spiritual values and theological orientation have changed. The objective nature of the symbol can perhaps be best understood through its visual representation.

Eliade and Geertz would appear to be searching for meaning in religion from opposing standpoints, the one from the nature of the sacred, the other that of material culture. Mary Douglas's observation "that the most exalted definition of religion starts with the subjective experience of the sacred" would seem germane here. "Worldview and ethos are analytical categories devised by social scientists for social descriptions and analysis but perhaps not fully adequate for the understanding of religious experience."[10] Perhaps an informed exposure to the religious art of the great world traditions would be the place to start. For vision is as much a subjective as objective experience. For example, the icon of the Buddha fashioned according to the canonical rules of iconometry is indeed a material object, but at the same time the viewer brings to it his own understanding of its meaning, as well as, for the devotee, the transformative experience of meditation. It is commonly believed that a Buddhist image that has been properly worshipped holds the sacredness vested in it by previous devotees.

Images and symbols are tools of the spiritual life, a means to an end and not the end in itself. They are archetypes that emerge from the individual consciousness and re-enter the collective subconscious, where the members of the community respond and react. The study of sacred art "can lead when it is undertaken with a certain openmindedness to a more or less profound understanding of the spiritual realities that lie at the root of a whole cosmic and human world."[11]

Visual forms are not discursive. They do not represent their message sequentially but simultaneously, while the meaning given through visual forms is understood only by perceiving the whole at once. Langer calls the visual arts "presentational symbolism," meaning that we understand art by feeling and conceive written narratives through reasoning.[12] The "Dance of Shiva," an iconography that evolved in the medieval period in South India, is considered by many to be the perfectly realized visual representation of a very complex theology. According to Coomaraswamy "whatever the origins of Shiva's dance, it became in time the clearest image of the *activity* of God which any art or religion can boast of."[13] Shiva Nataraja, Lord of the Dancers (Fig. 1) is typically represented in motion, his jeweled, braided hair whirling in the dance. In his hair are a writhing cobra, a skull, the mermaid figure of the river goddess Ganga; upon it rests the crescent moon. In his right ear is a man's earring, a woman's is in the left. Adorned with jewelry, he is wearing tightly fitted breeches, a fluttering scarf, and the sacred thread. Four-armed, one right hands holds a drum, the other is uplifted in the sign of do not fear; one left hand holds fire, the other points down to the demon Muyalaka, a dwarf holding a cobra; the left foot is raised. An encircling halo, fringed with flame, rises from a lotus pedestal.

From the wealth of contemporary literature, we can explain not only the general significance of the dance, but also the details of its concrete symbolism. Some belong to the general conception of Shiva, such as the braided locks of the yogi, the skull of Brahma, and the figure of Ganga, which is the Ganges fallen from heaven and lost in Shiva's hair. His dual nature, embracing male and female, is symbolized by the two different earrings.[14]

Cosmic activity is the central motif of the dance. "Creation arises from the drumbeat: protection proceeds from the hand of hope; from fire proceeds

Figure 1. Shiva as Lord of the Dance.
Bronze, 12th c., South India. Photograph from
the Los Angeles County Museum of Art.

destruction; the foot held aloft gives release." The fourth hand points to this lifted foot, the refuge of the soul. "He dances to maintain the life of the cosmos and to give release to those who seek Him."[15]

In India, life, art, and religion are one. "The process of creating a work of art is also an act of worship, one through which the invisible manifests as the visible, and the artist who 'invokes' gives form to the formless, seeking to discover the unknown through the known."[16] In the monotheistic religions of the West, however, religious symbols and icons are not to be taken literally but are rather containers for ideas and emotions. Sacred icons are to be venerated, not worshipped. Iconoclasm, the rejection of the power of the icon, a prevailing, often disruptive theme in Western religions, became a central credo of the Protestant Reformation. Before, for more than a millennium, the image of Jesus on the cross had held center stage in cathedrals and churches, the focus of the Christian liturgy. With the Reformation when such worship was deemed idolatry, Jesus was removed from his cross, that stark form alone signifying his death and redemption.

The Christian cross by itself is a sign evoking a historical event basic to the history of salvation, the crucifixion of Jesus at Calvary, but it is not an icon. An icon includes the anthropomorphic representation of the deity, of which the crucifix is a prime example. The incorporation of the suffering and dying Jesus with his instrument of torture and death endows the cross with transcendence. The creation of an iconic form that adequately expressed the profundity of the mystery of salvation took almost a thousand years. In the early Christian and Medieval experiments the body of Jesus was awkwardly positioned against his instrument of torture and death; the crucifix represented his triumph and victory. For the first time in the tenth-century Gero Crucifix, we find a portrayal of the death of Jesus that is fully realistic. His

Figure 2. Edilberto Merida, Crucifix.
Clay and wood, 20th c., Peru.

heavy body, life-sized, hangs distorted on his outstretched arms and his eyes are closed. But "it is not the sign of his outward pain that makes this so deeply moving, but the inner suffering which shows on his face."[17]

A millennium later, Edilberto Merida, a Peruvian Indian, fashioned a small wooden cross and attached the image of Christ, molded from the clay of the soil, in the image of his own long-suffering people. This icon, brought to the United States by Maryknoll missionaries who had long worked so closely to support these oppressed indigenous peoples, was copied and widely distributed here. The face of Merida's Jesus is deeply etched in anguish, his mouth hanging open wide in pain, his work-worn hands and feet disproportionately large, a characteristic of peasant art and a most eloquent symbol for an activist Liberation Theology (Fig. 2).

The history of a religion provides the chronological development of facts and dates. Traditionally theology was the means of explicating religious meaning. Iconography is the analysis of the image in its cultural context. Iconographical analysis can also document the evolution of doctrine. In the study of religion, one notes the distinction between those which stress the iconographical representation of gods, and those which explicitly forbid to do this, and the implications of such policy.

"The choice of one of these positions is closely linked with the idea of transcendence of the gods or their immanence. Those religions which accentuate the immanence of the gods usually do not object to their representation in iconographical objects, which have a mediating function for the believers.

Important characteristics of the gods become manifest in their iconographical representations which can catch the attention of the devotees and evoke experience and emotions in them. The situation differs in principle from those religions which emphasize the idea that the gods are highly transcendent. Judaism, Islam and Christianity have given expression to this idea; on account of revelations, noted in their sacred books, it is forbidden to the believers to make an image of god by representing him in an iconographical object."[18]

Iconoclasm in Judaism has long been associated with the prohibition against graven images in the Second Commandment (Exod 20:4–6). A more nuanced understanding suggests that this attitude reflected the desire of a marginal people with a radically new faith to differentiate themselves from the practices of the surrounding peoples for whom the worship of images was central in their religious practice. They were not against figural art. For example, the biblical description of Solomon's Temple includes three-dimensional images of the cherubim who guarded the ark. Twentieth-century archeology has recovered a wealth of art in the synagogues of the Late Roman and Sassanian periods, the most notable of which is from the remains of Dura-Europus, a third-century Roman outpost on the Euphrates. The murals recovered from the three surviving walls of the structure are a picture book of biblical narratives. In the wall above over the Torah niche are four primary symbols of Judaism that are also frequently used elsewhere in synagogue floor mosaics of the period: the menorah, the seven-branched candlestick, the palm branch (*luluv*) and citron (*estrog*), both reminders the Harvest Festival of Succoth, and the Akedah, the Sacrifice of Isaac (Fig. 3).

Analysis of the contextual meaning of each of these symbols and symbolic scene reveals elements of Jewish theology in the post-Temple period when the prayer hall became the place of congregational worship. The story of the Sacrifice of Isaac is a dramatic reminder of the binding covenant between God and his people, a jealous God who demanded absolute allegiance, the defining relationship of every Jewish male with his God.

Jo Milgrom reminds as that as always, the Akedah of our own lifetime has been influenced by all the art movements and social and religious concerns of the current generations.

> The archetypal struggle between the generations which we have heretofore interpreted as an individual passage, part of the mythic shaping of the individual to the aims and ideals of the group, has acquired perhaps the cruelest possible meaning.... Particularly in Israel do Jews see themselves as Abrahams and Isaacs, in a country whose elders display concentration numbers on their forearms and whose youth serve forty days a year in reserves after a three-year tour of duty.[19]

George Segal's sculpture commissioned by the city of Tel Aviv is a "haunting scene of cruel isolation, bringing Abraham and Isaac back home," as it

Figure 3. Symbols over Torah Niche.
Mural painting. 3rd c., Dura-Europus, Syria

were, to Israel, "where the Akedah story is as commonplace as the Nativity is in every Christian country."

> The resultant furor provoked by the sculpture was...brought to conscious-
> ness because of Segal's middle-aged flabby Abraham in jeans. Ironically the
> Yom Kippur war broke out just a few months later, and no substitutes were
> found for the Isaacs. Segal's Akedah swept aside all cherished notions of Abra-
> ham's sage nobility. He was in fact our self-indulgent neighbor, overweight and
> underexercised.[20]

The Yom Kippur war had made his work all too prophetic. Segal created another version of the sacrifice for Kent State commissioned to commemo-rate the killing of the student protestors by the National Guard during the Vietnam War. Both sculptures were rejected as being too painful a reminder of the sacrifice the older generation was making of their young.

The theological disapproval of figural art combined with a propensity in Islam for symbolic thought meant that even the divinity could be symbolized visually.[21] In the mosque, the divine presence is symbolized by the hanging lamp placed in a niche, a powerful image invoked by the Koranic verses: "God is the Light of the heavens and the earth; the likeness of His Light is as a niche wherein is a lamp. This lamp is in a glass; and the glass is as a radiant star.... God guideth to his light whom He will" (24:35).[22]

The dome of the mosque symbolizes the firmaments as does its two-dimensional counterpart, the sunburst medallion which decorates the opening of many illuminated manuscripts.

The myth of a primordial paradise like the Garden of Eden as the reward of the faithful in the afterlife is a common theme in the religious imagination. In Islamic thought and art one of the most powerful images is the concept of Paradise as a verdant walled garden with flowering plants and fruit trees sanctioned as it is by the sacred words of scripture: "This is how the garden shall be, that await those who fear God: a garden refreshed with flowing water. The food of its fruits is never ending and its shade is permanent" (Koran 12:3).[23]

The image and symbol of the garden (*bagh*) is a manifestation of the center, figurally oriented form of the macrocosm: and a cipher for the unity, harmony, order, and plenitude of Being. The architectural conception of garden reflects the essence of place, the garden being viewed as a defined space encompassing within itself a reflection of the cosmos. Here mutually complementary aspects of place foster order and harmony. These features can be quite clearly seen in the arrangement of the *chahar bagh* (four gardens) with an octagonal pool at its center, and often a tomb or pavilion at one side, providing a series of beautiful perspectives.[24]

Paradise is further described in the Koran as being four gardens: "These are interpreted esoterically as four stages through which the mystic travels on the inward journey. The four gardens are called the Garden of the Soul, the Garden of the Heart, the Garden of the Spirit and the Garden of Essence.... The garden contains three things: a fountain, flowing water and the fruit of trees" (55:45–75).[25]

The garden as the blissful Paradise, the reward for the afterlife, was the model for both Persian and Mughal gardens, an oasis of pleasure in both the actual and ideal world. Miniature painters documented both the physical beauty of the garden with its tall slender cypresses, flowering plants and flowing fountains, as well as the sensual delights to be experienced there while lounging on soft bolsters, listening to music and poetry, drinking wine and when in the heavenly realm being entertained by *houris,* the beautiful angelic women of the afterlife.

This theme was also manifest in the garden tomb. "These are the Gardens of Eden," declared the inscription over the gateway of the Emperor Akbar's tomb at Sikandra, "enter them to dwell therein eternally."[26] That a great many mausoleums to both saints and secular rulers are found in Islamic lands is something of a paradox, for the glorification of the dead is foreign to the spirit of Islam, but it is made legitimate by the hope that the soul of the deceased shall benefit from the prayers offered by the visitors to the tomb. The community of believers wished to honor the saints.

It was also the ambition of secular rulers to perpetuate their names. While princely mausoleums were found as early as the Seljuks, it was the Mughal Emperors of India who brought the garden tomb to its greatest glory, with the Taj Mahal not only the crowning monument of their dynasty but also one of the great wonders of Indian civilization, and ranking with the pyramids as the world's finest funerary monuments. Built by the Shah Jahan as a mausoleum for his dearly beloved wife, Mumtaz Mahal, who died giving birth to their fifteenth child, the elegant white marble structure, its perfect formal symmetry framed by four minarets, is reflected in the waters of a long garden pool through the mists of its flowing fountains. The dominant decorative motif on both the outer and interior walls of the tomb is flowers once inset with brilliant precious stones.

Theories and Categories of the Sacred

What is the nature of the divine image? Is it to be considered intrinsically sacred? Is it a symbol of the sacred? A mediation of the sacred? Differing religions throughout history created different cultural expressions of common themes though which the holy and the sacred manifest. I selected the following areas of general exploration, applicable in each of the five traditions:

symbol	myth	sacred space
icon	sacred narrative	sacred architecture
archetype	ritual	pilgrimage

These themes play out in the analyses of the iconographies around which the course is designed. They provide the structure through which sacred narrative, theology doctrine, and popular belief are introduced. Some like the symbol have been discussed at length above; others will be commented on below.

Archetype

Eliade constructed an archetypal schema for sacred symbols that he saw as universals (28). His theoretical work was based primarily on ethnography of archaic and primal religions, but can also be used most fruitfully for the analysis of the symbols and iconographies of world religions. For example, the tree, which is one of the most potent archetypes, is the embodiment of life; the point of union of the three realms: heaven, earth, and the underworld; and a world axis around which the entire universe is organized. Ancient peoples widely believed the tree to be infused with an abundance of divine creative energy. Tree worship was widespread in nearly all parts of the globe where the climate was favorable to tree growth. In three of the world religions, despite elaborately evolved theology and iconography, the archetypal symbol of the tree remains paramount. In Christianity it becomes the wooden cross, in Buddhism the heart pillar of the pagoda, and in Hinduism the *yupa*, the sacrificial post. In popular religion of village and tribal India, the tree is worshipped in its natural form or as a post as the *devi* (the goddess). The two columns encircled with vines and leaves that stood outside of Solomon's temple so widely reproduced in the art of all three monotheistic faiths are yet another manifestation of the tree *cum* cosmic pillar.

The cosmic mountain, another archetype taken from nature, is the primordial mound of creation, the place where the dry land of the continents was first formed to create the continents. Worshipped in its natural form in the Himalayas by both Hindus and Buddhists, it was transmuted into the symbols system of sacred architecture in the towering structures of the cathedral, the Hindu temple and the Japanese pagoda, where traditionally its seven stories mark the stages of the ascent to heaven.

The cave, a symbol of the womb, is clearly identified as such in the Hindu temple where innermost chamber that houses the principle deity is named *grabhagrha,* womb chamber. This holy of holies takes the form of a cube in the Hindu temple, as it does for the sacred center in all three monotheistic faiths: the Jerusalem Temple, the Ka'ba in Mecca, and the crossing of the transept and nave in the Gothic cathedral. "The cube is linked to the idea of the idea of the cosmic center, since it is a crystalline synthesis of the whole of space, each face of the cube corresponding to one of the primary directions, namely the zenith, the nadir and the four cardinal points."[27] Appropriately in Buddhism where the goal is nirvana, nothingness, the interior of the stupa is a pile of rubble, and in its most highly elaborated form, that of Borobudur, with its small stupas enclosing the image of the Buddha, the stupa at the highest point of ascent is empty.

The human body is yet another natural symbol, an inexhaustible treasure to be mined for meaning. In the contemporary feminist discourse of the West, the gender of the Judeo-Christian god is controversial considering the Genesis narrative where God creates humankind in his own image. In the male dominant culture of monotheistic religions, the gender free Hebrew is always translated as male, and God the Father is imaged as an old man with a long white beard as in Michelangelo's depiction of creation on the ceiling of the Sistine Chapel.

Sacred Narrative

Sacred narrative relates the life stories of the gods. Christian narrative art selects those events that best exemplify the miracle of Jesus' incarnation and his teaching. Buddhist steles illustrate the four life experiences of Shakyamuni central to his mission: the miracle of his Birth out of the ribs of his mother,

Queen Maya; his Enlightenment under the bodhi tree; his First Preaching of the Sacred Law in the Deer Park at Sarnath; and his Nirvana, or death. Christians can follow the Stations of the Cross so vividly portrayed on the walls of cathedrals and churches. These narrative scenes orient the devotee, directing her worship to their theological meaning.

Another way that depictions of narrative illuminate faith is through the creation of an updated version that brings the life story of the sacred person into the time and place of the viewer. Albrecht Dürer made several series of prints of the Life of the Virgin, setting her story in the context of life of the German middle class of his day, in this way celebrating the mystery of Jesus' incarnation as an ongoing drama. Dürer was working at a critical period of Christian history. During the Protestant Reformation, with its claims of the direct relationship between human and divine and with the development of the printing press, cheap broadsides made sacred art available to the ordinary worshipper for the first time.

Central American artists, by bringing the life and teachings of Jesus into the world of their people, depicting him as one of their own, reified the gospels as ammunition for their revolutionary struggle, even going so far as to represent him with a machine gun slung over his shoulder.

Ritual

Ritual, the established form of worship, individual and collective, the ceremony that embodies liturgy, is most fully documented through video and film which makes more palpable to the student what is often abstract in text. Ritual objects like those used in the Hindu *puja* make more sense when viewed contextually. Body language can express the depth of feeling and emotion in the worshippers' encounter with the sacred. All Muslims, no matter where they are in the globe, prostrate themselves in prayer in the direction of Mecca: "The convergence of all gestures of adoration upon a single point becomes apparent, however, only in the proximity of the Ka'ba, when the host of believers bows down in common prayer from all sides toward a single center; there is perhaps no more immediate and tangible expression of Islam" (see Fig. 4 on the following page).[28]

Sacred Space

A sacred space is a defined space distinguished from all other spaces focusing attention on the forms, objects, and actions in it and revealing them as bearers of religious meaning. Sacred spaces vary in kind, including places that are constructed for religious purposes, such as temples or *temenoi*, and natural sites that are religiously interpreted, such as mountains or rivers. It includes spaces that can be entered physically, as the outer geography of the

Figure 4. Pilgrims before the Ka'ba, Mecca. Photograph by Robert Azzi.

holy land, imaginatively, as the inner geography of the body in Tantric yoga, or visually, as in the space of a mandala.[29]

The monumental stupa at Borobudur in Java was configured as a giant three-dimensional mandala which the pilgrim would circumnavigate passing along the lower galleries, on the walls of which were carved scenes from the life and teachings of the historical Buddha, Shakyamuni, as well as the stories from the Jataka tales of the miracles of the preceding Buddhas (Fig. 5).

He would then continue upward to the four circular terraces, above walking around the seventy-two small stupas, each pierced with diamond, and square-shaped openings to reveal the presence of the meditating Buddha within. The culmination of his journey, both physical and spiritual, was the topmost stupa, standing alone on the uppermost level and empty symbolizing *nirvana,* nothingness or the void, the final liberation of all sentient beings. Louis Frederic commenting on the theological meaning of Borobudur quoted from the *Dhamapada,* "He who considers the world a bubble, a mirage, becomes invisible to the King of Death" indicating that "at one and the same time the center and the immanent nature of all things insofar as the visible is only the apparent structure and form of the invisible."[30]

The orientation of the buildings is as important as their space and form, and their shape and geometry. The direction where the sun rises is the point of orientation for Christian worship because the sun is the image of Christ reborn at Easter. All Muslim prayers and sacred places on earth face in the direction of Mecca because this is where heaven and earth meet, and every sacred precinct is a replica in miniature of the Ka'ba itself. The *mihrab,* a

Figure 5. Plan of Borobudur.

niche in the wall of the mosque facing Mecca, toward which the believers pray, can be seen literally as the niche mentioned in the Koran as the gateway to Paradise. Every Muslim faces the Ka'ba to recite the canonical prayers, and every mosque is accordingly oriented in this direction.

> It is the only worked object that plays an obligatory part in Muslim worship. If it is not a work of art in the proper sense of the term — being no more than a simple cube of masonry — it belongs rather to what might be termed "proto-art," whose spiritual dimension corresponds to myth or revelation.... This means that the inherent symbolism of the Ka'ba, in its shape and the rites associated with it, contains in embryo everything expressed by the sacred art of Islam.[31]

The proscription for orientation toward Mecca is graphically illustrated in a painted Persian tile on which a disk-shaped world is sliced like a pie into wedges named for major Muslim centers, all converging at the central point of Mecca.

Sacred Architecture

The Gothic cathedral, the most familiar example of sacred architecture for a Western audience, can perhaps best be understood as an image, more precisely, as the representation of supernatural reality. Otto von Simpson points out the problem that contemporary students have in grasping the meaning and function of the symbol from the medieval world view.

> To those who designed the cathedrals, as to their contemporaries who worshipped in them, this symbolic aspect or function of sacred architecture overshadowed all others. To us, it has become the least comprehensible.... What experience did these great sanctuaries inspire in those who worshipped in them? And what theme did those who built them wish to convey?[32]

The cathedral was the house of God, "this term understood not as a pale commonplace but as a fearful reality. The Middle Ages lived in the presence of the supernatural, which impressed itself upon every aspect of human life."[33]

For Abbot Suger, the twelfth-century French prelate who created the prototype of the cathedral, at the Royal Abbey of St. Denis, the cathedral was the Heavenly Jerusalem. By enlarging the interior space to accommodate pilgrims and opening up the stone walls for the stained glass windows that would let in the heavenly light, he transformed the Romanesque into the Gothic. In the opening passages of his treatise in which he described the new building and interpreted the important elements of its design, he laid out his aesthetic of the sacred.

> A mystical vision of harmony that divine reason has established throughout the cosmos... As the "symbol of the kingdom of God on earth," the cathedral gazed down upon the city and its population, transcending all other concerns of life as it transcended all its physical dimensions.[34]

In order to more fully understand the significance of the cathedral for the medieval Christian, we must consider the changed meaning and function of the symbol in the Middle Ages and now: "For us the symbol is an image that invests physical reality with poetical meaning. For medieval man, the physical world as we understand it has no reality except as a symbol.... For us the symbol is the subjective creation of poetic fancy; for medieval man what we would call symbol is the only objectively valid definition of reality.[35] The origins of the Gothic cathedral lie in the religious experience, the metaphysical speculation, in the political and even the physical realities, of twelfth-century France, as well the genius of those who created it."[36]

Pilgrimage

Pilgrimage directly relates to the life of the founder and his intimates. Pilgrims walk the Stations of the Cross in Jerusalem, reimaging Christ's Passion, and make the month-long circumambulation through Braj, the Holy Land of Krishna, the site of his many lilas, or journey to Mecca where Mohammed lived and preached for the *Hajj*. The pilgrim's goal is "to make their faith brought to them from afar, more vivid by immersing themselves in its geographical setting; in allowing the landscape in which the founder lived to animate his message, otherwise received at second or third hand through books, sermons and so on."[37]

Conclusion

Images are what we live by. Throughout most of human history, the power of the arts for personal and cultural transformation has been acknowledged in the ongoing traditions of the sacred arts, ceremonials, and rituals through which society reclaimed its wholeness and expressed its vital spirit. Traditional peoples understood that the process of art brings each individual into the present, into contact with the body and the senses, into experiencing the life flow. Through the arts we connect deeply with one another and the community regenerates itself at the wellspring of reality: "The more we can seize of the different aspects of the phenomenal world, often contradictory, through which the Divine can be approached, the more we come near to a general, a 'real' insight into the mysterious entity we call God."[38] Eliade's archetypes provide access to a cosmic view of history, a perhaps universal set of multivalent symbols which posit a common ground for global humanity. If analyzed in their cultural context, shared meaning and values can be identified.

Furthermore, as Geertz has charged us, "The view of man as a symbolizing meaning-seeking animal . . . opens up a whole new approach, not only to the analysis of religion as such but to the relations between religion and values. The drive to make sense out of experience, to give it some form and order is evidently as real and pressing as the more familiar biological needs. . . . [Symbols] provide orientation for an organism which cannot live in a world it is unable to understand — implying a greater emphasis on analysis of such beliefs in terms of concepts — explicitly designed to deal with symbolic matter."[39]

We are challenged to offer a more wholistic approach to the study of world religions. The writing of history has always been from the standpoint of the victors; and historiography is always of its time, but in approaching the study of world religions through the visual arts we might at least be trying to understand religion and culture from the worldview of those who practice it.

And besides, it's more fun that way.

Notes

1. Rudolf Arnheim, *Visual Thinking* (Berkeley: University of California Press, 1983), 20.

2. Suzanne K. Langer, *Philosophy in a New Key,* 3rd ed. (Cambridge: Cambridge University Press, 1942), 145.

3. A. K. Coomaraswamy, "Meister Eckhart's View of Art," in *The Transformation of Nature into Art* (New York: Dover Publications, 1934, 1956), 64.

4. Arnheim, *Visual Thinking,* 17.

5. Herbert Read, Michael Fordham, and Gerhard Adler, eds., *The Collected Works of C. J. Jung,* Bollingen Series 20 (New York: Pantheon Books, 1953–92), 464–65.

6. Clifford Geertz, *The Interpretation of Cultures* (New York: Basic Books, 1973), 87–125.

7. Ibid., 126–27.

8. Diana Eck, *Darshan: Seeing the Image in India* (Chambersburg, Pa.: Anima Books, 1985), 10.

9. Mircea Eliade, *The Sacred and the Profane: The Nature of Religion* (New York: Harcourt, Brace, 1959).

10. Mary Douglas, "The Effects of Modernization on Religious Change," *Daedalus* 111 no. 1 (1982): 6.

11. Titus Burckhardt, *Art of Islam: Language and Meaning* (London: World of Islam Festival Trust, 1976), 1.

12. Langer, *Philosophy in a New Key*, 9.

13. A. K. Coomaraswamy, "The Dance of Shiva," in *The Dance of Shiva* (New York: Noonday Press, 1954), 67.

14. Ibid., 69.

15. Ibid., 75.

16. Eck, *Darshan*, 38.

17. Rudi Weber, *On a Friday Noon* (Geneva: World Council of Churches, 1980), 29.

18. Laurens P. van den Bosch, "Representations of Gods: Introduction," in *Visible Religion* (Leiden: Brill, 1983), 2:vii.

19. Jo Milgrom, *The Binding of Isaac: The Akedah — A Primary Symbol in Jewish Thought and Art* (Berkeley, Calif.: BIBAL Press, 1988), 276.

20. Ibid., 279.

21. Burckhardt, *Art of Islam*, 91.

22. Ibid.

23. Walter B. Denny, "Reflections of Paradise in Islamic Art," in *The Garden in the Arts of Islam* (South Hadley, Mass.: Mount Holyoke College Art Museum, 1980), 34.

24. Ibid., 41.

25. Ibid.

26. Mircea Eliade, "Methodological Remarks on the Study of Religious Symbolism," in Mircea Eliade and J. M. Kitagawa, eds., *The History of Religions: Essays in Methodology* (Chicago: University of Chicago Press, 1973).

27. Burckhardt, *Art of Islam*, 4.

28. Ibid., 5.

29. Mircea Eliade, "Sacred Space," in *The Encyclopedia of World Religions* (New York: Macmillan, 1987), 12:526.

30. Louis Frederic, *Borobudur* (New York: Abbeville, 1994).

31. Burckhardt, *Art of Islam*, 3.

32. Otto von Simpson, *The Gothic Cathedral: The Origins of Gothic Architecture and the Medieval Concept of Order* (London: Routledge, Kegan Paul, 1957), xiv.

33. Ibid.

34. Ibid., xv–xvi.

35. Ibid., xviii.

36. Ibid., xx.

37. Burckhardt, *Art of Islam*.

38. Victor and Edith Turner, *Image and Pilgrimage in Christian Culture* (New York: Columbia University Press, 1978), 156.

39. Geertz, *Interpretation of Cultures*, 141.

PUBLICATIONS BY HARVEY COX

Books

The Secular City: Secularization and Urbanization in Theological Perspectives. New York: Macmillan, 1965, 1971.

God's Revolution and Man's Responsibility. Valley Forge, Pa.: Judson Press, 1965; London: SCM Press, 1969.

Technology and Culture in Perspective. Cambridge, Mass.: Church Society for College Work, 1967. [With others, including the members of the Seminar on Technology and Culture at MIT.]

On Not Leaving It to the Snake. New York: Macmillan, 1967.

Edited, with an introduction, *The Church amid Revolution.* New York: Association Press, 1967. [A selection of the essays prepared for the World Council of Churches, Geneva Conference on Church and Society, 1966.]

Edited, with "Introduction and Perspective," *The Situation Ethics Debate.* Philadelphia: Westminster Press, 1968. [Response to *Situation Ethics: The New Morality*, by Joseph Fletcher (Philadelphia: Westminster Press, 1966).]

The Feast of Fools: A Theological Essay on Festivity and Fantasy. Cambridge: Harvard University Press, 1969, 1971.

Edited, *Military Chaplains: From a Religious Military to a Military Religion.* New York: American Report Press, 1971.

The Seduction of the Spirit: The Use and Misuse of People's Religion. New York: Simon & Schuster, 1973, 1977.

Turning East: The Promise and Peril of the New Orientalism. New York: Simon & Schuster, 1977.

Just as I Am. Knoxville: Abingdon, 1983.

Religion in the Secular City. New York: Simon & Schuster, 1984.

The Silencing of Leonard Boff: The Vatican and the Future of World Christianity. Oak Park, Ill.: Meyer-Stone Books, 1988.

Many Mansions: A Christian's Encounters with Other Faiths. Boston: Beacon Press, 1988.

Fire from Heaven: The Rise of Pentecostal Spirituality and the Re-Shaping of Religion in the Twenty-First Century. New York: Addison-Wesley, 1994.

Articles, Reviews

"Is There an Alternative to Our Foreign Policy?" *Christian Association (C.A.) Advocate* of the University of Pennsylvania, Philadelphia (March 1951): 1, 3.

"Religion in Oberlin." *The Oberlin Alumni Magazine* 53 (1957): 4–6.

"Obscenity and Protestant Ethics." *Christian Century* 76, no. 14 (April 8, 1959): 415–16.

"Biblical Evangelism in the Twentieth Century." *Foundations* 2 (1959): 101–10.

"Discoveries in Evangelism." *The Baptist Leader* (September 1959): 7ff.

"The Changing Scene in Evangelism." *Andover Newton Bulletin* 52, no. 5 (June 1960): 23–30.

Review of *The Reconciling Gospel* by Culburt G. Rutenber (Nashville: Broadman Press, 1959), in *Foundations* 3 (1960): 262–64.

"Playboy's Doctrine of the Male." *Christianity and Crisis* 21, no. 6 (April 17, 1961): 56–58, 60. Reprinted widely, including: *The Intercollegian* 79, no. 5 (March 1962); *Church in World* 2, no. 1 (October 1963): 1; *Catholic Mind* 61 (December): 1178; *National Newman News* 4, no. 7 (March 1964): 1, 11 ["What? 'Playboy' Basically Anti-Sexual?"]; *New Christian* (Incorporating *Prism*) (1964): 6–7.

"To See the Connection." *The Baptist Leader* (May 1961): 5–6.

"Miss America and the Cult of the Girl." *Christianity and Crisis* 21, no. 14 (August 7, 1961): 143–46. Reprinted in *Motive* 22, no. 4 (January 1962): 2–5 and *Zeitwende die Neue Furche* 32, Jahrg. 693–96 (1961) ["Miss Amerika und der Kult des Mädchens"].

"Ouch!" Review of *The Noise of Solemn Assemblies,* by Peter Berger (New York: Doubleday, 1961). *The Intercollegian* 79 (October–November 1961): 12ff.

Review of *We Hold These Truths,* by John Courtney Murray, S.J. (New York: Sheed and Ward, 1960). *Cross Currents* 11, no. 1 (Winter 1961): 79–83.

"Rome, Delhi and the Council." *Commonweal* 75, no. 14 (December 19, 1961): 362–64.

"Theological Reflections on Cinema." *Andover Newton Quarterly* 3 (November 1962): 28–40.

"A Baptist Intellectual's View of Catholicism." *Harper's* (December 1962): 44–50.

"German Ecumenism: Politics and the Dialogue." *Commonweal* 76, no. 25 (March 15, 1963): 635–39.

"The Church in East Germany." *Christianity and Crisis* 23, no. 13 (July 22, 1963): 135–39.

"A Theological Travel Diary: East Germany and Czechoslovakia, June 1963." [Christian Peace Conference, Prague.] *Andover Newton Quarterly,* n.s., 4, no. 2 (November 1963): 26–36.

"Letter from Williamston." [North Carolina Blacks Struggle for Civil Rights.] *Christian Century* 80, no. 49 (December 4, 1963): 1516–18.

"Facing the Secular." *Commonweal* 79, no. 21 (February 21, 1964): 619–22.

Review of *The Finality of Faith, and Christianity Among the World Religions,* by Nels Ferre (New York: Harper & Row, 1963). *Andover Newton Quarterly* (March 4, 1964): 44–46.

"Christians behind the Wall." *Fellowship* 30, no. 3 (March 1964): 11–12. [Published by Fellowship of Reconciliation.]

"Evangelical Ethics and the Ideal of Chastity." *Christianity and Crisis* 24, no. 7 (April 27, 1964): 75–80. Reprinted in: *Prism* 92 (December 1964): 7–17; "The New Protestant Debate over Sex," *Redbook,* October 1964, 56–57, 104–6; *Witness to a Generation: Significant Writings from Christianity and Crisis, 1941–1966,* edited by Wayne H. Cowan (New York: Bobbs-Merrill,

1966), 156–60; "Playboy's Doctrine of the Male," *New Christian* 1, no. 1 (December 4, 1964): 6–7.

"Coca-Cola and Champagne." *The Intercollegian* 81, no. 6 (April 1964): 13.

Review of *The Deputy* by Rolf Hochhuth [Translated by Richard and Clara Winston, Preface by Albert Schweitzer (New York: Grove Press, 1964)]. *Foundations* 7, no. 3 (July 1964): 309–11. [First appeared in the Bulletin of the National Conference of Christians and Jews.]

"God, Marx and Communism." *Think* 30, no. 3 (May–June 1964): 20–23. Reprinted in: *Gospel Herald* 57, no. 23 (June 16, 1964): 513–14; "Will the Communists Drop Atheism?" *Catholic Digest* (September 1964): 64–47; *The Watchman Examiner* 52, no. 43 (November 19, 1964): 723–25; *Church of the Brethren Leader* (December 1964): 11–14; "Gud, Marx och Kommunismen," *Dagen* [newspaper] (February 5, 1965): 2.

"A Denomination-Wide Lay Training Program." *Laity* [World Council of Churches] 17 (June 1964), 19–26.

"The Challenge of the Christian Faith." *The YWCA Magazine* (June 1964): 11–12.

"Kafka East, Kafka West." *Commonweal* 80, no. 20 (September 4, 1964): 596–600. [Revised version appears in *The Secular City*.]

"The Responsibility of the Christian in a Technicized World." *My Covenant Is Life and Peace (Malachi 2:5): Documents and Informations from the Second All-Christian Peace Assembly in Prague June 28–July 3, 1964* (Prague: International Secretariat of the Christian Peace Conference, 1964), 60–74.

"Using and Misusing Bonhoeffer." *Christianity and Crisis* 24 (October 19, 1964): 199–201.

"War on Poverty." *Christianity and Crisis* 24 (November 16, 1964): 224.

"Mississippi: The Closed Society," review of *Crisis in Black and White*, by Charles Silberman (New York: Random House, 1964). *Social Action*, 31, no. 3 (November 1964): 39–43.

"The Gospel and Postliterate Man" [implications of electronic media for Christian witness]. "Mindful of Man" Series. *Christian Century* 81, no. 48 (November 25, 1964): 1459–60.

"They Have Overcome." *Boston Sunday Globe* (December 20, 1964): 8A.

"Musts on the Domestic Agenda." *Christianity and Crisis* 24, no. 23 (January 11, 1965): 270–71.

"The Playboy and the Christian." [CBS TV, February 7, 1965] *Theology Today* 22, no. 4 (January 1966): 491–99.

"Apathy, Abdication and Acedia." *Renewal* 5 [issue entitled "Apathy in the Metropolis"] (January–February 1965): 18–20. Reprinted as "Age of Apathy" in *Perspectives* 10, no. 2 (March–April 1965): 58–60, and in *The Quill* 5 (December 1965).

"Sociology of Religion in a Post Religious Era." *The Christian Scholar* 48, no. 1 (Spring 1965): 9–26.

"Communism and Civil Rights." *Christianity and Crisis* 25, no. 7 (May 3, 1965): 90–91.

"Dirksen Amendment [on apportionment]." *Christianity and Crisis* 25 (May 17, 1965): 101–2.

"What's Involved in Being Both Christian and Open?" *The YWCA Magazine* (May 1965): 12ff.

"The Statute of Limitations on Nazi Crimes" [A Theological and Ethical Analysis]. *Background Reports* (June 1965). Published by the National Conference of Christians and Jews Project, Religious Freedom and Public Affairs. Appears as Addendum to *On Not Leaving It to the Snake*. Reprinted as "US Cleric Asks Forgiveness for Nazis." [Response to John Cogley] *New York Times*, July 4, 1965.

"The Church and the City." *Man in Community* 1 (July 1965): 13–20. [Published by United Church on the Green, New Haven, Conn.]

"The Restoration of a Sense of Place: A Theological Reflection on the Visual Environment," *The Living Light* 2, no. 3 (Fall 1965): 104. Reprinted in: *Let's See* 1 (January 11, 1966): 80; *Town and Country Church* 190 (September–October 1966): 3; *Ekistics/Oikistikh* 25, no. 151 (June 1968): 422–24; *On Not Leaving It to the Snake*.

"Beyond Bonhoeffer? The Future of Religionless Christianity." *Commonweal* 82, no. 21 (September 17, 1965): 653–57.

Review of *Social Humanism: An International Symposium,* edited by Erich Fromm (New York: Doubleday, 1965). *The Saturday Review* (September 19, 1965): 107–8.

"Ferment in the Churches: The New Christian Soldiers." *The Nation* 201, no. 11 (October 11, 1965): 216–20. Reprinted in *Information Service* 45, no. 12 (June 4, 1966).

"New Phase in the Marxist-Christian Encounter." *Christianity and Crisis* 25, no. 18 (November 1, 1965): 226–30. Reprinted in *On Not Leaving It to the Snake*.

"Bigotry in Boston." *Christianity and Crisis* 25, no. 20 (November 29, 1965): 250–51.

"Sex: Myths and Realities" [Hugh Hefner and Harvey Cox at Cornell University]. *Motive* 26, no. 2 (November 1965): 7–11.

"Cox on His Critics — Colloquy." [Reply to reviews of *The Secular City,* July 12, 1965] *Christianity and Crisis* 25, no. 21 (December 13, 1965): 274–75.

"The Changing Church." *Current* 66 (December 1965): 46–50.

"What Are We Celebrating and Why?" *Redbook* (December 1965): 40–44. Reprinted in *Hi Way* 8, no. 12 (December 1966): 11–13.

"Die Verantwortung der Christen in einer technisierten Welt." In *Anruf und Aufbruch: zur Gestalt der Kirche in Gegenwart und Zukunft. Festgabe für Günter Jacob* (Berlin: Evangelische Verlagsanstalt GmbH, 1965), 139–59.

"The Place and Purpose of Theology." *Christian Century* 83, no. 1 (January 5, 1966): 7–9. Reprinted widely: "The Prophetic Purpose of Theology" in *Frontline Theology*, edited by Dean Peerman (Richmond, Va.: John Knox Press; London: SCM Press, 1967), 149–55; "Das prophetische Ziel der Theologie," *Theologie im Umbruch: Der Beitrag Amerikas zur gegenwartigen Theologie*, edited by Dean Peerman and Malcolm Boyd (Munich: Christian Kaiser Verlag, 1968); *On Not Leaving It to the Snake*.

"World Apartheid." Letter to the Editor, *Commonweal* 83, no. 14 (January 14, 1966): 423, 450–51.

"An Imaginary Interview with Louise Day Hicks." *Renewal* (February 1966): 10.

"We Protest the National Policy in Vietnam." [Cox and others] *Christianity and Crisis* 26, no. 3 (March 7, 1966): 33–34.

"Theology in Ferment: The Death of God and the Future of Theology." *El Gaucho*. Special Supplement [Associated Students, University of California, Santa Barbara] (March 23, 1966): 9ff. Reprinted as "The Death of God and the Future of Theology" in *The New Christianity*, edited by William E. Miller (New York: Delacorte Press, 1967), 377–89. Also appears as a chapter in *On Not Leaving It to the Snake*.

" 'Secular' No Longer a Bad Word Nor Bad Influence." *The Churchman* (March 1966): 14.

"Maturity and Secularity." *Religion in Life* (Spring 1966): 215.

"Secularization and the Secular Mentality: A New Challenge to Christian Education in the Secular City." *Religious Education* 61, no. 2 (March–April 1966): 83–87.

"Introduction." *The Grass Roots Church: A Manifesto for Protestant Renewal*, by Stephen Rose (New York: Holt, Rinehart & Winston, 1966). Reprinted in *Renewal* 7 (January 1967): 22–23.

"The Ungrateful Poor." *Christianity and Crisis* 26, no. 8 (May 16, 1966): 93–94.

"Sex and the Secular Man." *Dominion* (June 1966): 51–57.

"Mission in a World of Cities." *International Review of Missions* 55 (July 1966): 273–81.

"Geneva, 1966." *Commonweal* 84 (August 19, 1966): 525.

Review of "The Future of Belief," by Leslie Dewart. *Herder Correspondence. Book Supplement* (New York: Herder and Herder, September 1966), 282A–282B. Reprinted as "Show Biz in Church." *Life* (October 21, 1966): 70ff [photos].

"How to Kill God." Review of *The Bible* (film by John Houston). *Look*, October 18, 1966, 104. Also, "Holy, Holy, Holy." Review of the same film in *Renewal* 6 (October–November 1966): 19–21.

"On Columns and Cities." *Commonweal* 85, no. 5 (November 4, 1966): 134–36.

"Let's End the Communist-Christian Vendetta." *Christian Century* 83, no. 45 (November 9, 1966): 1375–79. Reprinted in *Hi Way* 8, no. 12 (December 1966): 11–13. Also appears as a chapter in *On Not Leaving It to the Snake*.

Review of *The Church Inside Out*, by J. C. Hoekendijk (Philadelphia: Westminster, 1966). *Christian Century* 83, no. 146 (November 16, 1966): 1412–16.

"Detente for What?" *Christianity and Crisis* 26 (November 28, 1966): 264–65.

"Where Is the Church Going?" *United Church Herald* [Ohio edition] 10 (January 1, 1967): 34–38. Reprints: "Where Is the Church Going and How Is It Going to Get There?" *The Observer*, 1967, Centennial Reference Issue; *Church and Home*, 4, no. 4 (February 15, 1967): 14–17; *On Not Leaving It to the Snake*.

"The Epoch of the Secular City." [Address delivered to the Canadian Institute of Public Affairs.] Also appeared in *Plan* 8, no. 1 (January 1967): 16–21 and *Social Compass* 15, no. 1 (1968): 5–12.

"Revolt in the Church." *Playboy* (January 1967): 129ff.

"Dream City (Almost)." *Commonweal* 35, no. 15 (January 20, 1967): 426–27.

"The Biblical Basis of the Geneva Conference." *Christian Century* 84, 14 (April 5, 1967): 435–37.

"Discussion: Communist-Christian Dialogue." [With Roger Shinn and Paul Lehman] *Union Seminary Quarterly Review* 22, no. 3 (March 1967): 213–27.

"The 'New Breed' in American Churches." *Daedalus* [Religion in America issue] 6, no. 1 (Winter 1967): 135–50. Reprinted in *Harvard Today* (Spring 1967): 12–15 [edited version]. Also reprinted as "The 'New Breed' in American Churches: Sources of Social Activism in American Religion." *Religion in America* [The Daedalus Library, vol. 12], edited by William G. McLoughlin and Robert N. Bellah (Boston: Houghton Mifflin, 1968), 368–84.

"The Medium Is the Word." Review of *The Presence of the Word*, by Walter Ong, S.J. (New Haven: Yale University Press, 1967). *Christian Century* 85, no. 15 (April 10, 1968): 456.

"Reappraising the Draft." *Christianity and Crisis* 27, no. 6 (April 17, 1967): 73–74.

"An Open Letter to Allen Ginsburg." *Commonweal* 86, no. 5 (April 21, 1967): 147–49. Reprinted in *Information Service* 46, no. 12 as "What Is Christianity Going to Do about the Hippies?" and in *The Mennonite* 82, no. 39 (October 24, 1967): 649–51.

"Our Own Guernica: Guernica to Vietnam — The Capacity for Horror." *Commonweal* 86, no. 6 (April 28, 1967): 164–65.

"McLuhanite Christianity at Expo '67." *Commonweal* 86, no. 10 (May 26, 1967): 277–79.

"Evolutionary Progress and Christian Promise." *The Evolving World of Theology* [*Concilium. Theology in the Age of Renewal: Fundamental Theology,* 26:6, no. 3], edited by Johannes Metz (New York: Paulist Press, 1967).

"Religion and the New Morality" [panel]. *Playboy* (June 1967): 55ff.

"Penance: From Piety to Politics: Reparations as a Religious and Political Issue." *Renewal* 7 (June 1967): 18–19.

"The Riots: No Winners — Only Losers." *Christianity and Crisis* 27, no. 14 (August 7, 1967): 181–82.

"The Christian Pavilion." *Hi Way* 9, no. 9 (September 1967): 26–27.

"Tradition and the Future: I." *Christianity and Crisis* 27, no. 16 (October 2, 1967): 218–20. Also appears as part of "Tradition and the Future: The Need of New Perspective" in *On Not Leaving It to the Snake.*

"Tradition and the Future: II." *Christianity and Crisis* 27, no. 17 (October 16, 1967): 227–31. Also appears as part of "Tradition and the Future: The Need of New Perspective," in *On Not Leaving It to the Snake.*

"Introduction." *Man on His Own: Essays in the Philosophy of Religion,* edited by Martin Marty and Dean Peerman (New York: Herder and Herder, 1970). Also appeared as "Ernst Bloch and 'The Pull of the Future,' " *New Theology* 5, edited by Martin E. Marty and Dean G. Peerman (New York: Macmillan, 1968), 191–203.

"The Significance of the Church-World Dialogue for Theological Education." [Reply, Martin E. Marty, 280–82] *Theological Education* 3, no. 2 (Winter 1967): 270–79.

"Saculares Reden von Gott." *Die Zeichen der Zeit* 7, no. 21 (1967): 241–54.

"Pluralism in Higher Education." *Christianity and Crisis* 27, no. 14 (January 22, 1968): 323–24.

"Let's Face It: Are We Having a Nervous Breakdown?" *McCalls,* January 4, 1968, 6ff.

"God and the Hippies." *Playboy* (January 1968): 93ff.

"Cambridge Teach-In on COCU." *The Ecumenist* 6, no. 2 (January–February 1968): 113–25. [Addresses by McCord, Cox, Spivey, Baum. Given at Episcopal Theological School, October 21–22, 1967.]

"What About Detroit?" *Social Action and Social Progress* 34 (January–February 1968): 5–11. [Entire issue devoted to "Christians Confront Current Revolutions: Reflections from the United States Conference on Church and Society," 1967.]

"Who's Next?" [Regarding the indictment of the "Boston Five."] *Commonweal* 87, no. 17 (February 2, 1968): 524–25.

"The Christian Life Style in a Secular Age." *The Church Woman* 34, no. 3 (March 1968): 5–8.

"Dialogue on Christ's Resurrection." [Replies to J. Anderson, March 29, 4–9; rejoinder, 11–12; reply C. Pinnock, 6–11; with Lawrence Burkholder and Wolfhart Pannenberg.] *Christianity Today* 12 (April 12, 1968): 5–11.

"A Republic of Virtue — Where Will the University Get Its Values?" *Commonweal* 88, no. 5 (April 19, 1968): 138–42.

"Balancing the Book." *Commonweal* 88, no. 8 (May 10, 1968): 235–36.

"Radical Hope and Empirical Probability." *Christianity and Crisis* 28, no. 8 (May 13, 1968): 97–98.

"I Am for Kennedy." *Christianity and Crisis* 28 (June 10, 1968): 132–33.

"Technology, Modern Man, and the Gospel." [With Carl F. H. Henry — Panel; American Baptist Convention, May 30, 1968] *Christianity Today* 12 (July 5, 1968): 3–7.

"Christian Realism: A Symposium." [With John C. Bennett, Harvey G. Cox, Tom F. Driver, Alan Geyer, Robert Shaull, Roger L. Shinn] *Christianity and Crisis* 28, no. 14 (August 5, 1968): 175–90.

"Aloha and All That." *Commonweal* 88, no. 18 (August 9, 1968): 528–29.

"Enough Is Enough." [Replies, T. F. Driver and others, October 14, 232–38, 241–43]. *Christianity and Crisis* 28 (September 16, 1968): 193–94.

"Tongues of Flame: The Trial of Dan Berrigan and the Catonsville Nine." *Tempo* (October 31, 1968): 3. [A publication of the National Council of Churches]

"The Secular Search for Religious Experience." [With replies by Richard Luecke, William Hamilton, 330–40] *Theology Today* 11, no. 3 (October 1968): 320–32.

"Amnesty for America's Exiles." *Christianity and Crisis* 28 (November 25, 1968): 286–88.

"Christmas in a Troubled Time." *Long Lines* [Publication of American Telephone and Telegraph Company], 48, no. 4, November–December 1968, 12–17. [Illustrated by Corita Kent]

"Reinvesting the Churches' Wealth." *Christianity and Crisis* 28, no. 21 (December 9, 1968): 294–95.

"Underground Churches, Underground Schools." *Commonweal* 89, no. 11 (December 13, 1968): 376–78.

Letter to the Editor. [Reply to an article by Ernest Lefever, "A Humane Liberal Speaks," *Christianity and Crisis* (November 25, 1968)]. *Christianity and Crisis* 28, no. 22 (December 23, 1968): 321–22.

"The Spectrum Is Wider Than We Thought." [Reply to E. W. Lefever, November 25, 288–89] *Christianity and Crisis* 28 (December 23, 1968): 321–22.

"In Memory of Karl Barth." *Commonweal* 89, no. 13 (December 27, 1968): 24–25.

"The Christian-Marxist Dialogue: What Next?" *Dialog* 7 (Winter 1968): 18–26. Reprinted in *Marxism and Christianity: A Symposium,* edited by Herbert Aptheker (New York: Humanities Press, 1968), 15–28.

"Discussion: Communist-Christian Dialogue." [Harvey G. Cox, Paul Lehmann, Roger L. Shinn] *Union Seminary Quarterly Review* [Social Action, US] 22 (March 1967): 223–27; 35, no. 3 (November 1968): 23–25 [Reply to Roger Garaudy, 205–12].

Review of *Exploration into God,* by John A. T. Robinson (Stanford: Stanford University Press, 1967). *Harvard Divinity Bulletin* 1, no. 2 (Winter 1968): 17.

"The Mythology of Development." *Risk* 4, 2 (1968): 31–35.

"Corita: Celebration and Creativity." In *Sister Corita,* by Mary Corita Kent, Harvey Cox, and Samuel A. Eisenstein [34 color plates] (Philadelphia: Pilgrim Press, 1968). *New Book Review* (December 1968): 18–19.

"The Decent Society: Religion and Morality." [A symposium with articles also by Theodore C. Sorensen, John V. Lindsay, Kenneth B. Clark, Peter Matthiessen, Jerome B. Wiesner, Charles H. Percy, William Sloane Coffin, Edward P. Morgan, Kenneth Tynan, William O. Douglas] *Playboy* (January 1969): 91f.

"End of an Era: The New Deal." *Christianity and Crisis,* 28, no. 23 (January 6, 1969): 325–26.

"A Celebration of Conscience." [Report on the visitation to Allenwood Federal Prison Farm, December 20–21, 1968.] *Tempo* (January 15, 1969): 2–3.

"Mythologie der Entwicklungshilfe." [Berichte und Analysen] *Evangelische Kommentare [Stuttgart],* 2. Jahrg. (February 1969): 82–83.

Film reviews for *Tempo.* [A publication of the National Council of Churches.] "Bullitt" (February 1, 1969): 12. "Romeo and Juliet" (February 15, 1969): 12. "Greetings" (March 1, 1969): 12. "Shame" (March 15, 1969): 12. "The Killing of Sister George" (April 1, 1969): 12.

"Issues for the '70's." *Commonweal* 90, no. 1 (March 21, 1969): 18–20.

"Penance: From Piety to Politics." [Reparation as a religious and political issue] *Renewal* (June 1969): 18–19.

"Beyond Discreet Silence." *Christianity and Crisis* 29 (Sept 15, 1969): 225–26.

"Kinesthetic Happening: Art or Atrocity?" *Commonweal* 87, no. 2 (October 13, 1969): 44–45.

"Rubem Alves: Hopeful Radical." Review of *A Theology of Human Hope* by Rubem Alves (Washington, D.C.: Corpus Books, 1969). *Christian Century* 86 (November 5, 1969): 1417–19.

"Politische Theologie." *Evangelische Theologie* 29, no. 11 (1969): 565–72.

"A Yuletide Toast to Ebenezer Scrooge or How Christians Have Made Humbug out of Christmas." *Playboy* (December 1969).

"Preventive War against the Black Panthers." *Christianity and Crisis* 29 (January 5, 1970): 337–38.

"For Christ's Sake." *Playboy* (January 1970): 197ff.

"Issues for the '70s." [Reprint] *Church and Society* 60 (January–February 1970): 43–47.

"Looney Toons, Merry Melodies, Keystone Cops and the Wave of the Future: Mickey Mouse and Porky Pig." *Renewal* 10, no. 2 (February 1970): 4–6.

"Tired Images Transcended: An Interview with Myself." *Christian Century* (April 27, 1970): 384–86.

"Barbie Doll and the Specter of Cultural Imperialism." *Christianity and Crisis* 30 (April 27, 1970): 81–82.

"The Future of Christianity and the Church." *The Futurist* (August 1970): 122–29.

"Bird in the Hand." *Christianity and Crisis* 30 (September 21, 1970): 178–80.

"Tora! Tora! Tora!" [Article] *Christianity and Crisis* 31 (February 8, 1971): 9–10.

"Little Big Man." [Article] *Christianity and Crisis* 31 (March 22, 1971): 51.

"Trash." [Article] *Christianity and Crisis* 31 (April 5, 1971): 61–62.

"Love Story." [Article] *Christianity and Crisis* 31 (April 19, 1971): 75–76.

"The Cultural Captivity of Women." [Review of Stephen Sondheim's musical, "Follies"] *Christianity and Crisis* 31 (May 31, 1971): 111–12.

"The Virgin and the Dynamo Revisited: An Essay on the Symbolism of Technology." *Soundings* 54 (Summer 1971): 125–46.

"Eight Theses on Female Liberation." *Christianity and Crisis* 31 (October 4, 1971): 199–202.

"The Mass Media: A Theological Critique." [CELAM-USCC Inter-American Seminar, Mexico City, May 19–26, 1971] In *IDOC Internazionale* 35 (November 13, 1971): 24–37.

"McGovern in California: Campaign '72." *Christianity and Crisis* 32 (May 29, 1972): 139–40.

"What's at Stake in '72?" *Christianity and Crisis* 32 (October 16, 1972), 223–24.

"Churches and the Future of Religion." [Insearch Conference, Chicago, 1973] *Christianity and Crisis* 33, no. 1 (February 5, 1973): 9–11.

"Last Tango in Paris." [Film review] *Christianity and Crisis* 33 (March 5, 1973): 30–31.

Review of *Ethics and the Urban Ethos,* by Max L. Stackhouse (Boston: Beacon Press, 1972). *Andover Newton Quarterly* 13, no. 4 (March 1973): 288–91.

"An American Family." [Television documentary] *Christianity and Crisis* 33 (April 30, 1973): 80.

"On Coming of Age in Malvern." [Excerpt from *Just as I Am*] *Christian Century* 90 (August 1–8, 1973): 776–80.

"The Wisest and the Justest and the Best," review of *From Time to Time* by Hannah Tillich, and of *Paulus* by Rollo May. *New York Times Book Review* (October 14, 1973): 32.

"Toward Religious Pluralism." *Dialogue* 6, no. 4 (November 4, 1973): 42–44.

"Pluralism and the Open Society." *Religious Education* 69 (March–April 1974): 150–59.

Review of *From Primitives to Zen,* by Mircea Eliade. *New York Times Book Review* (August 11, 1974): 17–18.

"Viewpoint: Who Needs Rockefeller?" *Christianity and Crisis* 34 (November 11, 1974): 246–47.

"The Country Is Full of Ideolects." Review of *Religious Movements in Contemporary America,* by Irving I. Zaretsky and Mark P. Leone. *New York Times Book Review* (December 22, 1974): 13–14.

"Militant Sisters of Another Age." Review of *Purity Crusade: Sexual Morality and Social Control, 1868–1900,* by David J. Pivar. *The Review of Books and Religion* 3, no. 8 (1974): 1.

"Secular City: Ten Years Later." *Christian Century* 92 (May 28, 1975): 544–47.

"Most Maligned Theologian Award." *Christian Century* 93 (January 21, 1976): 36–37.

"All Things Are Possible." Review of *The Healing and Charismatic Revivals of Modern America,* by David Edwin Harrell, Jr. *New York Times Book Review* 81, no. 8 (February 22, 1976): 6, 22

"Ethics and Journalism" [with Krister Stendahl and Jerald F. ter Horst]. *Nieman Reports* 30, no. 1 (Spring 1976): 25–28.

"Theology aus der Praxis." *Evangelische Kommentare* 9, no. 6 (June 1976): 344–45.

"Blessed Rage for Order." [Review] *Review of Books and Religion* 5 (July–August 1976): 1f.

"The National Debate over Abortion." *Los Angeles Times,* Opinion Section, Part IV (September 16, 1976): 1, 5.

"Wrong to Make It a Political Cause" [abortion debate]. *Los Angeles Times,* part 4 (September 19, 1976): 1, 5.

"As though God Does Not Exist ... " *LOKAZ,* a Journal from Narga Institute. Garden City, N.Y.: Anchor Books (1976): 99–104.

"Boston Affirmations, 6 January 1976," [et al.]. *Study Encounter* 12, no. 1–2 (1976): 44–47. *Church and Society* 66 (May–June 1976): 55–58. Widely reprinted: "Boston Affirmations" [with some critical evaluations], Cox et al. *Theology Today* 33 (April 1976): 101–7. *Worldview* 19 (March 1976): 45–47. *Engage/Social Action* 4 (February–March 1976): 50–53. *Christianity and Crisis* 36 (February 16, 1976): 23–27.

"Light from the East: A Report from Naropa." *Christianity and Crisis* (January 24, 1977): 326–29.

"More on 'A Dual-Sex Eucharist.' " *Commonweal* 104, no. 4 (February 18, 1977): 112.

"Phenomenology of a Culture: Fellini's Casanova." *Christianity and Crisis* (March 21, 1977): 55–56.

"Four Big Ones." *Journal of Current Social Issues* 14, no. 2 (Spring 1977): 26–29.

"Eastern Cults and Western Culture: Why Young Americans Are Buying Oriental Religions." Excerpt from *Psychology Today* 11, no. 2 (July 1977): 36.

"Ethnic Me." *National Catholic Reporter* (October 14, 1977): 7.

"The Portable Sabbath: Why Americans Have Turned to Meditation." *Washington Post,* October 23, 1977, C1, C3.

Review of *Theology and the Philosophy of Science,* by Wolfhart Pannenberg. *Religious Studies Review* 3, no. 4 (October 1977): 213.

"Real Threat of the Moonies." *Christianity and Crisis* 37 (November 14, 1977): 258–63.

"Rediscovering the Sabbath through Meditation." *Boston Sunday Globe,* November 27, 1977, A2.

Review of *Daniel Martin,* by John Fowles (Boston: Little, Brown, 1977). *Commonweal* 104 (December 9, 1977): 794–95.

"A Dual-Sex Eucharist." *Commonweal* (December 1977): 8–9.

"Theologian of the Cosmos." Review of *Faith and Reality,* by Wolfhart Pannenberg. *The New Review of Books and Religion* 2, no. 4 (December 1977): 7.

"Die Reformation und die Stadt." *Auftrag und Werk* (1977): 3–11.

"Von Christus dem Clown." *Auftrag und Werk* (1977): 23.

"Turning East." [Excerpt from book] *Saturday Evening Post,* 250 (April 1978): 38f.

"The Rise of Fascism, Movie Style." *National Catholic Reporter* 14, no. 31 (May 26, 1978): 9.

"God Sets the Agenda: In Retrospect Books of the 1960's: [*The Secular City*]." *Christian Century* 95 (August 2–9, 1978): 741–43.

"Japan in Search of its Soul: Again, *The Chrysanthemum and the Sword.*" *Christianity and Crisis* (October 2, 1978): 225–29.

"Pope John Paul II and Polish Jokes." *Commonweal* 105 (November 24, 1978): 754–55.

"A Harvard Professor's Frightening Day in Iran." *Boston Herald American* (January 4, 1979): 8.

"What Happened at Puebla." [With Faith A. Sand] *Christianity and Crisis* 39 (March 19, 1979): 57–60.

"Limping Marxism." [Reply to Peter Berger] *Christianity and Crisis* 39 (July 23, 1979): 191.

"Science and Religion." *Think* 45, no. 6 (November–December 1979): 5–7.

"Theological Education and Liberation Theology: A Symposium of Response." *Theological Education* 16 (Autumn 1979): 25–29.

"Theological Reflections on Lay Ministry." *The NICM Journal* (National Institute for Campus Ministries) 5, no. 2 (Spring 1980): 18f.

"The Political Theology of John Paul II." *Michigan Quarterly Review* 19, no. 2 (Spring 1980): 140–55.

"Paradoxical World Situation a Challenge to Church, Theologian Says." *Arkansas Gazette,* July 2, 1980, 88.

"Theology: What Is It? Who Does It? How Is It Done?" *Christian Century* 97 (September 24, 1980): 874–75.

"In the Interest of Survival." *The Fayetteville Times,* November 14, 1980, 4–A.

"Avoiding Dogmatisms." [Letter to the Editors] *Commonweal* 107 (November 21, 1980): 656–58.

"Harvey Cox on the Conservative Religious Trend." *Peacework* (December 1980): 6–7.

"Defining the Religious Principle." *Back to Godhead* [magazine of the Hare Krishna Movement] 15, no. 10 (1980): 6–8, 29.

"Teens and the Religious Revival: The Real Thing or Rip-Off?" *Parents,* 1980, 52–53, 72, 80–81.

"Understanding Islam: No More Holy Wars." *The Atlantic* 247, no. 1 (January 1981): 73–80.

"Enough." *Report from the Capital* (March 1981): 4–5.

"The Battle of the Gods: A Concluding Unsystematic Postscript." In *The Other Side of God,* edited by Peter Berger (Garden City, N.Y.: Anchor Press/Doubleday, 1981), 284–302.

"Who Is Ernesto Cardenal?" *Christianity and Crisis* 43, no. 5 (April 4, 1983): 108–9, 126–27.

"The Heart of Heartless World." *Essays in Arts and Sciences* 12, no. 2 (May 1983): 5–16.

"Cambridge Stays Nuclear: The Pope, the Scientists, and the Dollar." [Editorial] *Christianity and Crisis* 43 (December 12, 1983): 470–72.

"Religion in the Secular City: A Symposium." *Christianity and Crisis* (February 20, 1984): 35–45.

"The Family: Between Myth and Promise." *American Baptist Quarterly* 3, no. 1 (March 1984): 31–41.

"God's Laughter Breaks Through." *Boston Sunday Globe* (April 22, 1984): A-7.

"Baptist Faith and Public Discourse." *Light* [Christian Life Commission of the Southern Baptist Convention] (May 1984): 9–12.

"Response to Commentators" [B. Johnson, P. Lehmann, P. Hegy, C. Bourg, 79–105]. *Sociological Analysis* 45 (Summer 1984): 77–113.

Review of *The Naked Public Square: Religion and Democracy in America,* by Richard John Neuhaus. *New York Times Book Review* (August 26, 1984): 11.

"Christian Radicals and the Failure of Modern Theology" [Reprint from *Religion in the Secular City,* 1984.] *Religion and Intellectual Life* 2, no. 1 (Fall 1984): 104–14.

"Vision for a Bright Economic Future." *New York Times* (November 18, 1984).

"Religious Pluralism and Political Discourse." *Harvard Divinity Bulletin* 15, no. 1 (October–November 1984): 2–4.

Response to Robert N. Bellah, "The Triumph of Secularism" [The First Noble Lecture, 13–26]. *Religion and Intellectual Life* 1, no. 2 (Winter 1984): 27–28.

"Religion Returns to the Secular City." In *Images of Man* (Macon, Ga.: Mercer University Press, 1984), 93–109.

"Imagining an Economy Based on Shalom: The Bishops' Draft Pastoral." *Christianity and Crisis* 44 (January 21, 1985): 509–12.

"The Trial of Jesus." *New York Times* (April 5, 1985): A27.

"Preacher at the Riverside." Review of *Harry Emerson Fosdick: Preacher, Pastor, Prophet,* by Robert Moat Miller. *Washington Post Book World* (April 14, 1985): 5.

"Poor, Yet Making Many Rich." [Review] *International Bulletin of Missionary Research* 9 (April 1985): 83–84.

"The Sheriff and the Scofflaw." [Editorial on international law] *Christian Century* 102 (September 25, 1985): 821–22.

"Moral Reasoning and the Humanities." *Liberal Education,* 71, no. 3 (Fall 1985), 195–203.

"The Changing Images of Jesus." Review of *Jesus Through the Centuries,* by Jaroslav Pelikan. *Washington Post,* Book World section (December 22, 1985): 1.

"In the Pulpit and on the Barricades." Review of *Reinhold Niebuhr,* by Richard Fox. *New York Times Book Review* 91, no. 1 (January 5, 1986): 1, 24–25.

"Theology, Politics, and Friendship." [Reinhold Niebuhr and C. C. Morrison] *Christianity and Crisis* 46, no. 1 (February 3, 1986): 16, 18.

"The Congregation and Its FBI Spy, Will Rise." *New York Times,* March 3, 1986, Section A, 15.

"Bless Our Spy: [U.S. government, FBI informants in small Baptist Church]." *Other Side* 22, no. 6 (July–August, 1986), 31.

"Surviving with Style." *Commonweal* 113, no. 18 (October 24, 1986): 550.

"Of Jesus and the Kingdom of God." Review of *The First Coming*, by Thomas Sheehan. *Boston Sunday Globe*, October 26, 1986, B106, B109.

"Religion, Politics, Television." *Christianity and Crisis* 46, no. 17 (November 1986): 408–09.

"A Liberation Theology for North America." *The World* 1, no. 1 (January–February 1987): 9–11.

"Why I Stay." *Commonweal* (February 19, 1987).

"A Procura de um Cristo Soviético." [Translated by Sieni Maria Campos.] *Religião e Sociedade*, 14, no. 3 (March 14, 1987): 4–24.

"The Church Militant in Latin America." Review of *Liberation Theology*, by Phillip Berryman and *Will It Liberate?* by Michael Novak. In *Washington Post Book World* 17, no. 14 (April 5, 1987): 1, 4.

"God's Last Laugh." [Editorial] *Christianity and Crisis* 47 (April 6, 1987): 107–8.

"Harvey Cox and Martin Marty: Religion and the Public Realm." [Dialogue] *Humanities Discourse* [Newsletter of the Federation of State Humanities Councils] 1, (July 7, 1987): 4–6, 8.

"If You Think Rome Is Going Conservative, Look at US or the Baptists." *National Catholic Reporter* (September 4, 1987): 12–13.

"What does a Confessing Church Confess?" *Katallagete* 10, no. 1–3 (Fall 1987): 24–28.

Review of *Death of Christendom, Birth of the Church*, by Pablo Richard, translated by Phillip Berryman (Maryknoll, N.Y.: Orbis Books, 1987). *HAHR,* 70 (February 1, 1990): 212–13.

"Fundamentalism as an Ideology." In *Piety and Politics* (Washington, D.C.: Ethics and Public Policy Center, 1987), 287–301.

"Fidel and Religion: Thoughts on the Church and Cuba." *The Nation*, 244, no. 18 (May 9, 1987): 597, 606, 608, 609–12.

"Liberation Theology vs. Cardinal Ratzinger." *Tikkun* 3 (May–June 1988): 17–21f.

"The Cross and the Swastika." Review of *The Churches and the Third Reich*, by Klaus Scholder. *Washington Post Book World* (July 24, 1988): A5.

"Religious Tradition as 'Selective Retrieval.'" *Conservative Judaism* 40 (Summer 1988): 20–25.

"Many Mansions or One Way: The Crisis in Interfaith Dialogue." *Christian Century* 105 (August 17–24, 1988): 731–35.

"La Teología de la Liberación vs. El Cardenal Ratzinger." *Maj'shavot/Pensamientos* 27, no. 3 (July–September 1988): 52–67.

"The Cross and the Kremlin." *World Monitor* 1, no. 1 (October 1988): 52–61. Also appeared as a chapter in *Many Mansions*.

Review of *Theology for the Third Millennium*, by Hans Küng. *National Catholic Reporter* (October 21, 1988): 23.

"Jesus in Harvard Yard." *Religion and Intellectual Life* 6, no. 1 (Fall 1988): 72–78.

"Rabbi Yeshua Ben Joseph." *The Pennsylvania Gazette* 87, no. 3 (December 1988): 17–22. Also appeared as a chapter in *Many Mansions*.

"Complaining to God." In *Theodicea Oggi*, edited by Marco Olivetti. Reprinted as: "Complaining to God: Theodicy and the Critique of Modernity in the Resurgence of Traditional Religion — Latin America Liberation Theology." *Archivo di Filosofia* 56, no. 1–3 (1988): 311–25.

"Big Day in the Back Bay." [Installation of Bishop Barbara Harris] *Christianity and Crisis* 49, no. 4 (March 20, 1989): 78–79.

"Gustavo's Grandchildren." *Christianity and Crisis*, 49, no. 9 (June 12, 1989): 94–95.

"On the Role of the Church in El Salvador." *Boston Sunday Globe. Focus* (Commentary and Opinion), November 19, 1989, A21, A23.

Review of *Other People's Myths: The Cave of Echoes*, by Wendy Doniger O'Flaherty. *Christian Century*, 106, no. 39 (December 20–27, 1989): 1205.

"The Church in the Modern World." Review of *The Christian Tradition: A History of the Development of Doctrine. Vol. 5, Christian Doctrine and Modern Culture (Since 1700)*, by Jaroslav Pelikan. *Washington Post Book World* 19, no. 49 (December 3, 1989): 1, 18–19.

"The Spirit of the Soviet Christ: The Light of Faith in the Soviet People." *Sojourners* 18, no. 11 (December 1989): 18–21.

"The Cross and the Kremlin II." *World Monitor* 2, no. 12 (December 1989): 54–60.

"Christians and Muslims: The Road Ahead." *New World Magazine* (1989).

"La mort de Dieu et l'avenir de la théologie." *Lumière et Vie* (1989): 32–42.

"The Guns That Silenced Ignacio Martín-Baró." *Interamerican Public Opinion Report* (January 1990): 10.

"We Are One in the Lord: Christians and Muslims." *New World Outlook* 80, no. 2 (March–April 1990): 18–19.

"World Religions, Politics Aside." Review of *The Christ and the Faiths: Theology in Cross-Reference*, by Kenneth Cragg (Westminster Press, 1987). *Cross Currents: Religion and Intellectual Life* 40, no. 1 (Spring 1990): 120–24.

"Walter Rauschenbusch." [Review] *Cross Currents* 40 (Spring 1990): 120–24. Reprinted as: "Walter Rauschenbusch." [Review] *Journal for the Scientific Study of Religion* 29 (March 1990): 137–40.

"Avarice for Good." Review of *A Tenured Professor*, by John Kenneth Galbraith (Boston: Houghton-Mifflin, 1990). *Christianity and Crisis* 50 (July 2, 1990): 229.

"The Vatican Needs a Dose of Glasnost." *New York Times* (August 17, 1990): A29.

"Why the Vatican Errs in Muzzling Dissent." *Boston Globe,* Religion (August 5, 1990).

"The Secular City 25 Years Later." *Christian Century* 107 (November 7, 1990): 1025–29.

"Theology from the Underside." *Harvard Divinity Bulletin* 19, no. 4 (Winter 1990): 10–11.

"Inculturation Reconsidered." [Indigenization as form of continuing oppression] *Christianity and Crisis* (May 13, 1991): 140–42.

"Foreword" for *Christianity and Crisis* (May 24, 1991).

"Is a Hundred Years Enough?" *Newsday,* Op-Ed (May–June 1991).

"Buddhist Killing." *Boston Globe,* Op-Ed (August 21, 1991).

"Heresy Hunters." *Boston Globe*, Op-Ed (September 1, 1991): A21.

"Is Latin America Turning Protestant? The Politics of Evangelical Growth." Review of *Tongues of Fire: The Explosion of Protestantism in Latin America* (Oxford and Cambridge, Mass.: Basil Blackwell, 1990). *American Journal of Sociology* 97 (September 1991): 579–82.

"Thinking About Jesus." Review of *The Gospel According to Jesus. Tikkun* 7, no. 1 (January–February 1992): 83–86.

"The Secular City and the Sacred Earth." [With Timothy C. Weiskel; anthropologist and theologian on the environmental crisis and Isaiah] *Religion and Values in Public Life (Harvard Divinity Bulletin)* 1, no. 1 (Fall 1992): 4.

"Die Inkarnation des Mammon: Warenkult und simulation in der inszenierten Gesellschaft." *Lutherische Monatshefte* 32 (January 1993): 4–7.

"The Inaugural: Symbols and Images." *Christianity and Crisis* 53 (February 15, 1993): 29–30.

"Some Personal Reflections on Pentecostalism." *Pneuma* 15 (Spring 1993): 29–34.

"The Only Oysters in Town: [what *Christianity and Crisis* offered will be missed]." *Christianity and Crisis* 53 (April 12, 1993): 85–86.

"Insight and Encouragement." [James Luther Adams; spiritual mentors] *Christian Century* 110 (April 14, 1993): 391.

"Why God Didn't Die: A Religious Renaissance Flourishing Around the World — Pentecostal Christians Leading the Way." *Nieman Reports* 47 (Summer 1993): 6–8, 47–49.

"Pentecostalism at Harvard." [Course on Pentecostalism and liberation] *Christian Century* 110 (August 25–September 1, 1993): 806–08.

"A Theologian's Reflection." *Creation Spirituality* 9, 4/5 (Summer–Fall 1993): 22–23.

"Priesthood in the Post-Modern World." *Journal of Oriental Studies* 32, no. 2 (1993). [Translated into Japanese by N. Okamoto.] *Journal of Oriental Studies* 5 (1995): 33–37.

"Jazz and Pentecostalism." *Archives de Sciences Sociales des Religions* 38 (October–December 1993): 181–88.

"Religion and Responsibility." Readers' Forum, *Boston Review* (December–January, 1993–94): 33–34.

"The Bishop and the Rebels." *New York Times* (January 26, 1994): A21.

"Business in a New Age." [Response to Martha Nichols's article "Does New Age Business Have a Message for Managers?"] *Harvard Business Review* (May–June 1994).

"Reply to Genovese and Rivers Forum." *Boston Review,* October 1994.

"Lifting the Curse of Babel: Pentecostals Bridge 70 Years of Ethnic Division." *New York Times* 144, November 6, 1994, IV15.

"Healers and Ecologists: Pentecostalism in Africa." [Excerpt from *Fire from Heaven*] *Christian Century* 111 (November 9, 1994): 1042–46.

"Pentecostalism and the Future of Christianity." *Tikkun* 9 (November–December 1994): 43–46.

Review of *A History of God: The 4000-Year Quest of Judaism, Christianity, and Islam,* by Karen Armstrong (New York: Knopf, 1993). *Boston Globe* (December 20, 1994): A17.

"Fire from Heaven." [Excerpt from *Fire from Heaven*] *Harvard Divinity Bulletin* 24, no. 1 (1994): 8–11.

"World Religions and Conflict Resolution" [with Arvind Sharma and Masao Abe]. In *Religion, The Missing Dimension of Statecraft* (Oxford: Oxford University Press, 1994), 266–83.

Review of *The Politics of Virtue: Is Abortion Debatable?* by Alan Freeman (Durham, N.C.: Duke University Press, 1993). *Tikkun* 10 (January–February 1995): 82–83f.

"World Watches Mexico Harassing the Clergy." [Letter to Editor] *New York Times* (October 4, 1995): A20.

"The Warring Visions of the Religious Right." [Profile of Regent University] *Atlantic Monthly* 276 (November 1995): 59–69.

"Jesus the Jew: Jesus the Christian." *What Kind of God?* [Studies in the Shoah 11] (Lanham, Md.: University Press of America, 1995), 297–304.

"Rethinking Religion: The Transcendent Dimension." *The Nation* 2, no. 1 (January 1, 1996): 20–23.

"Beliefs," by Peter Steinfels. [Cox quoted extensively] *New York Times* (January 27, 1996): 10.

"Sacred Space in the Secular City." *Graduate School of Design News,* Harvard University (Fall 1996): 38–40.

"The Gospel/Culture Question: Hermeneutics in the Social Settings of Theological Schools." *Boston Theological Institute Newsletter* (June 1996): 3–4.

" 'With Malice toward None . . . ' Mixing Religion with Politics is Nothing New." *Sojourners* 25 (September–October 1996): 22–25.

"Letter to the People of Korea," in Korean publication of *Fire from Heaven,* 1996.

"Into the Age of Miracles: Culture, Religion, and the Market Revolution." Review of *Exporting the American Gospel,* by Steve Brouwer, Paul Gifford, and Susan D. Rose (New York: Routledge, 1996). *World Policy Journal* 14, no. 1 (Spring 1997): 87–95.

"En God Is Toch Niet Dood." *Parakleet* 61 (Spring 1997): 17–22.

"Religion and Technology: A New Phase." [With Dr. Anne Foerst] *Bulletin of Science, Technology and Society* 17, Nos. 2–3 (1997): 53–60.

"On Leaving Behind Useless Controversies: A Protestant Perspective on the Papacy of the Future." Review of *The Papacy and the People of God,* edited by Gary MacEoin (Maryknoll, N.Y.: Orbis Books, 1998). *Harvard Divinity Bulletin* 27, no. 1 (1997): 8–12.

"Three R's, Plus One." [Prayer in public schools] *New York Times* (June 5, 1998): A23.

"Harlequin Christ." [Revised from *Feast of Fools,* 1969] *Witness* 81 (July–August 1998): 12–15.

"The Market as God: Living in the New Dispensation." *Perspectives* 13, no. 3 (September 1999): 69–77.

"The Myth of the Twentieth Century: The Rise and Fall of 'Secularization.' " In *Harvard Divinity Bulletin* 28, no. 2–3 (1999), 6–8.

"So Gracious Is the Time." Beliefnet [Internet] (December 1999).

"I Do in Part Believe It," December 19, 1999.

"Jerusalem the Golden." Beliefnet [Internet] (January 30, 2000).

Peter Jennings Reports: "The Search for Jesus," April 2000.

"Miracles from All Over," Beliefnet [Internet] April 24, 2000.

"What if God Were One of Us?," Beliefnet [Internet] June 26, 2000.

"The Thane Struts Again," Beliefnet [Internet] July 3, 2000.

"Two Men, One City," Beliefnet [Internet], October 3, 2000.

"Double-Edged Sword," Beliefnet [Internet], January 11, 2001.

"Secular Judaism: Some Questions." *Sh'ma* (June 2000, Sivan 5760): 7–8.

Review of Kenneth L. Woodward, *The Book of Miracles: The Meaning of the Miracles Stories in Christianity, Judaism and Islam.*

Review of James Carroll, *Constantine's Sword* (January 2001).

Symposia/Speeches/Lectures/Sermons

"Ancestors and Descendants." [Speech notes, undated]

"The Responsibility of the Christian in a Technicized World." *Christian Peace Conference* (September 11–12, 1964): 262–67. Delivered to the Second All-Christian Peace Conference, Prague, July 1964.

"Sex: Myths and Realities." A discussion with Hugh Hefner, editor of *Playboy*, held at Cornell University on "The Sexual Revolution on the Campus," November 1965.

"Theology in Ferment." *El Gaucho,* March 1966.

"Secularization and the Secular Mentality: A New Challenge to Christian Education." *Religious Education* (March–April 1966).

"Tradition and Future: The Need for New Perspective." Union for Democratic Action, 25th Anniversary Conference, Warrenton, Va., October 9, 1966.

The Playboy Panel: Religion and the New Morality, 1967.

"The Substance of Things Hoped For" [An Interview on Ernst Bloch]. *Jubilee* 15, no. 5 (November 1967): 409.

"The Christian Life Style in a Secular Age." At conference of Church Women United, December 1967.

"The Secular Search for Religious Experience" and "Festivity and Fantasy: Celebration in Theological Perspective." William Belden Noble Lectures, delivered at Harvard University, March 5, 6, 7, 1968. [Later published as *The Feast of Fools.*]

"The Nature of Student Unrest." Excerpts from address given to the Minister's Institute at Harvard Divinity School. February 7, 1969, taped and transcribed. Published in *Concourse*, HDS, Harvard University, 1, no. 17 (February 13, 1969): 1–2, 8–14.

"The Hartford Appeal: A Symposium, Part I," [et al.] *Worldview* 18 (May 1975): 22–27.

"Debate on the Hartford Appeal" [with Richard John Neuhaus and William Sloane Coffin, Jr.] *Christianity and Crisis* 35 (July 21, 1975): 168–79.

Lecture. Baptist Seminary of Nicaragua and Centro Valdivieso, Managua, Nicaragua, January 1980.

Seminar on "Religion in Appalachia." West Virginia, July 1980.

Lecture. Utah Shared Ministry Conference. Provo, Utah, September 21, 1980.

"The Domestic Basis for a Non-Violent Foreign Policy." Symposium lecture. Harvard University, Cambridge, Mass., Spring 1981.

"Religious and Moral Discussions of Nuclear Weaponry." Talk. Northwest Chapter of Physicians for Social Responsibility, Portland, Ore., May 1982.

Guest and respondent for "The Kingdom of God and the City of Man: The Work of Harvey Cox." Society for the Scientific Study of Religion, Eastern Regional Conference, Providence, R.I., October 1982.

Talk. CBS TV's "Morning News." Response to President Reagan's speech in Orlando, Fla. March 1983.

"A Religious Perspective on the Modern World." A plenary address delivered to the Ohio State University Third Annual Symposium in the Humanities, May 14, 1983.

Panel member. Meeting of the Permanent People's Tribunal on the case of Guatemala. Madrid, Spain, January 1983; October 9, 1983.

"Testing the Church's Mission in the City." Lecture. Annual conference of Los Angeles District of the United Methodist Church. February 17, 1984.

"Prophecy and Liberation in Latin American Theology." Mead-Swing Lecture. Oberlin College, Oberlin, Ohio, Spring 1984.

"The Religious Perspective." *Religion and Political Campaigns.* Proceedings of "Religion and the Campaign for Public Office," conference sponsored by the Institute of Politics and the Harvard Divinity School, Cambridge, Mass. (June 10–11, 1984): 7–18.

Talk. ABC network program *Directions* devoted to "Ballots, the Bible, and Basic Beliefs." June 1984.

"Moral Reasoning and the Humanities." Lecture. Woodrow Wilson National Fellowship Foundation seminar. Princeton, N.J., Summer 1984.

Keynote address. Meeting of the National Council on Religion in Public Education. Indianapolis, October 2, 1984.

Featured speaker. Baptist Joint Committee on Public Affairs. Washington, D.C., October 3, 1984.

"Religion and Politics in America: The Prospects for Civility." The George Dana Boardman Lectureship in Christian Ethics. University of Pennsylvania, October 29, 1984.

Keynote address. The Society for the Scientific Study of Religion. Knoxville, Ky., November 5, 1984.

"Liberation Theology." Otis Lectures, Wheaton College, 1985.

"Education for Citizenship: The Humanities in the University of the Future." University of New Hampshire, October 1985.

"Is Peace Really Possible?" Talk. CBS Morning News, December 25, 1985.

"The Kingdom of God in America: The Influence of Religion in the USA Today," presented in Japan, 1985.

"A Lover's Quarrel: The Story of Religion and Science in the West." World Congress for the Synthesis of Science and Religion, Bombay, India, January 1986.

"Religion, Politics, and Television." Symposium for 350th/50th Anniversary of Harvard University/JFK School of Government, September 6, 1986.

"Baptists and Liberation Theology." Series of Lectures. Southwestern Baptist Theological Seminary, Wake Forest, North Carolina, Spring 1997.

"Citizen's and Believers." Conference on "Transforming Faith." University of Maryland, May 1–2, 1987.

"The Influence of Religion in America." Rider College, Lawrenceville, N.J., October 13, 1987.

"Transmitting Sacred Traditions in a Post-Modern Era." Address for the installation of the President of the Jewish Theological Seminary. New York, September 1988.

"Religion and Spirituality." Lecture. American Academy of Psychotherapists. October 1988.

Inaugural lecture for the new chair of Franciscan Theology and Spirituality. Catholic Theological Union, Washington, D.C., April 1989.

Ethics Discussion Panel. Nieman Foundation Seminar. Cambridge, Mass. May 6, 1989. Published in *Nieman Reports* 43, no. 3 (Autumn 1989): 7–10.

"Theology from the Underside." Harvard Divinity School Convocation Address. Harvard Divinity School, Cambridge, Mass., September 20, 1989. Published in *Harvard Divinity Bulletin* 19, 4 (Winter 1990): 10–11.

Jean Donovan Memorial Lecture. University College, Cork, Ireland, January 1990.

"The Human Dimension in Interfaith Dialogue." Kelly Memorial Lectures. Tulane University, March 1990.

"Christianity and Apocalypse." Lecture for a conference on "Facing Apocalypse: Apocalyptic Imagery and Secular Politics." Salve Regina College, Newport, R.I., June 15, 1990.

"The Liberation of the Spirit." Prepared for III Reunión Latinoamericana sobre Religión Popular y Etnicidad. Mexico City, May 29 to June 9, 1990.

Bible study facilitator. American Baptist Convention Conference on "Faith Faces Issues." October 1990.

Featured speaker at a conference on "Health and Spirituality: The Abundant Life." Danvers, Mass., October 12–14, 1990.

Lecture on the church in Latin America. Fairfield University, November 1990.

"God and Glasnost: Religion in the Soviet Union Today." Lecture. Harvard Club, Boston, December 9, 1990.

"Christians and People of Other Faiths." Lecture. University of Richmond, March 3, 1991.

"Religiopolis: Beyond the Secular City." Witherspoon Lecture. University of North Carolina, April 1991.

Lecture for the International Association for a Married Priesthood, New York, June 1991.

"Future of the City." Lecture for the Boston Mission Society conference, October 1991.

"The Coming of the Anti-City." Rauschenbusch Lectures, Colgate-Rochester Divinity School, 1992.

"The City and the Earth." Lecture. Bangor Theological Seminary, Hanover, N.H., October 1992.

Ferguson Lecture. University of Manchester, England, March 1992.

"Religious Response to Consumer Society." Lecture. Soka University, Tokyo, Japan, May 1992.

"Religion in the Twenty-First Century." Lecture. Soka University, Tokyo, Japan, May 1992.

"Der Geist des Protestantismus und die Mediengesellschaft." Seminar für Praktische Theologie. Universität Hamburg, June 17, 1992.

"The Recovery of the Russian Spiritual Tradition: Its Implications for America." Keynote address for the international conference at Dartmouth College, July 1992.

"Shamans, Demons, and Entrepreneurs." Lecture. Korea, September 1992.

Lecture on Christology at Ghost Ranch, a Presbyterian Conference Center in New Mexico, July 1993.

Member of panel on religious pluralism at the centennial of the World Parliament of Religions, Chicago, August 1993.

"The Gentle Breeze and the Breath of Fire." Response to Daisaku Ikeda. Harvard University, September 24, 1993.

"The Search for God in Harvard Square." 150th Anniversary of Old Cambridge Baptist Church, Harvard Square, October 31, 1993.

"Christianity in the Twenty-First Century." Tanner-McMurrin Lecture on the History and Philosophy of Religion. Westminster College, Salt Lake City, Utah, April 1994.

"Recovering the Prophetic Voice in a Culture of Disbelief." Talk in conjunction with Yale Law School Professor Stephen L. Carter for the Christian Conference of Connecticut, New Haven, September 11, 1994.

"Did Jesus Have a Health Plan?" Lecture. Georgetown Presbyterian Church, Washington, D.C., November 1994.

"Canterbury Tales from Virginia Beach: A Visit to Regent University," 1995.

"Beyond the Secular City." Lecture at invitation of Cardinal Carlo Maria Martini, Milan, Italy, 1995.

Inaugural lecture on Pentecostalism for the Asuza Lecture Series at Regent University, Virginia Beach, Va., April 24, 1995.

"The City: Peril and Promise." For the annual meeting of the Northwest Interfaith Movement, Philadelphia, June 1995.

"Repentance and Forgiveness: A Christian Perspective." Responsive Community Conference on Repentance. June 16–17, 1995, Washington, D.C.

"Urbi et Orbi: The City and the World." Four Lectures at the Waldensian Seminary, Rome, Italy, July 1995.

Lectures at seminaries, colleges, and universities in South Korea, September 1995.

"The Ambiguous Feast: Festivity in Biblical Faith." Biblia Conference, Florence, Italy, October 21–22, 1995.

Address to Society for Pentecostal Studies. Wheaton College, Wheaton, Ill., November 1995.

Lecture on Pentecostalism. Fuller Seminary, Pasadena, Calif., November 1995.

"Relationship between Religion and the Future State of the World." Iowa State University, Ames, Iowa, November 1995.

Lecture on Religion in the Twenty-First Century. University of Southern California, Los Angeles, Winter 1995.

"Jesus and Generation X." For "Jesus at 2000: A National Scholarly Symposium," sponsored by Trinity Institute and held at Oregon State University, Corvallis, Ore., February 8–10, 1996. [Other participants included Marcus Borg, Dominic Crossan, and Huston Smith.]

"The Ambiguity of Festivity." Part of lecture series on 25th anniversary of Revels, Inc., at Cambridge Adult Education Center, Cambridge, Mass., February 21, 1996.

"Religion and Politics After the Secular City." At University of South Florida, February 24, 1996.

"Religion and the City." Two lectures to Presbyterian Synod of the Northeast at Union League Club in New York City, 1996.

"Religion and Politics after the Secular City." Keynote address at conference on "Religion and the Political Order: The State and the Sacred in Classical and Contemporary Christianity, Islam, and Judaism," University of Southern Florida, February 24, 1996.

"What is the Holy Spirit Saying to Mainline Churches?" Seminar sponsored by the Massachusetts Conference of the UCC, Wellesley Congregational Church, Wellesley, Mass., April 17, 1996.

The Globalization of Pentecostalism Conference. San José, Costa Rica, June 10–14, 1996.

"The Christian Gospel and the God of the Global Market: Paul and Demetrius Revisited." University lecture, Seoul, Korea, August 1996.

"The Lord and Giver of Life." Paper presented at Fifth International Theological Conference, Yonsei University, Seoul, Korea, August 1996.

"Sacred Space." Lecture given at Architectural Forum (discussion of a new Orthodox Jewish Synagogue, a Korean Presbyterian church, and black churches recently burned in the South), New York City, New York, January 1997.

"Mission in a World of Cities." Overseas Mission Center, New Haven, Conn., January 1997.

"The Historical Jesus and Interfaith Dialogue." Tantur Ecumenical Institute, Jerusalem, Israel, March 1997.

Conference on the First Commandment, Hartman Center, Jerusalem, March 1997.

"Children of Abraham." Hiram College, Ohio, 1997.

Lecture. Youngstown State University, Youngstown, Ohio, 1997.

"Values and Religion in the Technological City." Annual Conference of the National Association for Science, Technology, and Society, Worcester, Mass., March 7, 1997.

"Mission in the Americas — Century 21 — Northern Perspective." Lecture given at Conference of Latin American Pentecostal Churches, San Juan, Costa Rica, April 1997.

"God and the Market Economy." Lecture at Polytechnical University, Managua, Nicaragua, May 1997.

Keynote address at a conference sponsored by the Institute for the Study of American Religion, Princeton, N.J., June 1997.

"Sacred Space and the City." Lecture for a summer architectural institute at Catholic University of America, Washington, D.C., July 1997.

Speech, University Jewish Leaders' Conference, Brandeis University, July 1997.

"Changing Ideas of God in the World-Wide Pentecostal Movement." At Harvard Conference on Expanding Notions of God, April 7–9, 2000.

"Jews and Muslims in American Society." Keynote address at symposium, Hartford Seminary, Fall 1997.

322   *Publications by Harvey Cox*

Keynote address at a conference sponsored by the Detroit Parliament for World
    Religions, Oakland University, Rochester, Mich., April 29, 1998.
"Artificial Intelligence and Human Embodiment: A Biblical Perspective," sponsored
    by MIT and the Boston Theological Institute, 1998.
"Abraham's Children: Jews, Christians, and Muslims in the United States." At Hiram
    College and at Youngstown State University in Ohio, 1998.
Lecturer on Spirituality and Business at symposium in Boston, sponsored by the
    Andover Newton Theological School, 1998.
Lecture at the retirement of Professor Roger Johnson from the Religion Department,
    Wellesley College, Wellesley, Mass., 1998.
Participant in seminar on monotheism, "No Other Gods," at the Osher Center for
    Religious Pluralism at the Shalom Hartman Institute in Jerusalem, Israel, 1998.
Lecturer, Harvard University Alumni Tour to Burgundy and Provence, Summer 1998.
Panelist at an inter-religious conference on "Religion, Spirituality, and Medicine" at
    St. Vincent's Hospital of New York City, June 26, 1998.
Lecturer at conference, Institute for Jewish Leadership, Brandeis University, July
    1998.
"Voices of Public Intellectuals" [fifth lecture in a five-part series], sponsored by the
    Radcliffe Seminars, December 8, 1998.
"Theology Today." Executive Staff, World Council of Churches, Geneva, Switzer-
    land, June 30, 1999.
"New Tales of the City." Convocation Address at Graduate Theological Union,
    Berkeley, Calif., September 8, 1999.
Panel: "Future of Jerusalem," sponsored by the American Friends of Sabeel,
    Lexington, Mass., October 30, 1999.
Guest Saxophone Soloist with the Aardvark Jazz Orchestra at American Academy
    of Religion, November 20, 1999.
Panel on Scott McLennan's *Finding Your Religion*, Harvard Divinity School,
    December 8, 1999.
Panel at MAKOR on "Religion in 2000," Jewish Cultural Center, New York,
    December 13, 1999.
"A Religious Perspective on the Modern World." Lecture at Inaugural Conference,
    Ohio State University Religious Studies Program (2000).
"Changing Ideas of God in the World-Wide Pentecostal Movement," Harvard
    Conference on Expanding Notions of God, April 7–9, 2000.

CONTRIBUTORS

ROBERT N. BELLAH is Elliott Professor of Sociology Emeritus at the University of California, Berkeley. He was educated at Harvard University, receiving a B.A. in 1950 and a Ph.D. in 1955. His long-term research interest is in religious evolution. A recent essay coming out of this project is "Max Weber and World-denying Love: A Look at the Historical Sociology of Religion," in the *Journal of the American Academy of Religion.*

LEONARDO BOFF received his doctorate in theology and philosophy from the University of Munich. He was Professor of Systematic Theology for many years in Petrópolis, in the state of Rio de Janeiro, Brazil. He is currently Professor of Ethics and Ecology at the University of Rio de Janeiro and is investigating the relationship between social ecology, theology, and ethics. His most recent publications are *Ecologia: Grito de la tierra, grito de los pobres* (Ecology: Cry of the earth, cry of the poor), *Ethos mundial: Un consenso mínimo entre los humanos* (World ethos: A consensus among humans), and *Tiempo de Trascendencia: El Ser Humano Como Proyecto Infinito* (Time of Transcendence: The Human Being as an Infinite Project).

ROBERT MCAFEE BROWN was Professor Emeritus of Theology and Ethics at the Pacific School of Religion. He was educated at Amherst College, Union Theological Seminary, and Columbia University. In the course of his academic career he served first as Auburn Professor of Systematic Theology (1953–62) and subsequently as the Professor of Ecumenics and World Christianity (1976–74) at the Union Theological Seminary. He also served as Professor of Religious Studies (1962–76) at Stanford University and as the Professor of Theology and Ethics (1979–86) at the Pacific School of Religion. He acted as the Protestant Observer at the Second Vatican Council and has been actively associated with the World Council of Churches over the years. His numerous publications include books on Elie Wiesel, Gustavo Gutiérrez, and Reinhold Niebuhr, as well as on biblical and theological themes.

SATHIANATHAN CLARKE is Associate Professor in the Department of Theology and Ethics at the United Theological College, Bangalore, India. He was educated at Madras University (B.A., M.A.), United Theological College (B.D.), Yale University (S.T.M.), and Harvard University (Th.D.). He is a Minister of the Church of South India and taught for a year at the Harvard Divinity School (1995). He is the author of *Dalits and Christianity: Subaltern Religion and Liberation Theology in India.*

JAMES H. CONE is the Charles A. Briggs Distinguished Professor of Systematic Theology at Union Theological Seminary in New York City. He attended Shorter College (1954–56) and holds a B.A. degree from Philander Smith College (1958). In 1961, he received an M. Div. degree from Garrett Theological Seminary and later earned an M.A. (1963) and Ph.D. (1965) from Northwestern University. He is best known for his ground-breaking works, *Black Theology and Black Power* and *A Black Theology of Liberation,* and for *Martin and Malcolm and America: A Dream or a Nightmare?* and *The Spirituals and the Blues: An Interpretation.* His most recent publication is *Risks of Faith.* His research and teaching interests continue to explore the relationships between human structures and divine purpose in the quest for justice.

JOHN C. CORT is a freelance writer; author of *Christian Socialism: An Informal History;* former co-editor of *Religious Socialism;* and has contributed to eight books, including several encyclopedias. His most recent contribution is a chapter on social justice in *The Catholic Church in the Twentieth Century.* He is a former labor editor of *Commonweal* and a frequent contributor to Catholic and left-wing periodicals. He worked with Dorothy Day at The Catholic Worker in the thirties and has been an official in the AFL-CIO, the Peace Corps, and anti-poverty agencies.

ANNE FOERST pursued her graduate studies in Protestant theology at Wupperthal, further studies in computer science and philosophy at the University of Bonn, and doctoral studies in Systematic Theology at the Ruhr-University of Bochum under Professor Christofer Frey, where she obtained her Ph.D. in 1995. She was a postdoctoral fellow at the MIT AI-Lab from September 1995 until August 1999, where she conducted research on artificial intelligence that was supported by the German Research Society and Sir John Templeton Foundation. She won a Templeton award for the course proposal "God and Computers," taught at MIT in 1997. She has published several papers on related topics, two of which have appeared in *Zygon:* "Cog, A Humanoid Robot, and the Question of the Image of God" and "Artificial Intelligence: Walking the Boundary."

ELINOR W. GADON has a Ph.D. from the University of Chicago, Committee on the History of Culture. Her research and publications have focused on the analysis of myth and symbol in its cultural context. A nontraditional and innovative educator, she has created and taught multidisciplinary courses in the Art, Religion, and Culture of India, World Religions, and Women's Studies at Harvard, Tufts, University of California, Santa Barbara, and the New School for Social Research. She is the founder and retired director of a socially committed Women's Studies graduate program at the California Institute of Integral Studies based on the integration of body, mind, and spirit, and currently an associate scholar at the Mills Women's Leadership Program. She is also the author of *The Once and Future Goddess: A Symbol for our Time* and the forthcoming *The Wounded Minotaur: Recalling the Sacred Male*. She is featured in Cathleen Rountree, editor, *Women Turning Seventy: Voices of Wisdom* and CBC's TV series "The Face of God in the New Millennium."

ARTHUR GREEN is the Philip W. Lown Professor of Jewish Thought at Brandeis University. He is a historian of Jewish Mysticism as well as a theologian and his work seeks to serve as a bridge between these two distinct fields of endeavor. His books include *Seek My Face, Speak My Name: A Contemporary Jewish Theology* and *These Are the Words: A Vocabulary of Jewish Spiritual Life*. Green is former president of the Reconstructionist Rabbinical College in Philadelphia and was a founder of Havurat Shalom, an experiment in Jewish community in Somerville, Massachusetts, in the late 1960s.

MARGARET ELETTA GUIDER, O.S.F., is Associate Professor of Religion and Society at the Weston Jesuit School of Theology in Cambridge, Massachusetts, where she has taught for the past eleven years. She holds degrees in education from the University of Illinois and degrees in theology from the Catholic Theological Union and Harvard University. She is the author of *Daughters of Rahab: Prostitution and the Church of Liberation*. She also has written numerous articles on topics related to missiology, contextual theology, Franciscan spirituality, and the rights of children. Her current research interests include intercultural hermeneutics, contemporary issues in Women and Christian Mission, and the thought of Paulo Freire.

WILLIAM HAMILTON is a radical theologian who has taught at both the graduate and the undergraduate level in New York, Florida, and Oregon. He currently resides in Sarasota, Florida. He is working on Melville and Shakespeare and recently published an Internet book on Shakespeare called *Shakespeare, God, and Me*. He is involved in the "Seminars for the Homeless" movement and has discovered that *Hamlet* is an almost perfect text for the homeless and the addicted.

HANS KÜNG pursued first philosophical and then theological studies at the Gregorian University, the Sorbonne, and the Institut Catholique in Paris. His doctoral dissertation dealt with Karl Barth's doctrine of justification. His academic career has been closely associated with the University of Tübingen, where he was Professor of Ecumenical Theology and Director of the Institute for Ecumenical Research from 1980 to 1996. Best known for his book *On Being a Christian,* he is currently engaged in campaigning vigorously for the adoption of a global ethic by the world's religions.

FRANK D. MACCHIA graduated from Union Theological Seminary in New York (M.Div.) and the University of Basel (D.Theol.). He serves as Associate Professor of Theology at Vanguard University, an Assemblies of God university, in Costa Mesa, California (he is ordained in the A/G). He is Immediate Past President of the Society for Pentecostal Studies, and currently serves as Senior Editor of the Society's Journal, *Pneuma*. His dissertation on "The Message of the Blumhardts in the Light of Southern German Pietism" (1991) was released in the Wesleyan/Pietist Studies Series of the University Press of America. He has also published articles on pneumatology and ecumenical themes in various journals, such as the *Journal of Ecumenical Studies, Concilium, Transformation, Theology Today, Theology and Worship: Occasional Papers of the Presbyterian Church (U.S.A.), The Living Pulpit, Pneuma*, and the *Journal of Pentecostal Theology*. He has publications coming out in the *Encyclopedia of Christianity, The Encyclopedia of Worship and Liturgy, The Dictionary of Pentecostal and Charismatic Movements,* and *Ecumenical Trends*.

IAIN S. MACLEAN is a graduate of the Universities of Cape Town, Rhodes, South Africa, Princeton, and Harvard. He is Assistant Professor of Western Religious Thought at James Madison University, Harrisonburg, Virginia. His doctoral work in Religion and Society (under Harvey Cox) focused on social anthropology, theology, and political ethics. His present research includes the study of seventeenth-century Dutch mysticism and a comparative study of contemporary phenomena of national reconciliation commissions. Dr. Maclean has authored *Opting for Democracy: Liberation Theologians and the Struggle for Democracy in Brazil* and co-edited *The Encyclopedia of Religion in American Politics* and *God, Meaning, and Morality*.

WILLIAM MARTIN is the Harry and Hazel Chavanne Professor of Religion and Public Policy in the Department of Sociology and a Senior Scholar in the James A. Baker III Institute for Public Policy at Rice University. He received his B.A. and M.A. degrees from Abilene Christian University, a B.D. from Harvard Divinity School (1963), and a Ph.D. from Harvard (1969), where he was Harvey Cox's first graduate student. His books include *A Prophet with Honor: The Billy Graham Story* and *With God on Our Side: The Rise of the Religious Right in America*.

JÜRGEN MOLTMANN began the study of theology and philosophy as a prisoner of war in England 1946–48 (Theological School at Norton Camp, near Nottingham). He continued his studies after repatriation in 1948 at Göttingen University and finished them in 1952 with the first theological examination and promotion to a Dr. Theol. In 1957 he became a Dr. Theol. Habil. at Göttingen University with a historical study on Calvinism in Northern Germany and got the *venia legendi* for Systematic Theology. In 1967 he became professor at the Protestant Faculty of Theology at the University of Tübingen, where he has been professor emeritus since 1994. His main works have been translated into leading world languages. They include *Theology of Hope; The Crucified God; The Church in the Power of the Spirit; The Trinity and the Kingdom; God in Creation; The Way of Jesus Christ; The Spirit of Life;* and *The Coming of God.*

RODNEY L. PETERSEN is Executive Director of the Boston Theological Institute (BTI), the consortium of theological schools, seminaries, and university divinity schools in the Greater Boston area. Additionally, Dr. Petersen teaches in the areas of history and conflict resolution in the member schools and overseas. An ordained minister in the Presbyterian Church (U.S.A.) and serving in the United Church of Christ, he is a graduate of Harvard University, Harvard Divinity School, and Princeton Theological Seminary. He is author or editor and contributor of several works including *Preaching in the Last Days; Christianity and Civil Society: Theological Education for Public Life; Consumption, Population, and Sustainability: Perspectives from Science and Religion; Earth at Risk; Forgiveness and Reconciliation: Religion, Public Policy, and Conflict Transformation;* and *Theological Literacy for the Twenty-First Century.*

JORGE PIXLEY obtained his Ph.D. from the University of Chicago Divinity School and is currently Professor of Bible at Seminario Teológica Bautista, Apartado 2555, Managua, Nicaragua. His most recent book is a history of Baptists in Nicaragua entitled *Por una Iglesia Laica.* His latest book in English is *Biblical Israel: A People's History.* He is currently working on a Jeremiah commentary in English.

RICHARD L. RUBENSTEIN is President Emeritus and Distinguished Professor of Religion and Director of the Center for Holocaust and Genocide Studies at the University of Bridgeport. He received a Master of Hebrew Literature (M.H.L.) and rabbinic ordination from the Jewish Theological Seminary and Master of Theology (S.T.M.) and Ph.D. from Harvard University. Dr. Rubenstein is also Professor Emeritus of Religion at Florida State University where he served for twenty-five years. The Richard L. Rubenstein Professorship in Religious Studies has recently been established at Florida State University. There is general agreement among theologians that Rubenstein's first book, *After Auschwitz,* initiated the contemporary debate on the meaning of the Holocaust in religious thought, both Jewish and Christian. A revised, greatly expanded edition was published in 1992. His other books on the Holocaust are *The Cunning of History, The Age of Triage,* and *Approaches to Auschwitz,* co-authored with John K. Roth.

ARVIND SHARMA moved from India to the United States in 1968 to pursue higher studies first in Economics (Syracuse University) and then in Comparative Religion (Harvard Divinity School) and Sanskrit and Indian Studies (Harvard University). He taught for ten years in Australia (Queensland,

Sydney) and then moved to Canada in 1987, where he is currently Birks Professor of Comparative Religion in the Faculty of Religious Studies at McGill University. He is the author of several books and papers in the twin fields of Comparative Religion and Indian Studies and two books edited by him are widely used in teaching courses on world religions: *Women in World Religions* and *Our Religions*.

ELDIN VILLAFAÑE is Professor of Christian Social Ethics at Gordon-Conwell Theological Seminary (Boston, U.S.A.). He earned his Ph.D. in social ethics from Boston University. Current research interests include urban theology and ministry, Latino leadership development, and the public ministry of the church. Dr. Villafañe has been named as one of the nation's ten most influential Hispanic religious leaders and scholars by the *National Catholic Reporter*. Among his works are *The Liberating Spirit: Toward an Hispanic American Pentecostal Social Ethic; Seek the Peace of the City: Reflections on Urban Ministry; A Prayer for the City: Further Reflections on Urban Ministry*.

VICTOR F. WAN-TATAH lives in Youngstown, Ohio, where he is Professor of Philosophy and Religious Studies and Director of the Africana Studies Program at Youngstown State University. He is the author of *Emancipation in African Theology* and past president of the Youngstown Chapter of the Phi Kappa Phi Honor Society, and recipient of the Mary Bethune Award for Youth Advocacy of the Youngstown Chapter of the National Association of Negro Women. His current research interests are in the African American Catholic Congregation (AACC), or Imani Temple, under the leadership of Archbishop Stallings, and Contemporary African Christian Witness to North America.

CORNEL WEST received his B.A. from Harvard University and his M.A. from Princeton University. He has taught at Yale, Union Theological Seminary, and Princeton University, where he was Chair of the Department of Afro-American Studies. He is currently Alphonse Fletcher Jr. University Professor at Harvard University, teaching in the fields of Afro-American Studies and Philosophy of Religion. He is the author of numerous articles and books including *The Cornel West Reader* and *Race Matters*.